BIOLOGICAL ANTHROPOLOGY

MICHAEL ALAN PARK

CENTRAL CONNECTICUT STATE UNIVERSITY

MAYFIELD PUBLISHING COMPANY

Mountain View, California

London • Toronto

For Jan

Copyright © 1996 by Mayfield Publishing Company

Library of Congress Cataloging-in-Publication Data
Park, Michael Alan.
    Biological anthropology / Michael Alan Park.
       p. cm.
    Includes bibliographical references and index.
    ISBN 1-55934-424-5
    I. Physical anthropology.   I. Title.
  GN60.P35 1995
  573—dc20   95-39134
                                         CIP

Manufactured in the United States of America
10 9 8 7 6 5 4 3 2 1

Mayfield Publishing Company
1280 Villa Street
Mountain View, CA 94041

Sponsoring editor, Janet M. Beatty; production editor, Melissa Kreischer; art director, Jeanne M. Schreiber; manuscript editor, Sydney Baily-Gould; text designer, Anna George; cover designer, Susan Breitbard; illustrators, Jeanne M. Schreiber, John and Judy Waller; photo researcher, Brian J. Pecko; manufacturing manager, Amy Folden; cover photographs, top, © Robert P. Comport/Animals, Animals/Earth Scenes; center, © David Young-Wolff/PhotoEdit; bottom, © Ken Kelley/Zoological Society of San Diego. The text was set in 10.5/12 Goudy Old Style by University Graphics, Inc. and printed on 50# Chromatone Matte by Banta Book Group.

Photo and illustration credits appear on pages 344 and 345 which constitute an extension of the copyright page.

To the Instructor

Contemporary biological anthropology is a dauntingly broad field. It studies humans in the same way that zoologists study their subject species—from a perspective that includes *all* aspects of the species' biologies and that emphasizes the interrelationships among those aspects. In addition to the traditional topics of the human fossil record and human biological variation, bioanthropology includes primatology, modern technologies in molecular genetics, human demography, development of the individual, life histories, and such applications as forensic anthropology. Bioanthropology also appreciates that our cultural behavior is an integral part of our behavior as a species.

No wonder, then, that I (and others I have spoken to) have had difficulty in covering the entire field in a one-semester course. We have ended up leaving out important aspects (or paying them little more than lip service), or we have sacrificed a sense of bioanthropology as an integrated whole to a rushed and encyclopedic inventory of all the field's current topics.

As modern bioanthropology increased in breadth and complexity over the past several decades, so, too, did the size and detail of introductory texts. Several are now more than 600 pages long. To date, attempts to produce shorter introductory texts have consisted of simply cutting out parts of these existing tomes, resulting in rather uneven, sometimes oddly organized presentations of the field.

I wrote this text in order to present a diverse scientific field to beginning students. Here are the major assumptions that guided my writing:

- Because this is a text for introductory courses, I have tried to reduce the field to its most basic information. No part of the discipline has been left out; instead I have achieved brevity by managing the amount of detail and including only the information necessary to clearly and accurately convey the basic themes, theories, methods, and facts of bioanthropology.

- The text assumes that students have limited background knowledge of the material and little understanding of what science is and how it works. The text *explains* rather than simply itemizes facts and ideas, and it does so, as much as possible, in a narrative format. A lesson from the study of folklore is that a story is far more easily understood and retained than is a list of facts.

- I want students to feel that they are reading a text written by a real person who has participated in the field. I have tried to achieve a balance between an informal and formal style, and I have not shied away from the occasional colloquialism or personal comment.

FEATURES

I've included a number of features which I hope will make this text a more useful learning tool for students.

- *I've used the scientific method as a theme throughout the book to demonstrate the integrity and nature of bioanthropology.* I describe the scientific method and then, because this *is* anthropology, compare science to knowledge garnered from belief systems, discussing the relationship of these two spheres of inquiry and knowledge within cultures. I try to show specifically how scientific reasoning has provided us with the knowledge we have about the topics in bioanthropology. For example, I've presented an extended discussion of the origin and importance of bipedalism in hominid evolution by posing questions, suggesting answers, and then testing the logic of and evidence for those answers.

- *The text is organized to help students navigate their way through what is still a fairly hefty amount of information.* To help students feel a little less at sea in the midst of new facts and ideas, I regularly refer back to previous topics and ahead to topics that will be covered. The headings I use as signposts are as descriptive as possible (for example, "Natural Selection: The Prime Mover of Evolution"). The text is not cluttered with boxes, appendixes, or inserts; if it's important, it's in the body of the text.

- *Within chapters, a consistent format helps students better understand material new to them.* Each chapter starts with an **introduction** that sets the stage and context for what's to come, which is followed by a series of **questions** that the chapter will answer. Because science proceeds by asking and answering questions, this format is also used within the body of the text. Important **terms** are in boldface and are defined in the margins at their first appearance. Each chapter concludes with a **summary** that not only recaps the important points of the chapter but also provides some new ideas and thoughts that help put the chapter into context within the whole discipline. A list of **suggested readings,** made up mostly of nontechnical works, tells students where to find more information about the chapter topics.

- *Two glossaries, a bibliography, and a comprehensive index make information more accessible.* A Glossary of Human and Nonhuman Primates with a pronunciation guide defines taxonomic names for species discussed in the text. In additon to the running glossary within chapters, a comprehensive glossary appears at the back of the book. The bibliography gives complete references for the suggested readings and also lists technical works referred to within the text. The index helps students access information quickly.

- *The text's visual appeal enhances its readability.* Detailed, colorful charts and drawings, as well as full color photographs, underscore significant points in the text. Captions for the artwork add information rather than simply label the pictures.

SUPPLEMENTARY MATERIAL

The **Instructor's Manual** includes a test bank of about 500 multiple choice and short answer/essay questions, as well as chapter overviews, suggested activities, and lists of key words.

A **Computerized Test Bank** is available free of charge to qualifying adopters. It is a powerful, easy-to-use test generation system that provides all test items on computer disk for IBM-compatible or Macintosh computers. Instructors can select, add, or edit questions, randomize them, and print tests appropriate to their individual classes.

A set of **Color Transparencies** is also available for use on an overhead projector. Included are charts and diagrams from the text as well as several diagrams created just for classroom use.

ACKNOWLEDGMENTS

Because this is an introductory text that covers an entire field, I must go back to the very beginning of my career and thank my first teachers in bioanthropology at Indiana University, Robert Meier and Paul Jamison, and the late Georg Neumann.

In the present, special thanks to my friend, colleague, and ofttimes co-author, Ken Feder. Not only has he been a help with this project—supplying addresses, references, and computer advice—but he has, over the last nearly twenty years, been a catalyst, if not a major element in much of my professional activity, particularly my writing.

And thanks, as always, to the folks at Mayfield Publishing, particularly sponsoring editor Jan Beatty (always gentle with the bad news about some new deadline); production editor Melissa Kreischer (always adding a bit of whimsy to the same sort of bad news); art director Jeanne Schreiber (who ensured that my scribbles were turned into an attractive art program); copyeditor Sydney Baily-Gould (who fixed a sentence I wrote a dozen years ago and have always hated); and designer Anna George (who knows that design is indeed art).

I also thank all those who reviewed the manuscript: Lynne E. Christenson, San Diego State University; Dana A. Cope, College of Charleston; Norris M. Durham, University of Northern Iowa; David H. Dye; University of Memphis; Richard Effland, Jr., Mesa Community College; Deborah J. Overdorff, University of Texas at Austin; and Paul L. Schroeder, Whatcom Community College. Their suggestions and advice were invaluable. Any errors, of course, remain my responsibility.

To the Reader

The broad field of biological (or physical) anthropology deals with everything from evolutionary theory to the human fossil record to the identification of human skeletal remains from crime scenes and accidents. A detailed account of this whole field would result in an unwieldy text that would be a tough assignment for a one-semester introductory course, especially if it were assigned in its entirety.

This text is intended to truly be an *introduction* to biological anthropology. It will tell you about the many different kinds of studies bioanthropologists participate in and how they conduct them; you'll also learn about the scientific theories and data they use. All the important aspects of bioanthropology are covered here but with just the essential amount of detail. When you understand an idea from this book, then you should be able to delve more deeply into the subject if you are interested and have the basis for an even more profound understanding.

A major theme of this book is the scientific method. Biological anthropology is a science, so an understanding of how science works is essential. Because the field of anthropology studies the human species in its entirety, however, the text will examine science as a human endeavor, seeing where it fits in the realm of human knowledge.

HOW TO USE THIS BOOK

Each chapter starts with an **introduction** that sets the stage and context for what's to come, followed by a series of **questions** that the chapter will answer. Because science proceeds by asking and answering questions, this format is also used within the body of the text. Important **terms** are in boldface and are defined in the margins at their first appearance. Each chapter ends with a **summary** that not only recaps the important points of the chapter, but also provides some new ideas and thoughts that help put what you have just learned into the context of the whole discipline of bioanthropology. A list of **suggested readings** made up mostly of nontechnical works tells you where to find more information if you are interested in a particular topic.

A Glossary of Human and Nonhuman Primates defines taxonomic (scientific) names for species discussed in the text—names like *Homo sapiens* and *Australopithecus afarensis*—and tells you how to pronounce them. In addition to the running glossary within chapters, a comprehensive main glossary appears at the back of the book. The bibliography gives complete references for the suggested readings and also lists technical works referred to within the text. The index will help you more quickly access information.

Contents

To the Instructor   *iii*

To the Reader   *vii*

I   BIOLOGICAL ANTHROPOLOGY   *I*

In the Field: Doing Biological Anthropology   *2*
What Is Biological Anthropology?   *8*
Bioanthropology and Science   *12*
    The Scientific Method: "How Heaven Is"   *13*
    Belief Systems: "How to Get to Heaven"   *15*
Summary   *16*
Key Terms   *17*
Suggested Readings   *17*

2   THE EVOLUTION OF EVOLUTION   *19*

"On the Shoulders of Giants": Explaining the Changing
   Earth   *20*
"Common Sense at Its Best": Explaining Biological Change   *27*
Summary   *33*
Key Terms   *35*
Suggested Readings   *35*

3 EVOLUTIONARY GENETICS   37

How Genes Work   38

How Inheritance Works   46

Summary   48

Key Terms   49

Suggested Readings   49

4 THE PROCESSES OF EVOLUTION   51

Species: The Units of Evolution   52

Mutations: Necessary Errors   55

Natural Selection: The Prime Mover of Evolution   56

Gene Flow: Mixing Populations   59

Genetic Drift: Random Evolution   61

Sickle Cell Anemia: Evolutionary Processes in Action   63

Summary   67

Key Terms   68

Suggested Readings   68

5 THE ORIGIN OF SPECIES AND THE SHAPE OF EVOLUTION   71

New Species   72

Adaptive Radiation: The Evolution of Life's Diversity   75

The Shape of the Family Tree   80

Evolution Questioned: The Pseudoscience of "Scientific Creationism"   83

Summary   86

Key Terms   87

Suggested Readings   87

6 A BRIEF EVOLUTIONARY TIMETABLE   89

From the Beginning: A Quick History   90

Drifting Continents and Mass Extinctions: The Pace of
  Change   95

Summary   99

Key Terms   101

Suggested Readings   101

7 THE PRIMATES   103

Naming the Animals   104

What Is a Primate?   109
  The Senses   109
  Movement   111
  Reproduction   111
  Intelligence   112
  Behavior Patterns   113

A Survey of the Living Primates   117

The Human Primate   126
  The Senses   126
  Movement   126
  Reproduction   127
  Intelligence   128
  Behavior Patterns   128

Summary   128

Key Terms   129

Suggested Readings   129

8 PRIMATE BEHAVIOR AND HUMAN EVOLUTION   131

Studying Behavior   132

Baboons   136

Chimpanzees   140

Summary   146

Key Terms   147

Suggested Readings   147

9   STUDYING THE HUMAN PAST   _149_

Bones: The Primate Skeleton   _150_
Old Bones: Locating, Recovering, and Dating Fossils   _156_
How Fossils Get to Be Fossils   _161_
Genes: New Windows to the Past   _164_
Summary   _167_
Key Terms   _168_
Suggested Readings   _169_

10   EVOLUTION OF THE HOMINIDS   _171_

The Origin and Evolution of the Primates   _172_
The First Hominids: The Bipedal Primate   _178_
Bipedalism   _187_
The Hominids Evolve   _192_
The First Members of Genus _Homo_   _198_
Summary   _202_
Key Terms   _202_
Suggested Readings   _203_

11   _HOMO ERECTUS_   _205_

To New Lands   _206_
The Fossil Evidence   _214_
The Behavior of _Homo Erectus_   _217_
Summary   _222_
Key Terms   _223_
Suggested Readings   _223_

12   THE EVOLUTION OF THE GENUS _HOMO_   _225_

The First _Homo Sapiens_   _227_
The Neandertals   _233_

Modern Humans   *240*

The Origin of Modern *Homo Sapiens*   *247*
  The Multiregional Hypothesis   248
  The Population Replacement Hypothesis   249
  The Genetic Replacement Hypothesis   250

Summary   *256*

Key Terms   *256*

Suggested Readings   *257*

13 THE STUDY OF LIVING POPULATIONS   *259*

Genes in Populations   *260*

Evolution in Populations   *264*

Describing Populations   *268*

Human Adaptations   *274*
  Species Adaptations   274
  Variation in Adaptations   275
  Are All Polymorphisms Adaptively Important?   278

The Bioanthropology of Individuals   *282*

Summary   *286*

Key Terms   *287*

Suggested Readings   *287*

14 HUMAN BIOLOGICAL DIVERSITY   *289*

Sex and Gender   *292*

Race as a Biological Concept   *296*

Are There Human Races?   *300*

What, Then, *Are* Human Races?   *304*

Race, Bioanthropology, and Social Issues   *307*

Summary   *312*

Key Terms   *313*

Suggested Readings   *313*

15 BIOLOGICAL ANTHROPOLOGY: APPLICATIONS AND LESSONS   *315*

Forensic Anthropology: Reading the Bones   *316*
Lessons from the Past   *323*
Summary   *327*
Suggested Readings   *328*

Glossary of Human and Nonhuman Primates   329

Glossary of Terms   332

Bibliography   339

Index   346

Observe always that everything is the result of change, and get used to thinking that there is nothing Nature loves so well as to change existing forms, and to make new ones like them.

—Marcus Aurelius

BIOLOGICAL ANTHROPOLOGY

Anthropologists study
spiders, right?
—Anonymous caller

If you ask twenty different people to define anthropology, you will probably get twenty different answers. Anthropology is such a broad field that many people, understandably, are not sure just what an anthropologist studies. I have been brought rocks to identify, have been asked about the accuracy of the dinosaurs in *Jurassic Park*, and have even received a phone call from a man who wanted information about black widow spiders—and he was referred to me by someone within the university where I teach.

In this chapter, we will define anthropology in general and then focus in on the subfield of biological anthropology (or bioanthropology). Because fieldwork—where the anthropologists make their observations and collect their data—is perhaps the best known aspect of anthropology, and is the part that attracts many students to the discipline, I will begin with a brief description of two of my experiences.

As you read, consider the following questions:

What is anthropology, and what are its subfields?

What is biological anthropology?

How does the scientific method operate?

In what way is bioanthropology a science?

What are belief systems, and what is their relationship to scientific knowledge?

IN THE FIELD: DOING BIOLOGICAL ANTHROPOLOGY

The wheat fields on either side of the long, straight road in western Saskatchewan, Canada, stretched, as the cliché says, as far as the eye could see. I found myself wishing, on that June day in 1973, that the road went on just as far. I was on my way to an initial visit with my first real anthropological subjects, a colony of people belonging to a 450-year-old religious denomination called the Hutterian Brethren or Hutterites.

Up to this point I had not felt much anxiety about the visit. Accounts by other anthropologists of contacts with Amazon jungle warriors and New Guinea headhunters made my situation seem rather safe. The Hutterites are, after all, people who share my European-American cultural heritage, number English among their languages, and, far from being hostile, practice a form of Christianity that emphasizes pacifism and tolerance.

At this point, though, that didn't help. Nor did the fact that I was accompanied by the wife of a local wheat farmer who was well known and liked by the people of this colony. I simply had that unnamed fear that affects nearly all anthropologists under these first-contact circumstances.

Finally, the road we traveled—which had turned from blacktop to dirt about ten miles back—curved abruptly to the right, crossed a railroad track, and crested a hill, and I saw below us, at the literal end of the road, a neat collection of twenty or so white buildings surrounded by acres of cultivated fields. This was the Hutterite colony, or *Bruderhof,* the "place where the brethren live" (Figure 1.1).

We drove down the hill and into the colony. Not a soul was to be seen. My companion explained that it was a religious holiday, which required all but essential work to cease. Everyone was indoors observing the holiday, but the colony minister and colony boss had agreed to see me.

We entered one of the smaller buildings, which I recognized from pictures and diagrams of "typical" colonies as one of the residential buildings. The interior was darkened in conjunction with the holiday, and that, combined with my nervous excitement, have erased all first impressions from my memory. A few minutes later, however, with my bearings straight and the introductions made, I found myself explaining the reason for my visit to two men and a woman.

The men were dressed in the Hutterite fashion—black trousers and coats, white shirts—and they wore beards, a sign of marriage. The older, gray-haired man was the colony minister. The younger man, who happened to be his son, was the colony boss. The woman, the minister's wife, also dressed in the conservative style that has become a trademark of the Hutterites and related groups. She wore a nearly full-length sleeveless dress—a small floral pattern on a black background—with a white blouse underneath. Her head was covered by a polka-dot kerchief or "shawl," as they call it.

My contacts, the wheat farmer and his wife, had already given the Hutterites an idea of what I wanted to do, and my visit was arranged. But if they didn't like me or my explanation, they could still decline to cooperate. So I started from the beginning. The three listened in silence as I went through my well-rehearsed explanation. When I had finished, they asked me a few questions, far fewer than I had expected. Was I from the government? (My study involved using fingerprints as genetic markers, and they apparently knew about them only in the context of law enforcement and personal identification.) Did I know Scripture? (My equivocal answer created no problem.) What would I use this study for? Was I going to write a book? Did I know so-and-so who had been there two years ago and did medical examinations?

I expected that when they were done they would confer with one another or ask me to come back when they had decided if they would allow me to conduct the study. Instead, the Hutterite minister, who was

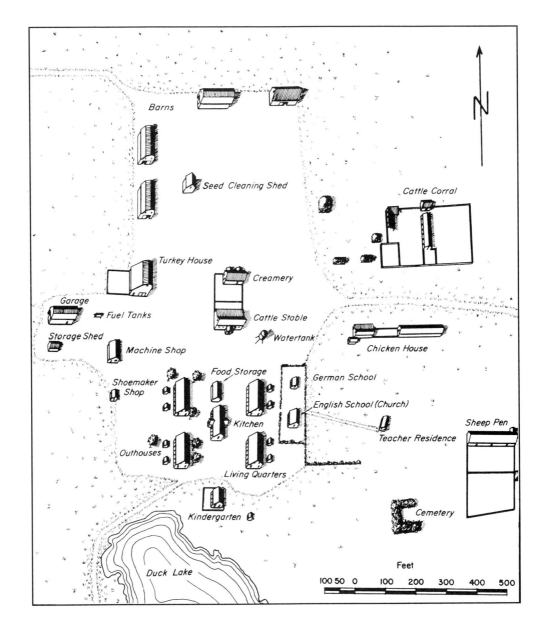

FIGURE 1.1

Diagram of typical Hutterite colony. The variety of buildings and their functions are indicative of the Hutterite's attempt to keep their colonies self-sufficient and separate from the outside world.

clearly in charge, simply said, "Today is a holiday for us. Can you start tomorrow?"

And so, for the next month, I took part in my personal version of the anthropological fieldwork experience—taking fingerprints, recording family relationships, observing colony life, and getting to know the Hutterites of this and one other Canadian *Bruderhof* (Park 1979) (Figure 1.2).

What exactly had brought me thirteen hundred miles from my university to the northern plains, to this isolated community of people whose way of life has changed little over the last 450 years and whose lifestyle and philosophy differ so from those of North American culture in general? Essentially, it was the same thing that takes anthropologists to locations from the highlands of New Guinea to caves in the Pyrenees to street corners in New York City: the desire to learn something about the nature of the human species.

In my case, I was pursuing an interest I had developed early in graduate school. An important facet of biological anthropology is the study of the processes of evolution and how they affect humans. I was curious about two of these processes: gene flow and genetic drift (see Chapter 4 for

FIGURE 1.2

Author (right) and Hutterite informant. I already had the beard, but it was suggested that I keep it so I would look more familiar to the Hutterite children.

FIGURE 1.3
Portrait of Henry Opukahaia.

details). Both topics had been described half a century earlier, but their workings and importance, especially with regard to human populations, were still poorly understood.

To examine the actions of these processes on human populations and to determine their roles in human evolution, I needed to find a human group with a few special characteristics. First, the group had to be isolated; that is, most members should find their mates within the group. The group had to be fairly small as a whole, hopefully with large individual families. It is also helpful if the people know and are interested in genealogical relationships and if their family relationships reflect genetic as well as cultural categories. (All societies have systems of family relationships, but few of these coincide completely with biological relationships.) Finally, individual populations within the group ideally would have been created through the splitting of earlier populations.

The Hutterites fit this description well. (I'll elaborate later.) I discovered them through library research on genetically isolated groups. My opportunity to study them was greatly enhanced by a stroke of luck. A fellow graduate student was the daughter of the wheat farmer and his wife who became my "public relations advisors."

Exactly twenty years later, I found myself standing over an open grave in an old cemetery in the wooded hills of northwest Connecticut. Our team of anthropologists was hoping to find the remains of a native Hawaiian who had been buried here in 1818 and who was now, after 175 years, going home.

A few weeks earlier, Nick Bellantoni, the Connecticut state archaeologist (and a former student of mine) had called me with a fascinating story. In 1808 a young Hawaiian named Opukahaia (O-pu-ka-ha-EE-a) escaped the tribal warfare that had killed his family by swimming out to a Yankee whaling vessel where he was taken on board as a cabin boy. Two years (and many adventures) later he ended up at Yale University in New Haven, Connecticut. He took the name Henry, converted to Christianity, and became a Congregational minister who helped build a missionary school in Cornwall, Connecticut. His dream was to return to Hawaii and bring his new faith to the people there (Figure 1.3).

Sadly, Henry's dream was never realized. He died in a typhoid epidemic in 1818 at the age of twenty-six, but his vision inspired the missionary movement that was to change the history of the Hawaiian Islands forever. His grave in Cornwall became a shrine both for the people of his adopted land and for visiting Hawaiians, who would leave offerings atop his platform-style headstone.

Nearly two centuries later, a living relative of Henry's had a dream in which she envisioned honoring Henry's final wish to once more see his native land. After almost a year of raising funds and making the necessary

arrangements, her dream was to come true. And this is where anthropology comes in.

Old New England cemeteries vary widely in the exact placement of headstones relative to the bodies buried beneath them, and the acidic New England soil is unkind to organic remains. Both logically and legally, this was a job for the state archaeologist, and Nick wanted my help in recovering and identifying whatever remains we might be lucky enough to find. He also wanted my help, it turned out, in moving several tons of stone.

Henry's tomb had been carefully and lovingly assembled by the people of Cornwall. They placed the inscribed headstone on a pedestal of field-stone and mortar. We dismantled this with care, labeling each stone and diagramming its position, since it was to be rebuilt by a stone mason. Under the pedestal, and going down about three feet into the ground, we uncovered three more layers of fieldstone that acted as a foundation for the monument and protection for the coffin and the remains we hoped were still below. When all the stones had been removed and we were into a layer of sandy soil, Nick worked alone, delicately scraping away the dirt inch by inch (Figure 1.4).

Late on the second day of our excavation, the remnants of the coffin came into view. In fact, the wooden coffin itself had long since decayed.

All that was left was the dark shadow of its outline in the soil. We began to despair of finding much else, but an hour later Nick's trowel grazed something hard, and in a few minutes the apparent remains of Henry Opukahaia saw the light of day for the first time in 175 years.

We soon learned that the skeleton was virtually complete. But *was* it Henry? As Nick slowly freed each bone from the soil and handed it up to me, we recorded it and compared it with what we knew of Henry from written descriptions and a single portrait. The skeleton was clearly that of a man and, at first glance, conformed to that of a person in his late twenties of about the right size. Henry had been described as being "a little under six feet," and the long bones of the arms and legs appeared to be just a bit shorter than mine, though much more robust. The skull, however, confirmed our identification. As the dirt was brushed away, the face of Henry Opukahaia emerged, the very image of his portrait. (Incidentally, the family has requested that, for religious reasons, photographs of Henry's remains not be published.)

We spent two more days with the bones, this time in the garage of a Hartford funeral home. We cleaned, photographed, measured, and de-

FIGURE 1.5

Reverend David Hirano, from Hawaii, speaks over the remains of Henry Opukahaia at his "homegoing" celebration in Cornwall, Connecticut. The koa wood coffin, ti leaves, and flowered lei all have symbolic meaning in Hawaiian culture.

scribed each bone. Closer analysis supported our graveside conclusions, and more. On the inside surface of the ribs, we found the telltale ashy texture that can be symptomatic of typhoid. The original diagnosis, done in the days before medicine even understood about microörganisms, had been correct.

Finally, we placed each bone in correct anatomical position in spaces cut into heavy foam rubber with which we had lined the bottom of a *koa* wood coffin, specially made and shipped from Hawaii. The following Sunday we attended a memorial service in Cornwall, and then Henry's remains began their long journey back home (Figure 1.5).

WHAT IS BIOLOGICAL ANTHROPOLOGY?

My experiences as a biological anthropologist range from examining the esoteric detail of evolutionary theory to using my knowledge of the human skeleton for a very personal and human endeavor. These are just two examples of the many things that biological anthropologists do.

Biological anthropology, or bioanthropology, needs to be defined within the context of anthropology as a whole, and doing this is both simple and complex. **Anthropology,** in general, is defined as *the study of the human species.* Simply put, we study the human species as any zoologist would study an animal **species.** We look into every aspect of the biology of our subject—genetics, anatomy, physiology, behavior, environment, adaptations, and evolutionary history—stressing the interrelationships among these aspects.

This kind of approach—examining a subject by focusing on the interrelationships among its parts—is called **holistic.** The holistic approach is the hallmark of anthropology. We understand that all the facets of our species—our biology, our behavior, our past, and our present—interact to make us what we are. We need to study some topics separately, since they can be so complex. Thus, you may be taking courses in history, economics, psychology, art, anatomy, and so on. What anthropology does is seek the connections among these subjects; for, in real life, they are not absolutely separate.

But here's where it gets complicated. The most characteristic feature of our species' behavior is **culture,** and cultural behavior is not programmed in our genes, as is, for example, much of the behavior of birds, or virtually all of the behavior of ants.

Human culture is learned. We certainly have a biological potential for cultural behavior in general, but exactly how we behave comes to us through all our experiences. Take language, for example. All humans are born with the ability to learn a language. Which language each of us

anthropology: The study of the human species.

species: A group of organisms that can produce fertile offspring among themselves but not with members of other groups.

holistic: Assuming an interrelationship among the parts of a subject.

culture: Ideas and behaviors that are learned and transmitted. Nongenetic means of adaptation.

actually speaks is determined by what country we are born in and what language is spoken in our family.

Moreover, cultural knowledge involves not just specific facts, but, more importantly, ideas, concepts, generalizations, and abstractions. For example, you were able to speak your native language fairly fluently before you were ever formally taught the particulars of its grammar. You did this by making your own generalizations from the raw data you heard and the rules they followed, that is, from the speech of others and from trying to make yourself understood by them. Even now when you speak, you are applying those generalizations to new situations. And each situation—every conversation you have, every essay you write, every book you read—is a new situation.

In short, culture is highly variable and flexible. It differs from society to society and from one time period to another. It even differs, in its details, from one individual to another. We continually modify our cultural behaviors to fit the unique circumstances of our lives.

All this variability makes the study of the human species complex and challenging, and so anthropology, the discipline that takes on this challenge, is typically divided into a number of subfields.

Biological anthropology (or physical anthropology) looks at our species from a biological point of view. This includes all the topics covered

FIGURE 1.6
The subfields of anthropology.

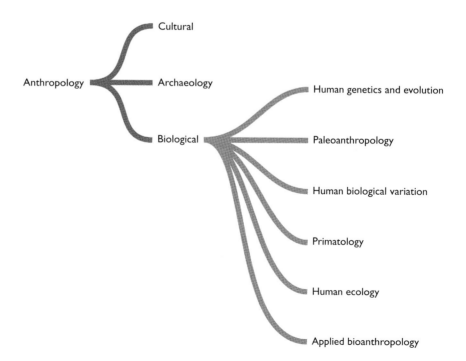

in this book. **Cultural anthropology** is the study of culture as a characteristic of our species and of the variation in cultural expression among human groups. This includes human language, although sometimes anthropological linguistics is considered a separate subfield. **Archaeology** is the study of the human cultural past and the reconstruction of past cultural systems. It also involves the techniques used to recover, preserve, and interpret the material remains of the past.

All anthropologists, then, are trying to do the same thing: learn about the human species. The enormity and complexity of the subject requires several starting points or focuses. These are the subfields of anthropology.

Each subfield has many specialties. For biological anthropology, these specialties are best expressed in terms of the questions we seek to answer about human biology:

1. What are the *biological characteristics* that define the human species?
2. How do our *genes* code for these characteristics? Just how much do genes contribute to our traits? How much is environmental?
3. How does *evolution* work and how does it apply to us? (These were the questions I was pursuing in my study of the Hutterites).
4. What is the *physical record* of our evolution? This is the specialty referred to as **paleoanthropology,** the study of human *fossils*.
5. What sort of *biological variation* do we see in our species today? What genetic variations does it reflect? How did this variation evolve? What do the variable traits mean for other aspects of our lives? What do they *not* mean?
6. What can we learn about the biology of our close relatives, the nonhuman **primates,** and what can it tell us about ourselves? This specialty is called **primatology.**
7. What do we know about **human ecology,** the relationships between humans and their environments?
8. How can we apply all this knowledge to matters of current concern? This is often called **applied anthropology.** (The story of the exhumation of Henry Opukahaia is an example.)

The place of biological anthropology and its subjects within the whole discipline of anthropology may be diagrammed as in Figure 1.6.

Individual biological anthropologists undertake numerous and diverse studies. I took fingerprints of members of a centuries old Christian group to learn something about the processes of evolution that have affected our species. Paleoanthropologist Donald Johanson led the team that discovered and identified the famous fossil of "Lucy," a 3.2-million-year-old hu-

biological anthropology: Subfield of anthropology that studies humans as a biological species.

physical anthropology: The traditional name for biological anthropology.

cultural anthropology: Subfield of anthropology that focuses on human cultural behavior and cultural systems.

archaeology: Subfield of anthropology that studies the human cultural past.

paleoanthropology: Specialty that studies the human fossil record.

primates: Large-brained, tree-dwelling mammals with three-dimensional color vision and grasping hands. Humans are primates.

primatology: Specialty that studies nonhuman primates.

human ecology: Specialty that studies the relationships between humans and their environments.

applied anthropology: Anthropology used to address current practical problems and concerns.

man ancestor. Elwyn Simons, another paleoanthropologist, studies fossil nonhuman primates that go even further back in evolutionary time—to the dawn of the apes more than thirty million years ago. Other anthropologists study living nonhuman primates. Shirley Strum, Barbara Smuts, and Linda Fedigan, for example, have all observed troops of baboons to understand what their behavior can tell us about our own.

Clyde Snow is a **forensic anthropologist.** He applies his knowledge of the human skeleton to solving crimes and identifying missing persons. He has worked to identify the remains of the victims of death squads in Argentina and has tried (so far without success) to locate the bones of Butch Cassidy and the Sundance Kid in Bolivia.

Melvin Konner has examined the lifestyles of contemporary **hunter-gatherers,** including diet and exercise, to show how they differ (mostly for the better) from those of people in industrial societies.

We'll meet these people and their studies, and many more, as we survey the field of bioanthropology. As we do, keep in mind that what connects these varied activities is their focus on *learning about human beings as a biological species.*

The studies of bioanthropologists are also connected in that they are all scientific. In many cases, they may not seem to fit the common conception of science. Most anthropologists don't wear white lab coats and work with test tubes and chemicals. Many anthropologists study things that can't be directly observed in nature or recreated in the lab because they happened in the past. But bioanthropology *is* a science, just as much as chemistry, physics, and human biology. We'll see how this is so, and we'll also look at some nonscientific ways in which people try to understand their world.

BIOANTHROPOLOGY AND SCIENCE

A popular image of a scientist is that of a walking encyclopedia. Science is often seen as fact-collecting. While it's fair to say that scientists know a lot of facts, so do a lot of other people. Champions on the TV quiz show *Jeopardy* are not usually professional scientists.

Facts are certainly important to science. They are the raw material of science, the data scientists use. But what scientists really do is *explain* facts, not simply collect them. **Science,** in other words, is *a method of inquiry; a way of answering questions about the world.* But how does science work? Is science the only valid and logical method for explaining the world around us?

The Scientific Method: "How Heaven Is"

The world is full of things that need explaining. We might wonder about the behavior of a bird, the origin of the stars in the night sky, the identity of a fossil skeleton, the social interaction of students in a college classroom, or the ritual warfare of a society in highland New Guinea. As people, we strive to understand such phenomena, to know why and how these things occur as they do. As scientists we must answer these questions according to a special set of rules—the **scientific method.**

We begin by asking the question we wish to answer or describing the phenomenon we wish to explain. We then make what are essentially educated guesses about possible explanations. These are **hypotheses.** We say "educated" guesses because they are based upon real, tangible information—*specific* pieces of data from which we try to propose a *general* principle. This process is called **induction.**

Next comes the essence of science. We must attempt to either support or refute our hypothesis by *testing* it. Tests may take many forms, depending on what we are trying to explain, but basically we reverse the process of induction and go from the general back to the specific by making predictions: *If* our general hypothesis is correct, *then* what other specific things should we observe? This process is called **deduction.** For example, we look for:

1. *Repetition.* Does the same phenomenon occur over and over?
2. *Universality.* If we vary some aspect of the situation, will the phenomenon still occur?
3. *Explanations for exceptions.* Can we account for cases where the phenomenon doesn't apppear to occur?
4. *New data.* Does new information support or contradict our hypothesis?

If we find one piece of evidence that conclusively refutes our hypothesis, we consider it disproved. But if the hypothesis passes every test we come up with, we elevate our idea to the status of a "very good hypothesis." In science, we call this a **theory.**

Notice that I didn't say we "proved" the hypothesis. Scientists should always be skeptical, always look for new evidence, always be open to and even invite change. The best we can honestly say about a theory is that *so far* no evidence has been found that *disproves* it.

Of course, some theories are so well supported that we are safe in considering them to be facts and in using them as a basis for further investigation. The theory of gravity, the theory of evolution, and the theory of relativity are all concepts central to many aspects of our lives because they are ideas supported by every test applied to them and refuted by none.

forensic anthropologist: One who applies anthropology to legal matters.

hunter-gatherers: Societies that rely upon naturally occurring sources of food.

science: The method of inquiry that requires the generation, testing, and acceptance or rejection of hypotheses.

scientific method: The process of conducting scientific inquiry.

hypotheses: Educated guesses to explain natural phenomena.

induction: Developing a general explanation from specific observations.

deduction: Suggesting specific data that would be found if a hypothesis is true.

theory: A hypothesis that has been well supported by evidence and testing.

FIGURE 1.7
Light bent by gravity. Einstein predicted that a strong gravitational field could bend light. His prediction was verified when light from stars that should have been blocked by the sun could be seen during a solar eclipse.

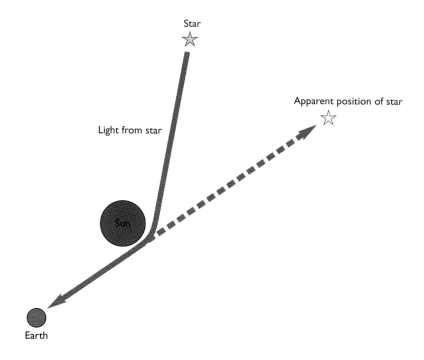

We don't stop investigating when we have developed a theory, however. No theory is complete. The theory of gravity establishes that some force that we call gravity exists, but we still don't understand exactly what gravity is and how it works. Science is now testing several hypotheses that attempt to explain the nature and operation of gravity.

Science is often popularly conceived of as the study of visible, tangible, and present-day objects—chemicals, living organisms, planets, and stars. But notice that gravity, for example, is decidedly *not* visible or tangible. We can't see gravity, but we know it exists because all our deductive predictions support its existence (Figure 1.7).

Similarly, past events can't be seen or touched. They can't be experimented upon directly or repeated exactly. The evolution of plants and animals is an example. But again, we know that evolution occurred because the idea has passed all our tests. The idea of evolution explains observations of the real world. We have observed everything we predicted we would *if* evolution occurred. We'll look more closely at how science has derived and supported the theory of evolution in Chapters 3 through 6.

Finally, we often think of the scientific method as applying only to stereotypical scientific matters like gravity, chemistry, and evolution. In fact, we all use the scientific method every day for issues somewhat more down-to-earth than gravity. Remember, science is *a way of thinking.*

Anytime you solve some problem—say, how to most efficiently organize all your activities for a certain day or how to repair a broken household item—you use a version of the scientific method.

Science answers questions about our lives and about the world in which we live. For an answer to be defined as scientific, it must be testable. Put another way, it must be possible to find data that would refute it. As Galileo said—speaking in metaphor—and as Pope John Paul II repeated centuries later, scientific inquiry tells us "how heaven *is*." That is, science tells us what the world is really like and how it works. In contrast to science are belief systems. They tell us how the world *should* be, or, as Galileo put it, "how to *get* to heaven."

Belief Systems: "How to Get to Heaven"

Some questions about the world, even in a technologically complex society like ours, remain beyond the scope of science.

Scientific inquiry, as powerful and important as it is, doesn't answer everything. Though we have some well-established theories about how the universe evolved once it began, the origin of the universe remains, for the moment at least, outside the realm of science. For most human societies throughout most of our species' history, many questions could not be addressed scientifically.

Nor does science tell us how to behave. In our society, for example, we treat medical matters scientifically. But science does not, and cannot, inform us how best to apply medical knowledge. Who should practice medicine? How are medical practitioners trained and administered by society? How should they be compensated? What should their relationship be with their patients? Is everyone equally entitled to medical care? It is the Hippocratic Oath, taken by all doctors, that addresses such questions. It says, for example, that "I will not permit considerations of religion, nationality, race, party politics or social standing to intervene between my duty and my patient; . . ."

Finally, there are questions that can never be answered by science—matters like the meaning of life, the existence of a higher power, the proper social relationships among people within a society, or the purpose of one's own life.

All these sorts of questions are addressed by **belief systems**—religions, philosophies, ethics, morals, and laws. Belief systems differ from science in that they cannot be tested, cannot be disproved. Their truths are taken on faith, and that, of course, is the source of their power. They provide stable bases for our behavior, for explanations of what is beyond our science and for the broad, existential questions of life. Belief systems change,

belief systems: Ideas that are taken on faith and cannot be scientifically tested.

but they only change when *we* decide to change them, either as a society or as individuals.

The existence of a supreme being is an example of a value inherent in one's belief system. Two of us with opposite views on the subject could debate the issue endlessly, but no scientific test could support or refute either view. If I were to change my mind on the matter, it would be because of personal decisions not because of a chemical reaction in a test tube or an observation through a telescope.

Belief systems don't apply only to these big questions. I had a friend in graduate school from a west African society that was polygynous—men could have several wives. Having more than one wife is normal for his society, whereas in mine, one wife (at least one at a time) is the norm. We discussed the pros and cons of these two systems at length one day, but we never, of course, arrived at any "answer." His belief was right for his society as was mine for my society. We each took it on faith that this was so.

Although we often perceive science and belief systems as being eternally and inevitably at odds with one another, nothing could be further from the truth. Conflicts do arise, as they do among facets of any society. But it should be apparent that, for a society to function, it needs both scientific knowledge and beliefs because neither, by itself, addresses all the questions.

To repeat Galileo's statement, while science tells us "how heaven *is*," belief systems tell us "how to *get* to heaven." Or, in the words of biologist John Maynard Smith, science tells us what is "possible" and beliefs tell us what is "desirable." No culture can function without both.

SUMMARY

Anthropology is the study of the human species. Because our species' most characteristic feature today is our cultural behavior and because culture is expressed in such great variety, most anthropologists specialize in cultural anthropology, the study of culture, cultural systems, and their variation.

Most human cultural systems existed in the past and have left us only meager physical remains of their presence and nature. A second major subfield of anthropology recovers and interprets these remains; this subfield is archaeology.

Biological anthropology (or physical anthropology) studies the human species the way biology studies any species, examining our biological characteristics, our evolution, our variation, our relationship with our environment, and our behavior, including our ability to have culture.

Bioanthropology, as a scientific discipline, asks questions about the human species and then attempts to answer them by proposing hypotheses and by *testing* those hypotheses, looking both for evidence in their support and for anything that would refute them.

Scientific knowledge is important for any society, but it must be mediated by the nonscientific values of belief systems—the untestable ideas of philosophy, law, and religion that are taken on faith. Societies need both, interacting in harmony, to fully function.

KEY TERMS

anthropology

species

holistic

culture

biological
    anthropology

physical anthropology

archaeology

cultural anthropology

paleoanthropology

primates

primatology

human ecology

applied anthropology

forensic
    anthropologist

hunter-gatherers

science

scientific method

hypotheses

induction

deduction

theory

belief systems

SUGGESTED READINGS

For more information on the Hutterites, see John Hostetler's *Hutterite Society.*

For a longer discussion of the nature of science and the scientific method, see Kenneth L. Feder's *Frauds, Myths and Mysteries: Science and Pseudoscience in Archaeology.* The relationship between science and belief systems is nicely covered by John Maynard Smith's article "Science and Myth" in *Natural History.*

The field of anthropology in general is covered by Emily Schultz and Robert Lavenda in *Anthropology: A Perspective on the Human Condition,* and, in a series of contemporary articles by Aaron Podolefsky and Peter Brown in *Applying Anthropology: An Introductory Reader.*

THE EVOLUTION OF EVOLUTION

One touch of Darwin
makes the whole
world kin.
—George Bernard
Shaw

A central theme of bioanthropology is the theory of evolution and its application to the human species—how we descended from nonhuman ancestors and how we have changed over time into modern *Homo sapiens*. **Evolution** is called a "theory" because the idea has passed every scientific test applied to it. Scientists are still debating the details of evolution, but *that* evolution occurred is so well-supported as to be considered fact.

How did our knowledge of the history of living organisms move from the realm of belief systems to the realm of science?

How did the scientific evidence for evolution develop?

"ON THE SHOULDERS OF GIANTS": EXPLAINING THE CHANGING EARTH

The Englishman Charles Darwin (1809–1882) is usually, and correctly, associated with our understanding of biological evolution (Figure 2.1). He is also popularly given credit for the very idea of evolution and for explaining and therefore proving it. However, this is not entirely correct. Like any great scientific accomplishment, Darwin's was based on the work of many who came before him. He stood, as Isaac Newton said of himself, "on the shoulders of giants." Darwin's genius was in being able to take massive amounts of data and assorted existing ideas and, using an imagination possessed by few humans, put them all together into a logical, cohesive theory that made sense of the world and that could be examined by the methods of science.

The idea of evolution is simple enough: Species of living things change over time, and sometimes this change is extensive enough to produce new forms of living organisms. This idea is not a new one now nor was it new in Darwin's time. Anaximander, a Greek of the sixth century B.C., proposed that humans had arisen from other forms of life. He incorrectly thought we arose directly from fish, but he explained his idea using reason rather than the supernatural; and his reasoning was based on the question of how animals survive in their environments, a question that would form the cornerstone of Darwin's idea (Harris, 1981).

Many others over the next two thousand years also contemplated the origins of living things, but the modern story really begins in Europe in the seventeenth century, where the influence of the Bible was felt in all aspects of life, including science. Specifically, the ancient Judeo-Christian creation story—Adam and Eve, the Garden of Eden, the flood and Noah's ark—was generally considered to be literally true. It followed, then, that the entire universe was created by supernatural powers over a period of six days and that, except for the matter of the great flood, the earth and its inhabitants were pretty much the same now as they were when created. One scholar, Irish Archbishop James Ussher (1581–1656), even used the assumption of biblical truth, as well as certain historical records, to help him calculate the date of creation, and thus the age of the earth. In 1650 he reckoned that the creation began at noon on Sunday, October 23 in the year 4004 B.C. The earth was thus about six thousand years old.

The literal interpretation of the Bible, in turn, was probably influenced by two old but persuasive ideas that go back to Plato and Aristotle, the Greek scholars of the fourth and fifth centuries B.C. One idea is called "essentialism." It is the notion that there is an ideal or essential form of every natural entity and that the entities we see are mere "things," copies of the ideal. The variations we see, for example, among the members of some species of living organism—for example, breeds of dogs—are just deviations from the essential dog form. Applied to biblical creation, essentialism promoted the idea that one ideal form of each living thing had been created and that the present-day variations—breeds of animals or races of people—are departures from those ideals.

The second idea is called the "chain of being." It says that the ideal or essential forms of things are not just a list of equals but are arranged in a ladder or chain, from least complex to most complex and from least perfect to most perfect. There are two different creation stories in Genesis, one where humans are created last, after all the animals (Gen. 1), and one where humans are created first (Gen. 2). Whichever order one accepts, however, there is the clear implication that humans are the most perfect form of creation. These two philosophical ideas would also have a strong influence on the later science of evolution, as we will see.

Dependence upon the Bible for knowledge of the natural world was not to last. About the time Ussher was making his calculations, others were beginning to seek knowledge about the earth from the earth itself. What these "natural scientists" or "natural philosophers" saw forced them to begin changing their minds about what seemed to be the obvious lessons from the book of Genesis.

For example, **fossils** of plants and animals—once thought to be mere quirks of nature—were recognized by another seventeenth-century scientist, Robert Hooke (1635–1703), as the remains of creatures that had become extinct or that still existed but in different form. Living things, in other words, had changed.

Moreover, Hooke attributed these extinctions and changes to the fact that the earth itself had been continually undergoing change since the creation. He even proposed a naturalistic explanation for Noah's flood; it was, he said, probably caused by earthquakes. So, since the earth is in a continual state of change, so are its inhabitants, changing as their environments are altered or becoming extinct if that alteration is too great.

evolution: Systematic change through time; here, with reference to biological species.

fossils: Remains of life forms of the past.

FIGURE 2.2
Geological strata at Provo Canyon, Utah. Data such as these convinced scientists that the history of the earth consisted of a series of events and that the earth and its life had undergone change over long periods of time.

Evidence for this idea of a changing earth came from the examination of the layers of rock and soil below the earth's present surface. These are the earth's **strata** (singular, stratum) and their study is called **stratigraphy** (Figure 2.2). One of the earliest scientists to discuss this was a Dane, Nicholas Steno (1638–1686). He suggested that the strata represented layers of sediments deposited by water in a *sequence*, the lower layers earlier and the higher layers later. The nature of the rock and soil of each stratum, and its fossil contents, showed the natural conditions at the time the stratum was deposited: what creatures existed, whether the area was under sea or on land, and so on. It became clear that neither the earth nor its inhabitants were stable and unchanging. It was also clear that the record of change could be read by observing the present-day world.

Steno and Hooke, however, still believed in a biblical chronology. The water-deposited layers of Steno's stratigraphic sequences represented basically two events—the original water-covered earth on which God created land and plants and animals (Gen. 1), and the waters of Noah's flood (Gen. 6–8). The geological record, however, shows a vast amount of change and the Bible only provides six thousand years of the earth's history. To bring about such change in so short a time, thought Steno and Hooke, required the presence of global catastrophic events associated with the creation and the flood—such as earthquakes and volcanos. Steno and Hooke and others who ascribed to this explanation are often referred to as **catastrophists.**

One well-known proponent of catastrophism was the French naturalist Georges Cuvier (1769–1832). Cuvier thought that a "prototype" of each creature had been created and that it and its environment had been planned to fit each other. The influence of essentialism is obvious here. Differences in climate, felt Cuvier, could bring about alterations in these prototypes, but such changes were limited, producing minor variations in the created types. He also thought that he could reconstruct the prototypes by using fossil remains of creatures. He compared the fragments of ancient creatures to living ones to try to picture what the whole organism looked like. In doing this, he pioneered the method known as **comparative anatomy,** still used today to infer missing parts of fossil organisms.

Cuvier also knew that life on earth had undergone major changes as well because, he felt, the entire plan of creation had been changed several times by the creator. These changes were manifested in a series of global catastrophes that brought about the extinction of existing forms of life and prepared the way for newly created forms. Thus, as science historian John Greene put it, Cuvier "recognized change but not development." In other words, he accepted that the world had changed but not that it had evolved, with new forms of life being modifications of older forms. Moreover, since humans were only included in the latest creation (although Cuvier did admit to the possibility that they might have been around before), there was the implication that humans were somehow the creator's highest, most perfect form of living thing—an idea clearly influenced by the chain of being concept.

Catastrophism enjoyed a degree of popularity because it seemed to reconcile natural evidence with a biblical timeframe. But strict catastrophism did not stand up to further scientific observation and examination. The French scholar Georges Buffon (1707–1788) concluded that, although catastrophic events do occur, they are rare and so "have no place in the ordinary course of nature." Instead, the earth's history is mainly explained by "operations *uniformly* repeated, motions which succeed one another without interruption [emphasis mine]" (Greene 1959:63–64). The motions Buffon spoke of were mainly the motions of the sea—tides

strata: Layers; here, the layers of rock and soil under the surface of the earth.

stratigraphy: The study of the earth's strata.

catastrophists: Those who believe the history of the earth is explained by a series of global catastrophes.

comparative anatomy: Comparing the anatomical features of various species. Used to reconstruct a fossil species from fragmentary remains.

and currents—operating to form the earth while the earth was still completely covered by water and while the strata were still being deposited. Phenomena such as wind and water erosion, occurring on land, he thought were not particularly important. But he did establish a new model: Much of the earth's geological history could be explained by normal, everyday, uniform processes—the things we can see taking place before our eyes. This idea is called **uniformitarianism.** For such processes to account for all the changes recorded in the earth's strata, however, more than six thousand years is required. Buffon was among the first to propose a longer history for the planet.

It was a Scotsman, James Hutton (1726–1797), who brought uniformitarianism onto the land. Hutton said that the history of the earth, as seen in its strata, is the result of three general processes: (1) the deposition of strata under the waters of the oceans; (2) the compacting of these strata by pressure and their uplifting above sea level by subterranean heat; and (3) the erosion of land by water, wind, and decay.

Hutton saw these processes as part of a self-regulating system: Erosion produced soil in which plants grew. Plants, in turn, fed animals and humans (for whom, he thought, all this had been created in the first place). New land was continually being formed under the sea from sediments produced by erosion, which would ultimately provide new sources of soil, and so on.

Again, such a system would require far more than six thousand years, and Hutton suggested that the earth was much older. Indeed, he thought it was virtually timeless, having "no vestige of a beginning—no prospect of an end" (Gould 1983:85).

Charles Lyell (1797–1875) was born in Scotland the year Hutton died, and it is his name that is usually associated with uniformitarianism. This is in part because his version of that idea was so extreme. He advocated, as had Hutton, the uniformity of processes throughout time, that is, that present-day processes are the key to explaining the past. He also believed that the rate of geological change was uniform—slow and steady through countless eons, with no need to invoke global catastrophes.

Furthermore, he believed that the earth itself was fairly uniform through time. The earth has been, and will be, always basically the same. Changes certainly occur, but they occur, said Lyell, just in the details, not in the overall appearance of the earth or in its life forms. Moreover, these changes occur in great cycles. He thought, for example, that dinosaurs, though extinct at the moment, would eventually reappear.

At this point, it would be a good idea to briefly describe where modern scientific knowledge stands on all these issues. We now agree with the major parts of the uniformitarian position, which are as follows:

FIGURE 2.3
Utah's Bryce Canyon shows the results of geological processes, especially the laying down of strata and subsequent erosion, over millions of years.

1. Processes that formed and changed the earth—as seen in its stratigraphic record—are the same processes that take place in the present.

2. By studying the stratigraphic record, we can reconstruct the past history of the earth (an idea that goes back to Steno).

3. For known geological processes to account for the changes recorded in the strata, an immense amount of time is required; we know now that the earth is about 4.5 billion years old (Figure 2.3).

We also now understand that Lyell was far too restrictive in his idea about uniform rate. Not all processes are slow and steady. Catastrophic events may seem relatively rare to us, but they do take place and have taken place many times during the history of the earth. Even Lyell acknowledged that most are localized events like volcanos and earthquakes that affect the geology and life of a particular area. However, some events are catastrophic on a global scale. At least five times during the four-billion-year history of life on earth, a major catastrophe has taken place,

uniformitarianism: The idea that present-day geological processes can also explain the past history of the earth.

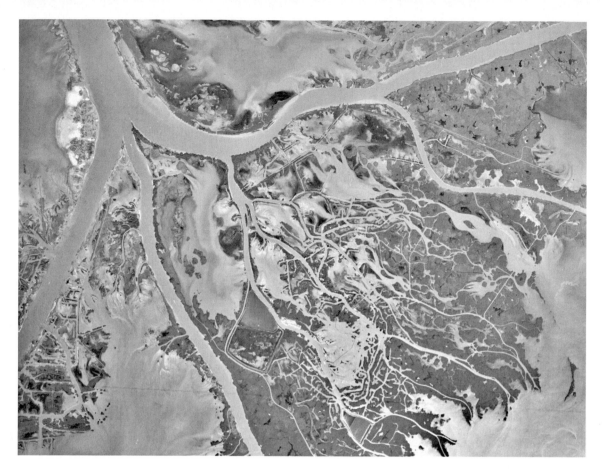

FIGURE 2.4

Aerial view of the Mississippi Delta. By estimating the amount of material deposited in the delta, Charles Lyell concluded (although incorrectly) that it was 100,000 years old.

bringing about the extinction of, in one case, over 90 percent of the earth's species. The most famous of these cataclysms (though not the biggest) occurred sixty-five million years ago when a comet or asteroid collided with the earth and caused such radical environmental change that 75 percent of the world's marine species became extinct along with many terrestrial species, including the dinosaurs. (See Chapter 6.) These are not the series of biblically associated catastrophes of Steno, Hooke, and Cuvier; they occur irregularly and are of natural origin. They have, nonetheless, radically altered the history of the planet.

Today we understand that Lyell's idea about the earth changing only in its details and in great cycles is also incorrect. The earth's history is a complex chain of events leading to other events, a continual sequence of changes—major and minor—never to be repeated. The dinosaurs are extinct; they will never return.

Despite what turned out to be some incorrect notions, Lyell's influence was great. Not only did he expand upon the work of Hutton and others, he also began the explicit examination of geological data, bringing it fully into the realm of natural science. For example, he attempted to estimate the age of the Mississippi Delta (Figure 2.4). Because the rate of deposition of sediments at the mouth of the river can be measured and because the size of the existing deposit in the delta can be estimated, the time required for the delta to be formed can be reckoned by assuming a uniform rate of deposition. Lyell arrived at a figure of about 100,000 years (1873:44–47). (Lyell was incorrect; the delta is not that old. Deposition rates are not constant nor were existing measurement techniques precise enough.)

Through the work of Hooke, Steno, Hutton, Lyell—and many others—the study of the earth was made natural rather than supernatural. Data about earth's history were sought in the earth itself, not within the presuppositions of belief systems. As a result, by the early nineteenth century, our world was viewed through the interacting perspectives of constant change brought about by observable processes over vast amounts of time.

Lyell put these ideas down in a major scientific work, his three volume *Principles of Geology*, first published between 1830 and 1833. The book was highly influential. It was enthusiastically received by supporters of the uniformitarian approach, strongly criticized by those who continued to explain earth's history as a series of global catastrophes, and pored over by those still examining the data. Among the latter was a young British naturalist who took the first volume of Lyell's book with him as he embarked, in 1831, on a 'round-the-world voyage of scientific exploration. This was Charles Darwin.

"COMMON SENSE AT ITS BEST": EXPLAINING BIOLOGICAL CHANGE

Robert Hooke recognized that fossils represented the remains of extinct creatures or of creatures that still existed but in different form. Steno showed that the earth's strata, and therefore the fossils in those strata, indicated a sequence of changes. Life on earth had undergone change, as had the earth itself.

This idea—then referred to as the "transmutation of species"—was a somewhat more controversial matter than the idea of a changing earth. For if other forms of life had arisen and changed over eons of time by uniform natural processes, then it followed that the same should apply to humans. It was, in part, in reaction to this idea that Cuvier attempted to apply catastrophism with a divine basis to an explanation of biological change. So, even after it became obvious that life had "evolved" (as we now phrase it), just *how* this had taken place mattered a great deal.

FIGURE 2.6
Biological variation. Variation within a population represents the raw material for natural selection. The tiger swallowtail butterflies (upper right and bottom) are members of the same species. The dark one is a mimic of the pipe-vine butterfly (left) that is protected from predation by its foul taste.

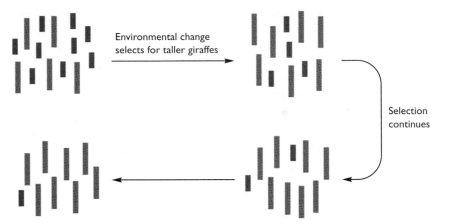

FIGURE 2.7
Schematic diagram of Darwin's model of evolution.

Environmental change selects for taller giraffes

Selection continues

the H.M.S. Beagle (1831–1836), Darwin realized the incredible degree of variation that exists within each living species (Figure 2.6). If Lamarck were correct, one would expect every member of a particular species to look pretty much the same because they all would have responded identically to the same environmental circumstances.

Darwin saw this was clearly not the case. Variation always exists, no matter how well-adapted a species might be. What tipped Darwin off to this fact of nature were his observations of domestic species like pigeons, carefully bred for certain features but still showing physical variation every generation. Therefore, in each generation, breeders would have to choose for mating only those individuals possessing the features they desired, using the assumption that offspring tend to resemble parents. The goal was to eliminate undesirable traits and accumulate desirable ones.

Darwin reasoned that the same thing happened in nature. Some of the natural variation within a species would make a difference in the success, or **fitness** of individuals. The better adapted individuals would tend to be more reproductively successful. Their traits would be passed on to more offspring than would those of the less well adapted. Over time, then, some traits would accumulate while others would decrease in frequency or even be eliminated. If the environment to which a species is adapted changes, it stands to reason that the fitness value of certain traits might change, so the process described might proceed in a different adaptive direction—what was once adapted might now be neutral or perhaps even poorly adapted.

So, while Lamarck thought that variation arose *when it was needed*, Darwin understood that variation *already existed*. Because Darwin lived before genetics were known, he did not understand where this variation came from, but his observations showed it was a fact; and he realized that nature, like a plant or animal breeder, "selects" the better adapted individuals for more successful reproduction. Darwin called this process **natural selection** (Figure 2.7).

fitness: The relative adaptiveness of an individual organism, measured ultimately by reproductive success.

natural selection: Evolutionary change based on the differential reproductive success of individuals within a species.

Several important ideas follow from natural selection:

1. It becomes clear that evolution by natural selection has no particular direction. Organisms do not "progress" to increasingly complex forms as Lamarck thought but evolve to simply stay adapted to their environments or, if possible, become re-adapted to changed environments. Variation is not "willed." It results from random processes that we now understand as the processes of genetics (see Chapter 3).

2. It is also clear that such a process, using random rather than directed or "willed" variation, is not foolproof. It doesn't always work. Species do become extinct, usually when the environment changes so extensively or rapidly that none of the existing variation within a species is adaptive. Extinction is, in fact, the norm. Nine–tenths of all species that have ever lived are now extinct.

3. It follows that *new* species can arise from this basic process. If populations within a species become environmentally separated, these populations will be under different selective pressures—different traits will be differently adapted in each environment. Moreover, the production of variation will be different in each population. Natural selection will have different raw materials to work with. Over time, then, a single species may give rise to one or more new species. This, in fact, was what Darwin was ultimately trying to explain, as indicated by the title of his most famous work, *On the Origin of Species by Means of Natural Selection*, first published in 1859.

Darwin's idea generated some controversy which was perhaps what caused him to delay publishing it. We know he understood natural selection sometime in the late 1830s, yet it was not until over twenty years later that he made it public. Even then, he only did so because a younger, less well-known naturalist, Alfred Russel Wallace (1823–1913), independently came up with the same idea and Darwin was urged by friends to rush his conclusion into print.

The controversy centered not around the idea of uniformitarian evolution itself—which was generally well accepted by that time—but around the fact that Darwin's idea, unlike Lamarck's, did not involve a particular progressive direction nor the direct control or will of the organism. Darwin also acknowledged extinction. These ideas were not always comfortable. But, to Darwin's surprise, by the time his book sold out on its first day of publication, the scientific community and much of the informed public were ready to accept the idea, even with its implications. Natural selection—the mechanism of evolution—was hailed as a major scientific breakthrough and remains today a classic example of scientific reasoning, what Darwin's friend Thomas Henry Huxley called "common sense at its best."

At about the time Darwin was writing *Origin of Species*, a monk in what is now the Czech Republic was answering Darwin's question about the source of variation. After years of undocumented research on several species of plants and animals, Gregor Mendel (1822–1884), derived the basic laws of genetics by experimenting with the pea plants in the garden of his monastery. These laws (which we'll cover in the next chapter) not only explained one source of biological variation, but also showed why and how offspring tend to resemble their parents. Basic laws of genetics and biological variation are crucial to natural selection and the origin of new species.

Mendel died in relative obscurity (Darwin never learned of his work) and his writings languished in libraries until 1900 when he was rediscovered independently by three European scientists. They realized that Mendel's work carried implications far beyond some interesting facts about pea plants. (This had been the reaction to his work during Mendel's life—that he had found some interesting facts about peas.) They understood that genetics filled in those pieces that Darwin acknowledged were missing from his process.

During the twentieth century, many scientists have added to Darwin's natural selection and Mendel's genetics. There have been new details, changes of emphasis, and major discoveries, such as the breaking of the genetic code in the early 1950s. But all the work of the last nearly one hundred years has been built upon the thoughts and discoveries of people like Darwin and Lyell and Hooke, and many others. All the men and women whose investigations have led to our modern theory of evolution (which we will cover in the next three chapters) would freely agree that they have stood on the shoulders of these giants (Table 2.1).

SUMMARY

The Judeo-Christian belief system, as set down in the Bible, was long seen as informing its followers not only "how to get to heaven" but also "how heaven is." That is, it was seen as both a belief system and as a source of literal knowledge. As scholars began looking more objectively at nature itself, however, their observations and the rational conclusions they drew from them showed clearly that knowledge of the heavens, the earth, and the earth's inhabitants required the methods of science. As the scientific method was applied to the study of the earth, scientists gradually learned to give up their presuppositions.

TABLE 2.1
Chart of Important People and Ideas Associated with Evolution

	Approx. Date of Publication	Contribution
James Ussher (1581–1656)	1650	Calculated age of earth using biblical data.
Robert Hooke (1635–1703)	1660s-90s	Fossils as evidence of change. Importance of environmental change.
Nicholas Steno (1638–1686)	1669	Stratigraphy.
Georges Buffon (1707–1788)	1749	Uniformitarianism. Longer timeframe.
James Hutton (1726–1797)	1795	Uniformitarianism. Natural cycles. Longer timeframe.
Jean Baptiste de Lamarck (1748–1829)	1809	Adaptation. Inheritance of acquired characteristics. Progressive evolution.
Georges Cuvier (1769–1832)	late 1700s early 1800s	Ideal prototypes. Climatic alterations. Extinction. Catastrophism.
Charles Lyell (1797–1875)	1830-33	Uniformitarianism. Scientific investigation.
Charles Darwin (1809-1882)	1859	Natural selection. The origin of species.
Alfred Russel Wallace (1823–1913)	1859	Natural selection.
Gregor Mendel (1822-1884)	1860s	The laws of inheritance.

Charles Darwin, adhering faithfully to the spirit of scientific methodology, was able to synthesize his observations and thoughts with those of many others and to formulate a theory that literally made possible the work that has led to our modern knowledge of the nature and evolution of living things.

KEY TERMS

evolution	uniformitarianism	comparative anatomy
fossils	adapted	fitness
strata	progressive	natural selection
stratigraphy	inheritance of	
catastrophists	acquired	
	characteristics	

SUGGESTED READINGS

The history of the study of evolution is covered in C. Leon Harris's *Evolution: Genesis and Revelations*, which contains numerous sections from original works, and in John C. Greene's *The Death of Adam*. The impact of Darwin's work on modern knowledge in general is the theme of Philip Appleman's *Darwin: A Norton Critical Edition*.

A new biography of Darwin that focuses on the man as well as the scientist, and nicely shows how the two aspects of his life were related, is John Bowlby's *Charles Darwin: A New Life*.

Paleontologist and science historian Stephen Jay Gould has written many wonderful essays about the history of evolution and the personalities involved. These can be found throughout his books *Ever Since Darwin*, *The Panda's Thumb*, *Hen's Teeth and Horse's Toes*, *The Flamingo's Smile*, *Bully for Brontosaurus*, and *Eight Little Piggies*. These are all highly recommended.

EVOLUTIONARY GENETICS

The laws governing
inheritance are for the
most part unknown.
—Charles Darwin

Two important features of Darwin's natural selection were the seemingly contradictory facts that offspring tend to resemble their parents but that, at the same time, there is continual production of biological variation among members of a species and from generation to generation. Both facts were obvious enough to careful observers like Darwin and others. But, as Darwin freely admitted, science was largely ignorant of the source of those facts, in other words, of how inheritance worked.

A popular idea of Darwin's time assumed that inheritance was "blending"—a mixture of some material from both parents. Certainly there are sufficient examples of offspring with combinations of parental traits to make this idea seem logical. For example, new flower colors can be produced by crossbreeding other colors, much like paints are mixed to make new shades. Breeds of dogs can be crossbred to get combinations of the parents' physical and behavioral characteristics in the hybrid offspring. But offspring are often born with characteristics that resemble neither parent or, as with one's sex, are definitely *not* mixtures.

Observations of nonblending traits may have led Gregor Mendel to begin experiments to determine just how inheritance operates. The laws he derived are still recognized today as the basis of genetics although, of course, they have been added to greatly. The most basic and perhaps most important of Mendel's contributions was his conclusion that inheritance did not involve the blending of substances but, rather, was **particulate.** He showed that traits are passed on by individual particles according to very specific principles. Mendel called these particles "factors;" we call them **genes.** We'll now survey our modern knowledge of basic genetics by addressing the following questions:

How do genes produce the traits that make a pea plant or a human being?

What are the basic laws of inheritance?

What processes bring about the variation we see among members of a species and between parents and offspring?

HOW GENES WORK

We begin to see how genes work with something Mendel could not possibly have understood. Although he concluded that the particulate factors we now call genes produce the features of an organism, and he provided us with the basic model for how traits are inherited, Mendel possessed neither the background knowledge nor the technology to figure out just how the genetic code operates at the chemical level.

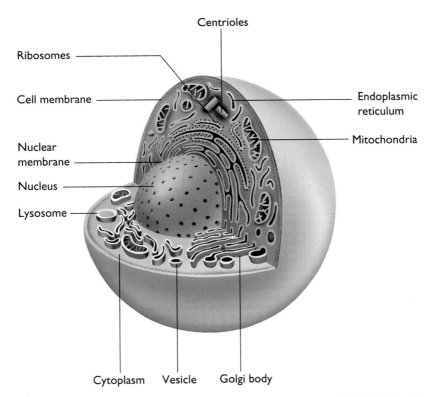

Centrioles

Ribosomes

Cell membrane

Nuclear
membrane

Nucleus

Lysosome

Endoplasmic
reticulum

Mitochondria

Cytoplasm   Vesicle   Golgi body

FIGURE 3.1

A typical cell and its important parts. This cell represents all types of cells from
the more complex single-
celled organisms like ameo-
bas to the cells in the human
body.

We understand today that a gene is a chemical code for the production
(synthesis) of a **protein.** Proteins are the basic building blocks of an organism's cells and, in a form called **enzymes,** are responsible for the cells'
chemical reactions. All organisms are composed of cells (Figure 3.1) so it
can logically be said that all living things are, in fact, proteins. Even the
inclusion of nonprotein substances—like the calcium in your bones—is
regulated by proteins.

The genetic code is found in the nucleus of cells, on long strands
called **chromosomes.** A chromosome is made up of a protein and a nucleic
acid. It is the nucleic acid—**deoxyribonucleic acid (DNA)**—that carries
the code.

DNA is like a ladder with the ends twisted in opposite directions
(Figure 3.2). This shape is referred to as a double helix. The sides of the
ladder are for structural stability. The rungs of the ladder are the code.
They are made up of pairs of bases (a family of chemicals). Only four bases
are involved: adenine (A), thymine (T), cytosine (C), and guanine (G),
and they are only paired in A-T or T-A, and C-G or G-C combinations.
Each base and the portion of the side of the ladder to which it is connected
is called a **nucleotide.**

The strings of these bases are divided into groups of three, called
codons. Codons are like words made up of three letters. Each word stands

particulate: The idea that
biological traits are controlled by individual factors
rather than by a single hereditary agent.

genes: Those portions of
the DNA molecule that
code for specific traits.

protein: One of the family
of molecules that makes
cells and carries out cellular functions.

enzymes: Proteins that
control chemical processes.

chromosomes: Strands of
DNA in the nucleus of a
cell.

**deoxyribonucleic acid
(DNA):** The molecule
that carries the genetic
code.

nucleotide: The basic
building blocks of DNA
and RNA, made up of a
sugar, a phosphate, and
one of four bases.

codons: The sections of
DNA that code for specific
amino acids.

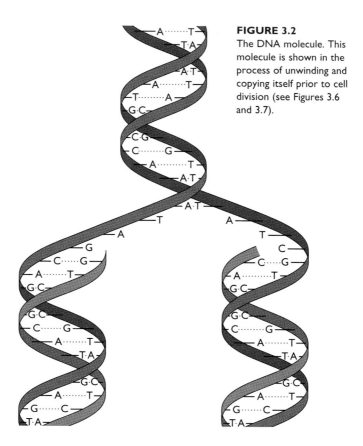

FIGURE 3.2
The DNA molecule. This molecule is shown in the process of unwinding and copying itself prior to cell division (see Figures 3.6 and 3.7).

FIGURE 3.3
The process of protein synthesis as described in the text. In reality, no protein is only four amino acids long, but the process works exactly as shown.

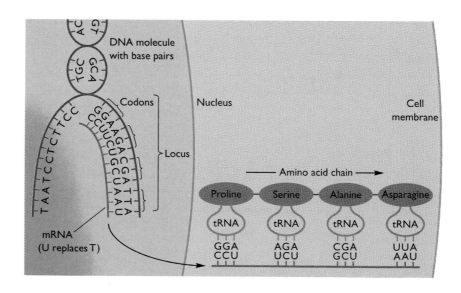

for a particular **amino acid.** A string of words—a genetic sentence—thus stands for a chain of amino acids. A chain of amino acids is a protein. Therefore, a sequence of codons codes for the linking together of amino acids to make a protein. This process is known as **protein synthesis** (Figure 3.3).

We can carry our analogy further. Because sentences need beginnings and ends, some codons serve the function of punctuation, separating one codon sentence from the next. Most human codons, however, perhaps as many as 90 percent, *appear* to do nothing. They are either copies of functioning codons or are meaningless, so-called junk genes. Exactly what purpose they serve, if any, and how they originated remains a matter of continuing debate.

A gene, therefore, is that portion of the DNA molecule that carries the codon sentence for a particular protein. Because *gene* is used in so many different ways, we also use the term **locus (pl. loci)** for this sequence of codons, referring to the position (locus) of those codons on a chromosome. To summarize then:

FEATURE	ANALOGUE	MEANING
base (A, T, C, G)	letter	
codon	word	amino acid
gene (locus)	sentence	protein

How does protein synthesis work? As you read this description, follow along in Figure 3.3. First, the code must be read. The DNA molecule unwinds, breaking apart at the middle of the "rungs" where the bases are joined. Only half of the DNA molecule, that is, only one base of each pair, carries the code. Another nucleic acid, **messenger ribonucleic acid (mRNA)**, in which uracil (U) replaces thymine (T), transcribes the code by lining up its bases to match their complement bases exposed on the unwound DNA. Remember, A must always pair with T (or U), and C with G. The mRNA, now a mirror image of the DNA code, then moves out of the nucleus into the cytoplasm of the cell.

In the cytoplasm are free amino acids (there are only about twenty different amino acids in all living organisms) and yet another nucleic acid, **transfer ribonucleic acid (tRNA).** The tRNA bases are in the original code letters (but with U still replacing T). The tRNA molecules pick up the corresponding amino acids and then line up along the mRNA with bases paired as in the original DNA molecule back in the nucleus. The lined-up amino acids bond to form the specified protein, which can now perform its functions in the cell.

It's still a long way from a protein to a trait—the observable, measurable physical or chemical characteristics of an organism. Some traits are

amino acid: The chief component of proteins.

protein synthesis: The process by which the genetic code puts together proteins in the cell.

locus (plural, loci): The location on a chromosome of the genetic code for a specific trait.

messenger ribonucleic acid (mRNA): The molecule that carries the genetic code out of the nucleus for translation into proteins.

transfer ribonucleic acid (tRNA): RNA that lines up amino acids along mRNA to make proteins.

FIGURE 3.4
Skin color variation in modern humans provides an example of a polygenic trait with a wide range of phenotypic expressions.

fairly simple. Hemoglobin, the chemical on red blood cells that carries oxygen, *is* protein. It is made up of two chains of 141 and 146 amino acids. In other words, it is coded for on two loci—two gene sentences with 141 and 146 words.

Skin color, by contrast, is not a simple trait. It involves three different pigments (including red hemoglobin) and other factors such as skin thickness. The color of a person's skin is thus a trait produced by the complex interaction of many proteins and so is coded for on many loci (Figure 3.4). Such traits are **polygenic.** Traits coded for by a single locus are, obviously, **monogenic;** however, most traits of most organisms are polygenic.

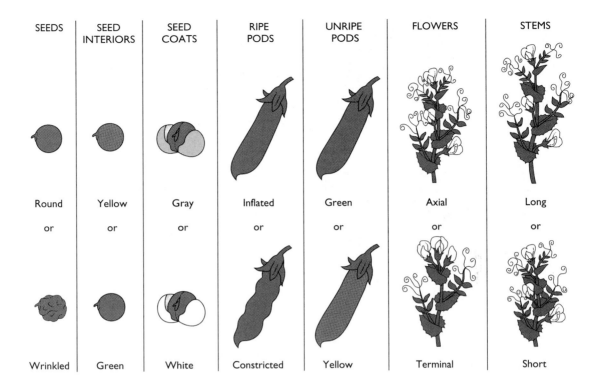

SEEDS	SEED INTERIORS	SEED COATS	RIPE PODS	UNRIPE PODS	FLOWERS	STEMS
Round	Yellow	Gray	Inflated	Green	Axial	Long
or	or	or	or	or	or	or
Wrinkled	Green	White	Constricted	Yellow	Terminal	Short

FIGURE 3.5
The traits of the pea plant that Mendel observed in his famous experiments.

Now, if Mendel possessed neither the technology nor the background knowledge to understand the structure of the genetic code and the process of protein synthesis, what then did he discover about the processes of genetics? We refer to his contribution as **Mendelian genetics.** It involves the basic laws of inheritance, which we will take up in the next section, and the general structure and operation of the genetic code.

Mendel conducted at least eight years of extensive breeding experiments, mostly on pea plants, crossing plants that exhibited different expressions of a trait and then crossing hybrids with each other and back with the original plants.

Mendel only used traits that were monogenic (Figure 3.5). He carefully picked these after considering other traits, many of which were polygenic and so were rejected because, like skin color, they did not appear in simple either/or variation. In a sense, Mendel "fudged" his experiment (no modern scientists would simply leave out what didn't fit their expectations), but we forgive him because, in fact, all *genes* work the way he thought even if some *traits* are more complex.

Mendel reached the conclusion that *each organism possesses two genes for each trait—one from each parent.* Not only does each organism possess two of each gene (or locus) but loci may come in different versions. We

polygenic: A trait coded for by more than one locus.

monogenic: A trait coded for by a single locus.

Mendelian genetics: The laws of inheritance, discovered by Gregor Mendel in the nineteenth century.

call these **alleles.** Although Mendel used pea plants, it might be more interesting for us to use a human example. There is a chemical called PTC (phenylthiocarbamide) that people can either taste or not. (For those who can, it has a dry, bitter flavor. If you find brussels sprouts bitter, you are tasting a thiocarbaminde.) This "taster trait" is monogenic, but the locus for the trait has, as you might suspect, two alleles: *T*, that codes for the ability to taste PTC, and *t*, that codes for the inability to taste the chemical.

Because every human possesses two loci for the taster gene—one from their father and one from their mother—we each have one of three possible combinations. These combinations are called **genotypes.** We may have two of the same allele: *TT* or *tt*, a condition known as **homozygous** (from *homo*, the same), or we may also have a pair of nonmatching alleles: *Tt*. This is **heterozygous** (from *hetero*, meaning different).

These genotypes are responsible for producing either a taster individual or a nontaster. The observable trait—the result of the genetic code—is the **phenotype.** What phenotype does each genotype here produce?

Genotype	Phenotype
TT	taster
tt	nontaster
Tt	taster

Why does the heterozygote *Tt* produce the same phenotype as the homozygote *TT*? Because, as Mendel also worked out, some alleles are **dominant** and some are **recessive.** In this case the allele for tasting is dominant (that's why it's a capital letter) and so, in the heterozygous genotype, it hides the action of the allele for nontasting. The only way a phenotype can reflect a recessive allele is if the genotype is homozygous for the recessive (*tt*).

It is very important to understand that the words dominant and recessive have no value attached to them. Dominant alleles are not necessarily better or more common. There are, for example, quite a few human genetic diseases, some lethal, caused by dominant alleles. The terms dominant and recessive simply mean that if two alleles in this relationship are in a heterozygous genotype, the action of the dominant will be expressed and the action of the recessive will be hidden.

Alleles for most traits do not, in fact, work this neatly. In most cases heterozygote genotypes result in phenotypes that exhibit some action of both alleles. (This is, in part, what led to the mistaken concept of "blending" inheritance.) Such alleles are said to be **codominant,** and they result in a greater number of possible phenotypes. In addition, many loci have more than two possible alleles, resulting in even more potential phenotypes. (Remember, however, that each individual can only possess a *pair* of alleles.)

A single example can demonstrate both these facts. Your blood type for the ABO system is coded for by a single locus, the *I* locus, but there are three possible alleles: I^A, I^B, and I^O. So, we have six possible genotypes but only four possible phenotypes. (We can designate the genotypes using only the superscript, but remember that these are alleles of a single locus, not separate genes.)

GENOTYPE	PHENOTYPE
AA	type A
AO	type A
BB	type B
BO	type B
AB	type AB
OO	type O

It's clear that both A and B are dominant over the recessive O. The AB genotype, however, expresses the action of both alleles. The A and B alleles are codominant. (We will discuss the ABO system in greater detail in Chapter 13.)

Most phenotypic traits, of course, are coded for by multiple loci, some of which may have even more alleles. In addition, some alleles are in an even more complex relationship, where the action of both is expressed in the phenotype, but one more so than the other.

Some of the pea plant traits that Mendel rejected were probably traits like these. He rejected them because their phenotypic expressions were too complex for him to easily see any regularities in inheritance. We still have this problem today although, of course, we don't simply ignore data we can't explain. The genetic bases for most phenotypic traits have eluded us because there are multiple loci involved and because the alleles of those loci are not in a simple dominant/recessive relationship to one another.

There is a further complication, and it's an important one. The path between the genetic code and the resultant phenotypic expression can be influenced by outside factors, that is, factors that are not directly part of the reading of the genetic code and the synthesis of proteins. We can call these nongenetic influences **environmental.** Certainly, some traits are unaffected by environmental influences. Your ABO blood type is determined by relatively simple proteins (called **antigens**) on the surface of your red blood cells. Because they are direct products of your genetic code, there's nothing that can change what those genes code for except a change in the code itself. Such a change is called a **mutation,** literally a mistake in the genetic code. (We will discuss mutations in the next chapter.)

Other traits, however, are influenced by environmental factors. Your skin color, for example, is certainly coded for in your genes (there are at

alleles: Variants of a genetic locus.

genotypes: The alleles possessed by an organism.

homozygous: Having two of the same allele.

heterozygous: Having two different alleles in a gene pair.

phenotype: The chemical or physical results of the genetic code.

dominant: The allele of a pair that is expressed in the phenotype.

recessive: The allele of a pair that is not expressed.

codominant: When both alleles of a pair are expressed in the phenotype.

environmental: Here, any nongenetic influence on the phenotype.

antigens: Proteins used by the body's immune system to distinguish between "self" and "nonself."

mutation: Any mistake in an organism's genetic material.

THE PROCESSES OF EVOLUTION

> I am convinced that
> Natural Selection has
> been the most
> important, but not the
> exclusive, means of
> modification.
> —Charles Darwin

One of the scientists who "rediscovered" Mendel's work in 1900 was the Dutch botanist Hugo de Vries (1848–1935). De Vries had been trying to explain the variations that sometimes spontaneously appeared in plants (and, of course, in animals)—such as a single flower of the wrong color or an individual that was far smaller or larger than other members of its species. Breeders called these oddities "sports." De Vries called them mutations. When he read about Mendel's experiments, De Vries realized that these mutations were the results of sudden changes in Mendel's "factors." We would now say that a mutation is any change in the genetic mechanism.

With De Vries's contribution, all the major pieces were in place to articulate a *basic theory of evolution*, which may be stated as follows:

A particulate genetic code is initially responsible for the form and function of an organism. Mutations in this code continually add genetic, and therefore phenotypic, variation to a species. Segregation, recombination, independent assortment, and crossing-over shuffle existing genotypic combinations at reproduction and thus provide additional genetic and phenotypic variation. Phenotypic variation is affected by the process we call natural selection, where the better adapted individuals will be more reproductively successful and will thus disproportionately pass on their phenotypic traits to future generations. The results of natural selection are the maintenance of a species' adaptive relationship to existing environmental conditions, the alteration of a species' phenotypic variation under circumstances of changing environmental conditions, and, ultimately, the development of new species.

As research continued throughout this century, it was realized that there are other processes that also play roles in the production of the variation on which natural selection acts. Research still goes on into the relationships and relative importance of all these processes in the evolution of species.

What are species?

What are the processes of evolution?

How do they interact to bring about evolution as we understand it today?

SPECIES: THE UNITS OF EVOLUTION

We observe evolution as the change in species over time and the development of new species. Evolution does not take place in individuals. You and I don't evolve in this sense. Evolution takes place in *populations* of organisms, and the basic population in nature is the species.

A species is *a population of organisms whose members can, under natural circumstances, freely interbreed with one another and produce fertile offspring.* Humans and chimpanzees, despite our 99 percent genetic similarity, cannot (even under *un*natural circumstances) interbreed and produce offspring because our two species have different numbers of chromosomes. But any two normally healthy humans of the opposite sex, no matter how different they may appear phenotypically, can reproduce, and their offspring are fertile. Thus, humans and chimps are different species, but all human beings are members of a single species, *Homo sapiens.*

Horses and donkeys can mate and produce offspring, known as mules. But mules are sterile. Two mules can't reproduce and make more mules. Thus, horses and donkeys are separate species.

In captivity, lions and tigers have been known to produce hybrid offspring that are, in many cases, fertile. But lions and tigers don't interbreed in the wild. Though their ranges overlap (in India), the specific environmental **niche** of each animal is different, as are their behaviors, including mating behavior. Thus, lions and tigers are separate species.

Similarly, domestic dogs and wolves can reproduce and the hybrid offspring are fertile. Indeed, in a genetic sense, dogs and wolves are still identical. But dogs and wolves do not freely interbreed under natural circumstances; wolves are wild and dogs are domestic (and thus, in a sense, unnatural). Dogs have been manipulated by humans for about 12,000 years and have become adapted to *our* environment. We have even produced some breeds that, because of their size, could not possibly mate with a wolf, or with other breeds of dogs, or carry and give birth to the fetuses from such matings.

It is not surprising to us that humans and chimps are separate species because, very simply, we don't *look* like the same species, although we do differ in only 1 percent of our genes. Horses and donkeys, on the other hand, do look pretty similar and yet are different species. Lions and tigers look like different species but can still produce fertile offspring, although only under artificial conditions. And some breeds of dogs look so similar to wolves as to obviously belong to the same species, although other breeds only faintly resemble their wild ancestors (Figure 4.1).

If the species is the basic natural unit of evolution, then why is the distinction among various species sometimes so vague? Why aren't all species equally distinct—separate from one another to the same degree and for the same reasons? And why are scientists who specialize in classifying species (called **taxonomists** or **systematists**) sometimes at odds with one another over which populations belong to the same species?

The answer to all these questions is that while the origin of new species from existing species usually happens fairly quickly, it does not happen instantly. It is a *process* that takes place over time (a subject we'll examine in Chapter 5). Thus, there is usually a period when two or more

niche: The environment of an organism and its adaptive response to that environment.

taxonomists: Those who classify and name living organisms.

systematists: Synonym for taxonomists.

emerging species still blend with one another and are therefore difficult to define—as is the case with dogs and wolves.

In addition, all species did not emerge at the same time. They appeared at different times, they evolve at different rates, and they continue to evolve. Species thus change in relation to one another as time goes on.

We established in the last chapter that, although evolution results in phenotypic change, it must also involve genetic change. So, if species change over time, we need to characterize populations within a species in genetic terms in order to fully examine their evolution. We do so by using the concept of **gene frequency,** also, and more accurately, called **allele frequency.**

Going back to our example of the taster trait, suppose every human on earth was homozygous for the dominant (T) allele. The allele frequency would be $T = 1.0$ (or 100 percent). The phenotypic result of this would be that every member of the species would be a taster.

Now, suppose that a mutation occurred somewhere that changed a T allele to a t allele and that, over time, the mutated allele was passed on to many generations of offspring so that at some point 25 percent of the alleles at the taster locus in our species were recessives (t). Now the gene (allele) frequencies for this locus would be .75 (75 percent) T, and .25 (25 percent) t.

This alteration in frequency would, of course, have a phenotypic effect. Most individuals will still be tasters since T is still the most frequent allele and, as you recall, heterozygotes are also phenotypically tasters. But there will be some homozygous recessives (tt) who will be nontasters. The species will have changed phenotypically over time as a result of a genetic change. Thus, evolution operates by *changes in gene (allele) frequency through time.* Anything that changes allele frequency is therefore a process of evolution.

We will now describe those processes that produce evolutionary change within species and that, ultimately, bring about the origin of new species.

MUTATIONS: NECESSARY ERRORS

A mutation is any change in the genetic code. Some mutations involve a single incorrect base in a codon (one letter of one word). These are known as **point mutations.** Some point mutations may be inconsequential, but some might result in the wrong amino acid in a protein, which could have disastrous results for the organism. (An example is sickle cell anemia, a genetic disease, which we'll cover at the end of this chapter.)

Other mutations may involve a whole chromosome or a large portion of one. These are called **chromosomal mutations.** They are almost always deleterious because many genes are affected. For example, humans who have three of the Number 21 chromosome, instead of the usual pair, have Down Syndrome or Trisomy 21, which results in mental retardation and other phenotypic effects (Figure 4.2).

Mutations are random; that is, a specific mutation doesn't occur for a specific reason or at a specific time. Mutations occur continually, but exactly *what* mutation occurs is totally unpredictable, nor do mutations occur *because* they are needed. Some mutations are the results of environmental influences, like cosmic radiation and other forms of radioactivity, or chemical pollutants. Most, however, are simply mechanical errors that occur during the complex process of gene replication at cell division or during the even more complex process where the genetic code is read, translated, and transcribed into proteins.

As you might imagine, then, mutations are frequent. They are occurring in the cells of your body as you read this. The mutations that occur during the reading of the code just affect the individual. The process of aging, for example, is partly a result of the accumulation of cells with mutations that make them in some way abnormal, though they are still alive and able to divide.

The only mutations that concern us in an evolutionary sense are those that occur in the gametes or in the specialized cells that produce gametes. These mutations are the ones that are passed on to future generations and thus bring about genetic change through time. Therefore, mutation changes gene frequency through time by making new versions of a gene (as in the taster trait example above) or by otherwise altering the details of the genetic code. Mutation is a process of evolution.

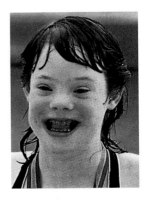

FIGURE 4.2
A child with Down syndrome, showing the characteristic facial features that are some of the multiple phenotypic effects of the presence of the extra chromosome. This girl has just won a medal in swimming at the Special Olympics.

gene frequency: The percentage of times a particular allele appears in a population.

allele frequency: The same as gene frequency, and the preferred term.

point mutations: Mutations of single codons.

chromosomal mutations: Mutations of a whole chromosome or a large portion of a chromosome.

Because mutations are mistakes—deviations from the normal genetic code—many are deleterious. They produce a phenotypic result that is abnormal and therefore, to one degree or another, maladaptive. Individuals with such traits may not be as reproductively successful as most members of their species, and so the mutant gene or genes will not be passed on as often, if at all. In other words, natural selection will select *against* those genes. But mutations may also produce alleles that are neutral, making no difference to an individual's fitness, or they may produce alleles that result in even *better* adapted phenotypes and are thus selected *for.*

Mutation, in other words, changes gene frequency and, as it does so, adds genetic variation to a species' **gene pool.** Mutations are the price living things pay for the process of evolution. Without mutation—if the first life forms reproduced themselves absolutely without error—nothing would have changed, and the first living things would be the *only* living things. Mutations are the "natural resources" for evolution.

NATURAL SELECTION: THE PRIME MOVER OF EVOLUTION

By now, you should have a pretty good idea how natural selection operates. The genetic variation produced by mutation, segregation, and recombination results in phenotypic variation within a species. Much of a species' phenotypic variation may make little difference to the fitness and reproductive success of individuals. We have come to see that nature is more tolerant of variation than Darwin thought. He felt that *every* variation made a difference. We know this is not the case.

At the same time, however, some phenotypic variation does make a difference. How much of a difference, of course, depends upon what traits are important for the adaptation of a particular species to a particular environment at a particular time. What's adaptive for one species—say, large size or a certain color—will not necessarily work for another species, and, as environments change, a trait that *was* adaptive for a species may no longer be adaptive.

Perhaps the most famous example of natural selection demonstrates the basic features of the process. There is a moth in England called the peppered moth, because when it was first described, before the Industrial Revolution, most members of the species were multicolored. This color pattern provided the moths with camouflage when they landed on tree trunks covered with lichens (a plant that is a combination of an algae and a fungus). Birds, the moth's major predators, had a hard time seeing them.

Every generation, however, some peppered moths would appear that would be uniformly dark in color, the result of a different allele (or alleles)

FIGURE 4.3
Peppered moths. Where trees are light and covered with lichens, the light form of the moth has an obvious selective advantage in being better camouflaged. Where trees are blackened by soot, the dark form has the advantage.

for coloration. These moths were more easily seen by the birds, so relatively fewer of them survived and reproduced. Thus, the multicolored moths were more common and the dark moths were rare (Figure 4.3).

When extensive coal burning in the nineteenth century killed off the sensitive lichens and blackened the tree trunks, the once rare dark moths had an adaptive advantage. Less easily seen by predators, they now reproduced relatively more successfully than the multicolored members of their species and so passed on more of the allele(s) for dark coloration. The frequency of the alleles involved changed over time causing the average phenotype of the species to change.

Recently, by the way, with less coal burning and better pollution control, the lichens are returning and, as you probably guessed, the multicolored moths are becoming increasingly frequent.

gene pool: All the alleles in a population.

The example of the peppered moths makes two very important points:

1. Adaptation within a species is *relative to a specific set of environmental circumstances*. Mixed coloration was adaptive under one set of environmental conditions, while dark color was adaptive when those conditions changed.

2. Notice that the dark coloration did not appear *when* it was needed. It was, perhaps fortunately for the peppered moth, *already present* as a result of genetic variation within the species. If the color variation of the moths had been of a different sort, or if there had been no variation in color, natural selection would have had different materials to work with and a quite different series of evolutionary events would have taken place. Natural selection does not create adaptive variation. It uses the variation already present.

It follows from these points that natural selection is not always successful in maintaining a species' adaptation and survival in the face of environmental change. If a change is too rapid and/or too extensive, the natural variation within a species simply may not be enough to provide any individuals with sufficient reproductive success to keep the species going. When that comet or asteroid hit the earth 65 million years ago and radically altered the earth's climate, perhaps hundreds of thousands of species, the dinosaurs and many others, were unable to adapt and thus became extinct. Natural variation within a species cannot predict what environmental change may take place in the future. Adaptation to change is a matter of luck. Indeed, for over 90 percent of all species that have ever existed, their luck ran out; they are extinct.

Recognition that extinction is commonplace was another reason for Charles Darwin's delay in making his idea of natural selection known to the public. Natural selection does not produce change in a particular direction (as Lamarck thought), nor does it always work to ensure the survival of a species. Darwin thought, perhaps correctly at first, that these implications were too uncomfortable for most people to accept. By 1859,

FIGURE 4.4

The processes of evolution. A species is in an adaptive relationship with its environment. This relationship is maintained by natural selection. Environments, however, are constantly changing, so the adaptive characteristics of species change through time. In addition, the gene pool of a species is always changing, altering the phenotypes upon which selection acts. Processes that alter a species' gene pool are also, by definition, processes of evolution because they change allele frequency. Mutation provides new genetic variation by producing new alleles or otherwise altering the genetic code. Flow and drift mix the genetic variation within a population, continually supplying new combinations of the genetic variables.

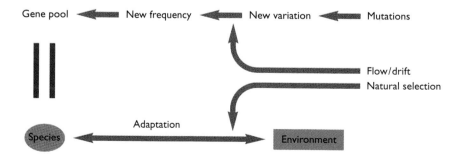

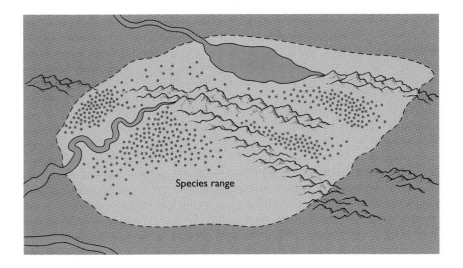

FIGURE 4.5
Demes. The members of a species of lowland, non-aquatic animal (dots) are un-evenly distributed within that species' range because of mountain and water bounda-ries. The separate population concentrations—the demes—may be phenotypi-cally distinguishable from one another.

however, the Victorian world of rapid social, industrial, economic, and political transformation had come to accept change as the norm, for itself as well as for nature. Moreover, the logic of *Origin of Species* was so lucid and well presented that its conclusions were seen as obvious. Darwin's book was a bestseller, and his idea was, except for a few holdouts, well accepted, at least within science.

Mutation and natural selection are the major processes of evolution. Mutation provides new genetic variation. Natural selection selects phenotypes for reproductive success based on their adaptive relationship with the environment. But because evolution is technically defined as change in allele frequency, two other processes must also be considered as processes of evolution (Figure 4.4).

GENE FLOW: MIXING POPULATIONS

By definition, members of a species can and do interbreed with one another. The members of a species, however, are usually unevenly distributed over that species' range. Populations within a species can be to some degree separated from other populations by environmental barriers, geographic distance, or, in the case of our species, social and cultural distinctions like political, religious, and ethnic boundaries. Such populations are called **breeding populations,** or **demes.** Individuals tend to find mates within their own deme (Figure 4.5).

Although belonging to the same species, demes may exhibit genetic distinctions. There are two reasons for this. First, demes may exist in some-

gene flow: The exchange of genes among populations through interbreeding.

breeding populations: Populations within a species that are genetically isolated to some degree from other populations.

deme: Same as breeding population, but sometimes implies physical distinctions.

what different environmental circumstances from each other, as in Figure 4.5. Natural selection will have been favoring different phenotypes, and thus different gene frequencies, in adaptive response to these environments.

Second, other genetic events (such as mutations, recombination, and the processes to be covered below) tend to be concentrated within demes because that is where breeding is concentrated. What happens genetically in one deme will differ from what happens in another.

However, because demes *are* still members of one species, interbreeding between them does take place. When members of different demes interbreed, new genetic combinations may be produced in the offspring. Genes within a species, in other words, "flow" among the populations of that species, altering the allele frequencies in those populations and adding still more genetic—and thus phenotypic—variation to the species as a whole (Figure 4.6).

This process of evolution is particularly effective in a mobile species like ours, where our populations are continually moving around and mixing genes. For example, half of all Hutterite marriages take place between colonies, the bride moving to the colony of her husband. The woman thus brings her genes into the population and contributes them to subsequent generations. In one of the colonies I visited, 70 percent of the female parents came from other colonies, and marriages involving these women produced nearly 60 percent of the children of the next generation. In the other colony, 75 percent of female parents "flowed" in, and their marriages produced 47 percent of the next generation. Changes from one generation to the next in a Hutterite colony are greatly affected by this continual mixing or flowing of genes among populations, and it is the same for the human species as a whole.

FIGURE 4.6
Gene flow.

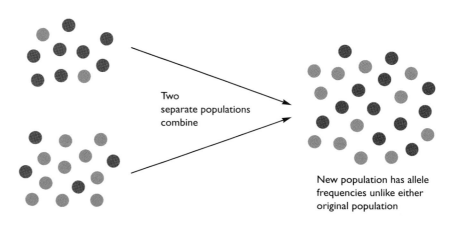

Two separate populations combine

New population has allele frequencies unlike either original population

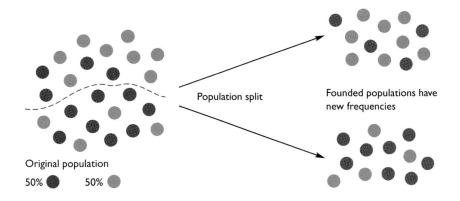

Population split

Founded populations have new frequencies

Original population

50% ●   50% ○

GENETIC DRIFT:
RANDOM EVOLUTION

The several processes that fall under this heading can be demonstrated by the following experiment: Take 100 coins and arrange them so you have fifty heads and fifty tails. Mix them up and without looking (that is, at random) select ten coins. They will probably *not* be five heads and five tails, 50 percent of each as in the original group. The odds are against it. Keep trying and you will get some idea just how bad the odds are. (In fact, the odds are about 4 to 1.) Your sample of ten is not usually representative of the whole population of coins. It is usually a nonrepresentative sample, and this effect is called **sampling error.**

Similarly, when a population within a species splits, each new population will most likely exhibit a nonrepresentative sample of the genes, and therefore the phenotypes, of the original. The splitting of a population is called **fission** and is the opposite of gene flow. The result—the production of two new sets of gene frequencies and phenotypic variation—is referred to as the **founder effect** (Figure 4.7).

The Hutterites again provide an example. Hutterites have one of the highest recorded birth rates, an average of about ten children per family. After such rapid population growth for about fifteen or twenty years, a colony becomes so large (130 to 150 people) that social and administrative problems arise, and there is increasing duplication of labor specialists. The colony will then fission or, as they call it, "branch out," half the colony families staying in the original location and half founding a new colony. As a result, the three original North Amercan Hutterite colonies, founded in 1874 and 1875, have now become over 300, and the original 300 Hutterite immigrants have become 30,000.

sampling error: When a sample chosen for study does not accurately represent the population from which the sample was taken.

fission: Here, the splitting up of a population to form new populations.

founder effect: Genetic differences between populations produced by the fact that genetically different individuals established (founded) the populations.

FIGURE 4.9
Normal (right) and sickled
red blood cells.

the body's tissues. Hemoglobin, as you recall, is made up of two pairs of amino acid chains, the alpha chain of 141 amino acids and the beta chain of 146. If a mutation occurs in the code for the sixth amino acid in the beta chain—one particular wrong word in a sentence of 146 words—an abnormal form of hemoglobin results.

When this abnormal form is present and stress, high altitude, or illness lowers an individual's oxygen supply, the red blood cells take on peculiar shapes, some resembling sickles (Figure 4.9). When in these shapes, the cells cannot carry sufficient oxygen to nourish the body's tissues. The results include fatigue, retarded physical development in children, increased susceptibility to infection, miscarriage, fever, and severe pain. Sickle cell kills about 100,000 people a year, who usually die before their twenties. Even if they do live longer, they have very low reproductive rates. In terms of evolutionary fitness, sickle cell anemia may be considered 100 percent fatal.

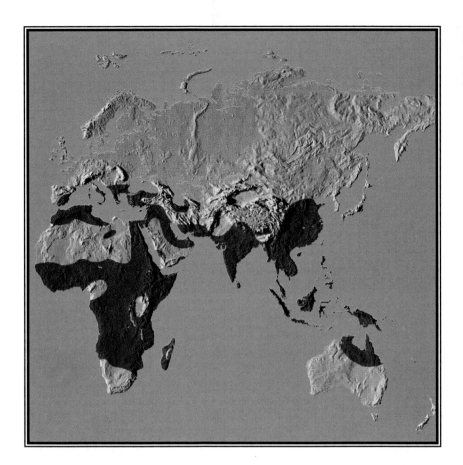

FIGURE 4.10
The distribution of high frequencies of malaria. Compare with the map of sickle cell anemia (Figure 4.8).

The abnormal allele for sickle cell is an example of a codominant allele. An individual who is homozygous for the allele will have sickle cell anemia. A heterozygote, who inherits one sickle cell allele and one allele for normal hemoglobin, will possess only about 40 percent abnormal hemoglobin. These people are said to have the sickle cell *trait*. In extreme conditions of low oxygen, they may experience symptoms of the disease, but usually not as severe as homozygotes and with a great deal of variation from person to person. The heterozygote condition is not normally fatal.

For a disease that kills its victims, usually without allowing them to pass on their genes, sickle cell is found in unexpectedly high frequencies in parts of the world (see Figure 4.8), in some areas as high as 20 percent. One would expect such an allele to be selected against and to virtually disappear.

The answer to this puzzle is a perfect example of the complexity of natural selection. Not only do heterozygotes experience less severe epi-

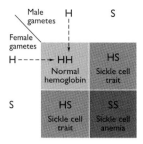

FIGURE 4.11

Punnett Square for sickle cell anemia showing the potential offspring of two heterozygotes. Because heterozygotes have an adaptive advantage in malarial areas but stand a one-quarter chance of producing an offspring with sickle cell anemia, the allele for sickle cell is maintained and passed on in such populations and the disease exhibits high frequencies.

sodes of the disease, they also have a resistance to malaria, an often fatal infectious disease caused by a parasitic single-celled organism and transmitted by mosquitoes. Malaria, though now treatable, still kills about a million people a year. Red blood cells with abnormal hemoglobin (recall that heterozygotes have about 40 percent of this) take on abnormal shapes when infected by the malaria parasite and die, thus failing to transport the parasite through the body. Sickle cell is found in highest frequencies where malaria is found in highest frequencies (Figure 4.10).

In no environment is there any advantage to being homozygous for sickle cell. In most environments, being heterozygous also confers some disadvantage. But in malarial areas, heterozygotes do have an advantage. They are resistant to malaria and they exhibit a variable and nonfatal form of the anemia. If heterozygotes are the healthiest in such environments and thus are relatively more successful at passing on their genes, then more sickle cell alleles will be inherited than would be expected if sickle cell had no benefit in any environment. Whenever two heterozygotes mate, they stand a one-quarter chance of producing an offspring who will die from sickle cell, but a one-half chance of producing an offspring who will die neither from sickle cell nor from malaria and who will possess one sickle cell allele (Figure 4.11). This shows dramatically how adaptive fitness is related to specific environmental conditions. Even a lethal allele may be adaptive under certain circumstances.

The connection between sickle cell and African Americans is an example of the founder effect. African Americans can trace at least some of their ancestry back to the populations from west Africa that provided much of the slave trade to North America. The African American population was thus, in part, founded by individuals from an area where sickle cell already existed in high frequencies.

But sickle cell is less frequent among African Americans than it is in Africa. Moreover, sickle cell is not limited to persons of African descent in this country. One only has to have the alleles to have the disease. Persons of largely European-American background can also have sickle cell. Both these facts can be explained partly as a result of gene flow. There has been a good deal of genetic mixing between European Americans and African Americans over the last several hundred years. The addition of European genes would lessen the frequency of the sickle cell allele in African Americans because Europe is largely free of the disease. The presence of the disease among a small number of persons of largely European descent might be the result of their having, sometime in the past, an ancestor of African descent who carried the allele. Of course, the mutation that produces the sickle cell allele can occur in people of any geographic or ethnic backgrounds, European Americans included.

Secondly, because malaria is virtually nonexistent in the United States and Canada, there is no adaptive advantage in possessing the sickle cell trait. Natural selection has been at work on this continent, selecting against the allele and thus producing lower frequencies, even in persons whose ancestors are from one of the areas of highest frequency.

Finally, while we're on the subject, there is evidence (Relethford 1994) that the frequency of malaria increased when people began farming in Africa several thousand years ago. Clearing and planting the land provides the sunlight and the pools of stagnant water that are ideal breeding grounds for the mosquitos that carry the malaria parasite. An increase in malaria would result in an increase in selection for the sickle cell allele, which, in heterozygotes, confers an immunity to the infectious disease.

Thus, the full story of this lethal disease shows the interaction of the forces of evolution and involves not only the genetics behind the cause of the disease, but also a single-celled parasite, an insect, and a human cultural practice. The story of sickle cell is a perfect example of the holistic perspective of anthropology.

SUMMARY

A basic theory of evolution involves the production of new genetic variation by mutation and the continual recombination of that variation at reproduction. Gene flow, and the forms of genetic drift (fission, its result, the founder effect, and gamete sampling), act to randomly change gene frequencies within populations of a species. The resulting phenotypic variation becomes the raw material for natural selection that selects individuals for reproductive success, thus accumulating adaptive traits across generations and decreasing the frequency of poorly adapted traits.

The basic unit of evolution is the species, an interbreeding population that is reproductively isolated from other populations. Because the evolution of new species is a process that occurs over time and at differing rates, species are not always equally distinct from one another and can often be difficult to define. Species are characterized genetically by gene (allele) frequency, the percentage of times each possible allele of a gene occurs. Evolution is thus technically defined as a change in allele frequency over time.

CHAPTER

5

THE ORIGIN OF SPECIES AND THE SHAPE OF EVOLUTION

. . . endless forms most
beautiful and most
wonderful have been,
and are being evolved.
—Charles Darwin

The examples of evolution in action that we discussed in the previous chapter—the peppered moth responding to a human-caused environmental change and populations of our own species interacting with malaria—have focused on changes within single species. Darwin's book, however, was called *The Origin of Species*. What Darwin was ultimately trying to explain was how new species arise, the "mystery of mysteries," as he called it in his introduction.

How do existing species give rise to new species?

How do the processes of evolution contribute to the origin of new species?

How do species diversify?

What does the "family tree" of species look like?

Are there any challenges to the idea of evolution? Are they valid?

NEW SPECIES

Species are, by definition, reproductively isolated from other species. Members of two species cannot mate and produce fertile offspring. Members of the same species can. What prevents interbreeding between species?

Any difference that prevents the production of fertile hybrid offspring between two populations under natural conditions is called a **reproductive isolating mechanism.** These isolating mechanisms fall into several general categories (based on Dobzhansky 1970):

1. *Ecological.* Members of the populations are adapted to different environmental niches. Even though their ranges may overlap, their specific environments don't—as is the case with lions and tigers. Ecological isolation probably explains the origin of the **hominids,** the group to which our species belongs (see Chapter 10).

2. *Seasonal.* Mating within each population or the flowering of plants of two related species takes place at different times of the year.

3. *Sexual.* Behaviors that attract one sex to the other (called courtship behaviors) are different in the two populations.

4. *Mechanical.* The organs of reproduction (genitalia or flower parts) are incompatible.

5. *Different pollinators.* In flowering plants, different species, even though closely related, attract different insects to facilitate pollination.

6. *Gamete isolation.* The cells of reproduction may be incompatible or may not be able to survive within the body of a member of the other species, thus preventing fertilization even if mating takes place.

7. *Hybrid inviability.* Fertilization may occur, but the hybrid zygotes do not survive.

8. *Hybrid sterility.* Hybrids survive but do not produce functional gametes. Mules are an example.

The origin of new species, then, is the evolution of *any* of these differences between populations that prevent the production of fertile offspring. As biologist Edward O. Wilson puts it, "In order to spring forth as a species, a group of breeding individuals need only acquire *one* difference in *one* trait in their biology. . . . When that happens, a new species is born [emphases mine]" (1992:68).

How do such differences arise? It is important to understand that reproductive isolating mechanisms do not evolve *in order to* produce a new species. It is an accident that the differences in traits end up as isolating mechanisms. The differences themselves evolve through the processes of mutation, flow, drift, and natural selection as we discussed before. The traits are part of the adaptive response of populations to their environments.

Suppose, to take the clearest model, a species inhabits a wide geographic range and populations (demes) at opposite ends of the range exhibit slightly different adaptive responses to the particular environmental circumstances found there. Now, some environmental change—say, a river changing its course, the destruction of some important resource, or the advance of a glacier—splits the species, geographically isolating one deme from another. Over time, each population will continue to adapt to its environment but without being able to exchange genes with the other deme. In other words, there is no gene flow. Each population will accumulate different genetic and phenotypic traits and quite possibly one or more of these will, by chance, be a reproductive isolating mechanism. If, at some point, the geographical barrier were removed and the two populations *could* mix, they would not be able to interbreed. They would be separate species, and we would say that **speciation** has occurred (Figure 5.1).

Even if a species is adaptively homogeneous, with very little variation, speciation can occur if a small population becomes isolated from the rest of the species. As in the example above, the processes of evolution, responding to the local environment of that population and acting just on that population, may evolve a trait or traits that end up as reproductive isolating mechanisms. Over time, the descendants of the small population will become a separate species from the parental population. Even if reunited, they will not be able to interbreed and produce fertile offspring.

reproductive isolating mechanisms: Any difference that prevents the production of fertile offspring between members of two populations.

hominids: Modern human beings and our ancestors, defined as the primates who stand erect.

speciation: The evolution of new species.

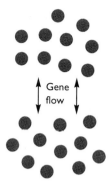
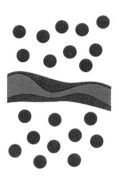
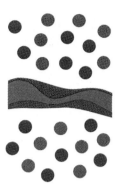
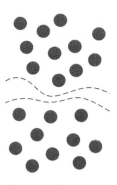

Two demes of
a single species

Environment barrier
isolates demes

Genetic and phenotypic
differences accumulate
over time

Even with barrier
removed, populations
are reproductively
isolated and are
separate species

FIGURE 5.1
Diagram of speciation.

Speciation may be accelerated when a breeding group within a species shares a mutation with extensive phenotypic effects. Such mutations are called **macromutations.** The mutation for sickle cell anemia is an example. Although the mutation itself is small (a point mutation), its phenotypic results are numerous and substantial. Like the sickle-cell mutation, most macromutations are, as you would expect, deleterious. But, by chance, some macromutations might be neutral or even beneficial. In such a case, they would be retained by natural selection, and they might serve to very rapidly make a small population within a species adaptively isolated from the rest of the species. Speciation is given a "head start" by the macro-mutation.

A famous example is that of the salamanders, who begin life as aquatic larvae much like tadpoles. Eventually they develop functioning lungs and legs and spend their adult life on land. The axolotl from Mexico (Figure 5.2) is a salamander that never grows up. Because its pituitary gland fails to supply its thyroid with a certain hormone, the axolotl becomes sexually mature but does not finish developing physically and retains into adult-hood the external gills and fully aquatic lifestyle of salamander larvae. It is a separate species. If injected with the missing hormone, the axolotl will mature and live on land. The difference, in other words, is a simple one—the presence of a hormone—but the mutation that brought about the difference served to immediately reproductively isolate its possessors from the rest of their species. The speciation that produced the axolotl was nearly instant. (Obviously, more than one salamander would have to have shared the mutation. Perhaps the mutation occurred during the production of a group of eggs and so all the salamanders that developed from those eggs were actually axolotls.)

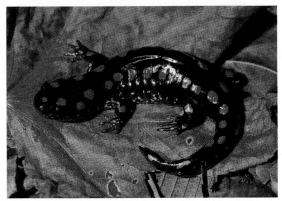

FIGURE 5.2
An axolotl (upper left) with larval (lower left) and adult salamander (upper right). Note the similarity between the axolotl and the immature salamander. The axolotl is, in a sense, a salamander that never completely matured.

The processes of evolution that bring about genetic and phenotypic variation (see Figure 4.5) are constantly in action. So are the processes that alter environmental circumstances. It stands to reason, then, that the conditions that produce new species are ever-present and that speciation must be a very common occurrence indeed.

ADAPTIVE RADIATION: THE EVOLUTION OF LIFE'S DIVERSITY

No one is sure how many species of living things inhabit the earth, and we have no idea how many have *ever* lived on this planet. There are about one and one-half million *named* species living today, and scientists estimate that the total may actually be ten times that number (Figure 5.3).

macromutations: Mutations with extensive and important phenotypic results.

FIGURE 5.3
Estimated number of living
species for major groups of
organisms.

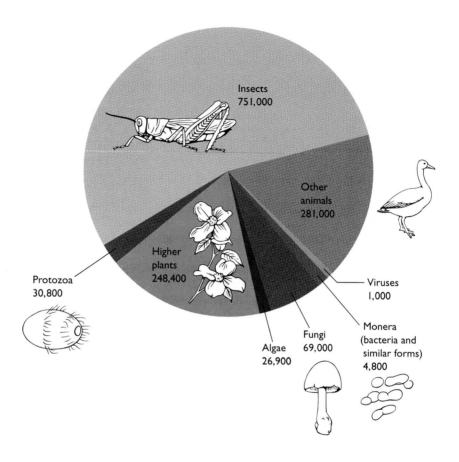

Insects
751,000

Other
animals
281,000

Protozoa
30,800

Higher
plants
248,400

Viruses
1,000

Monera
(bacteria and
similar forms)
4,800

Algae
26,900

Fungi
69,000

Even in modern times, new species are still being discovered. Edward Wilson (1992) notes that in 1988 five new mammal species—three of them primates—were described and named, and in 1990 a new species of South American monkey was discovered on an island only forty miles from São Paulo, Brazil. Since 1908, eleven species of cetaceans (whales and porpoises) have been discovered. New species of small mammals, mostly rodents and bats, are described at an average rate of sixteen per year. New species of bacteria are being found by the thousands. Recently, a whole new type of bacterium was discovered deep within the earth's crust.

Despite the great array of living creatures, however, there is a great degree of similarity among them all. All living things, for example, use the same genetic code; they are built from the proteins that are the products of that code using the same basic twenty amino acids. We assume, then, that life on earth had a single origin. This being the case, all those millions upon millions of species have descended from a common ancestor and have come about by the process of speciation.

For a potential new species to persevere, it must survive the adaptive trials of natural selection. Put another way, it must have a place to go, an environment to which its traits are adapted, an "ecological opportunity." When such opportunities are extensive, speciation may take place numerous times, and a group of related species may spread into a number of niches. This spread of related species is called **adaptive radiation.** Evolution has been a story of the adaptive radiation of species into different environments and the subsequent actions of the processes of evolution on those species.

Ecological opportunities come about, and can foster adaptive radiation, under these three general circumstances:

1. when an environment is empty, that is, when no similar and therefore competing species live there,

2. when extensive extinction empties a set of environments of competing species, and

3. when the new group of related species are adaptively **generalized** (as opposed to **specialized**) and are able to disperse successfully into different niches and displace species already there.

An example of the first situation is the famous case of Darwin's finches, a group of thirteen (some authorities recognize fourteen) related bird species that inhabit the Galápagos, a volcanic archipelago of some nineteen islands in the Pacific about 500 miles west of Ecuador (Figure 5.4). This was one of Darwin's stops on his voyage around the world.

From a small group of original migrants, blown out to the islands from the mainland of South America an estimated half-million years ago, these birds have radiated into niches that were unoccupied by other birds. Today there are species of ground-dwelling finches that feed on seeds of different sizes and have bills shaped accordingly. There are several species that feed on cactus, and several that live in trees and eat insects. Their bills, too, are adapted for the specific foods they eat. One species is a tool-user, holding a cactus spine or twig in its bill and using it to probe for insects in tree trunks. The ground finches on two of the smaller islands peck the skin of larger birds and drink the blood that results. Not surprisingly, they are referred to as "vampire finches."

In fact, birds in general are an example of adaptive radiation into empty niches. Birds first evolved some 150 million years ago from dinosaurs (Figure 5.5). There was little competition for species possessing the new attributes of feathers and, for some, flight. This evolutionary novelty radiated into a wide variety of niches resulting currently in about 9000

adaptive radiation: The evolution and spreading out of related species into new niches.

generalized: Here, species that are adapted to a wide range of environmental niches.

specialized: Species adapted to a narrow range of environmental niches.

FIGURE 5.4
The Galápagos Islands and the number of finch species on each island. (Data from Lack, 1947.)

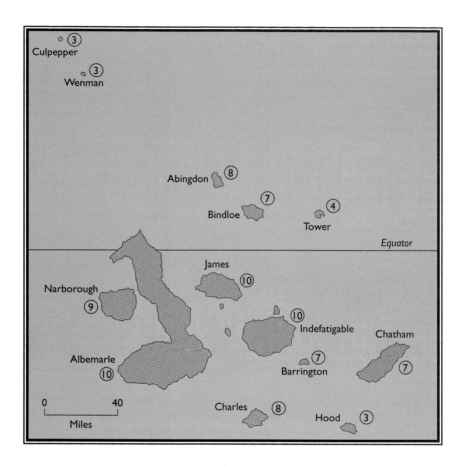

species of birds of incredible diversity. All are variations on the same basic theme.

The mammals are an example of a group of species that were able to take advantage of the niches opened up by a major extinction—the one that killed off all the dinosaurs and many other species. The mammals were among the survivors. At the time they were mostly small, **nocturnal,** rodentlike creatures, but they now had a world of niches open to them that were free of previous competitors. The mammals radiated rapidly, and by about 40 million years ago most major types of mammals we know today had evolved.

We can look to our own group of mammals, the primates, for examples of species that were able to radiate because they were generalized and could fairly easily disperse into diverse niches. When monkeys first evolved, over 35 million years ago, they proved more generalized than their **prosimian** ancestors, the so-called primitive primates. The monkeys were larger-brained, **diurnal,** and well adapted to an active **arboreal** life eating a mixed diet of leaves, fruits, and insects. As the monkeys underwent speciation

FIGURE 5.5
The fossil remains of Archeopteryx ("ancient bird"), a small upright dinosaur with feathers, modifications of reptilian scales. The fossil is evidence that birds are descended from dinosaurs and that this change took place fairly rapidly.

and radiated into new niches, they displaced the prosimians. In the New World (Central and South America), there are only monkeys; the North American prosimians apparently became extinct. In the Old World (Europe, Africa, and Asia), prosimians were pushed into marginal areas. A few species live on the mainland of Africa, but most inhabit isolated islands of Southeast Asia and the island of Madagascar (the Malagasy Republic) that had separated from mainland Africa prior to the monkeys' evolution (see Chapter 10 for more detail).

On the scale of a single species, we will see this pattern repeated when we look more closely at our own evolution. At least once during the evolution of our group of primates, a new and more generalized species of hominid spread geographically and ecologically, displacing an existing hominid species (see Chapters 10, 11, and 12).

nocturnal: Active at night.

prosimian: Primate with primitive features, most closely resembling the ancient primates.

diurnal: Active during the day.

arboreal: Adapted to life in the trees.

THE SHAPE OF THE FAMILY TREE

What is the pace of speciation and what, as a result, is the shape of the evolutionary "family tree" of species?

Charles Darwin felt that natural selection was responsible for speciation and that it was a process of almost unlimited power. He said that natural selection brought about "the accumulation of innumerable slight variations, each good for the individual possessor," and he added:

> What limit can be put to this power, acting during long ages and rigidly scrutinizing the whole constitution, structure, and habits of each creature,—favoring the good and rejecting the bad? I can see no limit to this power, in slowly and beautifully adapting each form to the most complex relations of life. (1898:267)

In other words, Darwin saw natural selection as "fine-tuning" each species to its environment, constantly favoring or rejecting any difference among individuals, no matter how "slight." This constant selection eventually changes one species so much it may be considered a new species. In the process, selection can produce "varieties" within each species as populations become differently adapted to slightly different environments. These varieties will eventually become so distinct that they will be separate species. For Darwin, this process was slow and steady. Indeed, we refer to it as **Darwinian gradualism.**

According to this model, the family tree of species has gracefully diverging branches. These represent the slow but steady pace at which individual species change through time and at which populations within species slowly become distinct from one another under the "scrutiny" of natural selection. The tree of evolution represents, in Darwin's words, "an interminable number of intermediate forms . . . linking together all the species . . . by [fine] gradations" (1898:271–72) (Figure 5.6).

Here, however, Darwin was uncharacteristically incomplete. For one thing, the fossil record has failed to show intermediate forms with fine gradations for all evolutionary lines. Instead, fossil species often tend to remain relatively stable for long periods of time and changes—new species—show up rather suddenly. For example, the first bird we know of for sure in the fossil record is not a mix of birdlike and dinosaurlike traits, a 50/50 combination as one might expect if evolution were slow, gradual, and steady. Rather, Archeopteryx (see Figure 5.5) is a perfectly good dinosaur but with perfectly good feathers. Clearly, evolution here was not a slow, steady accumulation of many small changes, but was focused on the evolution of feathers and may have occurred fairly quickly. ("Quickly" in evolutionary perspective is, of course, a relative term and may mean thousands of years.)

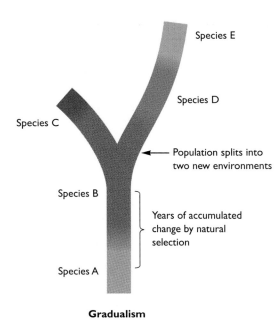

FIGURE 5.6
Darwinian gradualism.

Gradualism

Similarly, the origin of our own group, the hominids, did not occur slowly and steadily, gradually producing a humanlike form from an apelike one. The first fully accepted hominid fossils, from 3 to 4 million years ago, are, to exaggerate only slightly, apes that stood upright (see Chapter 10). The change was not gradual, but was focused on bipedalism and was quick enough so that few other evolutionary changes had time to occur.

A second problem is more theoretical. If, as according to Darwin, each "slight variation" that natural selection favors is "good for the individual possessor," then we have to assume an adaptive benefit for *each small step* in the development of some trait. But can one-hundredth of a feather, then one-tenth of a feather, then one-quarter of a feather, and so on, each benefit its possessor enough to make a reproductive difference? It could happen, but we have come to realize that natural selection is not as creative as Darwin imagined. It cannot "scrutinize" a species, as if through a powerful microscope, and favor or reject each little difference among individuals. If this were the case, species would not show as much variation as they do and still be well adapted. Rather, natural selection acts only on differences that make a difference in reproductive success.

So, natural selection is a conservative force, rejecting what doesn't work and allowing whatever does to reproduce. The role of natural selection is basically to maintain the adaptation of a species to its environment. Natural selection is not the author of evolution so much as the editor. Thus, species normally change very little over the course of their tenure on earth, and new species seem to arise fairly quickly as a result of the

Darwinian gradualism:
The view, held by Darwin, that evolution is slow and steady with cumulative change.

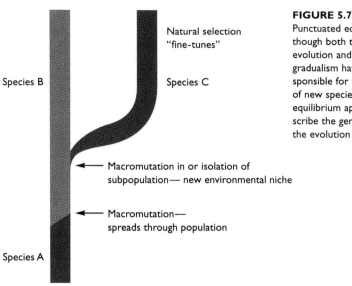

Species B

Species C

Natural selection "fine-tunes"

Macromutation in or isolation of subpopulation— new environmental niche

Macromutation— spreads through population

Species A

FIGURE 5.7
Punctuated equilibrium. Although both this mode of evolution and Darwinian gradualism have been responsible for the evolution of new species, punctuated equilibrium appears to describe the general picture of the evolution of life on earth.

Punctuated Equilibrium

isolation of populations within species through geographic separation, mutation, or a combination of both. Natural selection, of course, *then* plays an important role in screening the isolated population in terms of adaptive fitness.

We may describe this model of evolution as follows: The adaptive equilibrium of species with their environments is punctuated (interrupted) by the evolution of a new species from a population of the parental species. The parental species, in the meantime, may remain unchanged, at least for a time. This model is called **punctuated equilibrium** and is represented not by a tree with gracefully diverging branches but by a bush with many twigs. These twigs are evolution's experiments, potential new species. Many twigs are short, since the species they represent became extinct in a short time. Some are longer, however, and give rise to yet more new species (Figure 5.7).

No doubt, both modes of evolution—Darwinian gradualism and punctuated equilibrium—occur. It is currently being debated whether one or the other is the more common mode. Likely, we will find examples of both as the fossil records of various evolutionary lines become better understood.

At any rate, the evolution of life on earth cannot be depicted as a ladder or a chain representing the steady march of progress toward complexity, as Lamarck and other early scientists believed. Nor is it a gracefully branching tree, as Darwin pictured it. Instead, it is, in the words of Stephen Jay Gould (1994:91), a "luxuriant bush," more complex than we will probably ever know—a "blooming and buzzing confusion," says Gould (1985:355) or, to use Darwin's words, like the "tangled bank" of a stream.

EVOLUTION QUESTIONED: THE PSEUDOSCIENCE OF "SCIENTIFIC CREATIONISM"

All the information about the theory of evolution presented in these last two chapters has been developed and tested, using the methods and principles of science, over the past several hundred years by many people and from many different perspectives. Evolution is a fact, and it is the central concept of all biology, although we continue to apply the scientific method to our investigation of specific details. Our ideas about the generation of genetic variability, adaptation by natural selection, and the origin of species from existing species—all these explain everything we observe and understand about the living world.

We benefit from this knowledge every day of our lives. We eat foods from species of plants and animals bred according to the principles of genetics and selection. We know the causes of many of the illnesses that beset us because we understand the genetic operations of our cells, and we have insight into how some organisms (like viruses and bacteria) are adapted to other organisms (like us), and vice-versa. Many of the antibiotics and other medicines that help us treat those illnesses work only because of the interrelatedness of all life. And this interrelatedness has also allowed us to manipulate the genes of other organisms, like bacteria, to "trick" them into producing human insulin for the treatment of diabetes, human growth hormone, and interferon, a chemical in our body's immune system.

So it is truly astounding that some people, even today, question the fact that evolution actually occurred. Think back to our discussion of science from Chapter 1. Science and belief systems are both important for the operation of any society, and ideally, they operate in harmony with one another. They are still, however, distinct realms of knowledge, distinguished by the *testability* of science and the *faith* of belief. What about ideas that have characteristics of both?

Suppose someone holds a scientific idea (an idea that is testable) but treats it as a belief by taking it on faith and by not testing it or recognizing the results of tests that have been applied to it, even if those tests refute it.

Here's an example: There are people who believe that the lines in the palms of your hands and on your fingers hold information about your personal character and even, perhaps, about your future. This belief is called palmistry, and its precepts are quite scientifically testable. I tested

punctuated equilibrium: The view that species tend to remain stable and that evolutionary changes occur fairly suddenly.

them (Park 1982–83), and not surprisingly, they failed. But will palmists all over the country close up shop because some anthropologist says their ideas are false? Hardly. Palmists take their ideas on faith. In other words, they treat a scientifically testable idea like a belief system. Thus, palmistry is a **pseudoscience** or "false science."

Although pseudoscientific ideas like palmistry, astrology, or the power of crystals may be harmless enough, other examples contain implications that may not be so benign. Some pseudoscientific ideas find support within established belief systems. There are—believe it or not—still people who want to think the earth is flat and who refuse to acknowledge the masses of scientific evidence to the contrary (Schadewald 1981–82). It turns out that a major source for this belief comes from literal interpretations of several biblical passages; for example, in Matthew 4:8:

> Again, the devil taketh him [Jesus] up into an exceedingly high mountain, and sheweth him all the kingdoms of the world . . . .

How, the flat-earthers ask, could Jesus have seen all the kingdoms of the earth unless the earth were flat?

Although most people recognize the allegorical sense of this and similar passages in both testaments, there is a danger that some might find the issue terribly confusing. On the one hand, scientific evidence tells us unequivocally that the earth is a sphere. On the other hand, an interpretation of the chronicles of two major religions seems to say the earth is flat. Must one choose between science and religion? There are those who think so and, in the process, both science and belief suffer.

The idea of a flat earth is utterly ridiculous, but there is another pseudoscience, relevant to our topic here, that is far more complex and difficult to evaluate. It's called **scientific creationism.** It proposes that the entire universe, including the earth and all its inhabitants, were created spontaneously by untestable forces around 10,000 years ago. Except for minor changes within "kinds" of plants and animals (breeds of dogs, for example, or regional varieties of a wild species), no changes in living organisms have occurred. Certainly no *new* species have arisen. What about the layers of rock and soil and the fossils they contain? Those are the results of "a primeval watery cataclysm" (Morris 1974:22), a great flood, in other words (Figure 5.8).

Sound familiar? It should. It is derived directly from a literal interpretation of the first eight chapters of the Book of Genesis, and it is clearly in direct opposition to all the data and ideas accumulated and tested by science. A hundred years of scientific inquiry tell us that the universe, including the earth and its inhabitants, arose through knowable, natural processes. The universe is at least 8 billion years old, the earth 4.5 billion, and life nearly four billion years old. Living organisms do change through

FIGURE 5.8
Strata of the Grand Canyon in Arizona. Scientific creationists contend that these strata and all the fossils they contain are the results of the biblical flood. Real scientific data show that the canyon's strata represent geological and biological events over nearly 2 billion years of time.

time, and species give rise to new species. The geological and fossil records are the records of these billions of years of change.

"Scientific creationism" is thus a pseudoscience—a testable set of ideas that, even in the face of contrary evidence, are accepted on faith. But scientific creationism goes further. Its proponents claim its ideas are, indeed, supported by scientific evidence that also refutes the accepted theory of evolution. That the creation model coincides with one interpretation of Genesis merely shows, they say, the scientific accuracy of the Bible. Because advocates of scientific creationism claim both models are scientific, they feel both should be taught in science classes as viable alternative explanations for the origin and diversity of life.

The argument is persuasive, especially in a society like ours, concerned with religious freedom and with our American senses of fair play and equal time. *But equal time is for equivalent things.* There is not a single shred of scientific evidence in support of the creation model.

To teach scientific creationism alongside evolution would be to violate the religious freedoms of those who do not subscribe to a strict creationist interpretation. It would also badly confuse those trying to learn how science really operates and what conclusions about our world science has arrived at. The distinction between science and belief would be blurred, interfering with the harmonious and important relationship between the two.

The quality of our lives now and in the future depends on the continued progress of our testable scientific knowledge, mediated by the values

pseudoscience: Scientifically testable ideas that are not tested but are taken on faith, even if shown to be false.

scientific creationism: The belief in a literal biblical interpretation regarding the creation of the universe, with the connected belief that this view is supported by scientific evidence.

of our belief systems. We need to understand what these two areas of knowledge are and how they interact, and we must promote free access to, and sharing of, all knowledge.

SUMMARY

The evolution of new species is an obvious result of the interacting processes of genetic variation, natural selection, and environmental change. New species arise when a population within an existing species becomes isolated. Isolation is usually geographic but may also be the result of a macromutation. In isolation, this new population experiences the processes of genetic variation and phenotypic adaptation separate from the parent species. Among the differentiating traits that result may be characters that act as reproductive isolating mechanisms, meaning that even if the populations once again have the opportunity to interbreed, they will probably not be able to do so. They are separate species.

The process of speciation, occurring countless times over the billions of years of life's history, has produced the incredible array of living forms we know today and we see in the fossil record. The species we know about only hint at the variety that exists today and has existed in the past. When species have the opportunity, they are able to adaptively radiate into new niches, and the diversity of living forms is the result. It must be remembered, however, that all these forms are variations on the single theme of life that originated on this planet. All life, through speciation and adaptive radiation, is descended from a single origin.

We can depict evolution as a luxuriant bush, dense with innumerable twigs, each representing a new species. We use the bush as a metaphor and icon of evolution for two reasons. First, we realize that the conditions for speciation are continuously being produced, so that speciation has probably taken place more often than we can imagine. Second, we understand that Darwin's model of the origin of species driven by the steady, gradual, "fine-tuning" of natural selection is not entirely accurate. Natural selection is a conservative force, acting largely to maintain a species' adaptation. What produces new species is geographic and/or genetic isolation, and these processes act relatively quickly.

The evidence for evolution is overwhelming. We are still examining the specific details of evolutionary theory, but the fact of evolution and our knowledge of the essential processes involved are hypotheses that have passed numerous scientific tests and have failed none. They are theories in the scientific sense of the word. The evidence for evolution is as strong as, say, the evidence for the idea that the earth revolves around the sun and not the other way around. Nonetheless, there are those who, for reasons that have nothing to do with science, claim that evolution did not occur. These claims have, in the true spirit of science, been examined, and they have been shown to be scientifically invalid. Their proponents, however, continue to insist on their accuracy. These claims are thus pseudosciences, and they confuse the important relationship between science and belief systems; for, in fact, there is no necessary conflict between the two.

KEY TERMS

reproductive isolating mechanisms
hominids
macromutations
adaptive radiation
generalized

specialized
nocturnal
prosimian
diurnal
arboreal
Darwinian gradualism

punctuated equilibrium
pseudoscience
scientific creationism

SUGGESTED READINGS

You should certainly have a look at the book that began our modern understanding of evolution, Darwin's *Origin of Species*. The last chapter, "Recapitulation and Conclusion," nicely summarizes his arguments and provides a good idea of his style.

Again, a wonderful book on evolutionary processes, the origin of new species, and the variety of living things is Edward Wilson's *The Diversity of Life*.

For more on Darwin's finches, see Jonathan Weiner's *The Beak of the Finch*.

One of the originators of the model of punctuated equilibrium is biologist Stephen Jay Gould, and many of his articles concern that model. Try "The Episodic Nature of Evolutionary Change" and "Return of the Hopeful Monster," both in *The Panda's Thumb*.

Gould has also addressed the shape of the evolutionary bush. See his informative book *Wonderful Life* and his article in the October, 1994 *Scientific American*, "The Evolution of Life on the Earth."

For an idea of the arguments of the scientific creationists, try *Evolution: The Fossils Say No!* by Duane T. Gish. For a refutation of scientific creationism, go once again to Stephen Jay Gould and a series of articles on the subject in *Hen's Teeth and Horse's Toes*.

CHAPTER

6

A BRIEF
EVOLUTIONARY
TIMETABLE

... and there is no new
thing under the sun
—Ecclesiastes 1 : 9

FIGURE 6.2
Stromatolites in Australia, formed when mats of blue-green algae, single-celled organisms, are covered with sand, silt, and mud, which the algae cement down and then grow over. Fossil stromatolites, and thus the organisms that made them, have been dated to 3.5 billion years ago.

organisms preserved in stone, many of which were probably already capable of **photosynthesis.**

Just how life came about on the earth is also a matter of debate. For over forty years, scientists have been able to produce carbon-rich **organic** compounds from **inorganic** compounds with a fairly simple laboratory procedure, showing that the process could have occurred quite easily. In fact, they have been able to produce amino acids, which, as you recall, are the building blocks of proteins. But, as you also recall, proteins cannot be built without a nucleic acid code. Evidence now suggests that RNA formed very early in earth's history. RNA was able to replicate itself and act as a code for the synthesis of proteins. Later, DNA took over this role (Orgel 1994). It is still, of course, a long way from amino acids and RNA to a living organism, and the details of this path remain unclear.

Whatever happened, it happened fast (a billion years from the formation of the earth to life *is* fast, in the geological time scale), but once established, life at first evolved slowly. The world's first organisms were simple single cells like bacteria (Figure 6.3). It wasn't until about 2 billion years ago that complex single-celled organisms evolved containing nuclei and organelles (see Figure 3.1).

All these early single-celled organisms reproduced **asexually** by splitting and making copies of themselves. Evolutionary change relied entirely on mutations. About a billion years ago, some organisms had begun to reproduce **sexually.** Sexual reproduction may have begun as a mechanism of genetic exchange to replace defective genes. Soon, however, it proved to be an accelerator of evolution. Now, in addition to mutation, recombination also provided genetic and phenotypic variation, and evolutionary change quickly started to gain speed. Figure 6.4 summarizes the major events in the history of life on earth and gives the names of the major time periods.

All life still remained single-celled for another half billion years. As long ago as 590 million years, we find the first hints of organisms made up of more than a single cell, and then, about 535 million years ago (mya), multicellular organisms burst on the scene. Some even possessed hard parts like shells. So sudden and rapid was this event that it is referred to as the Cambrian Explosion. In a mere 5 million years, all major body plans of multicellular animals had evolved, including ancestors of the **vertebrates,** animals with backbones (Figure 6.5). In fact, there are Cambrian fossils representing several body plans that no longer exist. So far, there are no explanations for this "explosion" that everyone agrees upon, but it is clearly a major event in the history of life. The evolution of animals since the Cambrian has been, essentially, variations on the themes set during that relatively brief time (Gould 1989, 1995).

By 425 mya, fish had evolved, and plants and animals began to colonize the land. Insects appear about 400 mya; by 350 mya, some of them

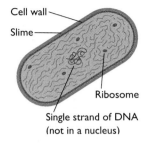

Cell wall
Slime
Ribosome
Single strand of DNA
(not in a nucleus)

FIGURE 6.3
A typical bacterium, representing some of the earliest forms of life on earth and, in terms of time and numbers, the dominant forms.

photosynthesis: The process where plants manufacture their own nutrients from carbon dioxide and water, using chlorophyll as a catalyst and sunlight as an energy source.

organic: Here, molecules that make up living organisms. They are rich in carbon.

inorganic: A molecule not of organic origin.

asexually: Reproducing without sex, by fissioning or budding.

sexually: Reproducing by combining genetic material from two individuals.

vertebrates: Organisms with backbones.

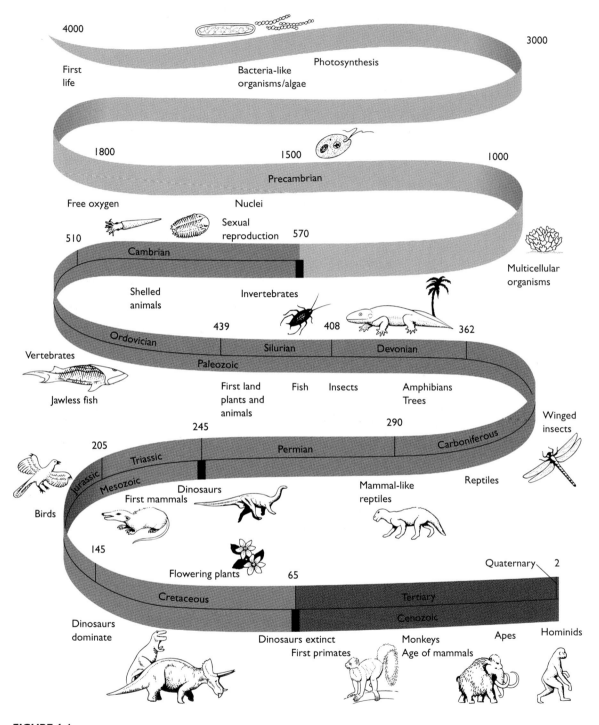

FIGURE 6.4

Time line showing the major events in the history of life on earth. The placement of sample organisms is approximate and some are stylized representations. Time is in millions of years. The last 570 million years are drawn to scale.

FIGURE 6.5
Cambrian fauna, mostly arthropods, the group consisting of modern day insects, spiders, and crustaceans. The large creature in the center grew to three feet long. The flowerlike animals on the right are unclassified.

had evolved wings. Reptiles show up around 350 mya as well, and the reptilian form that is thought to have given rise to the mammals is found at about 250 mya. Dinosaurs began evolving around 235 mya, with true mammals appearing about 220 mya. Sometime around 150 mya, a small dinosaur with feathers signals the beginning of the evolution of birds (see Figure 5.5). Flowering plants appear only a little more than 100 mya.

DRIFTING CONTINENTS AND MASS EXTINCTIONS: THE PACE OF CHANGE

During all this time, life was not the only thing evolving on earth. The earth itself was also evolving as the continents changed shape and position, a phenomenon known as "continental drift" that operates through the process of **plate tectonics.** The outer layer of rock on the earth, the "crust," is not solid and permanent. It is broken into some sixteen pieces

plate tectonics: The movement of the plates of the earth's crust caused by their interaction with the molten rock of the earth's interior. The cause of continental drift.

FIGURE 6.6
Continental drift. Movement of the earth's land masses over the last 200 million years caused by the processes of plate tectonics.

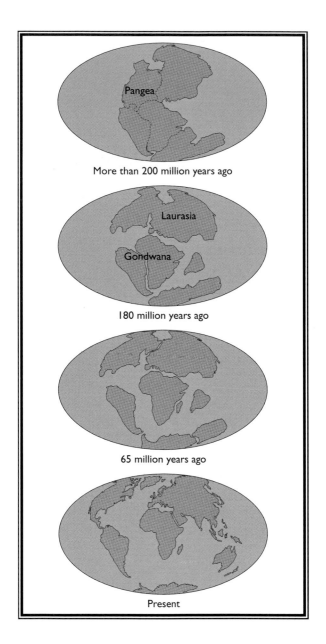

More than 200 million years ago

180 million years ago

65 million years ago

Present

of various sizes called "plates" that fit together like a huge spherical jigsaw puzzle. But the motion of the molten rock (magma) below the crust causes the plates to change. In some areas, magma seeps up between the plates where it solidifies, pushing the plates apart. Something has to give, of course, and at other boundaries, called "subduction zones," one plate is pushed under the other and plunges deep within the earth where it melts and adds to the magma. Clearly, then, the continents—those parts of the plates that protrude above sea level—have shifted over time, and will continue to do so (Figure 6.6). It should also be noted that plate tectonics accounts for important geological phenomena. Where the plates meet and move against one another, tremendous forces are produced that cause earthquakes, volcanos, and mountain building.

By the time the dinosaurs and early mammals had appeared, all the continents had drifted together to form a huge "supercontinent" we call **Pangea,** literally "all lands." This is why, for example, we find fossils of the same type of dinosaur in what are now such widely separated places as China, North America, and Antarctica. Around 200 mya, Pangea began to break up, and the resulting land masses—the ancestors of our present-day continents—drifted over the globe, producing a diversity of environments and geographical boundaries that has profoundly affected the nature of life on earth as we know it today.

From all we've discussed so far, it would seem that the evolution of the earth and its life—influenced by continental drift and the environmental changes it brings about—has been a slow, steady process. And basically, it has been—relative to the immense amount of time involved. But the fossil record shows that at least five times in the planet's history, some change has taken place that was so rapid and extensive that it radically altered the course of biological evolution by causing a mass extinction.

For example, about the time the continents were drifting together forming the supercontinent of Pangea—at the end of the Permian era—over 95 percent of all species of marine and terrestrial organisms suddenly became extinct. Some changes occurred to which none of the variants within all those species was adapted. The cause for this greatest of all mass extinctions is not known for sure, but a new hypothesis suggests it was the result of massive volcanic eruptions in what is now Siberia that altered the planet's climate. At any rate, such a catastrophe certainly had a major effect on the future course of life's evolution.

Other mass extinctions did not have such a "down-to-earth" explanation, and one of these directly affected the evolution of our small section of the evolutionary bush. About 65 million years ago, the dinosaurs were the dominant form of land animals and were present in the oceans as well. Mammals, as mentioned in Chapter 5, were also around, and had been for nearly as long as the dinosaurs. In terms of ecological niches, however, mammals didn't have many places to go because those niches were already occupied (Figure 6.7).

Then one day—literally—a comet or an asteroid, thought to measure six miles across, crashed through the earth's atmosphere and into the crust where the north coast of the Mexican Yucatán is now. The impact made

Pangea: The supercontinent that included parts of all present-day land masses.

FIGURE 6.7
Rudolph Zallinger's Pulitzer Prize-winning mural, at Yale University, showing some of the dinosaurs that once virtually dominated the earth's environments. (Mr. Zallinger passed away while this book was in production.)

a crater 112 miles in diameter. The comet or asteroid may have broken apart on impact with the atmosphere and pieces may have hit in other locations as well.

This collision created a blast like that of a nuclear explosion. Thousands of cubic miles of vaporized rock, water vapor, and small particles and dust were shot into the atmosphere and distributed worldwide. Heat from the impact caused massive forest fires that created smoke and ash. One hypothesis suggests that the impact produced shock waves that bounced inside the earth and were focused on the opposite side of the planet, causing large-scale volcanic activity that put even more smoke and ash into the air. It has recently been noted that the area of the Yucatán is rich in sulfur, and this suggests that the impact might have produced sulfuric acid in the atmosphere. All this matter would have created a blanket that blocked sunlight, cooling the earth and preventing the photosynthesis of green plants.

These extensive environmental changes proved disastrous (a word that means, appropriately, "bad star"). Dinosaurs became extinct, along with every other species of land animal weighing more than about 55 pounds, many plants, and much of the ocean's plankton, the small organisms that provide a great deal of the world's oxygen and that act as an important source of food at the base of the food chain.

Somehow, many of the mammals survived. Perhaps, by a stroke of luck, they were adapted to withstand adverse, changing conditions already. Now, with the dinosaurs suddenly gone, a whole world of new niches was open to them and to many other creatures that made it through the ca-

tastrophe. This group included the birds, thought by many to be the dinosaurs' only living direct descendants (Figure 6.8).

So rapid was the mammals' adaptive radiation that within about 25 million years, all major types of mammals we know today had appeared—everything from bats to whales to a group of tree-dwelling creatures possessed of acute eyesight, dexterous hands, and large, inquisitive brains. These are the primates, and it is this group that we shall focus on in the next chapters.

SUMMARY

This narrative of the history of the universe has been necessarily brief, but it does point out three themes that are important to remember as we continue.

First, it could be said—by virtue of our numbers (5.6 billion) and our impact on the planet—that we are the dominant species on the earth today. But our evolutionary history makes up a small fraction of the whole history of the universe and even of the earth (see again the figures at the beginning of the chapter). We are the new kids on the evolutionary block, and we have not as yet even proved ourselves successful by the criterion of longevity. Cockroaches have been around hundreds of times as long as

FIGURE 6.8
The ostrich shows a striking similarity to bipedal dinosaurs, further evidence of the evolutionary relationship between dinosaurs and birds.

we have; bacteria have been around since the beginning of the fossil record. By these standards, our species is in its infancy.

Second, as the Bible says, "there is no new thing under the sun." Indeed, although we often speak of the "origin of the earth" or the "origin of life," the only *real* origin is that of the universe itself. All the events listed above have been *rearrangements* of what already existed: matter condensing from cooling energy; large atomic particles forming from smaller ones; stars coming together from cosmic dust, and heavy elements created from lighter ones in the nuclear furnaces of those stars; the elements of inorganic molecules rearranged to form the molecules of life; and the shuffling of the genetic code to produce the extraordinary multitude of living things that have inhabited this planet.

Third, and perhaps the most humbling thought, the specific history of the universe, including the earth and its life, could have happened in countless other ways. Each event in our story is contingent upon preceding events. For example, our evolution as we know it is dependent upon the specific sequence of events that came before it. If those events had been different, *we* might be different—or we might not be here at all. Imagine if that comet or asteroid had *not* hit the earth 65 million years ago. In other words, the evolution of humans—or anything else for that matter—was not inevitable. We're lucky we're here.

KEY TERMS

photosynthesis	asexually	plate tectonics
organic	sexually	Pangea
inorganic	vertebrates	

SUGGESTED READINGS

There are many good books on the subject of the history of the universe, the earth, and life. I especially recommend Timothy Ferris's *Coming of Age in the Milky Way* for a discussion of the science behind our understanding of this history. *The Book of Life*, edited by Stephen Jay Gould, is an especially complete and beautifully illustrated book. For a more technical, but still readable work, try *History of Life* by Richard Cowen.

The Cambrian Explosion is covered in Stephen Jay Gould's *Wonderful Life* and in an article by R. Gore in the October 1993 *National Geographic*, "Explosion of Life: The Cambrian Period."

The subject of mass extinctions is discussed in E. O. Wilson's *Diversity of Life* and in an article in the June 1989 *National Geographic*, "The March Toward Extinction."

Evolution as a series of contingent events is a second theme of Stephen Gould's *Wonderful Life* and of his article in the October 1994 *Scientific American*, an issue devoted to the subject of "Life in the Universe."

CHAPTER

7

THE PRIMATES

I confess freely to you,
I could never look long
upon a monkey,
without very mortifying
reflections.
—William Congreve
(1695)

"The proper study of mankind is man," said the poet Alexander Pope. The last few chapters should have convinced you that even biological anthropologists, who by definition focus on the study of mankind (or, more properly, humankind) simply cannot limit their interests to just our own species. The processes that have produced modern *Homo sapiens* are the processes that have produced every single species that has ever inhabited this planet. Additionally, all those species are part of an integrated whole, comprised of all environments and all living things in complex interaction with one another across geographical space and through evolutionary time.

Moreover, were we to limit our study just to our species, or even to the hominids in general, we would lose a great deal of perspective. We need to compare ourselves to other forms of life to see in what ways we are similar and in what ways we differ. This comparison is made all the more important because we *are* the species we are studying, and so it can be difficult to be objective about ourselves. Thus, the study of primatology is an important part of anthropology.

In this chapter we will address several important questions:

What is our place in nature; that is, where do we fit—from a scientifically objective point of view—in the world of living things?

What are the characteristics of the primates—the group of animals of which we are a part?

In what ways are humans like the other primates? In what ways are we unique?

NAMING THE ANIMALS

We have already discussed the concept of the species, the "natural" unit of classification in nature. Each organism belongs to a specific species (the words come from the same root), a group of potentially interbreeding individuals that are reproductively isolated from other groups.

The most cursory examination, however, shows clearly that there are larger units of classification of living things. Some species are more similar to one another than they are to other species. The Book of Genesis, for example, does not name each species that God creates, but lists general categories: "the fish of the sea," "the fowl of the air," "every herb of the field," "every beast of the earth."

TABLE 7.1
Taxonomy of Five Familiar Species

	Human	Chimpanzee	Bonobo	Gorilla	Wolf
Kingdom	Animalia	Animalia	Animalia	Animalia	Animalia
Phylum	Chordata	Chordata	Chordata	Chordata	Chordata
Class	Mammalia	Mammalia	Mammalia	Mammalia	Mammalia
Order	Primates	Primates	Primates	Primates	Carnivora
Family	Hominidae	Pongidae	Pongidae	Pongidae	Canidae
Genus	Homo	Pan	Pan	Gorilla	Canis
Species	sapiens	troglodytes	paniscus	gorilla	lupus

This fact so struck Swedish botanist Karl von Linné (1707–1778) that he devised a taxonomic system to name and thus categorize all living creatures. A **taxonomy** is a classification based on similarities and differences. I have, for example, accumulated thousands of notes, articles, and other important individual pieces of paper in my years as a bioanthropologist. If I simply stored all these together randomly, I'd never find anything when I need to refer to it. Instead, I file my papers according to general categories and subcategories nested within them. For instance, I have a file cabinet marked "Biological Anthropology." One of its drawers is marked "Evolution," and within that drawer is a file folder marked "Taxonomy" where I keep notes and copies of articles on Linné and the related matters I'm now writing about.

Similarly, Linné (who used Latin names and even latinized his own name to Carolus Linnaeus) devised a system, published in final form in 1758 and amended by his immediate disciples, that used seven nested categories. Table 7.1 shows a Linnaean taxonomy for five familiar species. We'll detail the taxonomy of our species to show what Linnaeus's system accomplishes.

Humans are members of the group called Animalia within the largest category, called a kingdom. We share this grouping with the other four species on the chart by virtue of the fact that we all ingest our food, have sense organs and nervous systems, and are capable of intentional movement. We are not members of any of the other four kingdoms: simple single-celled organisms (bacteria), complex single-celled organisms (amoebas and the like), fungi (mushrooms, mildews, molds), or plants (roses, ferns, broccoli, pine trees).

taxonomy: A classification based on similarities and differences.

FIGURE 7.1
Amphioxus, a chordate, with a notochord but no bony spine. (Shown about four times life size.)

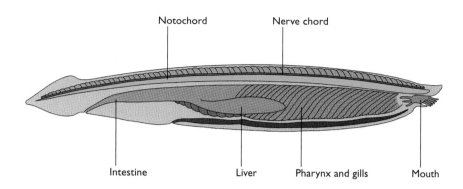

Within kingdom Animalia are about thirty phyla (singular, phylum), groups such as sponges, jellyfish, starfish, three types of worms, mollusks, arthropods (insects, spiders, crustaceans), and chordates. We are members of phylum Chordata because we have a bony spine, the evolutionary descendant of a **notochord,** a long cartilagenous rod running down the back to support the body and protect the spinal chord, the extension of the central nervous system (Fig. 7.1). Chordates with a bony spine are grouped into a subphylum, Vertebrata. Note that all five species on the chart are chordates and, more specifically, vertebrates.

There are seven classes within the vertebrates: the jawless fishes (an ancient group represented by only a few existing species), cartilagenous fishes (sharks and rays), bony fishes (guppies, tunas, and so on), amphibians (frogs, salamanders), reptiles (snakes, lizards, alligators), birds, and mammals. All our example species are members of class Mammalia because we maintain a constant body temperature (usually called "warm blooded"), have hair, give birth to live young, nourish the young with milk from mammary glands, and have relatively large, complex brains.

We need to stop here for a moment for an important point. You may have noticed that some of the traits listed for mammals are also possessed by other classes. Birds, for example, are also warm blooded; so, according to many, were some of the dinosaurs, and so are a number of other creatures including great white sharks. Some sharks, some bony fishes (like guppies), and some snakes give birth to live young. On the other hand, you might know two mammals that do not possess all the mammalian traits. The spiny anteater and the duckbill platypus, both from Australia, lay eggs. Obviously, though, birds, dinosaurs, and great white sharks are *not* mammals, while the spiny anteater and platypus *are*. What's the resolution to this seeming contradiction?

The answer is that inclusion into a taxonomic category is more than simply a matter of possessing a list of traits. The traits of an organism make possible that organism's *adaptation,* and it is adaptation, measured by reproductive success, that is the criterion of natural selection. Thus, taxonomic categories become statements about adaptation, with each taxonomic level becoming more specifically focused. Mammals, whether they lay eggs or not, are animals that are adapted through active lifestyles and a reliance on learned behavior. Their young, therefore, require a great deal of direct care and nurturing, and mammals require a constant body temperature to sustain their level of activity, and hair (or in the case of whales, a thick layer of fat) to maintain that temperature. That's not a very concise definition of a mammal, but the real world doesn't always make things easy for those of us who try to describe it.

Within class Mammalia are about nineteen orders—nineteen rather specific adaptive strategies. There are, for example: the flying bats; the fully aquatic whales and dolphins; the partially aquatic seals, seal lions, and walruses; two orders of hoofed plant eaters (the difference being a skeletal feature of the feet); the rabbits and hares; the rodents; the meat eaters; the insect eaters; the pouched marsupials (kangaroos, opposums); and a group of large-brained, tree-dwellers with 3-D vision and dexterous hands. These are the members of order Primates.

At the level of order, our five example species (from Table 7.1) differentiate. The wolf belongs to order Carnivora (the meat eaters) while the other four are primates. Humans split from the other primates at the level of family. The gorilla, while similar to the remaining two, is different enough to be placed in a separate genus (plural, genera). The chimpanzee and bonobo (or "pygmy chimp"), similar enough to once be considered members of the same species, are now recognized as different species within the same genus.

The Linnaean taxonomic system thus indicates the relative relationships among named organisms. Table 7.2 gives the taxonomic categories of five unidentified species you probably don't recognize. You should, nonetheless, be able to tell their relative biological relationships.

Linnaeus's goal was to describe the system that, as he believed, God had in mind when he created all the earth's living things. Linnaeus was a creationist as were just about all scientists of his time. But, as you can probably see, to modern scientists, his taxonomy indicates not only present day similarities and differences but evolutionary relationships as well. The *reason* the chimp is more similar to the bonobo than to a human is because the chimp and bonobo diverged more recently than the chimp and human. The chimp and bonobo are thought to have had a common ancestor from which they split about 1.5 million years ago. Humans and the chimp/bonobo line branched about 5 million years ago. Humans and chimps have had a longer time to evolve in different ways than have the bonobo and chimp, which is why they are more different *and* why they are placed in different taxonomic families.

notochord: The evolutionary precursor of the vertebral column.

TABLE 7.2
Taxonomy of Five Unidentified Species*

	A	B	C	D	E
Kingdom	Animalia	Animalia	Animalia	Animalia	Animalia
Phylum	Arthropoda	Arthropoda	Arthropoda	Arthropoda	Arthropoda
Class	Crustacea	Insecta	Insecta	Insecta	Arachnida
Order	Decapoda	Hymenoptera	Diptera	Diptera	Aranceae
Family	Nephropsidae	Apidae	Muscidae	Culicidae	Theridiidae
Genus	Homarus	Apis	Musca	Anopheles	Lactrodectus
Species	americanus	mellifera	domestica	quadrimaculatus	mactans

So, from a Linnean taxonomy, we may create a family tree, indicating when the classified species branched from one another in their evolutionary history. Of course, a taxonomy can't tell us the exact dates of divergence. Evolutionary rates differ in different evolutionary lines and at different times. But it can tell us the relative times of branching. Figure 7.2 shows a family tree for the five species in Table 7.1. You should be able to draw a tree for the species classified in Table 7.2.

FIGURE 7.2
Evolutionary tree for the five species in Table 7.1. We infer the evolutionary relationships from the taxonomic classifications.

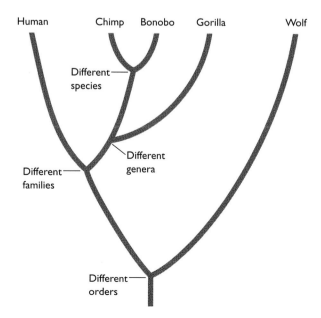

Linnean taxonomy has been the traditional way of classifying living things—categorizing based on relative degrees of biological similarity and difference, and then inferring evolutionary relationships based on that categorization. It works pretty well, too. Today, however, with increasing knowledge of the fossil record and with new techniques for comparing species by genetic as well as phenotypic differences, a new system of taxonomy is emerging. It is based on actual evolutionary relationships—*not what species look like now*. The new system is called **cladistics,** and we'll discuss it in Chapter 9. It has some fascinating implications for our view of nature. For the moment, however, we'll use the traditional method and the standard names.

Now, let's focus on the mammalian adaptive strategy that characterizes the members of order Primates.

WHAT IS A PRIMATE?

There are about 200 living species of primates. We're not sure how many have existed during the order's evolutionary history of around 55 million years. Primates range from the very small such as the mouse lemur of Madagascar which weighs less than three ounces, to the gigantic—an extinct ape from China and India that may have stood 12 feet tall and tipped the scales at half a ton (Figure 7.3). Some primates inhabit small, very specific environmental ranges and spend their lives slowly moving through the trees, eating fruits, leaves, or insects; one species of primate lives in every environment and produces its own food.

This wide variety makes it a bit difficult to define the primate order in a simple sentence. The primates are best defined by looking at the characteristics that they have in common and in seeing how these traits facilitate the primate adaptive strategy. We'll look at the primate traits by using the following categories: (1) the senses, (2) movement, (3) reproduction, (4) intelligence, and (5) behavioral patterns.

The Senses

Bats and dolphins live in worlds of sound. Dogs live in a world of smells. The primates live in a visual world. Vision is the predominant sense for the primates.

cladistics: A classification system based on order of evolutionary branching, rather than on present similarities and differences.

*By the way, the five species classified in Table 7.2 are, from left to right: lobster, honeybee, housefly, mosquito, black widow spider.

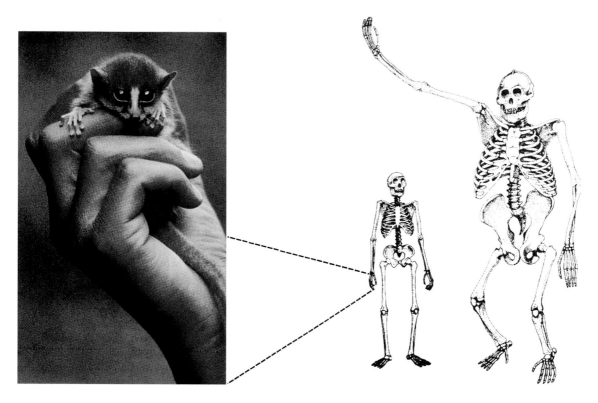

FIGURE 7.3
A mouse lemur, the smallest living primate compared to a human and to Gigantopithecus, now extinct, the largest primate ever (see Chapter 10).

Most primates see in color. If you look around the place you're now in, you're seeing it just as the majority of primates would. In addition to color vision, primates also see in three dimensions. They have true depth perception, technically called **stereoscopic vision**—possible because the eyes face forward and see the same scene from slightly different angles (Figure 7.4). The nerves and muscles of primate eyes are protected by enclosure within a bony socket.

Other senses are not as acute as in many mammals. Primates lack the auditory (hearing) and olfactory (smell) senses of such familiar animals as dogs, cats, and cattle. Furthermore, and obviously related to the less acute sense of smell, is the fact that primates tend to lack a snout and so are rather flat-faced in profile. There is, as you might expect for a group of 200 species, some variation. Many members of one group of primates (the prosimians that we'll discuss in the next section) are nocturnal and lack color vision, but they have better senses of smell and hearing than do monkeys, apes, and humans.

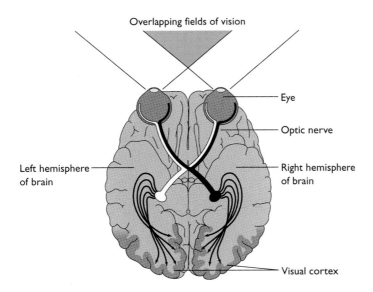

FIGURE 7.4
Stereoscopic vision. The fields of vision overlap and the optic nerve from each eye travels to both hemispheres of the brain. The result is true depth perception.

Movement

Primates, like most mammals, are, with one exception, **quadrupedal;** that is, they walk, climb, and leap using all four limbs. Although many primates can stand or even walk on two legs for short periods, humans are the only habitually **bipedal** primates. Unlike most mammals, the limbs of primates are extremely flexible, and the hands (and, in many cases, the feet) of primates have the ability to grasp objects. This is known as **prehensile** (Figure 7.5).

In addition, most primates are able to touch their thumbs to the tips of the other fingers, allowing them to pick up and manipulate small objects. This capacity is called **opposability.** Finally, most primates have nails rather than claws on the tips of the fingers and toes. These provide support for the sensitive tactile sense receptors of the fingers. In short, primates have manual dexterity. Some have a great degree of dexterity in the feet as well (see Figure 7.12 later in this chapter).

Reproduction

Nearly all primate species give birth to one offspring at a time. A few primates, such as some of the marmosets from South America and some of the lemurs from Madagascar, normally produce twins or triplets. As is typical of mammals, the primates take an active role in the protection,

stereoscopic vision: Three-dimensional vision; depth perception.

quadrupedal: Walking on all fours.

bipedal: Walking on two legs.

prehensile: The ability to grasp.

opposability: The ability to touch the thumb to the tips of the other fingers.

FIGURE 7.5
Prehensile grip. An orangutan holding its trainer's
hand demonstrates the prehensile grip of the primates,
both human and nonhuman.

nurturing, and socialization of their young. Mostly because of their large, complex brains and because of the importance of learning, the primates take a long time to mature. How long, of course, depends upon the size of the primate species. During this time, the young primates are dependent upon adults. The primates, relative to size, have the longest period of **dependency** of any mammal.

Intelligence

Intelligence can be defined as the relative ability of an organism's brain to acquire, store, access, and process information. These abilities are related to brain size and brain complexity. A bigger brain has more room for all the complex nerve connections that make it work, just as a very sophisticated computer must necessarily be larger than a simple one. But brain size must also be looked at in a relative way: How big is the brain compared to the body it runs? A sperm whale, with its 20-pound brain, has a brain size ten times that of the average human's. A sperm whale's body, however, is over five hundred times the size of ours. We have bigger brains than a whale *relative to* the size of our bodies; we run less body with more brain, which is true of the primates in general. Of all mammals, the primates have the largest relative brain sizes.

In addition, the primate brain is complex, especially in the neocortex, that part of the brain where abstract thought, problem solving, and attentiveness take place (Figure 7.6). In short, the primates are smart.

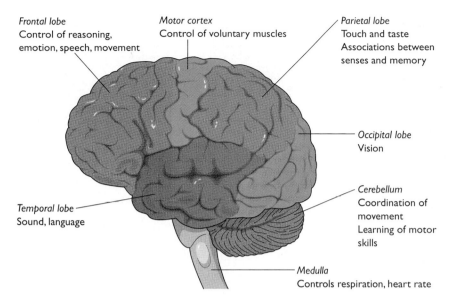

Frontal lobe
Control of reasoning,
emotion, speech, movement

Motor cortex
Control of voluntary muscles

Parietal lobe
Touch and taste
Associations between
senses and memory

Occipital lobe
Vision

Cerebellum
Coordination of
movement
Learning of motor
skills

Temporal lobe
Sound, language

Medulla
Controls respiration, heart rate

FIGURE 7.6
The human brain with major parts and their functions.

Behavior Patterns

Primates are social animals. Most primate species live in groups. Many other animals do too, but even those few primate species—like orangutans—that usually remain solitary, still interact with other members of their species in ways that are far more complex than between, say, members of a herd of antelope. The difference is that primates recognize individuals, and the individual primate holds a particular status relative to others in its group and to the group as a whole. A primate group (often referred to as a troop) is made up of the collective relationships among all its individual members. We will see these relationships in action when we examine primate behavior more closely in Chapter 8.

As physical evidence of the importance of these relationships, it may be noted that primates are among the most colorful of mammals, and most of the color patterns of primates are on their faces (Figure 7.7). The attention of one primate to another is drawn to the face, to the primate's identity as an individual.

In some primates—baboons and chimpanzees, for example—individuals may have rather specific statuses within the troop. Some have more social power and influence than others. They are said to be dominant, and this situation is called a **dominance hierarchy.** In addition, most primate species recognize a special status for females with infants, and these units are well protected by other members of the troop, regardless of their actual relationships (Figure 7.8). Among chimpanzees and baboons we even see lasting relationships that can only be described as friendship.

dependency: Here, the period after birth during which offspring are dependent upon adults.

intelligence: The relative ability of the brain to acquire, store, access, and process information.

dominance hierarchy: Individual differences in power, influence, and access to resources and mating.

FIGURE 7.7
Some colorful primate faces, including that of one primate that purposely enhances the color. Colorful faces are evidence of the importance of individual recognition within primate societies.

FIGURE 7.8
Male baboon protecting mother and young. The female holding her baby at left was being threatened by the boisterous play of a group of adolescent males, out of the picture to the right. The adult male in the center stepped in and barked at the group, which quickly took its play elsewhere.

Primate social groups are maintained through communication. Primates have large repertoires of vocalizations, facial expressions, and body gestures. Touch is also an important form of communication among primates, and often takes the form of **grooming,** an activity that serves the practical purpose of removing dirt and parasites, but also acts as a source of reassurance to maintain group harmony and unity (Figure 7.9).

How, then, may we characterize the primate adaptive strategy? First, it is important to acknowledge the environment that the primates are adapted *to*. The basic primate environment is arboreal—primates live in trees. To be sure, several species—gorillas, for instance—spend more time on the ground than in the branches, and we humans are thoroughly terrestrial. But most primates spend most of their time in the trees, and the primate traits in the preceding discussion all evolved in response to an arboreal environment. Even the partially and completely terrestrial primates possess features that are variations on the arboreal adaptive theme. So, we can define primates in the following way:

> The primates are mammals adapted to an arboreal environment through well-developed vision, manual dexterity, and large, complex brains that rely on learned behavior; the latter is aided by the birth of single offspring and the direct and extensive care of those offspring during a long period of dependency while they are socialized into groups based upon differential relationships among individuals.

Such a complex group of organisms requires a lengthy description.

grooming: The cleaning of the fur of another animal; promotes social cohesion.

FIGURE 7.9
Chimp vocalization and grooming. A chimpanzee exhibiting a "low open grin," an indication of moderate fright or excitement. Chimps grooming, an activity that rids them of dirt and parasites and, more importantly, helps maintain group unity and harmony.

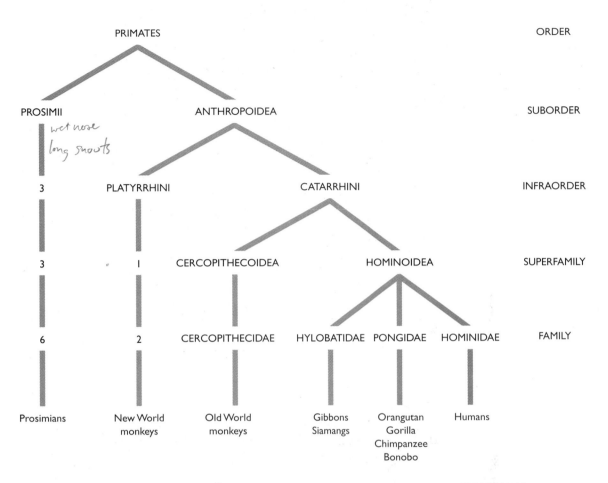

ORDER — PRIMATES

SUBORDER — PROSIMII, ANTHROPOIDEA

wet nose
long snouts

INFRAORDER — 3 (PROSIMII), PLATYRRHINI, CATARRHINI

SUPERFAMILY — 3 (PROSIMII), 1 (PLATYRRHINI), CERCOPITHECOIDEA, HOMINOIDEA

FAMILY — 6 (PROSIMII), 2 (PLATYRRHINI), CERCOPITHECIDAE, HYLOBATIDAE, PONGIDAE, HOMINIDAE

Prosimians; New World monkeys; Old World monkeys; Gibbons Siamangs; Orangutan Gorilla Chimpanzee Bonobo; Humans

FIGURE 7.10
Primate taxonomy. Numbers refer to living primate groups in that category.

A SURVEY OF THE LIVING PRIMATES

Figure 7.10 is a simplified taxonomy of the approximately 200 species of living primates. For the sake of space, some groups are indicated only by the number of those groups within a category; for instance, there are six families of prosimians. One of the first things you should notice is that there are new categories here. Suborder, infraorder, and superfamily have been added between the traditional Linnaean categories of order and family. Sometimes a **taxon** of organisms has many species adapted to a wide variety of geographical locations and environmental niches; consequently, additional taxonomic categories need to be added to accurately capture what seem to be natural divisions. (A complete taxonomy of insects, for example, a class with over three-quarters of a million *known* species is, as you can well imagine, incredibly complex.)

taxon: Any category within a taxonomic classification.

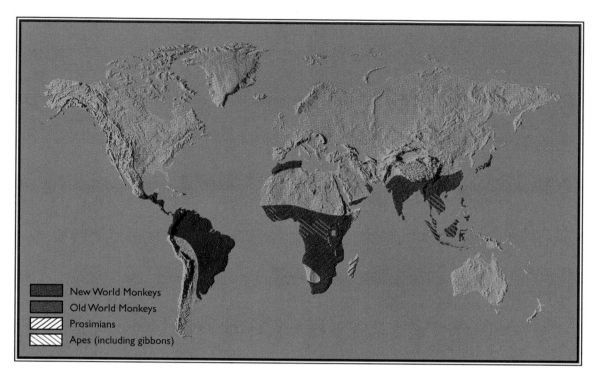

FIGURE 7.11

Distribution of the living primate groups.

Legend:
- New World Monkeys
- Old World Monkeys
- Prosimians
- Apes (including gibbons)

The order Primates is divided into two major suborders, Prosimii and Anthropoidea. Prosimians ("pre-apes") represent the most primitive primates, that is, those that most closely resemble the earliest primates. At first widespread, prosimians were pushed into marginal areas as newer, more adaptively flexible primates evolved. Some modern prosimians live on the mainland of Africa and India and on the isolated islands of Southeast Asia, but the majority inhabit the island of Madagascar (Figure 7.11).

The forty or so living species of prosimians exhibit a number of differences from the general primate pattern (Figure 7.12). About half of the prosimian species are nocturnal and so lack color vision, but they do have large eyes that can gather more light and better than average senses of smell and hearing. To aid their olfactory sense, they have a protruding snout with a large smell receptor area (the mucus membranes within the nose) and a moist, naked outer nose (like a dog or cat) to help pick up the molecules that make up the olfactory signal. Prosimians do have the stereoscopic vision characteristics of primates because they need to judge distances in bushes and trees, and many use their 3-D vision to help catch insects, a favorite food of many prosimian species.

Prosimians have prehensile hands and feet, but their opposability is limited. Many can only touch the thumb with all four other digits together; their digits don't move independently. Some prosimians have claws, instead of the typical primate nails, on a couple of fingers or toes. These are known as "grooming claws" and are used for that purpose.

A few species of lemurs from Madagascar give birth to twins or even triplets on a regular basis. Transporting them through the trees, however, is no problem because an adult male or an older brother or sister often helps the mother carry and care for her infants. At other times, the infants are kept in a nest.

A particularly interesting prosimian is the tarsier of Southeast Asia (Figure 7.13). Weighing just four or five ounces, this little insect eater has powerful hindlimbs for jumping, enlarged fingertips and toetips for added friction, and the ability to turn its head 180 degrees in either direction like an owl. Its name comes from its elongated ankle, or tarsal bones, that make its legs look like they bend too many times. Because of its flat face, upright posture when clinging to trunks and branches, and lack of a moist nose, combined with some recent genetic studies, a few authorities place the tarsier in the second primate suborder, Anthropoidea.

The anthropoid ("humanlike") primates include monkeys, apes, and humans. Suborder Anthropoidea is further divided into two infraorders,

FIGURE 7.12
A prosimian, the slow loris of Southeast Asia. Notice the large eyes, moist, naked nose, and the grooming claw on one toe of each prehensile foot.

Platyrrhini and Catarrhini. This division is based on a geographical separation of early primates into a Western Hemisphere, or New World group, and an Eastern Hemisphere, or Old World group. All the New World platyrrhine primates are monkeys. The Old World catarrhine primates are made up of monkeys, apes, and humans. Despite the fact that humans now inhabit the entire globe, the hominids first evolved in the Old World, in Africa.

Several features distinguish New World from Old World primates. The most obvious is the nose. Platyrrine means "flat nose," and the noses of the Central and South American monkeys have widely spaced nostrils separated by a broad septum (Figure 7.14). Compare this with a typical Old World catarrhine nose by looking in the mirror. (Again, although our species now lives all over the world, we are considered Old World catarrhine primates). Platyrrine monkeys have more teeth than catarrhines, twelve premolars (bicuspids) as compared to eight. Because New World monkeys are almost entirely arboreal, they have evolved long limbs, and some have clawlike nails. Several species also have evolved prehensile tails and so effectively have five grasping limbs. No Old World monkey evolved this adaptation. Finally, one group of platyrrhines, the marmosets, normally gives birth to twins.

The Old World primates are divided into two superfamilies. The monkeys of Europe (now limited to Gibraltar), Africa, and Asia make up superfamily Cercopithecoidea. Apes and humans are in superfamily Hominoidea, divided into three families.

There are about seventy-five species of cercopithecoids (Figure 7.15). They have the nasal shape and tooth number of all Old World primates, and most have tails. Males tend to be larger than females, a trait not common in New World species. Also unlike the platyrrhines, the Old World monkeys have fully opposable thumbs. The monkeys of the Eastern Hemisphere seem more adaptively flexible than those of the West. At home in the trees, many cercopithecoids are equally comfortable on the ground. They live everywhere from the deserts of Africa and the Middle East to the mountains of northern Japan.

Superfamily Hominoidea contains the larger, tailless primates. The hominoids, the apes and hominids, are generally larger than the monkeys and have larger brains, both relatively and absolutely. Their brains also have larger neocortexes meaning that the hominoids are more intelligent as we have defined that term. Finally, a series of traits make the hominoids good "suspensory climbers and hangers"; they are adapted to an arboreal environment through the ability to climb and hang from branches with their arms. The traits behind this ability are a flexible shoulder joint, a shoulder blade that is farther back than in monkeys, and a strong collar bone (clavicle) for added support. Although modern humans do not

FIGURE 7.14
A New World monkey—the wooly spider monkey, or muriqui, of Brazil. Notice the widely separated nostrils and the prehensile tail.

FIGURE 7.15
An Old World monkey, the rhesus of Asia. This is perhaps as close as one could come to an "average" primate. The rhesus has been important in medical and behavioral experiments. The Rh blood group was named after it.

FIGURE 7.16
A gibbon brachiating.

display this ability as often or as well as the apes, we still possess it, as is evident by watching athletes on the high bar or rings.

Family Hylobatidae includes the gibbons and siamangs of southeast Asia and Malaysia. Sometimes referred to as "lesser apes," they are noted for their mode of locomotion, arm-over-arm swinging through the branches called **brachiation** (Figure 7.16). They also have an unusual social organization for primates. Male and female hylobatids form a permanent monogamous pair.

There are four species within family Pongidae, the "great apes:" the orangutan of southeast Asia, and the gorilla, chimpanzee, and bonobo ("pygmy chimpanzee") of Africa (Figure 7.17). Some new genetic research implies that there may be a third chimp species, the versus chimp, from west Africa (Wildlife News 1995; Woodruff and Morin 1995).

brachiation: Locomotion using arm-over-arm swinging.

FIGURE 7.17
The great apes (clockwise from top left): orangutan of Southeast Asia; gorilla, bonobo, and chimpanzee of Africa.

FIGURE 7.18
Chimps using tools they have made to extract termites from their mound.

The pongids are large (a male gorilla in the wild may weigh 450 pounds) with heavy, powerful jaws used for eating a wide range of fruits, nuts, and vegetables. Chimps also eat meat on occasion. The apes are quadupeds although chimps, gorillas, and, especially bonobos, are fairly good at upright walking for short distances. Orangutans are solitary, but the other apes live in social groups marked by some degree of dominance but otherwise with fairly loose organization and changeable group membership.

The apes have relatively large brains; a large chimp, for example, may have a brain half the size of the smallest modern human brain. Apes are intelligent. They have, for example, an intimate knowledge of a large number of food sources, many of which ripen seasonally or grow in limited areas.

Some chimpanzees can make simple tools, the best known of which is their termite "fishing stick," a modified twig or blade of grass they insert into a hole in a termite mound and wiggle around to stimulate an attack by the insects. The termites cling to the "invader," and the chimps draw out a tasty meal (Figure 7.18). Other chimps have been seen to use rocks to break open hard-shelled nuts. Chimps are also known to cooperatively hunt small animals, including other primates, and meat is the one food source that chimps will share with one another.

Finally, apes have a large repertoire of calls, facial expressions, and body gestures with which they communicate information, mostly about emotional states. Though this form of communication is nothing like human language, some individuals from all the great ape species have been taught to use nonvocal versions of human languages, most notably American Sign Language (AMESLAN) for the hearing impaired. It is said by some researchers that with this skill they can communicate at the level of a four- or five-year-old human.

The third hominoid family is Hominidae, the hominids. This includes all living human beings and several extinct species. We need, of course, to detail the traits of this group.

THE HUMAN PRIMATE

Each of the 200 living primate species has its own unique expression of the primate adaptive strategy. Humans are no exception. Let's describe the hominids by using the same categories with which we characterized the primates in general.

The Senses

Our senses are essentially the same as those of the anthropoid monkeys and the apes. There may be some minor differences, but, basically, we all hear, smell, and, especially, see the same world.

Movement

This is the characteristic that, in broad evolutionary perspective, defines the hominids. We are the only primate that is habitually bipedal, and we have been for over 5 million years. (Our big brains came along much later.) The bones and muscles of our back, pelvis, legs, and feet are all structured to balance us and hold us upright. Because our legs are the limbs of locomotion, they are longer and more muscular than our arms—just the opposite of the apes. Completely freed from locomotor functions, our hands have become organs of manipulation. We have the most precise opposability of any of the primates and the longest and relatively strongest primate thumb.

FIGURE 7.19
A baboon in estrus. The skin around her genital area is swollen and brightly colored, a clear visual sign that she is fertile and sexually receptive.

Reproduction

Like most primates, we have one offspring at a time. Though we are not the largest primate (the gorilla is), we have the longest period of dependency and we take the longest time to mature. Chimps, for example, reach sexual maturity at about nine years and physical maturity at about twelve. For humans, the averages are thirteen and twenty-one. In addition, we are born even more helpless than other primates.

Our sexual behavior, too, is different. The other primates, like most mammals, engage in sexual activity, for the most part, only when it can lead to reproduction. Thus, mating occurs when a female has ovulated, has produced an egg that is ready to be fertilized. She undergoes hormonal changes that make her sexually receptive, and she gives off signals that sexually stimulate males. During this time, the female is said to be in **estrus** (popularly, "in heat"). In many mammals the estrus signals are in the form of olfactory stimuli; in primates, they are visual (Figure 7.19).

Humans, of course, have lost the signals of estrus, a condition sometimes referred to as "concealed ovulation." Human males don't automatically know when a human female is fertile. This may seem a rather inefficient way to perpetuate the species, but, as we are all aware, humans have replaced unconsious, innate sexual signals with sexual consciousness. Sexuality has become part of our conscious thought, tied up with all the other reactions and attitudes and emotions we have toward other members of our species and toward ourselves. You might say we are potentially continually in estrus. Although humans are perhaps the most

estrus: The period of fertility. The signals indicating this condition.

extreme example of this form of reproductive behavior, we will see it foreshadowed, in the next chapter, in some of our close relatives.

Intelligence

We are clearly the most intelligent primate, as we have defined that term. We can store, access, and process more information in more complex ways. Our cultural behavior—our languages, societies, belief systems, norms of behavior, and scientific knowledge—all attest to these abilities. Our intellect is made possible by our large, complex brains, especially our neocortexes, the outer layer where abstract thought takes place.

Behavior Patterns

Like most primates, humans live in societies that are based on the collective conscious responses of a group of individuals. The difference is that our groups are structured and maintained by cultural values—ideas, rules, and behavioral norms that we have created and shared through complex, **symbolic** communication systems.

SUMMARY

The study of the nonhuman primates has been a traditional aspect of biological anthropology. We *are* primates, after all, and the characteristics of our relatively new species have evolved out of the basic primate traits and the adaptive strategy that they facilitate. We can only fully comprehend ourselves as a biological species by understanding where we fit into the natural world.

Taxonomy provides us with a way of naming and categorizing species so as to indicate their biological relationships. It also gives us an idea as to the evolutionary relationships among species. In other words, a Linnaean classification shows us the basic shape of the "bush" of evolution.

The primates are one of nineteen orders of mammals. They may be characterized as adapted to arboreal environments through manual dexterity, visual acuity, and intelligence. There are about 200 living species of primates, each a unique manifestation of the general primate theme. The human primate's major uniqueness is in its form of locomotion; we are the only primate that is a habitual biped, a trait that evolved over 5 million years ago. Since then, our other distinguishing feature has

symbolic: Here, a communication system that uses arbitrary but agreed-upon sounds and signs for meaning.

evolved—our big brain, capable of such complex functions that we can create our own adaptive behaviors, expressed as our various cultural systems. It is to the possible precursors of our behaviors that we will turn next.

KEY TERMS

taxonomy	prehensile	grooming
notochord	opposability	taxon
cladistics	dependency	brachiation
stereoscopic vision	intelligence	estrus
quadrupedal	dominance hierarchy	symbolic
bipedal		

SUGGESTED READINGS

An excellent book on the primate order is by Napier and Napier, *The Natural History of the Primates*. For a look at the endangered lemurs of Madagascar, see the article in the August 1988 *National Geographic* by primatologist Alison Jolly called "On the Edge of Survival." The National Geographic Society has also produced a beautifully illustrated book on the great apes, *The Great Apes: Between Two Worlds*, by Nichols, Goodall, Schaller, and Smith, that discusses not only the four species of apes but also talks about the scientific studies conducted on them in the wild as well as the dangers they now face from their close relative.

A comprehensive and readable book comparing humans with other primates is Richard Passingham's *The Human Primate*. For an interesting, though somewhat speculative, discussion of the evolution of the human brain, try Carl Sagan's Pulitzer Prize winning *The Dragons of Eden*.

I'll recommend some more books on the behavior of humans and our fellow primates in the next chapter.

PRIMATE BEHAVIOR AND HUMAN EVOLUTION

Often I have gazed into
a chimpanzee's eyes
and wondered what
was going on behind
them.
—Jane Goodall (1990)

J ust as we look to the anatomy of our close relatives to get some idea about the basic set of phenotypic traits from which we evolved, we may also look at the behavior of the other primates to gain some insight into why we behave the way we do. Because we share common ancestors, some of our behavior patterns—just like some of our physical features—may be variations on the same evolutionary theme.

In this chapter we will look at two types of nonhuman primates in particular, the several species collectively called baboons (genus *Papio*) and the two species of genus *Pan*, the common chimpanzee and the "pygmy chimp" or bonobo. The reasons for choosing these primates will be discussed.

> **How do we organize a study of something as complex as behavior?**
>
> **What are some of the scientific cautions that must be exercised in doing so?**
>
> **What are some of the relevant behaviors of our close relatives?**
>
> **What light do they shed on the evolution of the behavior of the hominids?**

STUDYING BEHAVIOR

The idea of using behavioral patterns is based on the same premise as is our use of physical comparisons with other primates: We share a common heritage with the other primates and so have inherited our shared features from the same source, a common ancestor. It is not a coincidence, for example, that all the primates have prehensile hands. Our common prehensile ability comes from the same ancient ancestor and, in this case, serves the same basic function. Such traits, shared by multiple species through inheritance from a common ancestor, are called **homologies.** Thus, we gain some perspective on our prehensile hands by fully examining the prehensile appendages of species with whom we share an ancestor from whom we all derived the trait.

It should be noted that homologous traits need not share a common function. Your arms and the wings of a bat, though they are used for different things, are homologies. The traits are similar by virtue of having evolved from the same source, an early mammal.

The wings of a bat and the wings of an insect, however, though they share a similar function, have evolved independently and are not at all similar in structure. These functional but evolutionarily unrelated simi-

(a)

(b)

(c)

FIGURE 8.1
Analogy and homology. The wing of an insect (c) and the wing of a bat (b) are analogous—they share a function but are evolutionarily different. The wing of a bat and the arm of a human (a) are homologous—they have different functions but share the same evolutionary source.

larities are known as **analogies.** We can certainly learn something about the physics of flight by comparing these wings, but there is a limited amount of information we can get about the wings of *bats* by studying the wings of *insects* because they evolved quite separately from one another (Figure 8.1).

Just as organisms pass on anatomical and physiological features in their genes, they also pass on behavioral characteristics. In some groups—ants, for example—whole behavioral repertoires are passed on. Ants rely completely on built-in instinct; they don't really think or, in fact, have much of anything to think *with*. So, even though ants live in highly complex societies and act in elaborate ways, all their behaviors are coded in their

homologies: Traits shared by two or more species through inheritance from a common ancestor.

analogies: Traits shared by two or more species that are similar in function but unrelated evolutionarily.

genes, to be triggered by outside stimuli but with little or no flexibility or variation in the response.

Other organisms, with larger and more complex brains, can vary their behavior as needed to cope with specific situations. Their behavior is flexible. They have behavioral potentials or themes carried in their genetic codes, and they respond to their environments by building onto these potentials—taking in information from the outside, remembering it, retreiving stored information, and utilizing it in appropriate circumstances. In other words, they *think*.

The nature of the inborn behavioral potentials in complex organisms is still a matter of debate, especially when humans are the topic. There have been those who argue that we are born as "blank slates," or, in a more modern image, as computers with internal hardware but nothing programmed. The extreme opposite view says that our brains come equipped with *specific* behaviors that are only modified to a small degree by our individual experiences—like a computer with many basic programs already in the system.

The reality is no doubt somewhere in the middle. Certainly we come into this world with some basic behavioral responses built in. Facial expressions like smiling, nursing behavior among infants, the bond between a mother and her offspring, the drives to walk upright and learn language—these are all recognized as universal in our species and as preprogrammed in our biology. But just as certainly, we are not programmed for *particular* ways of expressing these and other behaviors. Language ability, for example, may be instinctive, but the specific language you speak is learned within a specific cultural and individual context.

There is a scientific study that looks for evolutionary explanations for behaviors, especially social behaviors. It is called **sociobiology,** and two of its ideas are particularly relevant here. The first is called **inclusive fitness.** It refers to the fact that your close relatives share many of your genes. As a result, the fitness of your *genes* is measured by your own adaptive success (the usual definition of fitness), but it "includes" as well the adaptive success of your relatives. Thus, any behavior that has evolved through time that causes you to aid your close relations also serves to help your genes get passed on.

A good example is the case of **altruistic** behavior. If, for instance, I perform some action that saves my sister's life, but costs me mine in the process, I might not pass on any more genes, but I have helped increase the possibility that some of my *genes* will get passed on, because my sister and I share, on average, 50 percent of our genetic endowment.

Of course, humans have moral reasons for altruistic actions, but altruistic behaviors are seen in many other species, where there could be no cultural motivation. It may not seem logical that a behavior that might endanger the individual could have evolved by natural selection. But, if we look at the genes, rather than just the "packages" they come in, we can see how this could be the case. The altruistic behavior was selected for because it helped individuals possessing genes for that behavior to be reproductively successful, even if a few individuals were sacrificed in the process.

The second idea concerns **reproductive strategies.** Put simply, individuals have evolved behaviors that maximize their reproductive success. Male and female mammals, however, differ in their contributions to reproduction, so their evolved behaviors may differ as well. Females, of course, carry, nurture, and raise offspring—largely by themselves in most mammalian species, including most primates. Males, on the other hand, contribute sperm. Thus, behaviors have evolved that help females raise healthy offspring and that allow males to try to impregnate as many females as possible.

If it is the case that at least behavioral themes can be inherited, then we can shed light on our behaviors by looking into those of other creatures. In doing so, however, we need to take into account the concepts of homology and analogy. In comparing the behaviors of humans and chimpanzees, it is highly likely that a behavior is shared because it is the *same* behavior, derived by both species from our common ancestor of 5 or 6 million years ago. Understanding the nature and function of that behavior in chimpanzees is likely to provide insight into the origin of the behavior in humans because the behavior in question is homologous.

A specific behavior similar in humans and baboons is less likely to be homologous. Our two species have evolved independently for over 20 million years, so there is a greater chance that the behaviors evolved separately, under separate environmental circumstances and for different adaptive reasons. Still, they may be variations on some *general behavioral pattern* common to the primates and inherited from an early common ancestor.

The chance of two behaviors being analogous increases as we compare species that are less and less closely related. Some investigators have compared the behavior of humans with that of social carnivores like lions, wolves, and African wild dogs. There are strikingly "human" behaviors in these species. All three hunt cooperatively. Wolves and wild dogs have complex social relationships, use vocal and gestural signs to maintain them, and both actively feed their young. Wolves, especially, are territorial.

These collections of similarities, however, are probably not derived from a common ancestor, but have, at most, evolved quite independently from some general mammalian traits of social interaction, care of young, and relatively large complex brains allowing for flexibility of behavior.

sociobiology: The scientific study that examines evolutionary explanations for social behaviors within species.

inclusive fitness: The idea that fitness is measured by the success of one's genes, whether possessed by the individual or by that individual's relatives.

altruistic: Behavior that benefits others without regard to one's own needs or safety.

reproductive strategies: Behaviors that evolve to maximize an individual's reproductive success.

What we do learn from the behavior of such species is that one possible route to adaptive success for mammals is through complex social behavior and that this behavior is common in species that include meat in their diet, especially meat from large animals. But it is only one route; other carnivores—the fox and the leopard, for example—are solitary hunters. Lions, though they hunt cooperatively, never share food with their young.

Comparing analogous behaviors, then, can be informative and can point out possible clusters of adaptive traits. But analogies must be used with the understanding that the more evolutionarily distant the species, the less useful is the comparison. Ants live in highly complex societies to which investigators often apply human names (slave, caste, queen, nurse, soldier), but studying the social behavior of ants probably tells us nothing directly about our own societies.

We can now look at the behavior of some other species that have, to varying degrees, been used as models for the origin and evolution of our own behavior. For years, nearly all our information about other species came from studies of their behavior in the artificial environments of zoos and laboratories. Only when the science of **ethology**—studying creatures in the wild, under natural conditions—became popular and possible could we see how they were *really* adapted. And only then did we begin to learn some of the truly remarkable adaptations that our fellow primates possess.

BABOONS

The five species of genus *Papio* have long been of interest to anthropologists because of the complexity of the baboon's social organization and because among baboon habitats are the **savannas** of east and south Africa—the very habitat of our early hominid ancestors (Figure 8.2).

Our common notion of baboon behavior, handed down since the 1950s, once provided us with what seemed like a reasonable model for the behavior of our hominid ancestors because baboon societies appeared to share a number of features we saw as characteristic of our own social systems. Baboon troops were seen as centered on and held together by a dominance hierarchy of males. Often twice as large as females and equipped with long, sharp canine teeth, male baboons were thought to compete with one another from youth for social position. The baboon who was the largest, strongest, most aggressive, and smartest became the dominant member, a position recognized and acknowledged by the whole troop. The dominant male was the leader and decision maker. He had first rights to food and to females. He produced the most offspring, perpetuating those traits that made him dominant.

FIGURE 8.2
Baboons on the savannas of
Africa. This scene would
have looked familiar to our
early ancestors.

According to this view, female baboons had a loose hierarchy among themselves but always ranked below males within the troop. A female's social position was often determined by that of the male she mated with during estrus. Her main function was thus to bear and raise offspring, and her identity was essentially based on this function.

Such a system, the thinking ran, was an obvious aid to surviving the rigors of savanna life. The vulnerable troop members—females and young—were an undifferentiated group found in the middle of the troop and surrounded by males, who held individually defined and recognized positions in the hierarchy. The males were thought to be organized in an almost military fashion to protect and defend the females and to pass on their genes through them.

The short duration of early studies, combined with the expectations and, perhaps, wishful thinking of some researchers to observe a hierarchical, male-oriented society, led to an overemphasis on the aggressive, de-

ethology: The study of the natural behavior of animals under natural conditions.

savannas: The open grasslands of the tropics.

FIGURE 8.3

Baboon threat. A male baboon shows his long canine teeth and flashes his white eyelids in a "threat gesture," probably directed at a less dominant male.

cision-making, mate-choosing role of the males. This perception made it hard in turn to see the females as possessing differentiated identities and roles. The logical conclusion was the prime importance of males and their competition for dominance.

This interpretation of baboon social organization has recently been questioned, if not put to rest (Fedigan and Fedigan 1988, Smuts 1985, Strum 1987). Studies over the last decade have verified that male baboons do have individual identities and differential social power and influence, and they do protect and defend the troop from members of other troops and from predators (Figure 8.3). But a formal, tightly structured dominance hierarchy among males does not exist. Rather, the structure of the troop is based on "a network of social alliances" (Fedigan and Fedigan 1988:14), including friendships between females and between females and males. These friendships may be so strong that a male will aid his female friend's infants even though he may not be their father (see Figure 7.8). Such friendships, rather than the social position of the males, may be what determines who mates with whom.

Differential social positions exist, but they are based not on those "masculine" traits mentioned previously but on an individual's "experience, skill, and . . . ability to manipulate others [and] mobilize allies" (Fedigan and Fedigan 1988:15). If there is any subgroup that is central to a troop and that ties generations together, it is that made up of related females, the males being more mobile and less a stable part of the troop than was previously supposed. In fact, the competition that may be most important to the troop is not that among males, but among females, competing with one another "over access to the resources necessary to sustain them and their offspring" (Fedigan and Fedigan 1988:5). Finally, it appears that mate choice is more a female prerogative. Males make overtures toward estrus females, but it is the females who decide with whom they will mate. These behaviors are examples of inclusive fitness and male reproductive strategy. The male baboons have evolved protective behaviors toward females and offspring in their troop because those offspring *may* be theirs, and perhaps because those females may one day bear their offspring. Moreover, they try to keep away males from other troops to prevent strangers from including their genes in the troop's gene pool. At the same time, males are more mobile than females and will also try to spread their contribution of sperm to females in other troops.

The females, on the other hand, by forming alliances with related females and by selecting the males with whom they will mate, are helping assure their own reproductive and child-rearing success, as well as the success of their genes via the reproductive success of their close relatives. Keep in mind, however, that the baboons don't have these results consciously in mind. The behaviors have evolved over time because they increase the fitness of the genes of the individuals who perform them. We don't really know what is going on in the minds of the baboons that motivates them to act in these ways.

The earlier version of baboon social organization indicated that to survive on the savannas a primate needed a tightly organized, male-oriented and dominated, almost militaristic society (the use of the term *troop* is not arbitrary). The obvious conclusion was that the early hominid savanna dwellers probably had a similar set of behaviors and that our modern social systems are, to one extent or another, variations on this theme.

Again, however, we must remember that we can share with baboons only the most general primate homologous traits. Similarities between humans and baboons exist because we have evolved variations of the same behavioral themes. Our specific expressions of those themes, though, are the results of separate and independent evolutionary histories.

Nevertheless, those separate histories have produced results that are similar in baboons and humans and, as we shall see, in chimpanzees; that is, the adaptive focus of a social structure built around a family unit, friendships, mutual aid within the group, defense of the group, and recognition of individuals. This social structure at least tells us that such a focus is one possible adaptive path among primates, and so it is conceivable to assume that something like it was the key to the survival of the early hominids. Given that our closest relatives, the chimpanzees, exhibit this cluster of traits, it seems an even more reasonable assumption.

CHIMPANZEES

Some of the most remarkable results of ethological observations have come from three landmark studies of the great apes: Jane Goodall's study of the chimpanzee, Dian Fossey's of the gorilla, and Biruté Galdikas's of the orangutan. Each of these studies is interesting in its own right and tells us something of the variations possible on the basic primate pattern of social organization.

The orangutan is an Asian ape and is separated from us by 12 million years or more. The gorilla, though according to some as close to us genetically as the chimp and while exhibiting many of the same basic social behaviors, is a rather specialized ape. Unlike the chimpanzee, it spends much of its time on the ground and its almost exclusively vegetarian diet is largely of ground plants. This species is not known to make or use tools. The species most relevant to our present subject, are the chimpanzee and bonobo.

Much of what we know of the ethology of the chimp comes from the more than thirty years of research at Gombe Stream National Park in Tanzania led by Jane Goodall (1971, 1986, 1990). Goodall's studies have shown that, in addition to physical and physiological traits, we share with chimps a number of behavioral characteristics. These are centered on aspects of social interaction, and this is instructive for our understanding of our own behavior.

The bond between mother and infant is strong in chimps, as it is in most mammals. These apes, though, have large, complex brains and have a lot to learn about their world before they can become functioning adults. Thus, the mother-infant bond is particularly long-lived and important, and the nature of that interaction can have a lasting effect on the rest of a chimp's life. Poor treatment by its mother, for example, often makes a chimp a poor mother herself when she bears young. Chimps have been seen to help their mothers with younger siblings, and siblings often remain close into adulthood. Chimps, in other words, *raise* their young, and the family bonds that result may last a lifetime.

The chimps in a group are arranged in a dominance hierarchy. Males are generally dominant over all females, but within females a loose hierarchy exists. Males actually compete with one another in an attempt to achieve the highest position possible. The rewards are access to feeding places and to females, the latter being another example of male reproduc-

FIGURE 8.4
A male chimpanzee showing a "full open grin." This is a sign of excitement, often used by a high-ranking chimp displaying close to a subordinate. Compare with the baboon in Figure 8.3.

tive strategy. Social position, though attained in males through violent-looking but seldom injurious actions (Figure 8.4), is maintained via a series of expressions, gestures, and vocalizations. One of the most important is grooming (see Figure 7.9), which maintains social cohesion, and on occasion is a sign of dominance when a subordinate male grooms his superior. Other expressions of social interaction include kissing, hugging, bowing, extending the hand, sexual gestures, grinning, and various vocalizations—and we can freely use these terms because the meanings of these actions in chimp society seem to be precisely what they are in human society.

FIGURE 8.5
A chimp in Tanzania, eating the carcass of a baboon he has recently hunted and killed. He may share some of his prize with close friends in his group.

A chimp society, however, is in no way some sort of dictatorship. Instead, it is marked by cooperation and mutual concern, which is seen mostly within the family unit of mother and offspring (because chimps are sexually promiscuous—a female may mate with a dozen males during estrus—the biological father is unknown). Throughout their lives, this family unit will protect and care for each other especially during illness and injury. Males have even been known to help brothers in their competition for dominance. Care also extends outside the family unit. Offspring are important to the group as a whole, and adults will come to the aid or protection of a youngster threatened with some harm, possibly risking their own welfare, even if the youngster is not necessarily theirs. Once, an adolescent male adopted an unrelated youngster who had been orphaned (Goodall 1990:202). This protectiveness may be another example of inclusive fitness, where genes contributing to a behavior have been selected for because they confer adaptive fitness to individuals as well as to those that individual aids, who may also share those genes.

Group membership is somewhat fluid. Chimps, for various reasons, will leave a group, and outsiders will occasionally enter it. Despite this fluidity, there is a sense of group identity and territory. Small bands of males will sometimes patrol the boundaries of their group's range; and when members of other groups are encountered, they are reacted to as outsiders. This is another case of males performing a behavior that serves to protect their reproductive investment.

With chimps, however, we may reasonably wonder about more conscious motivation for some of these behaviors. In one chilling series of events, for example, males from Goodall's main study group attacked and killed a female and all the males of a group that had broken away to establish its own territory. Goodall thinks the motivation may have been to reclaim the area.

Among the chimpanzee's wide range of food sources is meat. Chimps from some groups, including those studied by Goodall and associates at the Gombe Stream National Park in Tanzania, are hunters (Stanford 1995). Males, and occasionally females, will hunt and kill small pigs, antelopes, and monkeys, including young baboons (Figure 8.5). At Gombe, chimps, often hunting in cooperative groups, kill over 100 red colobus monkeys a year, nearly a fifth of that species within the chimps' range. Meat is the one food that chimps will share, and male chimps are more likely to share with friends. They will even withhold meat from rivals. There is evidence, too, that a male will hunt in order to get meat as an offering to an estrus female.

Much of our information about this species comes from Goodall's research, but work on other chimp groups amply bears out her observations and conclusions and lends support to the idea that chimp behavior is flexible, adaptable, and the result of intelligence and reasoning. For example, a chimp group in the forests on the west coast of Africa uses hammerstones to crack open nuts, something the Gombe chimps don't do, though the Gombe chimps are famous for their termite sticks (see Chapter 7). The west African chimps also have different hunting techniques, relying more on cooperation between hunting males than did the Gombe chimps (Boesch and Boesch-Achermann 1991).

Recently, even more intriguing information has come to light about the second species of chimpanzee, the "pygmy chimp" or bonobo (Kano 1990). The bonobo lives in the lowland forests of Zaire and has been

FIGURE 8.6
A bonobo walking bipedally.
Note that she is doing so because she is carrying some
leaves in her hands.

estimated by genetic studies (see Chapter 9) to have been separate from the common chimp for 1.5 million years. Not really pygmies at all, these chimps are as large as the common chimps, though more slender with smaller heads and shoulders. They walk upright more often than the common chimps (Figure 8.6). But there are even more striking differences.

The bonobos are more peaceful and gregarious than the common chimps. They have a hierarchy, but it is looser than the common chimp and much less male-oriented. They more readily share food with one another, and the food shared is not limited to luxury items like meat. They have never been observed to kill another of their kind, and their sexual behaviors play important roles in group cohesion.

A group of bonobos, especially when feeding, constantly posture toward one another, rubbing rumps or "presenting" themselves as if initiating sexual activity. When sex does follow it is usually face-to-face, unlike the position of other primates and like humans. Sexual activity is not limited to opposite sex partners. Females commonly rub genitalia with other females, and males will mount each other.

Moreover, the signs of fertility, the estrus signals, seem nearly always present in bonobo females. In all chimps the fertile and therefore sexual period is marked by a swelling and coloration of the skin of the genital area, which stimulates sexual interest on the part of the males. In common chimps, the swelling only occurs when the female has ovulated and is fertile. In bonobos, however, there is some swelling almost all the time, and they seem almost constantly sexually receptive. Sexual activity in this species has become separate from purely reproductive activity and is responded to on a conscious level. The motivation for sex may be as much psychological and social as it is reproductive.

The function of this friendly posturing and sexual receptiveness seems to be the same as grooming and as some of the expressions and gestures among all chimps: to prevent violence, to ease tension, especially while feeding, as a greeting, a sign of reconciliation, or to reassure another group member. Sex or some form of sexual activity, heterosexual or homosexual, has even been seen to precede food sharing.

Now, if all the behaviors of the chimp species sound more than vaguely human, the reason may be simple. We share certain behavioral patterns because we inherited them from a common ancestor. To be sure, our line and that of the chimps have been going their separate and independent ways for 5 or 6 million years, and even shared features have had the chance to become modified by all the processes of evolution—to be changed, eliminated, enhanced, and differently adapted to our species' different niches. Chimps are not "living fossils" stuck in some 5 million-year-old rut while our ancestors continued to evolve. But because our common ancestor is relatively recent and there is striking similarity between our bodies and behaviors, we can argue that our shared behaviors are homologous.

This does *not* mean that humans have specific genes for friendship, food sharing, territoriality, or continual sexuality. These are complex behaviors, and humans and chimps are complex species. It does hint that, as with the chimps, the focus of the human adaptation—the thing that adapted our earliest hominid ancestors and that has been the adaptive theme of our line—is social interaction based on individual recognition, a strong bond centered around family relationships (generally mothers and their offspring), long-term friendships, sexual consciousness, mutual care within the group, and recognition of and defense of the group. It seems reasonable to assume that our hominid ancestors behaved in similar ways. As Jane Goodall says,

> . . . the concept of early humans poking for insects with twigs and wiping themselves with leaves seems entirely sensible. The thought of those ancestors greeting and reassuring one another with kisses or embraces, cooperating in protecting their territory or in hunting, and sharing food with each other, is appealing. The idea of close affectionate ties within the Stone Age family, of brothers helping one another, of teenage sons hastening to the protection of their old mothers, and of teenage daughters minding the babies, for me brings the fossilized relics of their physical selves dramatically to life. (1990:207)

SUMMARY

As we noted in the last chapter, one way to guide us as we look at our own species is to understand the context from which our species evolved. This approach works for behavior as well as for physical adaptations. The importance of a well-defined social organization is seen among another savanna primate, the baboon, and is a good hint that an analogous behavior was a key to the survival of early savanna hominids.

More useful is the behavior of close evolutionary relatives, especially the chimpanzee and bonobo. Chimp behavior differs in specifics from ours and has been evolving separately from ours for 5 or 6 million years. All three species have adapted to different particular niches. The basic patterns for the behavior of all three species, however, are homologous. They are the same because we inherited them from a common ancestor. It is highly likely, then, that our remote hominid ancestors also used some manifestation of these patterns.

Such studies indicate to us that the early hominids of the plains of Africa may very well have been highly social creatures and that their social organization was built around differing interpersonal relationships, a family unit, conscious sexuality, recognition of group membership and territory, and mutual care at both the individual and the group level.

KEY TERMS

homologies	inclusive fitness	ethology
analogies	altruistic	savannas
sociobiology	reproductive strategies	

SUGGESTED READINGS

The latest thinking on baboon behavior can be found in Shirley Strum's *Almost Human* and in Barbara Smut's *Sex and Friendship in Baboons.* Jane Goodall's latest work on the chimps and her experiences studying them is *Through a Window: My Thirty Years with the Chimpanzees of Gombe.*

For more technical information on primate behavior, see *The Evolution of Primate Behavior* by Alison Jolly, and *Patterns of Primate Behavior* by Claud A. Bramblett.

Dian Fossey recounts her study of gorillas in *Gorillas in the Mist;* her own story in turn, including her murder, is told by Farley Mowat in *Woman in the Mists* and in the 1988 movie, *Gorillas in the Mist.* Biruté Galdikas tells about orangutans in *Reflections of Eden: My Years with the Orangutans of Borneo.*

The bonobos are described in the March 1995 issue of *Scientific American* in an article by Frans B. M. de Waal called "Bonobo sex and society."

STUDYING THE HUMAN PAST

> The present contains
> nothing more than the
> past, and what is found
> in the effect was
> already in the cause.
> —Henri Bergson

The study of the human past—our evolutionary history—is a central part of biological anthropology. To understand the human species today, we need to know where, when, how, and from what we evolved. But the past *is* the past. We can't see past events as they were happening. We can't make them happen again. All we have are the present-day results of series of past events, like the living species of primates we discussed in the last two chapters. In some cases, we have the physical remains of past events, such as the fossils of extinct species, but these have themselves undergone change since they were part of a living creature.

The present, however, can be a powerful tool. Recall, from Chapter 2, how Hooke and Steno used fossils and stratigraphy to plot the events of the past and how Hutton and Lyell used the idea of uniformitarianism—that the past can be explained by present-day processes—to understand how past events took place.

In this chapter, we will address the methods used by bioanthropologists to answer questions about our past.

What are the features of the primate skeleton and how can knowledge of them help us identify fossil remains?

How do we locate, recover, and date fossil remains?

How are fossils formed, and what affects the condition of the fossils we find?

What can we learn about our past from new technologies in the study of genetics?

BONES: THE PRIMATE SKELETON

Most of the physical remains we find of the evolutionary past are in the form of preserved bone. Only in rare cases are we lucky enough to discover soft tissue remains of an ancient organism (see Figure 15.1). Therefore, knowledge of the skeletal structure, or **osteology,** of the group of species in which we are interested is vital. The first thing we need to do, of course, is determine what species the skeletal remains are from. The human skeleton is a variation on the basic mammalian skeletal theme and, more specifically, on the primate skeletal theme. Figure 9.1 compares the skeletons (with the major bones labeled) of a domestic cat, a gorilla, and a modern human.

The bones are not separate from the muscles, nerves, blood vessels, and other soft tissues of the body. Rather, they all develop together and

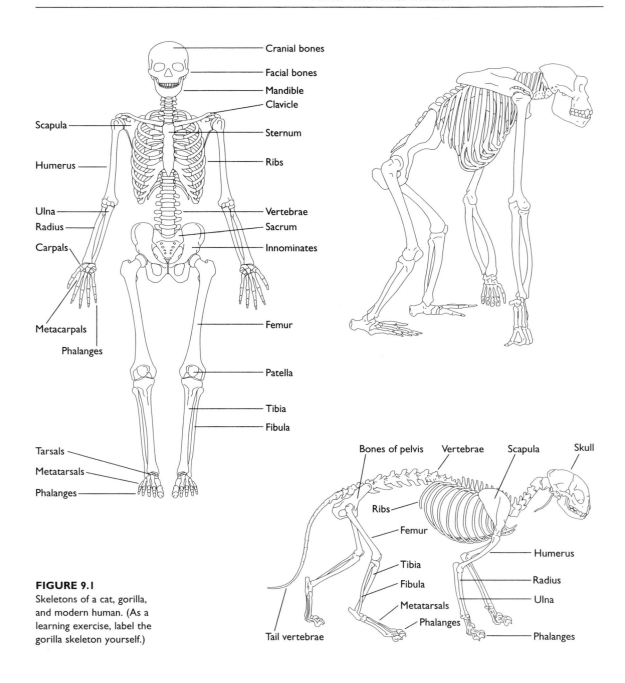

FIGURE 9.1
Skeletons of a cat, gorilla, and modern human. (As a learning exercise, label the gorilla skeleton yourself.)

osteology: The study of the skeleton.

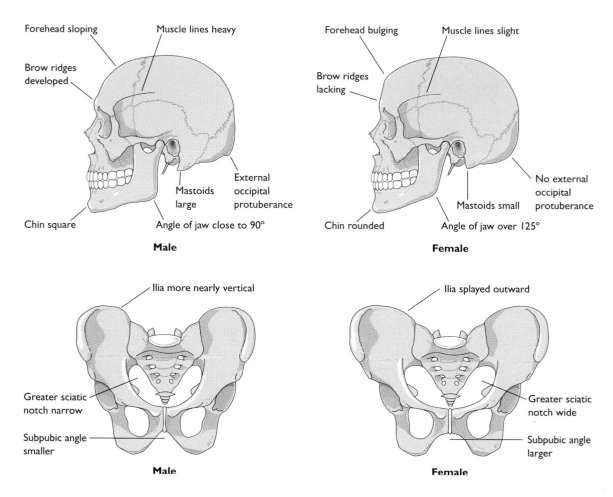

FIGURE 9.2
Sex differences in the skull
and pelvis.

are adapted to function together. For example, the skull serves to protect the brain; therefore, the skull is a good indicator of the shape and size of the brain it once protected. Muscles are attached to bones, and so the location, size, and shape of the muscle attachment point on a bone will provide some indication of the size and shape of the muscle even though the muscle itself may have decayed long ago. We can tell a lot about a creature from the bones it leaves behind.

One of the more obvious and important things we can tell about a human skeleton is its sex. Humans are a species that exhibits **sexual dimorphism,** notable physical differences between the sexes. In general, males tend to be larger and more heavily muscled than females, a fact that also applies to the apes and to extinct hominid species. The skull and especially, for obvious reasons, the pelvis are the best parts of the skeleton for determining sex (Figure 9.2).

Average dates for cranial suture closure (years)

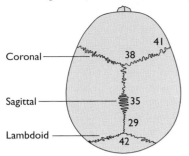

Coronal
Sagittal
Lambdoid

41
38
35
29
42

Ages of epiphyseal union (years)

Elbow	14
Hands and feet	15
Ankle	16
Thigh	17
Knee	18
Wrist	19
Shoulder	20
Hip	21
Clavicle	28

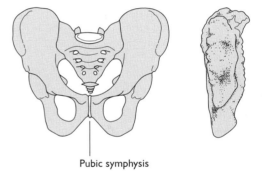

Epiphysis (cap)

Diaphysis (shaft)

Epiphyseal disc

Cranial Suture Closure. The bones of the cranial vault are separate at birth and gradually fuse during a person's lifetime. The numbers indicate the average age (in years) of complete closure at different points along the lines of attachment, the sutures. There are other dates as well, on locations not shown in this view. Because of the great degree of individual variation, this is not a particularly reliable technique.

Epiphyseal Union. The bones of the arms, legs, hands, feet, and other bones grow in sections: a shaft, or diaphysis, and caps, or epiphyses. When growth is complete, the cartilaginous disks between caps and shaft turn to bone and a single bone results. Ages for epiphyseal union are known and are uniform enough to provide a reliable aging method. The ages shown indicate that all sites at any one location fuse at about the same time. For example, at the elbow the far (distal) end of the humerus and the near (proximal) ends of the radius and ulna all fuse at 14 years.

Eruption dates of deciduous and permanent teeth

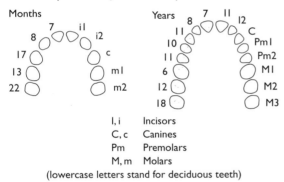

Months

7 i1
8   i2
17   c
13   m1
22   m2

Years

7 11
8   12
11   C
10   Pm1
11   Pm2
6   M1
12   M2
18   M3

I, i	Incisors
C, c	Canines
Pm	Premolars
M, m	Molars

(lowercase letters stand for deciduous teeth)

Pubic symphysis

Dental Eruption. Humans have two sets of teeth: deciduous, or "baby" teeth, and adult teeth. Each tooth "erupts" through the gum line at a certain average age. We determine age by seeing which tooth was the last to erupt and which unerupted tooth would have erupted next. We recognize this method in our use of the term "six year molar" for the first adult tooth to erupt. The degree of development of each tooth below the gum line (seen in broken bone or in x-rays) can also be used.

Pubic Symphysis. The inner surface of the bones where the pelvis meets in front is called the pubic symphysis. Between the ages of 18 and 50+, the appearance of this surface undergoes characteristic changes. By assessing the phase to which a specimen belongs, we can approximate age at death. The symphyseal face shown is a Phase VIII, giving an age of 40 to 44 years. (Redrawn from Todd 1920.)

Age at death may also be determined from skeletal remains. The body, including the bones, goes through many physical changes as it develops, matures, and ages, and many of these changes take place at fairly regular times. By determining, on a skeleton, which changes have already taken place and which have yet to take place, we may approximate the age at which these changes ceased, that is, the age at which the individual stopped living (Figure 9.3).

FIGURE 9.3
Aging techniques.

sexual dimorphism: Physical differences between the sexes of a species.

FIGURE 9.4

The skeletons of a gorilla and a modern human. Note the differences in shape and orientation of the pelvis, the relative lengths of arms and legs, and the shape of the feet. The size and shape of the muscles of posture and locomotion would also reflect the difference between quadrupedalism and bipedalism.

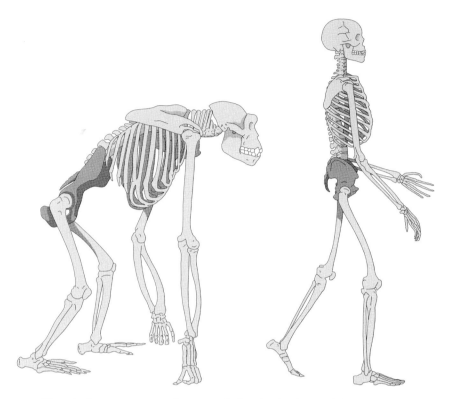

The skeleton acts as a framework for the body, and thus the size and shape of the bones can reveal something of the appearance of the entire living person. We know, for example, from the sheer size and ruggedness of their bones, that a group of humans from Ice Age Europe (the "Neandertals," who we will discuss in Chapter 12) were big, brawny, and extremely strong. Several investigators have attempted to reconstruct the faces of our ancestors from the shapes of skulls and facial bones. Using their knowledge of human anatomy, they artistically add missing bones, eyes, fatty tissue, cartilage, muscle, and skin to casts of ancient skulls, "fleshing out" our picture of early humans (see Figure 15.2). (This technique is also used in law enforcement to try to identify skeletal remains. We will discuss the application of human osteology to legal matters in Chapter 15.)

The skeleton can also tell us something about the behavior of the organism that possessed it. We have mentioned the importance of bipedal locomotion in our evolution and that this behavior is the first hominid trait to evolve. We know it is the first because the nature of the bones of the pelvis and femur, along with the position of the skull atop the spine, are all indications of posture and movement. Thus, our analysis of the bones of our most ancient ancestors includes indications of how they walked about (Figure 9.4).

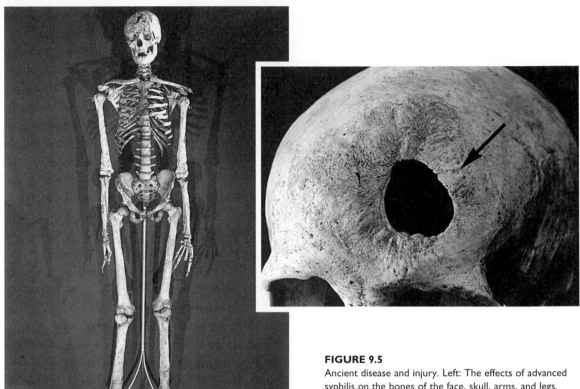

FIGURE 9.5
Ancient disease and injury. Left: The effects of advanced syphilis on the bones of the face, skull, arms, and legs. Right: A trephined skull. The arrow shows the outer margin of the surgery. The edge of the hole indicates that healing had taken place before the individual died.

Moreover, we can discern information about diet from dental and skeletal remains. The type of teeth are evidence. Look at the **carnivore** dentition of your dog or cat, and compare it to the **omnivore** teeth in your own mouth. The teeth of the dog or cat, although they show some differentiation, are all pointed and sharp, adapted for grasping, piercing, cutting, and crushing. Our teeth are adapted for a greater variety of operations and, thus, a greater variety of food types. More specifically, certain wear patterns on the teeth, when examined microscopically, can reveal whether the diet was made up of soft foods like fruits, or more abrasive, gritty foods like grains and roots. We can even examine the chemical content of ancient bones for their proportion of strontium and calcium to determine whether plants or meat made up the bulk of the diet of certain populations.

Finally, we may acquire information about the health status of our ancestors. Many diseases leave characteristic marks on the skeleton. These include such important disorders as arthritis, tumors and other cancers, tuberculosis, leprosy, anemias, syphilis, osteoporosis, and various infections. Injuries, too, leave their marks, as do other behaviors, including scalping and **trephination,** a prehistoric surgical procedure that involved cutting a hole in the skull (Figure 9.5). (We will take up these topics in more detail in Chapter 15.)

carnivore: An organism that is adapted to a diet of mostly meat.

omnivore: An organism with a mixed diet of animal and vegetable foods.

trephination: The cutting of a hole in the skull, presumably to treat some illness.

FIGURE 9.6
Olduvai Gorge, Tanzania, one of the world's most productive sites for paleoanthropologists. The strata represent two million years of evolution.

OLD BONES: LOCATING, RECOVERING, AND DATING FOSSILS

Most creatures that have ever lived, including humans, have left no remains. Fossilization (which we'll discuss in the next section) is a rare occurrence. A fossil, therefore, is really a priceless treasure, and finding one is an uncommon event even in those **sites** that, because of their geological history and nature, yield many remains. Olduvai Gorge in Tanzania has provided us with some of the most important hominid fossils, yet Louis and Mary Leakey lived and worked there for over twenty years before finding one. How then, do we even decide where to begin looking?

A lot, of course, depends upon just *what* we're looking for. If it's dinosaurs we're interested in, we wouldn't look in rock layers (remember the idea of stratigraphy) that are older or younger than the dinosaurs themselves. For hominid fossils, we need strata that were deposited in the last 5 or 6 million years.

FIGURE 9.7
A fragile fossil: the cast of a duck-billed dinosaur egg and hatchling. Below are the actual fossil eggs in their rock matrix.

It helps, too, if those strata are exposed by geological processes. Layers that are far under the surface might contain important fossils, but purely practical considerations would make it difficult, time-comsuming, and expensive to dig them up. A place like Olduvai Gorge is ideal. There, an ancient river cut a canyon 300 feet into the earth, exposing layers of soil and rock that go back about 2 million years. Walking down into the gorge is walking back in time (Figure 9.6). At Omo, in Ethiopia, another important early hominid site, the strata have been tilted by geological forces, so that layers from 1 million to 4 million years old are all on the surface. Here, walking back and forth on the ground is like walking through time. In addition, in such places, natural water and wind erosion helps expose new soil and whatever fossils they may contain.

Of course, just because a location *looks* like it might easily yield fossils doesn't mean that the conditions there were always conducive to fossilization. Paleoanthropologists might inquire as to whether fossils of *any* sort have been found in a potential area of investigation in strata from the time period they were interested in. Both Olduvai and Omo already had reputations as rich fossil areas before the search for hominid fossils began at those sites.

Recovering fossils once they are located can be a tricky business. Fossils are old and often very fragile. Many old bones are **petrified**—turned to stone—and so are hard to distinguish from the stone in which they were found (Figure 9.7). Raymond Dart, the discoverer of one of the most

sites: Places that contain evidence of human presence.

petrified: A fossil that has turned to stone.

FIGURE 9.8
Hypothetical stratigraphic sequence. The human remains are between two layers of volcanic rock that can be dated using the K/Ar method. They must be younger than the volcanic deposit below and older than the one above.

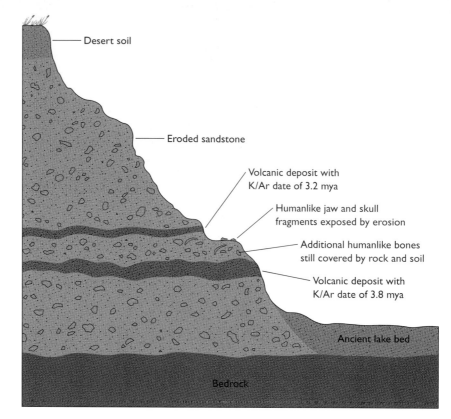

Desert soil

Eroded sandstone

Volcanic deposit with K/Ar date of 3.2 mya

Humanlike jaw and skull fragments exposed by erosion

Additional humanlike bones still covered by rock and soil

Volcanic deposit with K/Ar date of 3.8 mya

Ancient lake bed

Bedrock

FIGURE 9.9
Grid system diagram of a portion of an excavation from Ambrona in Spain, dated at around 350,000 years ago (see Chapter 11).

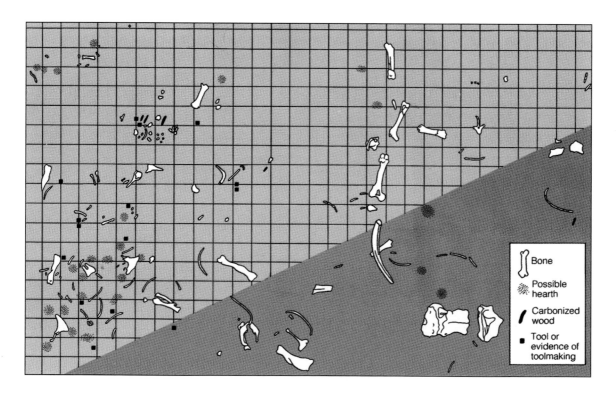

Bone

Possible hearth

Carbonized wood

Tool or evidence of toolmaking

famous hominid fossils (both of whom we shall meet in the next chapter), took seventy-three days to separate the tiny fossil from the limestone in which it was encased. The excavation tools of the paleoanthropologist, then, are not so much the backhoe or even the shovel, but rather the artist's brush, the mason's trowel, and the dentist's pick.

A fossil sitting on a shelf in a lab, or on display in a museum, may be beautiful, intriguing, and provocative, but it is scientifically useless unless we know precisely where it was found, its **provenience.** To keep track of the proveniences of fossils, recovery is carried out with the utmost care directed at detailed and accurate record keeping. After all, once fossils are removed, a site is destroyed, and we must have records of the relative locations of all the important items contained in that site.

Many early hominid fossils are simply found on the surface of the ground, exposed by wind and water erosion. Many, however, are dug out of the ground or are found associated with particular strata.

The depth at which a fossil is found relative to other fossils and to the natural strata of the soil or rock is, of course, an indication of relative age. This is the principle of stratigraphy, the idea that the deeper a layer is the older it is. It is an important dating method and is referred to as a **relative dating technique;** that is, it indicates the age of a fossil in comparison to another (Figure 9.8). In the absence of any natural stratigraphy, the excavator of fossils must establish one. For example, the investigator may dig down by regular increments, perhaps only centimeters at a time, recording the precise depth of any item of interest.

Similarly, the horizontal location of each fossil is important. Often a paleoanthropologist—like the archaeologist looking for human cultural remains—uses a grid system. A site is divided into squares or grids, and each grid is excavated separately (Figure 9.9). Again, the precise location of a fossil, relative to others at the same depth, is recorded through photographs and maps.

Besides relative dating, there are also **absolute dating techniques.** These tell us the actual age of a fossil. Among the best known and most useful are **radiometric** techniques, such as **carbon dating,** which can be used to date fossils back to about 60,000 years ago and so is relevant to the later period of human evolution. It works as follows: Carbon, in the form of carbon dioxide, is found in all living things, which continually exchange it with the environment through respiration and metabolism. Most carbon is ^{12}C, indicating that there are twelve particles in the nucleus (six protons and six neutrons). Some carbon, however, is "carbon 14" or ^{14}C because it has two extra neutrons and it is formed when cosmic radiation hits nitrogen in the atmosphere. We know the proportion of each form (called an isotope) of carbon in a living organism. Once an organism dies, however, it is no longer taking in new carbon and so its ^{14}C—an unstable or radioactive isotope—begins to decay back into nitro-

provenience: The precise location of something.

relative dating technique: Dating technique that indicates the age of one item in comparison to another.

absolute dating technique: Dating technique that gives a specific age, year, or range of years.

radiometric: Refers to the decay rate of a radioactive substance.

carbon dating: A radiometric dating technique using the decay rate of a radioactive form of carbon found in organic remains.

TABLE 9.1
Other Dating Methods

Dating Method	Age Range	Material Dated	Basis
Thermoluminescence	No effective limits	Fired clay, pottery, bricks, burned rock	Measure of amount of energy captured in material from decay of radioactive elements in surrounding soil; amount of energy captured is proportional to age
Paleomagnetism	2000 B.P.-present	Material with magnetic minerals	Movement of earth's magnetic pole and known dates of the position of the pole
Amino (aspartic) acid racemization	1,000,000-2000 B.P.	Bone	Shift in polarity of amino acids
Obsidian hydration	800,000 B.P.-present	Obsidian (volcanic glass)	Regular build up of "hydration layer" caused by chemical reaction of obsidian with water over time
Fission track dating	1,000,000-100,000 B.P.	Volcanic rock	Radioactive decay leaves microscopic damage "tracks" in rock at regular rate
Electron spin resonance		Cave deposits, bone	Electrons produced by natural radiation become trapped in crystalline materials at a regular rate

Overview of time range, application, and basis of dating methods not discussed in the text.

gen, and it does so at a constant rate called a **half-life.** The half-life of ^{14}C is 5730 years. In that time, one-half of the ^{14}C will have decayed. In another 5730 years, half of the remaining half will decay, leaving a quarter of the original, and so on.

Now, if we find some organic remains—bone, for example, or even burnt wood from a fire—we can test it to see how much ^{14}C is left compared to how much the organism contained when alive. We know how much ^{14}C a living organism should contain, and we test the amount left as we would test any radioactive substance, with a device like a Geiger counter that measures the amount of radiation emitted. Suppose that our specimen has one-quarter of the living amount. Two half-lives have passed, or 5730 times two, or 11,460 years. Beyond 60,000 years ago there is not enough ^{14}C left to accurately measure. So how do we date the really old fossils, like those of the early hominids?

We could use another important method called **potassium/argon,** or **K/Ar, dating.** Radioactive potassium (^{40}K), found in volcanic rock, decays into stable argon gas at a half-life of 1.31 billion years. Organic matter contains ^{40}K as well but loses the argon gas that it decays into. Volcanic rocks, formed during eruptions, have a crystalline structure that traps the argon. Using the same reasoning as for carbon dating, we test volcanic rock for the amount of argon, work backward, and date the rock. Now, organic remains may be dated relatively. Any fossils found in a layer of volcanic rock are as old as that rock. Fossils found just above are younger; those found just below are older, and so on (see again Figure 9.8).

There are other dating techniques that use the principle of radioactive decay or other chemical and physical laws. Several date volcanic rock; others can be used directly on organic remains (see Table 9.1). In many cases, more than one of these methods may be applied and, when they agree, we have a well-established date for a geological stratum or a fossil. Most of the dates that will be presented in the following chapters are reasonably well confirmed through the use of one or more of these techniques.

HOW FOSSILS GET TO BE FOSSILS

Most animals and plants that have inhabited the earth have left no fossil remains. There are probably whole taxonomic groups that we have no idea of because we've found no clues to their existence. Why is this so?

The conditions under which an organism, or some of its parts, can be preserved are quite specific. In New England, where I live, the soil is very acidic, due largely to the annual fall of leaves and pine needles. Organic remains tend to disappear very quickly. This is why we were surprised to find the entire, intact skeleton of Henry Opukahaia (see Chapter 1). His bones were preserved because he was buried on a hill in sandy soil, so water, with all its related chemical and biological decaying activity, could not accumulate around him, and probably because the cemetery was regularly cleared of leaves.

Organic remains tend to be preserved under several conditions. In cases of extreme dryness, even soft tissues, usually eaten by everything from bacteria to insects to scavengers, may mummify. Natural mummies were created in normal burials in the desert sands of ancient Egypt, even before the Egyptians began artificial mummification. In 1972, eight human bodies were found in graves in a rock overhang in western Greenland. These Inuits (Eskimos) had been naturally mummified by a combination of low temperatures, drying winds, and protection from the elements by the rock, and they had been preserved for over five hundred years (Figure 9.10).

Lack of oxygen also contributes to preservation. Such conditions are found in the thick mud at the bottom of some lakes and ponds. With no

half-life: The time needed for one-half of a given amount of a radioactive substance to decay.

potassium/argon (K/Ar) dating: A radiometric dating technique using the decay rate of radioactive potassium, found in volcanic rock, into stable argon gas.

FIGURE 9.10
Mummy of Inuit baby, about
six months old when he died.

FIGURE 9.11
Artist's reconstruction of a
leopard with the remains of
an early hominid in a tree
above the entrance to a
South African cave. This behavior probably accounts for
the accumulation of bones in
the area's caves, including
bones of our ancestors.

oxygen, there is little bacterial action, and organic remains decay very slowly. Many important fossils have been found in places that were once lake bottoms.

Of course, the longer ago the organism lived, the less likely we are to find remains, simply because there is more chance that they will have been crushed, dissolved, eaten, washed away, and so on. But in some cases, minerals may crystallize out of water around the bones or shells of a creature, or in rare cases around slowly decaying soft tissue, and may fill in the spaces left by the decay of organic matter. In this case, the fossil becomes petrified; it literally turns to stone and so is harder, more resistant to processes of decay and no longer edible although, naturally, some anatomical detail is lost. The dinosaur fossils with which we are so familiar as well as the remains of the earliest hominids are all stone. Luckily for us, the creatures that left these remains perished in just the right situations. Most creatures aren't so considerate.

A fossil is more than just an indication of the type of organism of which it was once a part. A fossil also contains clues as to how the animal died and what happened to it after its death. The study of these factors is called **taphonomy** (from *taphos*, dead), and it has been important in our understanding of our own evolution.

For example, some early hominid bones have been found in limestone caves in South Africa along with the bones of other mammals. These findings led investigators to believe that our early ancestors inhabited those caves and were hunters who brought their kills back home. More recent taphonomic analysis, however, reveals that the hominids were the hunted, not the hunters. The bones were the leftovers of leopard kills. Leopards often drag their prey up into a tree where no other predator or scavenger can get at it, and they eat it over several days. As the prey is eaten and, later, as the remains decay, the bones fall to the ground. Now, although much of South Africa is dry, the limestone caves hold moisture, and so trees tend to grow well around the mouths of the caves. As leopard kills hanging in these trees fell apart, the bones fell into the caves. Those bones included antelopes, baboons, and other animals leopards eat, and apparently, our ancestors were on the menu as well (Figure 9.11). One early hominid skull shows twin puncture wounds that appear to have been the cause of death. The lower canine teeth of a leopard fit exactly into these punctures, providing evidence for the preceding analysis. Taphonomy, although the study of the dead, has thus told us important things about how our distant ancestors lived. We will describe another important conclusion from taphonomy in the next chapter when we see how microscopic scratches on bones and teeth reveal something about the diet of the early hominids.

taphonomy: The study of how organisms become part of the paleontological record.

GENES: NEW WINDOWS TO THE PAST

We are beginning to be able to extract DNA from ancient bones and other preserved organic remains, such as insects trapped in amber (hardened tree sap) like in *Jurassic Park* (although the part where the dinosaurs were genetically reconstituted and grown is entirely fictional and, indeed, scientifically impossible. Sorry). Most genetic studies, however, must be done on living organisms. How, then, can such studies contribute to our understanding of the past?

Just as we can reconstruct evolutionary relationships by comparing the anatomical traits of living creatures, we may do the same with comparisons at the genetic level. In many ways, genetic comparisons are more accurate. Phenotypic traits are normally controlled by a complex interaction of multiple genetic loci, evolutionary processes, and environmental factors. As a result, a trait may look the same in two species, but the expressions of that trait in each species may be based on very different genetics, developmental processes, and environmental interactions, and the two traits may have different adaptive significances.

Stephen Jay Gould (1980) notes the example of the panda's "thumb," which looks like the thumb of primates and is used for grasping. It is actually, however, not a finger at all but an elongated wrist bone that is used solely to strip the leaves off bamboo stalks, just about the panda's only food. One might conclude from this striking similarity in a rather unique feature that pandas are closely related to primates, but the similarity is purely a coincidence. The thumbs of primates and the "thumb" of the panda are analogous, not homologous. The panda is a bear, in order Carnivora, not at all closely related to primates, as an examination of the genes themselves would clearly point out.

On the other hand, two species may look very different, but their differences may be the result of extensive phenotypic effects of a very small number of genes, and the species may actually be quite closely related. Humans and chimps are an example.

Comparing genetic differences among individuals, species, and higher taxa (genera, families, and so on) reveals actual biological relationships, no matter what the species look like or how seemingly similar or different some of their traits. In the 1960s, Vincent Sarich and the late Allan Wilson of the University of California at Berkeley pioneered research that used genetic comparisons to determine evolutionary relationships. Because the technology for comparing actual genes was still in the future, they compared the chemistry of blood proteins. These are large proteins, easily obtained and easy to work with, and, most importantly, are the direct products of the genetic code. This research provided some startling conclusions.

FIGURE 9.12
Human chromosomes, on the left in each pair, compared to chromosomes of chimpanzees. The similarities in banding pattern are clear. In the far lefthand pair, the pattern of human chromosome 2 is similar to that of two chimp chromosomes. The far righthand pair are virtually identical. This is one piece of evidence for the 99 percent genetic similarity between our two species.

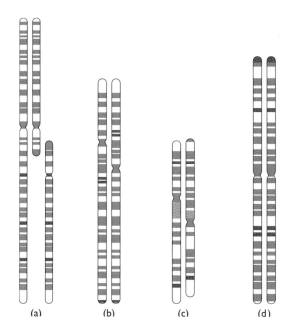

(a)   (b)   (c)   (d)

It had been assumed that humans and our closest relatives, the great apes, were separated by 12 to 15 million years of evolution. This estimate was based on the degree of phenotypic difference between us and them and on some fossils of that age that appeared to show the beginnings of hominid traits. Wilson and Sarich's research showed that the blood proteins of humans and chimps were almost identical. In other words, our genes, at least for those traits, are almost the same. Comparing this difference with that between species whose evolutionary divergence time was known, Wilson and Sarich calculated that our two species had branched apart a mere 5 million years ago. These 12-million-year-old fossils, they said, were not hominids, no matter what they appeared to be. They were right, as we will see in more detail in Chapter 10.

Other methods for making comparisons closer to the genetic level verified this hypothesis. A protein, you recall, is a genetically coded sequence of amino acids. Proteins may thus be compared for the sequence of amino acids that constitute them. Again, it turned out that humans and chimpanzees showed less than 1 percent difference in the amino acid structure of certain blood proteins—nearly identical. Comparison of a bonding reaction of the DNA of chimps and humans and of the pattern of bands on chromosomes of chimps and humans (an indication of the nature of their sequence of genes) revealed the same lack of difference (Figure 9.12).

Recently, we have developed the technology to compare the very structure of the genes themselves—the sequence of bases (A, T, G, and C) of the DNA. A multinational project known as the Human Genome Initiative (the genome is the total genetic endowment of a species) is attempting to map the locations of the 100,000 to 300,000 human genes and to determine the exact sequence of all the 3 billion bases that make up our species' genetic code.

The technology involved has allowed us to make great strides in such matters as personal identification in criminal and missing persons cases. For example, blood samples from crime scenes can be genetically compared with blood from suspects. DNA sequencing also helps in locating genes involved in various diseases. At least one gene on each of the twenty-three human chromosomes (except the tiny Y or male chromosome) has been found to be linked to a human ailment. Examples are ALS or Lou Gehrig's disease (a fatal degenerative nerve disease), some cases of breast cancer, a form of kidney disease, Tay-Sachs disease (a fatal metabolic disorder), one form of Alzheimer's, PKU (a metabolic disease that results in mental retardation), sickle-cell anemia, malignant melanoma (skin cancer), cystic fibrosis (a lung disease), Huntington's disease (a degenerative nerve disease), muscular dystrophy, kidney cancer, psoriasis (a skin disease), osteoporosis (thinning of the bones in women), and many more. For many of these diseases, we can test for the presence of the defective gene even if symptons have not yet appeared.

These new technologies have also been applied to the study of human evolution because we can now very specifically compare the genes of various living human groups (see Chapters 12 and 14) and other primate populations and compare the genes of humans with related species. Such detailed studies have shown us, for example, that the bonobos are genetically distinct enough from the common chimps to be considered a separate species. These techniques also further bear out what older studies indicated—that humans and chimpanzees differ by about 1 percent of their genetic make up and that this difference, when compared with differences among and between other species, points to a divergence time of about 5 million years.

Chapter 7 included information about a method of taxonomic classification called cladistics. Whereas the traditional taxonomy compares living species and infers evolutionary relationships, cladistics uses the new genetic technologies as well as information from our increasing ability to interpret the fossil record and classifies according to actual evolutionary relationships, no matter what the living creatures look like.

For example, based on phenotypic appearances, it makes sense to separate humans and the four great apes into different taxonomic groups, an ape group and a hominid group—traditionally family Pongidae and family Hominidae (Figure 9.13). This makes intuitive sense because, certainly,

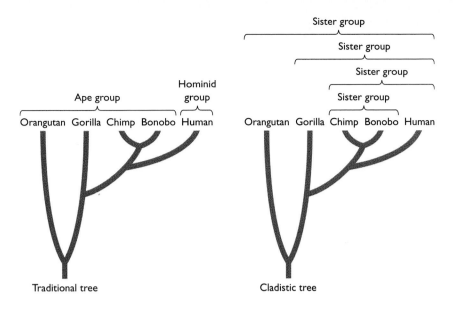

FIGURE 9.13
Traditional and cladistic taxonomies, as described in the text.

an orangutan and a chimp appear far more similar to each other than either does to you or me.

However, in terms of actual order of evolutionary branching, there's no such thing as an ape. The latest divergence is between the two species of chimpanzee, the common chimp and the bonobo, who thus form a "sister group." The next sister group, working back in time to the next branch, includes humans. Then comes the group made up of chimps, bonobos, humans, and gorillas, and so on. There is no sister group that *includes* the four great apes but *excludes* the hominids.

Adherents to cladistic taxonomies have thus proposed new classifications to better capture this idea. One version, for example, places only the orangutan in family Pongidae and lumps the gorilla, the two chimps, and humans in family Hominidae. We will continue to use the traditional taxonomic names and limit the hominids to the habitually bipedal primates.

In the next two chapters, we will outline the story of hominid evolution. All the above scientific techniques have been applied to studying this story and have allowed us to achieve what knowledge we have of our evolutionary history.

SUMMARY

Often, when we read a necessarily brief article in the popular media about some new fossil find, we get the impression that the scientists conducted some sort of magic to arrive at their stated conclusions. In the October 3, 1994, issue of *Time,* for example, we read that a small fossil tooth and a few other fragmentary bones from Ethiopia have been discovered and are heralded as "a new chapter in the history of human evolution" (Lemonick 1994). On the basis of these bones, a new species of hominid was established, and it is described as being about four feet tall, probably bipedal, having been "ravaged by carnivores," and having lived 4.4 million years ago in the forests. That's pretty specific information from a handful of bones turned to stone.

You should now understand that arriving at such conclusions is not magic at all. Though data like these bones are from a creature millions of years old, we may still use scientific methodology to interpret them. We know what modern mammalian skeletons look like and what previous fossil finds look like, so we can compare our new fossils to them in order to give them a taxonomic assignment.

As the fossils were being recovered, exhaustive data were recorded about their provenience, allowing us to generate hypotheses about their environment and, using technologies from physics, their date.

We understand how fossils are formed and what their specific condition can tell us about how the creature died and became part of the fossil record. We know, for example, what bones that have been "ravaged by carnivores" look like.

Finally, combining the preceding techniques with new methods from genetics, we have been able to piece together a tentative family tree of the hominids. When a new set of fossils are found, we have a context into which they may be placed and a taxonomic system that can supply them with a name. We will meet this new fossil species and many others in the next chapter, and see exactly how these fact-finding techniques are applied.

KEY TERMS

osteology

sexual dimorphism

omnivore

trephination

sites

petrified

provenience

relative dating
    technique

absolute dating
    techniques

radiometric

carbon dating

half-life

potassium/argon
    (K/Ar) dating

taphonomy

SUGGESTED READINGS

A detailed and beautifully photographed book on the human skeleton, with life-sized pictures, is *Human Osteology* by Tim White and Pieter Folkens. Analysis of the human skeleton in anthropological context is also covered nicely in William Bass's *Human Osteology: A Laboratory and Field Manual of the Human Skeleton*.

Techniques of excavation, interpretation, and dating are covered in more detail in Ken Feder and Michael Park's *Human Antiquity*, Second Edition, and in even more detail in *Archaeology: Discovering Our Past* by Robert Sharer and Wendy Ashmore and in *In the Beginning* by Brian Fagan.

Taphonomy is covered by Pat Shipman in *Life History of a Fossil: An Introduction to Taphonomy and Paleoecology* and by Lewis Binford in *Bones: Ancient Men and Modern Myths*.

The new techniques in genetics applied to human evolution is one of the topics in *Blueprints: Solving the Mystery of Evolution* by Maitland Edey and Donald Johanson. The issue of cladistics and its implications for our view of the relationships among species is in an article by Stephen Jay Gould in his book *The Panda's Thumb* called "The Telltale Wishbone." The title article of that book details the panda example discussed earlier in this chapter.

CHAPTER

10

EVOLUTION OF THE HOMINIDS

... there are no final
words. Human origins
will always be
enigmatic.
—Donald Johanson

Paleoanthropologists observe present day species and the fossilized remnants of other species to try to reconstruct the biological past. Similarly, physicists observe and measure the universe as we see it today in an attempt to understand its origin and evolution. Their methods of observation and measurement are highly technical and are considered essentially accurate. Therefore, we know the distances to the stars, the speed with which those stars are moving away from us, and even their chemical makeup.

When these individual pieces of data are put together, however, the story is often confusing and puzzling. Recently, for example, some new estimates of the age of the universe indicate that the universe is *younger* than some of the stars it contains. This obviously can't be. Either some of the observational or measurement techniques are wrong or less accurate than we thought, or different groups of scientists have interpreted the data differently, or—just maybe—the universe is more complicated than we have imagined.

The study of human evolution is also a complicated venture. We have many thousands of individual pieces of data, each observed, measured, dated, and analyzed according to the very latest technologies. But when we try to put them all together, we come up with disagreements, contradictions, and often several equally plausible interpretations. This chapter and the two that follow will give you the most current ideas about our evolution, including all the missing pieces and possible interpretations— at least the ones based on scientific inquiry. We will address the following questions:

What is the evolutionary history of the primates?

When, and under what circumstances, did the hominids evolve, and why was bipedalism so important?

What do we know about the first member of the genus *Homo*?

THE ORIGIN AND EVOLUTION OF THE PRIMATES

There are a large number of fossil specimens of the primates. Over half of all extinct primate species, however, are based on fragmentary remains, mostly pieces of jaw or sometimes just teeth. Although a particular extinct species may be represented by many specimens, fossils of its contemporaries are lacking, giving us no basis for comparison. There are large gaps in the primate fossil record. Some periods are represented by many fossils, but they all come from one or two sites. Still, we can put together a general, if tentative, picture of the course of primate evolution (Figure 10.1).

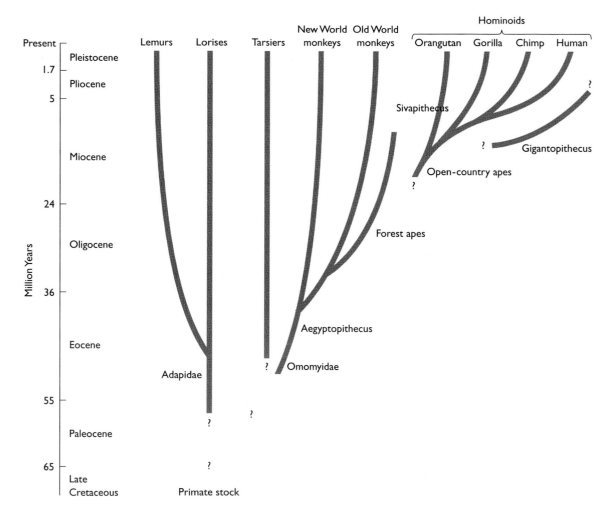

FIGURE 10.1

Simplified evolutionary tree for the primates, with major geological periods and dates. Question marks indicate insufficient data to establish evolutionary relationships.

Very few fossils exist to tell us about the earliest stages of primate evolution. Evidence includes only a few primatelike teeth from Montana dated at 65 million years ago (mya) and some 60 million-year-old bones from Wyoming that have primate features related to climbing behavior. Remember that, at the time, North America and Eurasia were still very close together and possibly still connected in some locations (see Figure 6.6), so the primates probably originated on the large northern landmass called Laurasia, not on what is *now* North America.

In addition, there is a large group of species from North America and Europe from about 60 mya, the plesiadapiforms, that were once thought to represent early primates, but are now generally considered to be ancestral to modern Southeast Asian gliding mammals, the colugos or "flying lemurs" (that are not really lemurs).

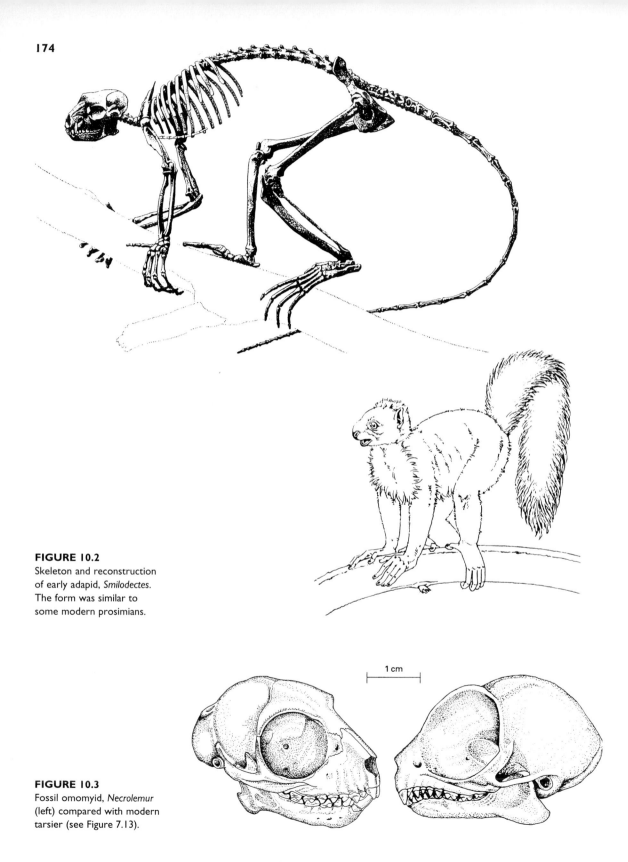

FIGURE 10.2
Skeleton and reconstruction of early adapid, *Smilodectes*. The form was similar to some modern prosimians.

1 cm

FIGURE 10.3
Fossil omomyid, *Necrolemur* (left) compared with modern tarsier (see Figure 7.13).

Undisputed primates appear about 55 mya. They are enough like modern primates that we place them in the suborder Prosimii. These early primates come in two groups, both found in North America and Europe. One group, the Adapidae, are lemurlike and so are thought to be ancestral to modern lemurs and lorises (Figure 10.2). The other group, the Omomyidae, are tarsierlike. They may date back as far as 60 mya, and may be ancestral to both tarsiers and anthropoids (Figure 10.3, and see also Figure 7.13).

By the time the omomyids were expanding into Asia, the eastern and western hemispheres were completely separate. We know that all modern New World primates are monkeys, but there are very few monkey fossils from the New World, mostly because the jungle environment leads to quick and complete scavenging or decay of dead animals. Thus, we don't know for sure how the evolution of the primates proceeded in the western hemisphere. There are two views on the subject. The first is that the New World prosimians moved into Central and South America when they joined North America, and that the prosimians subsequently evolved into modern platyrrhines.

The second view is that early monkeys from the Old World "rafted" over to the Americas, floating on logs and branches, or "island hopping" over a chain of volcanic islands when the two hemispheres were closer together. These early monkeys replaced any prosimians that still inhabited the New World, and they eventually evolved into the modern New World monkey species. Although there are some distinct differences (see Chapter 7), the basic similarity between the Old World and New World monkeys argues for a single origin and thus for the second scenario. In addition, although most of the fossils from the New World are incomplete and therefore hard to evaluate, a new find from Chile of a 20-million-year-old monkey skull is complete enough to show definite similarities to older monkey fossils from Africa.

We are most interested in primate evolution in the Old World. Most of the history of the Old World monkeys comes from a single site, the depression of an ancient lake in the desert southwest of Cairo, Egypt, called the Fayum. Paleontologist Elwyn Simons began extensive investigations there in the early 1960s that continue today. From this valuable site come a number of monkeylike forms dated from 40 to 25 mya. The most important, perhaps, is *Aegyptopithecus*, from about 33 mya (Figure 10.4). This 10-pound primate shows anthropoid traits as well as several features of the teeth, braincase, and skull that resemble later hominoids (apes and hominids). It may be ancestral, then, to all the modern anthropoid primates.

As the early anthropoids expanded, they outcompeted the prosimians and pushed these more primitive primates into marginal areas. Most prosimians now live—though they are endangered—on the island of

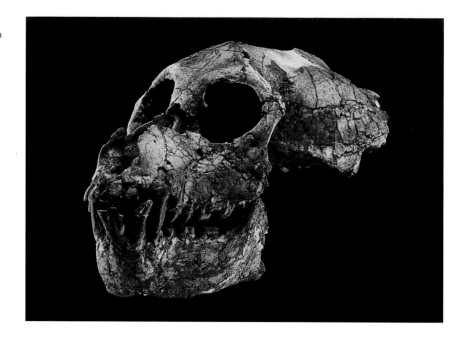

FIGURE 10.4
Skulls of *Aegyptopithecus* from the Fayum in Egypt. The form is considered an early monkeylike form that may be ancestral to later anthropoids.

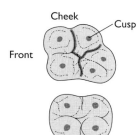

FIGURE 10.5
Y-5 cusp pattern found only in hominoids, and the four-cusp pattern found in all anthropoids. The chewing surface is shown. A look in the mirror will probably give you a first hand glimpse of a Y-5 tooth.

Madagascar, which they probably reached by rafting. No other primates invaded Madagascar until humans got there.

Apes appear in the fossil record about 23 mya. We refer to these earliest apes as "dental apes" because it is their teeth, rather than their overall anatomy, that resembles those of modern apes. Especially important is a feature of the molar teeth found only in hominoids and no other primates. It is called the Y-5 cusp pattern (Figure 10.5).

The earliest of these apes were arboreal forest-dwellers from Africa and Europe. Their small back teeth with thin enamel (the outer coating of the teeth) indicates a diet of soft fruits and leaves. They show a great deal of physical variation and a wide geographic distribution. None, however, resemble modern ape species, and their fossil record ends about 12 mya.

Starting about that time, we find fossils of more ground-living, open-country apes, whose larger back teeth with thicker enamel point to a more mixed vegetable diet that included harder foods, such as nuts. Fossils of these apes have been found in Africa, India, Pakistan, China, Turkey, Hungary, and Greece. The first fossils found were just teeth and partial jaws. One influential interpretation claimed they possessed hominid traits and so in fact represented the first hominids. This idea nicely fit the conjectured 12- to 15-million-year separation of apes and hominids.

The new genetic techniques, discussed in Chapter 9, showed that apes and humans are so closely related that they must have split much more recently, possibly 5 or 6 million years ago. As more complete fossils of the early apes have been recovered, it has become clear that they are indeed apes, not hominids. One form from India, Pakistan, and Turkey, *Sivapithecus* (that lent its name to the entire group), has detailed features of the face, teeth, and arms that it shares with the modern orangutan and so is most likely an ancestor of that species (Figure 10.6).

Another form, however, *Ouranopithecus,* so far only found in Greece and dated at between 9 and 10 mya, has some detailed features that it shares with hominids. Though clearly an ape, about the size of a female gorilla, it is thought by some to be a good candidate for a member of the ape line that eventually led to the hominids (De Bonis and Koufos 1994).

We can't leave this discussion without noting perhaps the most famous, and the biggest sivapithecid—indeed, the biggest primate ever. It is a giant ape whose fossils have been found in China, northern India, and Vietnam called, appropriately, *Gigantopithecus* (see Figure 7.3). So far, only jaws and teeth have been found, but estimates from these indicate this primate may have been 10 to 12 feet tall when standing upright, and may have weighed from 700 to 1200 pounds. Evidence from the teeth indicate that it was, like the gorilla, a vegetarian. Gigantopithecus lived from about 7 mya to perhaps as recently as 300,000 years ago, recently enough to have possibly encountered modern humans. (One can't help but wonder if these

FIGURE 10.6
Skull of *Sivapithecus* (left) compared to modern orangutan. They are essentially identical.

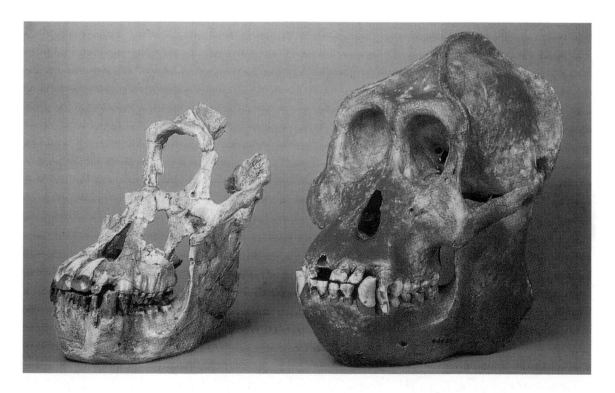

creatures, or at least their bones, may have given rise to legends of the famous "abominable snowman" or yeti from the Himalayas. In any case, however, there is absolutely no indication that they are still around.)

Current evidence indicates that apes evolved in Africa and Europe about 20 mya and diverged subsequently into a number of evolutionary lines all over the Old World. Gradually, these lines decreased, leaving relatively few forms to evolve into the modern hominoids. One line that we are fairly sure of is that from *Sivapithecus* to modern orangutans. Some African form or an African population of that form gave rise to the line leading to modern African apes which, about 5 or 6 mya, split into two more lineages that would become the chimpanzees and the hominids.

THE FIRST HOMINIDS: THE BIPEDAL PRIMATE

The first evidence from the dawn of hominid evolution came in 1925. South African anatomist Raymond Dart was given a fossil found in a limestone quarry at a site called Taung ("place of the lion"). This was the fossil mentioned in Chapter 9 that took seventy-three days to separate from its limestone matrix. When freed, the fossil revealed the face and braincase of a young apelike primate, but with two important differences (Figure 10.7). First, the canine teeth, long and large in apes with gaps to accomodate them when the jaws are shut, were no bigger than those of a human child. Second, the **foramen magnum,** the hole in the base of the skull through which the spinal cord extends from the brain and around the outside of which the top vertebra articulates, was well underneath the skull rather than toward the back as in apes. The foramen magnum's position indicated an upright, bipedal posture rather than a quadrupedal one (see Figures 9.1 and 9.4). Dart hypothesized that the Taung Baby, as it came to be known, was an intermediate between apes and hominids, and he named it *Australopithecus africanus,* the "southern ape of Africa."

Further finds in Africa substantiated Dart's assessment of the anatomy of the Taung Baby and his opinion that it represented a new type of primate. They also made it clear that *Australopithecus,* rather than being an intermediary, was, in fact, a hominid, a bipedal primate. (The rules of scientific nomenclature, or taxonomic names, require that first-used names are kept, even if they later prove to be descriptively inaccurate. Thus, these hominids are still named "southern apes.")

The story of the discoveries and various interpretations of the fossil hominids from this early period is fascinating in itself. Several of the books listed at the end of this chapter tell that story. For our purposes here, we'll

FIGURE 10.7
The "Taung Baby," the first specimen of *Australopithecus*. Note the naturally formed cast of the brain.

look at the story as it stands today. There is still no general agreement on exactly how this part of our evolutionary bush looks, but we do have some fossils with well-established dates (Table 10.1), and locations (Figure 10.8).

　　First, a general orientation. All the fossils discussed here belong to family Hominidae. Within that family are three commonly recognized genera, *Australopithecus*, *Paranthropus*, and *Homo*, each with several species. Only the last genus still exists; the other two are extinct. These groups may be distinguished by the following definitions, on which I'll elaborate.

foramen magnum: The hole in the base of the skull through which the spinal cord emerges and around the outside of which the top vertebra articulates.

TABLE 10.1
List of Early Fossil Hominid Species

	A. afarensis	A. africanus	P. robustus	P. boisei	H. habilis
Dates	4-3 mya	3-2.3 mya	2.2-1.5 mya (?)	2.2-1 mya (excludes "Black Skull")	2.2-1.6 mya
Sites (see Fig. 10.8)	Hadar Omo Laetoli	Taung Sterkfontein Makapansgat Lake Turkana (?) Omo (?)	Kromdraai Swartkrans	Olduvai Lake Turkana Omo	Olduvai Lake Turkana Omo Sterkfontein (?) Swartkrans (?)
Cranial capacity (in ml)	380–500 $\bar{x}=440$	435–530 $\bar{x}=450$	520 (based on one specimen)	500–530 $\bar{x}=515$	500–800 $\bar{x}=680$
Size (average, in lb.)	110	100	105	101	89
Skull	Very prognathous Receding chin Large teeth Pointed canine with gap Arcade between ape and human Hint of crest	Less prognathous than afarensis Jaw more rounded Large back teeth Canines smaller than robustus, larger than afarensis No crest	Heavy jaws Small canines and front teeth Large back teeth Definite crest	Very large jaws Very large back teeth Large crest	Flatter face Less sloping forehead Teeth similar to africanus No crest
Postcranial Skeleton	Long arms Short thumb Curved fingers and toes Bipedal	Similar to A. afarensis	Hands and feet more like modern humans Retention of long arms	Similar to P. robustus	Limited evidence Retention of long arms Maybe retention of primitive features of hand and foot

FAMILY HOMINIDAE: THE BIPEDAL PRIMATES

Genus *Australopithecus:* the small-brained, gracile hominids with a mixed vegetable diet

Genus *Paranthropus:* the small-brained, robust hominids with a grassland vegetable diet

Genus *Homo:* the large-brained, omnivorous hominid

It should be noted that authorities are about evenly divided on the issue of whether *Paranthropus* is a separate genus or is part of *Australopithecus*. I will use the first option here, in part because I think the evidence warrants it and in part because using a different name makes

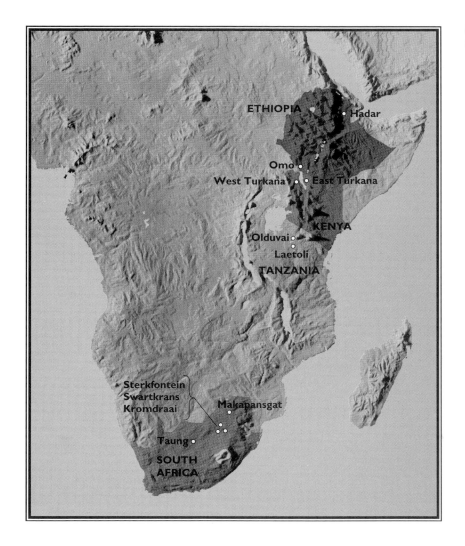

FIGURE 10.8
Map of early fossil hominids.

understanding the evolutionary trends of this complex period of time a little easier.

The earliest hominid fossils discovered so far are among the latest ones found. First discovered in Ethiopia in 1992 and 1993, the finds consisted of seventeen fossil fragments including some arm bones, two skull bases, a child's mandible, and some teeth (Figure 10.9). These fossils were different enough from any found previously to warrant creating a fourth hominid genus, and they were called *Ardipithecus ramidus* (the genus name means "ground ape" and the species name means "root" in the local language). The fossils are dated at 4.4 mya. (These are the fossils, mentioned in Chapter 9, that had been "ravaged by carnivores.") The only existing hominid remains found between 4 and 5 mya were few, fragmen-

FIGURE 10.9

Fossil tooth and a portion of jaw from *Ardipithecus ramidus*.

tary, in some cases poorly dated, and their taxonomy not generally agreed upon.

In 1994, more fossil bones were recovered in Ethiopia, close to the first site. These consisted of ninety fragments representing about 45 percent of a skeleton, including the telltale pelvis, leg, ankle, and foot. These new finds, however, still await analysis.

Ardipithecus ramidus is considered a hominid because the foramen magnum is more forward than in apes, and because of some detailed features of the elbow joint and the teeth. At the same time, it is "the most apelike hominid ancestor known" (White et al. 1994). Among other things, the canine teeth are larger, compared to the other teeth, than in later hominids. It seems, then, that *ramidus* is very close to the time when the hominids and the apes split and so may be, as the name implies, the "root" hominid species.

However, these fossils remain somewhat enigmatic for the moment. Although the evidence from the foramen magnum indicates that they were bipedal, conclusive evidence from the legs, pelvis, and feet must wait until the newest finds can be fully examined and the results published. Furthermore, along with the fossils of *ramidus* were those of many forest mammals as well as fossilized seeds and wood. It appears *Ardipithecus ramidus* lived in the forests and not on the open plains or savannas as did the later hominids. As you'll see, all our interpretations of early hominid evolution have been linked to a savanna environment. I'll address this potential interpretive problem later.

In August, 1995, the newest hominid species was announced. Called *Australopithecus anamensis*, it consists, so far, of twenty-one specimens from the Lake Turkana region of Kenya (*anam* means "lake"), including jaws, teeth, a skull fragment, a tibia, and a humerus. The specimens are dated at 4.2 to 3.9 mya. Although they exhibit apelike features such as large canine teeth, the root of the canine is vertical as in later hominids rather than angled as in apes, and the tooth enamel is thicker than in apes or in *Ardipithecus ramidus*, and more like later hominids. Most notably, the leg bones are clearly those of a biped. These finds are new, but there appears to be some consensus that they may represent the ancestor of all later hominids, with *Ardipithecus ramidus* representing a side-branch of the hominid family.

The next species, by contrast, is well established and its nature is more generally agreed upon. The species is *Australopithecus afarensis*, and its first and most famous specimen is the 3.2-million-year-old skeleton, also from Ethiopia, known as "Lucy" (Figure 10.10), found in 1974 by Donald Johanson and his team. Lucy is remarkable because, as old as she is, nearly 40 percent of her skeleton was preserved, and all parts of her body were well represented except the cranium whose remains are fragmentary. We know, based on modern criteria at least, that she was a female, and that she stood about 3 feet, 8 inches and weighed about 65 pounds. Although there is some disagreement about details, there is no doubt that Lucy and her kind were bipeds and that they can be grouped together as a distinct species.

Other fragmentary specimens, including a portion of a skull dated at 3.9 mya, have been unearthed in Ethiopia and Tanzania and assigned to this species. Based on this evidence, a reconstruction of the head of *A. afarensis* was attempted (once the genus name is noted, a capital letter can be used to abbreviate it), but a complete fossil skull continued to elude us until 1994. In March of that year, Donald Johanson and his team announced the discovery of an *A. afarensis* skull, AL 444-2, again from Ethiopia, that closely resembled both the previously discovered fragments (though it was larger than Lucy) and the reconstruction (Figure 10.11). It was dated at 3 mya.

The evidence, so far—over 300 specimens—indicates that there was a single hominid species, *A. afarensis*, from the period of 4 million to 3 million years ago. The great variation in size of the specimens has led some to suggest that there were several species, but the size differences fit the pattern of sexual dimorphism of apes and other early hominids. We are

FIGURE 10.10
The skeleton of "Lucy," the first specimen of A. afarensis.

FIGURE 10.11
The reconstruction by Drs. Tim White and William Kimbal of *A. afarensis* (top) was confirmed by the discovery of the first complete skull of the species (AL 444-2).

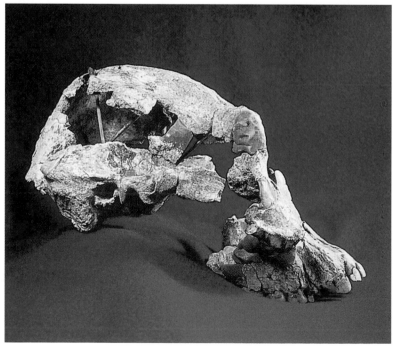

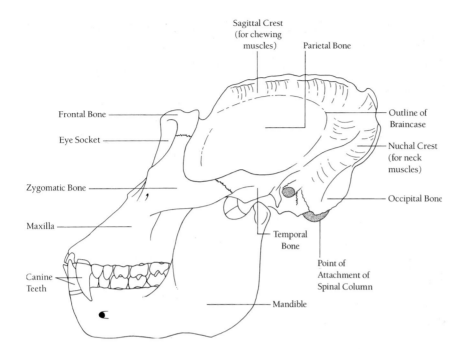

Sagittal Crest
(for chewing
muscles)

Parietal Bone

Frontal Bone

Eye Socket

Zygomatic Bone

Maxilla

Canine
Teeth

Outline of
Braincase

Nuchal Crest
(for neck
muscles)

Occipital Bone

Temporal
Bone

Point of
Attachment of
Spinal Column

Mandible

FIGURE 10.12
Skull of a male gorilla. Compare the sagittal crest with those in Figures 10.17, 10.19, and 10.20.

probably looking at the remains of both males (for example, AL 444-2) and females (for example, Lucy) of one species.

What did Lucy and her kin look like? They might be described as "bipedal apes." Their average brain size was about 440 ml (milliliters—a milliliter is about one-third of a fluid ounce), close to the average for chimpanzees and with the same maximum size of about 500 ml. They have the **prognathism** (projection of the lower face and jaws), the pointy canine teeth, and the gaps in the tooth rows characteristic of apes, though these canine teeth and gaps are not as pronounced as in apes. There is a hint of a sagittal crest, a ridge of bone along the top of the skull for the attachment of major chewing muscles. Gorillas have these crests (Figure 10.12). In modern humans, these muscles are attached on the side of the head. (Put your hand on your head, about 2 inches above your ears, and clench your teeth. You'll feel the muscle.)

The arms of A. *afarensis* are about in the same proportion to the body as in modern humans, but the legs are relatively shorter, making the arms functionally longer. The hands and feet were relatively longer and showed some curvature of the bones. The bones of the shoulders and arms show evidence of heavy musculature. These individuals, though adapted for bipedal walking on the ground, were still good tree climbers.

prognathism: The jutting forward of the lower face and jaw area.

At first, there was some disagreement as to just how bipedal *afarensis* was, especially considering the apelike nature of much of the rest of its anatomy. All the interpretations, after all, were based on fossilized bones; no one, obviously, had ever actually seen one walk. But in 1976, Mary Leakey recovered the next best thing at a site in Tanzania called Laetoli—a set of footprints made in a fresh layer of volcanic ash that quickly hardened and preserved for us a striking picture of an event that took place 3.7 mya. Two hominids, one large, one small, had walked side-by-side through the ash shortly after an eruption. The hominids' footprints show an anatomy and stride no different from ours today (Figure 10.13).

Clearly, then, bipedalism was the first hominid trait to evolve. We know this because it is, essentially, the only hominid trait in an organism that is otherwise an ape. If bipedalism had evolved slowly, one would expect other traits to have changed as well. Therefore, bipedalism may be seen as the adaptation that began our family of primates.

FIGURE 10.13
The Laetoli footprints from Tanzania, and the reconstruction of the probable scene of their origin at the American Museum of Natural History in New York City.

BIPEDALISM

What's the benefit of standing upright? Under what circumstances was it selected for in our earliest ancestors? Not many creatures use this form of locomotion. Kangaroos do, (and many dinosaurs did), but they also use their tails for balance and support. Birds are bipedal, but their feet are able to grasp; they can even sleep standing up. We, on the other hand, attempt to balance our bodies vertically on two small points of contact with the ground. When we walk, we throw ourselves off balance, swing one leg forward, and catch ourselves before we fall flat on our faces. We can't run particularly fast and we aren't very stable on rough or slippery surfaces. Let's work through an explanation of this early adaptation using the scientific approach of posing questions, suggesting answers, and then testing the logic of those answers.

Remembering that natural selection does not create new traits, but selects from variation already present, we can again look to our close relatives for clues about the beginnings of our family's characteristic posture and locomotion. Most primates, in fact, can walk bipedally on occasion. The best occasional bipeds are, not surprisingly, the chimpanzees and bonobos, and one of the most common motivations for these quadrupeds to walk upright is the need to use the arms and hands for something other than locomotion—usually to carry something (see Figure 8.6). Assuming that this behavior was true of our common ancestor, we may then offer a general explanation of our bipedalism by saying that this ability was selected for among some group of apes because it conferred an adaptive and reproductive advantage in their particular environment.

Except for the recently discovered fossils labeled *Ardipithecus ramidus*, nearly all specimens of hominids from Africa between 4 and 1 million years ago have been found in areas that are, or were at the time, savannas—the great open grasslands that characterize much of eastern and southern Africa today (Figure 10.14). The savannas were even more extensive during the period in question, as the great deserts of North Africa are fairly recent. How could bipedalism be related to this environment?

To a primate, the savannas present a very different set of problems than do the forests. Primates are basically vegetable eaters. Although there are plenty of plants on the savannas, there are not as many that can be

FIGURE 10.14
The climatic zones of Africa today, except for the large deserts of the north and south, are nearly the same as when hominid evolution began 5 mya.

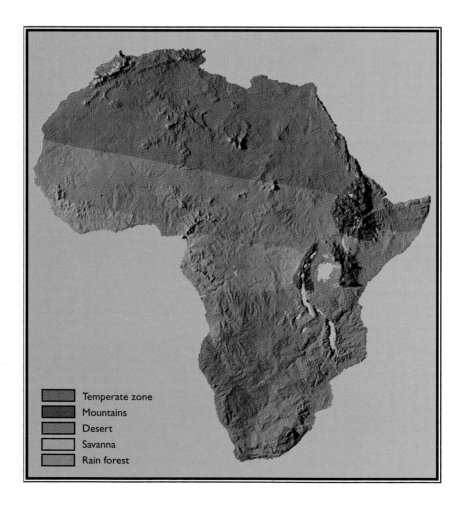

Temperate zone
Mountains
Desert
Savanna
Rain forest

utilized by the digestive systems of most primates. Most primates cannot digest cellulose as can the ungulates, grazing animals such as the African savanna antelopes. Edible plants or plants with edible parts are not as concentrated on the open plains, so primates have to travel over a wider area to find food. The savannas are more affected by seasonal change than are the forests, so there may be greater variation between the wet and dry seasons. Finally, there is more danger involved in acquiring these widely dispersed foods on the savannas. Lions, leopards, cheetahs, wild dogs, hyenas, and other predators are more than happy to make a meal out of a small primate, as we saw in Chapter 9.

There are, of course, sources of meat on the savannas. Chimpanzees are known to hunt, kill, and eat other mammals. They are even known to **scavenge** the kills of leopards found hanging in trees. It is unlikely, though, that our earliest savanna ancestors hunted, at least any large animal, and there is no physical evidence that they did. They may well, however, have scavenged kills, and there is evidence for this, which we will cover later. But, even so, the prey animals must be located, caught, killed, then taken away and kept away from other predators, or scavenged after the predators have finished. All these are dangerous enterprises on the plains.

Bipedalism, however, could have allowed our early ancestors to accomplish some of the above activities in greater safety and with greater efficiency. Freeing the arms and hands from locomotor activities means that food could be transported from open areas to safer locations like a grove of trees or a rock shelter. This would have been especially important if the food was part of an animal carcass, because other meat-eaters would also find it attractive. Children could be carried while mothers walked in search of food. Perhaps sticks and rocks were carried and thrown to scare predators and scavengers away from a kill.

It has also been proposed that bipedalism, by elevating the head, provides better views of potential sources of food and danger. The vertical orientation, according to another view, also helps cool the body by presenting a smaller target to the intense equatorial rays of the sun and by placing more of the body above the ground to catch what cooling air currents there may be. The savannas can be hot, and the heat built up by hours of steady walking in search of food needs to be dissipated. (This also may be the adaptive significance of another trait, at least of modern hominids—our relatively hairless bodies. Having no hair allows sweat to evaporate more quickly and cool the body more efficiently.) Finally, although bipedalism is not an energy-efficient way of running, it is efficient for walking. Thus, long periods of steady walking in search of food require less energy if done upright.

The above theories can be offered as a reasonable explanation why individuals who were better bipeds were better adapted to life on the

scavenge: To eat the flesh of an animal that is already dead.

savannas. Bipeds could search for, find, and transport food to safety, with greater energy efficiency, less heat buildup, and less danger. But does this explain why bipedalism would have made some individuals more reproductively successful? Remember that reproductive success is the measure of natural selection. Simple survival and longevity are only part of it.

Once again, we may get a clue from our close relatives, the chimpanzees and bonobos. Although chimps normally have no need to share resources, they do share meat from a hunt, possibly because it is—in some chimp way—considered a luxury item.

The bonobos, on the other hand, even share foods that are plentiful, which serves to avoid conflict and to establish and maintain peaceful coexistence within the group. Food sharing is, in a sense, a symbol of group peace and unity.

Moreover, as you recall from Chapter 8, the bonobos use sex—in various combinations and with a variety of techniques—to strengthen and maintain group unity and to defuse tension. Sex for them is separate from purely reproductive activity. It has social and psychological meaning as well.

Perhaps our early ancestors survived by the enhancement of adaptations that focus on peaceful cooperation and group unity. They shared resources, the acquisition of which was made easier and safer by selection for the ability to walk habitually upright. In addition, our sexual consciousness—the fact that, for us, sex is part of our psychological and social beings—may also, as in the bonobos, have both motivated and maintained group cohesion. Of course, sexual consciousness also contributed to the reproductive success of the individuals and thus, in the end, to the evolutionary success of the group.

Such a set of adaptations would certainly have been one way of surviving on the savannas. But two more questions come up. First, what about baboons, another successful savanna primate that survives in that environment *without* bipedalism and food sharing, and whose sexual activity is limited to the estrus periods of the females?

Second, what about *Ardipithecus ramidus?* We don't know for certain at this point that they were bipedal. Supposing they were, however, we need to ask *why* they were. Unlike all the subsequent early hominids, they appear to have lived in the forests.

The first question can be answered by remembering that adaptations are relative to a particular species at a specific point in time in response to a specific environment. Just as the primate adaptations are not the *only* successful way of living a life in the trees, neither are the hominid adaptations the only way to survive on the savannas. The different responses of the baboons and the hominids simply show that there is more than one way to adapt to the same environment—even within the same general group of organisms. Even so, despite the important differences, both types of primates still focus on social organization in adapting to the savannas.

The answer to the second question is that perhaps bipedalism was actually first selected for survival in the forests, not on the savannas. Bipedal walking is common among the bonobos, as is food sharing and sexual activity with social as well as reproductive meaning, yet the bonobos live in denser forests than do the chimpanzees. In fact, it has been suggested that the bonobos have undergone less evolutionary change than humans or chimpanzees and thus may most closely resemble the common ancestor of all three of these species (de Waal 1995). Their adaptations, then—focusing on social unity—may simply have been the particular manner in which our ancestral group of apes responded to a forest environment. Later, in response to some change that required life on the savannas, those adaptations turned out to work well in that environment too.

Indeed, there is continuing debate as to just what sort of environmental change would explain the evolution of the hominids. One view (Vrba 1993) suggests that a decrease in global temperature between 5 and 6 mya made Africa drier, shrinking the forests and producing savannas. These changes resulted in the isolation of some populations of our ancestors in that environment and selection for the traits that would become the hallmarks of our family. A further consequence of this drying trend would be an increased reliance on scavenged meat, a resource that would have been available year-round, in contrast to many plants that would have responded more to seasonal changes.

A second scenario (Coppens 1994) claims that the ancestors of the hominids and modern apes were isolated from one another not by a drastic climatic change but by a geological one—the formation of the Rift Valley in East Africa starting about 8 mya (Figure 10.15). Tectonic movements caused a sinking that formed the valley and a rising of a line of mountains on its western rim. This caused a localized climatic change resulting in the area west of the valley remaining moist and forested, and the east of the valley turning drier and becoming savanna. Today, chimpanzees are found only to the west of the valley. Early hominid fossils are found only to the east.

Yet another view says that at least one site in Kenya reveals no evidence of an abrupt change, but rather indicates that East Africa was a "heterogeneous mosaic" of environments from forests to open plains at the time in question (Kingston et al. 1994: 958). The early hominids may not have been so much forced out of the forests but instead may, in some more complex reaction, have taken advantage of new opportunities and less competition (at least from other hominoids) on the savannas. There, their bonobo-like forest adaptations proved equally useful and, over time, were enhanced by natural selection.

FIGURE 10.15
The Rift Valley. The formation of this valley some 6 million years ago produced major climatic changes that may have influenced hominid evolution.

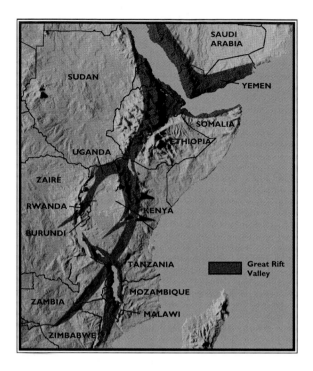

The details concerning where we stand with our knowledge of the early evolution of our hominid family and its characteristic traits are still being debated. We do know, however, that by 4 mya, the hominid line had been established and that it can be associated with a savanna environment. We also know that the major adaptation of the hominids—the trait that distinguishes it from the other primates—is bipedalism. We can hypothesize that accompanying upright locomotion was an emphasis on group unity and survival facilitated by food sharing and perhaps by sexual activity separated from purely reproductive functions and linked to emotional, social, and personal relationships.

Whatever happened, it was successful. At least one hominid species was well ensconced on the plains of East Africa by 3 mya and from there our family began its adaptive radiation.

THE HOMINIDS EVOLVE

Somewhere around 3 mya, *Australopithecus afarensis* branched into at least two lineages, one leading to an extinct form of hominid and the other to the line that would eventually lead to modern humans (Figure 10.16 and refer to Figure 10.8 and Table 10.1).

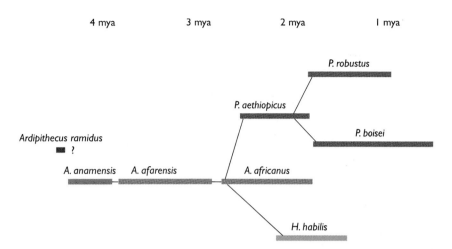

FIGURE 10.16
Family bush of the early hominids. Approximate time ranges of the species discussed in the text, showing hypothesized relationships. The chart will be completed in Figure 12.21.

The initial set of hominid features, as represented by Lucy and her kin, continued for another three-quarters of a million years. Though little changed from A. *afarensis,* the fossils representing this period are still called by their original name, A. *africanus* (Dart's "southern ape of Africa"). The remains of this species have been found mostly in South Africa, but there are some fossils from Kenya and Ethiopia as well. They have the same body size and shape and the same brain size as A. *afarensis.* There are a few differences, however. Their faces are a bit less prognathous and they lack a sagittal crest. Their canine teeth are smaller, there are no gaps in the tooth row, and the tooth row is more rounded, like a human rather than an ape.

The relative sizes and shapes of the teeth of *Australopithecus,* although on the whole larger than those of modern humans, indicate a mostly mixed vegetable diet of fruits and leaves. This is confirmed by taphonomic analysis of microscopic scratches and wear patterns on the teeth. Though there is no direct evidence of meat eating, it is probable that they ate some small creatures.

The essential similarity of A. *afarensis* and A. *africanus* suggests a plausible, and simple, interpretation. We may consider A. *africanus* as a continuation of A. *afarensis,* more widely distributed in East and South Africa, and showing some evolutionary changes. It should be noted that this interpretation is not agreed upon by all investigators and remains hypothetical.

Two distinctly different types of hominid, however, were found from about 2.5 mya. One type retains the chimpanzee-sized brains and small bodies of *Australopithecus,* but has evolved a notable robusticity in the areas of the skull involved with chewing. This is genus *Paranthropus.* As

FIGURE 10.17
The "Black Skull." Note the
large size of the sagittal
crest, the largest of any hominid.

noted before, many authorities place these fossils in genus *Australopithecus*,
but—although I have at the moment no strong opinion one way or the
other—I will use *Paranthropus* both for clarity and because I lean toward
that interpretation of current evidence.

The fossils representing the beginning of this genus are a single skull
from Lake Turkana, Kenya, dubbed the "Black Skull" because of its dark
color that is the result of minerals in the ground (Figure 10.17), and some
fragmentary fossils from Ethiopia. These fossils are grouped into a separate
species, *P. aethiopicus*, and are dated at between 2.8 and 2.2 mya.

The Black Skull is striking for several reasons. First, at only 410 ml,
it has the smallest adult hominid brain ever found. On the other hand, it
has the largest sagittal crest of any hominid, the most prognathous face,
and an extremely large area in the back of the mouth for the molar teeth.
Although no teeth were found, its molars appear to have been four or five
times the size of a modern human's.

The Black Skull represents the beginning of a second major type of
hominid, sometimes referred to as "robust" hominids. Although they were

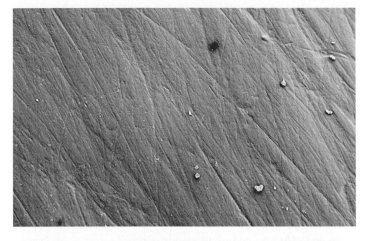

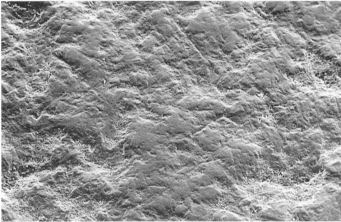

FIGURE 10.18
Scanning electron microscope pictures of the surfaces of the teeth of early hominids. The enamel of the teeth of *Australopithecus africanus* (above) is polished and scratched, while that of *Paranthropus* is pitted and very rough. This is evidence of the hard, tough, gritty foods eaten by the latter.

pretty much the same as *Australopithecus* in brain and body size, the members of genus *Paranthopus* were considerably more robust in all those features involved with chewing. The sagittal crests, broad, dished-out faces, large cheekbones, huge mandibles, and back teeth that are much larger relative to the front teeth—all point to a diet of large amounts of vegetable matter with an emphasis on hard, tough, gritty items like seeds, nuts, hard fruits, and tubers. This is confirmed by microscopic wear pattern analysis (Figure 10.18).

A little over 2 mya, two types of robust hominids appear. We may tentatively consider them two species that branched from the first robust form represented by *P. aethiopicus*. One species, *Paranthropus robustus*, is found in South Africa and dates between 2.2 and 1.5 mya or even later (Figure 10.19). It retains the body size of *Australopithecus*, but there is a slight increase in average brain capacity to about 520 ml. The jaws are heavy, the back teeth are large, and there is a sagittal crest—all indications of a mixed, tough vegetable diet. The crania, though, are obviously not as robust as *P. aethiopicus*.

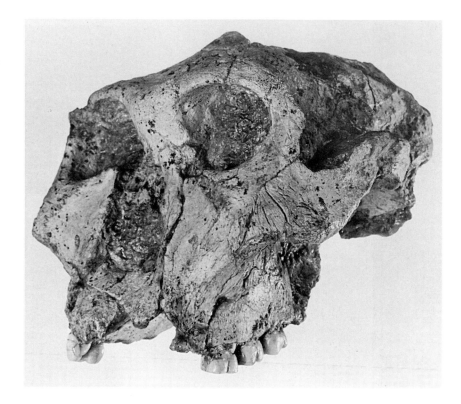

The second robust species continues the extreme ruggedness of
P. aethiopicus, though not quite as pronounced. Found in Tanzania, Kenya,
and Ethiopia and existing from 2.2 to 1 mya, *Paranthropus boisei* shows
features that, along with those of *aethiopicus,* are sometimes referred to as
"hyperrobust" (Figure 10.20). The specimen that defined the species is the
famous "Zinjanthropus," found by Mary and Louis Leakey in 1959.
Dubbed "Nutcracker Man," this specimen showed extremely large jaws
and back teeth and a large sagittal crest. Otherwise *P. boisei* has the body
and brain size of the South African robust hominids.

The second new hominid genus that appeared about 2.5 mya is the
one to which modern humans belong, *Homo.* We will discuss the first
species of our genus in the next section. For now, however, we need to
account for the overall shape of the early hominid family "bush" (see again
Figure 10.16). What might have caused the branching that founded the
new genera of *Paranthropus* and *Homo?* What caused the extinction,
around the same time, of genus *Australopithecus?* Finally, what might have
caused the extinction of the *Paranthropus* species about a million years
ago?

FIGURE 10.20
Paranthropus boisei from Lake Turkana, Kenya, similar to the first specimen of the species, originally called "Zinjanthropus."

We can't answer these questions with certainty, but there is evidence (Vrba 1993) that there were further drying trends, accompanied by a decline of forests and expansion of savannas, at about 2.8 mya and again at about 900,000 years ago. The first change may have selected for both the robust hominids, increasingly adapted to a diet of the tough vegetables found on the open plains, and the genus *Homo*, with its increased brain size and ability to make stone tools. Both these sets of adaptations proved useful on the savannas. The remaining populations of *Australopithecus*, though originally adapted to the savannas, may not have been able to cope with these further changes and may, at the same time, have been out-competed by the new hominid lines.

Although it is intriguing to picture some sort of direct and violent confrontation that caused the extinction of the first hominid genus, and, subsequently, of *Paranthropus*, such a scenario is not necessary. When the niches of several similar species overlap by too great an extent, those species find themselves in ecological competition with one another. As a result, often all but one are pushed out, maybe to the point of extinction. This phenomenon is called **competitive exclusion,** and, with the help of

competitive exclusion: When one species outcompetes others for the resources of a particular area.

the third climatic and vegetational change 900,000 years ago, probably also accounts for the fact that genus *Homo*, from that point on, was the only surviving type of hominid.

THE FIRST MEMBERS OF GENUS *HOMO*

When the Leakeys found Zinjanthropus in 1959, they found some simple stone tools at the same level of Olduvai Gorge (Figure 10.21). At first, they thought Zinjanthropus had made the tools, but they began to feel that "Zinj" was too primitive to have made something so sophisticated.

These tools, called "Oldowan" after Olduvai Gorge, seem very simple to us. Also called pebble tools, they are nothing more than water-smoothed cobbles, up to 3 or 4 inches across, modified by knocking off a few chips from one or two faces to make a sharp edge. But, unlike the termite sticks of the chimpanzees, there is nothing in the raw material—the stone—that immediately suggests the tools that can be made from it or the method of manufacture. Making even a simple Oldowan tool is a far more complex technological feat than stripping the leaves off a branch to make a stick narrow enough to fit down the hole of a termite mound. (I can attest to the difficulty.) A stone tool also requires the maker to be able to imagine within the stone the tool he wants to make and to picture the process needed to make it. This leap of the imagination and increase in technological skill are what make the first evidence of stone tool making so important.

In addition, there is evidence that the earliest stone tool makers also realized that the flakes chipped off the stone could be used as tools for

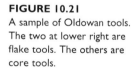

FIGURE 10.21
A sample of Oldowan tools. The two at lower right are flake tools. The others are core tools.

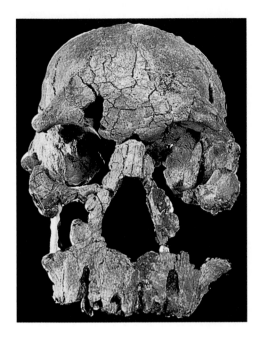

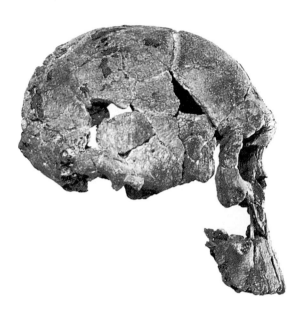

FIGURE 10.22
Homo habilis, the well-known skull 1470 from Lake Turkana, Kenya. Note the flatter face, smoother contours, lack of a sagittal crest, and more rounded braincase as compared to *Australopithecus* and *Paranthropus*.

finer work like scraping small pieces of meat off of a bone. In anthropological terms, they not only made **core tools** but **flake tools** as well.

There is still no accepted evidence that either *Australopithecus* or *Paranthropus* made any tools, although it is likely that, like chimps, they made simple tools from branches or may have used unmodified stone. A recent study has indicated that the hands of *Paranthropus* were more similar to those of modern humans than previously thought, and so they may well have had the manual dexterity necessary to make stone tools (Susman 1988). Furthermore, some simple stone tools have recently been found in Ethiopia that date to 2.6 mya, nearly half a million years earlier than the earliest fossil of *Homo*. Still, no hard evidence links any hominid other than *Homo* with the manufacture of stone implements.

It appeared then, and still does, that Zinjanthropus was not a good candidate for having been the maker of the pebble tools. Then, in 1961, the Leakeys found a second hominid from the same time period. Actually, they had found fragmentary fossils of this form in the same year as Zinjanthropus, but they had not been fully recognized as something different. They named the new form *Homo habilis*, "handy man" (Figure 10.22).

The reasons for including these fossils in genus *Homo* are twofold. First, there is a notable increase in brain size, from the average of about 480 ml for *Australopithecus* and *Paranthropus*, to an average of 680 ml with

core tools: Tools made by taking flakes off a stone nucleus.

flake tools: Tools made from the flakes removed from a core.

a possible maximum of 800 ml in *H. habilis*. Second, the presence of the stone tools indicated that those larger brains were capable of a complexity of thought not seen in the record of the other two hominid genera. Thus, *H. habilis* seems to mark the beginning of a new trend in hominid evolution—toward bigger brains and greater intelligence. Fossils of *habilis* have now been found in Tanzania, Kenya, and Ethiopia, and perhaps from southern Africa, and have been dated at between 2.2 and 1.5 mya. It should be noted that some authorities claim that certain of the fossils labeled *H. habilis* might represent separate species of our genus. One such fossil, in fact, is that pictured in Figure 10.22. We will treat all of these fossils as a single species.

Other than the larger braincase, *H. habilis* still resembles the other two hominids in many respects. The face is a bit less prognathous, but the back teeth are still relatively large, the arms are proportionately long, and the bodies are small. In fact, a partial skeleton of *H. habilis* from Olduvai may be the smallest adult hominid fossil known.

What is it about the stone tools that may have given *Homo habilis* an edge? Paleoanthropologist Richard Leakey, the son of Louis and Mary, suggests that sharp stone tools allowed these hominids to more quickly cut meat and bones off a carcass, making the addition of meat to the diet through scavenging safer and more efficient. There is evidence for this suggestion.

Ten sites have been identified at Olduvai from the *Homo habilis* period that contain Oldowan tools, flakes, and animal bones. Once thought to be some sort of "home base," these areas are now thought to be "stone cache" sites (Potts 1984), where hominids left supplies of stones and to which they took recently scavenged animal remains for quick, safe processing and eating. Analysis indicates that these sites were used repeatedly for short periods, as one would expect of such places.

Archaeologist Lewis Binford (1985) has analyzed the animal bones from these sites and has found that they are mostly the lower leg bones of antelopes. These bones carry little meat and, along with the skull, are about the only parts left after a large carnivore has finished eating. However, such bones are rich in marrow, so a major activity at the sites in question may have been to cut off what little meat remained on these bones and then to break them open for the nutritious marrow inside.

Finally, Pat Shipman has studied the taphonomy of these and other bones with a scanning electron microscope (1984, 1986). She found that marks left by cutting with stone tools were usually on the shafts of the bones as if pieces of meat were cut off, not near the joints as if an entire carcass had been butchered. Also, the hominid tool marks sometimes overlie carnivore tooth marks, showing that the carnivores had gotten there first (Figure 10.23).

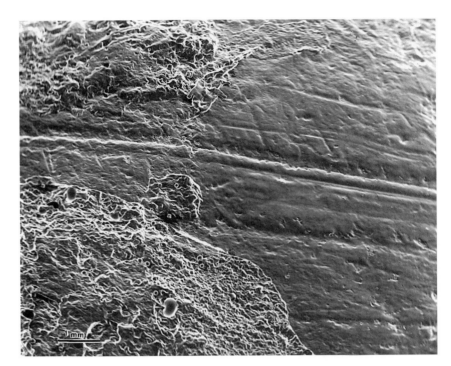

FIGURE 10.23
Scanning electron micro-
scope photograph of cut
marks, these on an elephant
bone from the Spanish site of
Ambrona about 350,000
years ago.

We may envision *Homo habilis* in small cooperative groups, maybe family groups, foraging on the savannas for plant foods and always on the lookout for a carnivore kill, watching for a group of scavengers gathered on the ground or a flock of vultures circling overhead. Their big brains allowed them to better understand their environment and to manipulate it, making imaginative and technologically advanced tools from stone. With these tools they cut apart the carcasses they found and took the pieces back to a safe place, maybe where they had stored more tools. There they cut the remaining meat off the bones and, using large hammer stones, smashed open the bones for marrow. It was no doubt a harsh life, but it was successful. The adaptive themes of large brains and the social organization and tool technology they made possible, set the stage for the rest of hominid evolution.

Homo habilis fossils indicate that this species was around for only about half a million years. Before *H. habilis* disappears from the fossil record, a new hominid species will come on the scene—one that continues and enhances the trends of big brains and tool technology, adaptations that would soon carry it all over the Old World.

◳   ◳   ◳

SUMMARY

The primates are one of the earliest of the existing mammal groups to evolve after the mass extinction of 65 mya. They appear to have evolved first in what are now North America and Europe, but the success of their adaptations allowed them to radiate over the Old World and into the New World.

About 23 mya, the hominoids appear in the form of primitive apes. This successful group has left fossils all over Africa, Europe, and Asia. It is from one of the African apes that our family, Hominidae, branched off some 5 or 6 mya.

The evolution of habitual bipedalism marks the beginnings of our family and was the major distinguishing characteristic of this family for the first half of its time on earth. Bipedalism may have begun as part of one group's adaptation to the forests. We still see this trait—along with food sharing and sexual consciousness—in today's bonobos. However, these adaptations also proved useful on Africa's open plains, and the hominids soon were well established in that environment and radiated into three distinct groups, now classified as separate genera: *Australopithecus*, *Paranthropus*, and *Homo*.

The first two genera, *Australopithecus* and *Paranthropus*, with their chimp-sized brains, remained largely vegetarians and persisted until nearly a million years ago. However, they eventually lost out to a combination of environmental change and competition from the third hominid genus, *Homo*, with its bigger brain and ability to manipulate its environment both mentally and technologically, including the making of stone tools. These adaptations allowed the earliest members of our genus to more safely and efficiently exploit an abundant and reliable new food source, meat scavenged from natural deaths among the great herds of savanna animals. This adaptive base led, as we will see in the next chapter, to the further radiation of this type of hominid, eventually to become one of the earth's dominant species.

KEY TERMS

foramen magnum	scavenge	core tools
prognathism	competitive exclusion	flake tools

SUGGESTED READINGS

The primates and their evolution are covered in John G. Fleagle's *Primate Adaptations and Evolution*. The intriguing story of *Gigantopithecus* is told in *Other Origins: The Search for the Giant Ape in Human History* by Russell Ciochon, John Olsen, and Jamie James. For a more technical account of early primate evolution, see R. D. Martin's article in the May 20, 1993 issue of *Nature* called "Primate Origins: Plugging the Gaps."

The story of the study of the human fossil record and of some of the major recent discoveries is told in *Lucy: The Beginnings of Humankind* by Donald Johanson and Maitland Edey, and in a sequel, *Lucy's Child: The Discovery of a Human Ancestor* by Johanson and James Shreeve. A slightly different perspective on much of the same material is found in Richard Leakey's *Origins Reconsidered: In Search of What Makes Us Human*. The most recent coverage of this topic is Ian Tattersall's *The Fossil Trail: How We Know What We Think We Know About Human Evolution*. All these are authoritative, readable, and quite enjoyable.

A beautifully illustrated treatment of the subject, based on a new exhibit at the American Museum of Natural History in New York is Ian Tattersall's *The Human Odyssey: Four Million Years of Evolution*. Also well-illustrated, though now a bit out-of-date, is the cover article in the November 1985 issue of *National Geographic*, "The Search for Our Ancestors" by Kenneth Weaver.

It would be a good idea to see what a primary report on an important fossil looks like. A good example is the first report on the discovery of *Ardipithecus ramidus* (at the time, lumped into genus *Australopithecus*). It's in the 22 September 1994 issue of the British journal *Nature*.

For a nice summary of the different views on the possible climate change influences on human evolution, see the May 17, 1994, *New York Times* article titled "Fog Thickens on Climate and Origin of Humans" by John Noble Wilford. A nicely illustrated description of the Rift Valley explanation is by Yves Coppens in the May 1994 *Scientific American* titled "East Side Story: The Origin of Humankind."

For a look at the new fossils of *Australopithecus anamensis*, see the September 1995 issue of *National Geographic*.

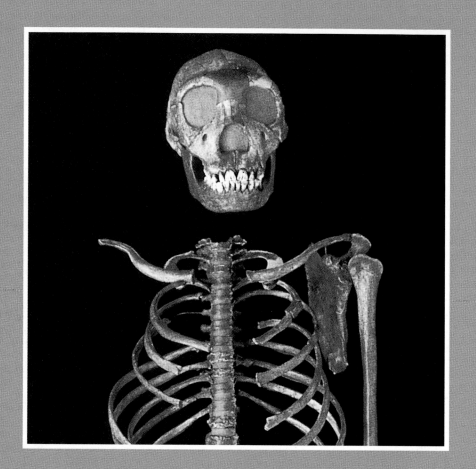

CHAPTER

11

HOMO ERECTUS

Behold, how great a
matter a little fire
kindleth!
—James 3:5

We take the control of energy pretty much for granted. As I'm writing this on my computer, I'm listening to music on my CD player and, when I'm finished, I'll fax some pages to my editor. Then maybe I'll take a break and put the dogs in the car and drive them to their favorite lake. All these devices, and dozens more that are common parts of our everyday lives, require external sources of energy, which we only really appreciate when we're left suddenly without it after a power failure or a mechanical break-down. When those things happen we can feel absolutely helpless.

The hominids we've discussed so far had gained some control of an energy source—their own energy. *Australopithecus* and *Paranthropus* were probably able, as chimpanzees are, to direct their energy to the manufacture of simple tools. *Homo habilis*, with their larger brains, had clearly acquired the control to make tools from stone. But the control of an outside energy source had to wait for the next species of hominid, *Homo erectus*, with even larger brains and with bodies that were perhaps better arranged to manipulate objects. Even then, it apparently took over a million years before that energy source—fire—was first brought under control and put to use. When it was, however, it not only changed the physical lives of the members of that species, but probably their psychological lives as well. The taming of fire may have set the stage for all the technology that was to follow and that would come to so define the lives of modern humans.

> **Who were the people we place in species *Homo erectus* and how were they able to spread all over the Old World?**
>
> **What is the fossil evidence for this species?**
>
> **What evidence do we have that allows us to reconstruct the lives of *Homo erectus*?**

TO NEW LANDS

The next species in our story is *Homo erectus*. The species name means "walking upright." The name was first applied to fossils of this group in the 1890s, when it was thought that they must represent the earliest bipeds. We know now, of course, that the hominids were bipedal for millions of years before *Homo erectus*. From an evolutionary perspective, however, *H. erectus* might be considered the most successful hominid species.

Homo erectus, according to the latest evidence, may have lasted well over one and one-half million years. This species evolved first in Africa, but soon after its emergence, it began to spread and by a half-million years ago was all over the Old World and living in a wide range of climatic

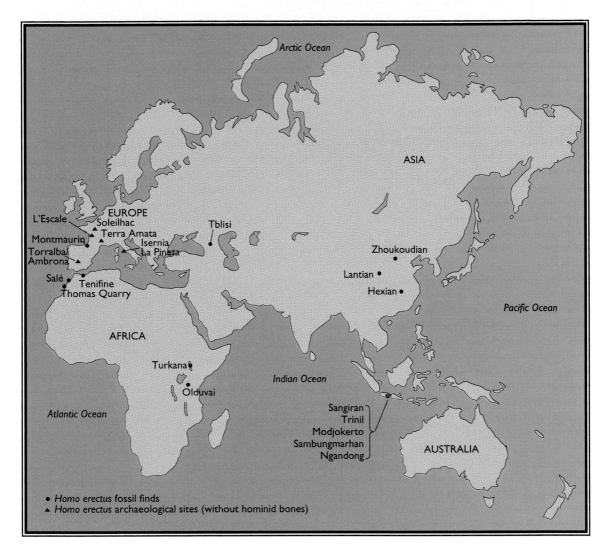

FIGURE 11.1
Map of *Homo erectus* sites.

Map labels:
Arctic Ocean
ASIA
EUROPE
L'Escale
Soleilhac
Terra Amata
Montmaurin
Isernia
La Pineta
Torralba
Ambrona
Tblisi
Zhoukoudian
Lantian
Hexian
Pacific Ocean
Salé
Tenifine
Thomas Quarry
AFRICA
Turkana
Olduvai
Indian Ocean
Atlantic Ocean
Sangiran
Trinil
Modjokerto
Sambungmarhan
Ngandong
AUSTRALIA

• *Homo erectus* fossil finds
▲ *Homo erectus* archaeological sites (without hominid bones)

conditions. Although it is still a matter of debate, some authorities consider *H. erectus* a very stable species, changing little physically or culturally during its tenure on earth.

Although lack of change, or stability may seem negative to us, it is positive in an evolutionary sense. Lack of change indicates that a species is in equilibrium with its environment, that its adaptations are successful under various and changing circumstances, and that it does not alter its environment to the extent that it must continually change in response. Recall that the punctuated equilibrium model of evolution says that most species remain stable during their time on earth.

Let's now look at how *H. erectus* has been understood up until recently. I will then indicate some of the new data and how these data may—if they prove correct—change our view of these important ancestors. Figure 11.1 shows the locations of *H. erectus* sites. Table 11.1 gives the locations, fossils, brain sizes, and dates of those sites.

TABLE 11.1
Overview of Major *Homo Erectus* Fossils

Country	Locality	Fossils	Specimen	Age	Brain Size (ml)
Java	Trinil	Skull cap, femur	"Java Man"	<1 million years	940
	Sangiran	Cranial and post-cranial	S-2	<1.6 million years (?)	800
		fragments from about	S-4	<1.6 million years (?)	900
		40 individuals	S-10	<1.6 million years (?)	850
			S-12	<1.6 million years (?)	1050
			S-17	<1.6 million years (?)	1000
	Ngandong	Cranial and post-cranial	N-1	100,000 years (?)	1170
		fragments from more	N-6	100,000 years (?)	1250
		than a dozen individ-	N-11	100,000 years (?)	1230
		uals	N-12	100,000 years (?)	1090
	Sambungmachan	Cranial fragment	Sambungmachan	100,000 years (?)	1000
	Modjokerto	Fragmentary remains of		1.8 million years (?)	
		a child		(age of Modjokerto)	
China	Zhoukoudian	Cranial and post-cranial	II	<.5 million years	1030
		remains of more than	III	<.5 million years	915
		40 individuals	VI	<.5 million years	850
			X	<.5 million years	1225
			XI	<.5 million years	1015
			XII	<.5 million years	1030
	Hexian (Lontandong)	Partial skull	"Hexian Man"	<.5 million years	1000
	Lantian (Gongwangling)	Cranial fragments,	"Lantian Man"	.7–.8 million years	800
		Mandible			
Tanzania	Olduvai	Cranial and post-cranial	OH 9	1.25 million years	1060
		fragments including	OH 12	.6–.8 million years	700-800
		mandibles and pelvis			
		and long-bone			
		fragments			
Kenya	East Turkana	Cranial and post-cranial	KNM-ER 3733	1.78 million years	850
		fragments including	KNM-ER 3883	1.57 million years	800
		mandibles and pelvis			
		and long-bone frag-			
		ments			
	West Turkana	Nearly complete	KNM-WT	1.6 million years	900
		juvenile individual	15000		
Algeria	Ternifine	Three mandibles and a		.5–.7 million years	
		skull fragment			
Morocco	Thomas Quarries	Mandible and skull		.5 million years	
		fragments			
	Sidi Abderrahman	Two mandible			
		fragments			
	Salé	Skull fragments	Salé	.4 million	880
				Mean	984.79

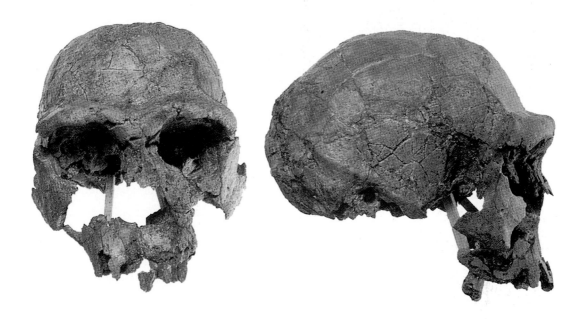

FIGURE 11.2
The *Homo erectus* skull of ER 3733 from Lake Turkana, Kenya, is fairly typical of the species.

As with all the other hominid species so far, *H. erectus* first evolved in Africa. We can imagine that its evolution was a further response to life on the savannas. As we will see, *H. erectus* is characterized by notably larger brains and more complex tools than its predecessor, *Homo habilis*. These adaptations may have given the species an edge in finding food safely and efficiently out on the open plains.

The oldest established fossil of *H. erectus* comes from East Turkana in Kenya and is dated at 1.78 mya (Figure 11.2). It is typical of *H. erectus* crania. It has heavy **brow ridges,** a prognathous face, sloping forehead, elongated profile, **sagittal keel,** sharply angled occipital bone with a pronounced **torus,** and a cranial capacity of 850 ml. (Figure 11.3). The average for the species is about 980 ml., just slightly under the modern human minimum of 1000 ml., but a considerable jump from the 680 ml. average for *Homo habilis*. Note that some fossils of *H. erectus* have cranial capacities within the modern human range. This oldest specimen is thought to be that of a female. A similar skull, also from East Turkana, is dated at 1.57 mya and is more ruggedly constructed. It is thought to be a male.

From the neck up, then, *H. erectus* is quite distinct from the preceding species, *H. habilis*, in overall size, ruggedness, and especially brain size. The skull, however, still retains primitive features that distinguish it from mod-

brow ridges: Heavy, bony ridges over the eyes.

sagittal keel: A sloping of the sides of the skull toward the top, as viewed from the front.

torus: A bony ridge at the back of the skull, where the neck muscles attach.

FIGURE 11.3
Cranial features of *Homo erectus* compared with those of modern *Homo sapiens*.

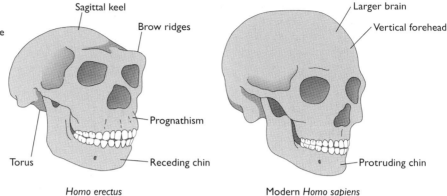

Homo erectus   Modern *Homo sapiens*

ern *Homo sapiens*. From the neck down, on the other hand, *H. erectus* is essentially modern, and apparently was so from its beginnings.

We know this because one of the oldest fossils of *H. erectus* is also the most complete. It is a nearly whole skeleton found at West Turkana in Kenya and dated at 1.6 mya (Figure 11.4). The shape of the pelvis indicates that it was a male. Based on dental eruption and lack of any epiphyseal union, it is estimated that he was twelve years old when he died. This, of course, assumes that aging criteria were the same over a million years ago as they are today. The boy was about 5½ feet tall and, again, if modern growth patterns were the same at that time, he might have been 150 pounds and six-feet tall had he lived to adulthood.

Other fossils of *H. erectus* have also been found in Africa. Except for OH 9 from Olduvai Gorge, dated at 1.25 mya, they are much younger—from 700,000 to 400,000 years old. This means that *Homo erectus* spread throughout the African continent and that populations of the species remained there for over a million years.

However, *H. erectus* did not remain only in Africa. According to traditional interpretations, members of the species had reached Southeast Asia and China by about three-quarters of a million years ago (see Table 11.1). What prompted the people of this species to leave the savannas to which they were apparently so well adapted?

We can't know the answer for sure, but a good guess is that the spread of *H. erectus* was simply an outcome of their adaptive success. Their big brains enabled them to exploit the savannas to a greater extent than had the other hominids to date. They had better and more varied tools (which will be discussed later in this chapter), the ability to learn more about their environment and to reason out the problems that their habitat presented, and, no doubt, a more complex social organization. With these adaptations, *H. erectus* would have rapidly increased in population size.

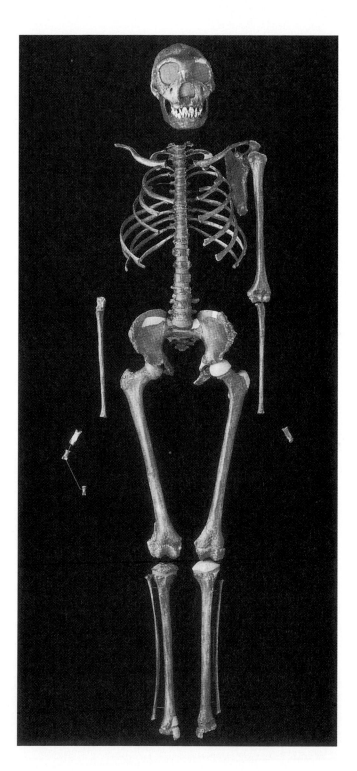

FIGURE 11.4
The "Turkana Boy," *Homo erectus* fossil KNM-15000, one of the most complete early hominid fossils ever found. The pelvis is clearly that of a male and the epiphyses at the top of his left femur are obviously not fused (see Figure 9.3).

Population increase, however, puts pressure on resources and, perhaps, on social harmony as well. So groups of *H. erectus* probably fissioned and moved outside of familiar areas, in search of less competition over food, space, and two other resources that may have been even more important factors—water and shelter.

Water can be scarce on the savannas. There are lakes, rivers, and waterholes, but many of these are seasonal and are dry for months on end. *H. erectus*, with bodies virtually the same as ours, were no longer good tree climbers and so had to seek shelter on the ground, in groves of trees or, if they could locate one, in a cave or rock shelter. Of course, a leopard or other animal may already be in residence in the cave and have to be dealt with.

In search of food, water, shelter, and perhaps, of space and social harmony, *Homo erectus* wandered the Old World. Those wanderings eventually carried them as far from their African homeland as what is now Beijing, China, and the Indonesian island of Java. Not only did these journeys take them to new climates, but the travels also brought them

FIGURE 11.5
Hubbard Glacier (right) meets the sea at Disenchantment Bay in Alaska. Note the person at lower left for scale.

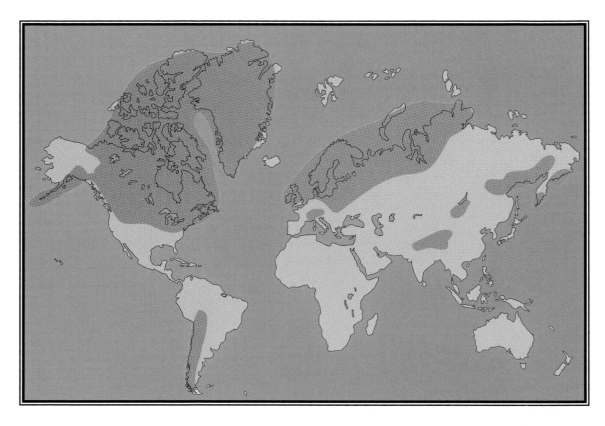

FIGURE 11.6
Maximum extent of the ice
sheets during the Pleistocene.

into contact with the changeable environments of the Ice Ages, known technically as the **Pleistocene.**

Beginning about 1.6 mya and ending 10,000 years ago, the Pleistocene was actually a complex series of extremely cold periods separated by warm phases, some warmer than today. There may have been as many as eighteen cold episodes during the Pleistocene, some lasting tens of thousands of years. We still don't know what caused these cold periods. Suggestions range from increased volcanic activity, with dust and ash blocking the sun's rays, to changes in the earth's orbit.

When the average world temperature drops, ice and snow accumulate over the years at the poles and in higher elevations. The pressure of this accumulation forces the movement of great sheets and rivers of ice. These are called **glaciers** (Figure 11.5). During periods of glacial advances, much of North America, Europe, and Asia were covered by ice, sometimes nearly a mile thick (Figure 11.6). Parts of the world not covered by the glaciers were nonetheless affected by cooler summers and wetter winters. The advance of the glaciers also had the effect of condensing the world's climatic

Pleistocene: The geological time period, from 1.6 million to 10,000 years ago, characterized by a series of glacial advances and retreats.

glaciers: Massive sheets of ice that expand and move.

zones into smaller spaces. Several times during the Pleistocene, where I now live, in the temperate oak and pine forests of Connecticut, was like the arctic **tundra** of Alaska and northern Canada. Moreover, with so much of the earth's water tied up in the great ice sheets, sea levels dropped as much as 400 feet, exposing large areas of land formerly under water. This allowed humans to migrate to areas previously inaccessible, North America, for example.

The world of the Pleistocene was the world through which *Homo erectus* was able to migrate and establish themselves and we find their remains in some of the far corners of the Old World. Naturally, they also inhabited the areas in between, but we have yet to uncover fossils in these areas.

THE FOSSIL EVIDENCE

The first finds ever of *H. erectus* were from Java, made by the Dutch physician Eugene Dubois in 1891. Dubois chose Java to look for hominid fossils largely because he was already stationed there with the military. But the choice was also a logical one for the time, since most people thought that humans had first evolved in Asia, despite Darwin's clear suggestion that Africa was the hominid homeland. The idea that our evolutionary line was originally African apparently did not sit well with many Europeans.

When Dubois found a skull cap and a diseased femur at the site of Trinil (Figure 11.7), he thought they represented the "missing link" between apes and humans, and he dubbed the specimens "Pithecanthropus erectus," the upright ape-man, popularly known as "Java Man." Since Dubois's work, numerous other fossils have been located in Java (refer back to Table 11.1) and are now recognized as fully hominid and assigned to our genus, *Homo*. The fossils found in Java are similar in phenotype to the African and other Asian specimens, although their average brain size is higher than some of the earlier fossils and many are over 1000 ml. Some new dates have recently been suggested for some of these fossils from Java, and we will return to them later.

Perhaps the most famous *Homo erectus* fossils are those from China, particularly from a cave outside of Beijing called Zhoukoudian. Starting in the 1920s, six nearly complete skulls, a couple dozen cranial and mandible fragments, over 100 teeth, and a few postcranial pieces were recovered from the cave. Stone tools and animal bones, including bones of horses, were also recovered. The hominid remains are clearly similar to other specimens of *H. erectus*. Dating indicates that the cave was first occupied about 460,000 years ago and was used until about 230,000 years ago.

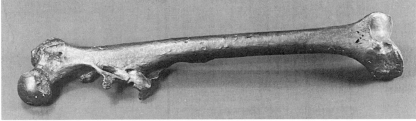

FIGURE 11.7
The skull cap and femur of the "Java Man" *Homo erectus.* The growth toward the top of the femur is the result of a pathological condition.

The fame of the Zhoukoudian fossils, called "Peking Man" (the old spelling of Beijing), lies mostly in the fact that they are missing. When Japan invaded China in 1937, U.S. marines, attempting to get the fossils out of the country, were captured by Japanese troops. The fossils were never seen again. Their whereabouts remain one of the great mysteries in anthropology. Fortunately, extensive measurements had already been made on the bones and accurate casts had been taken (Figure 11.8).

Several other Chinese sites, especially Lantian and Hexian, have also provided important fossils of *H. erectus.* Outside of Africa and Asia, however, there is only one established specimen of this species, a mandible fragment and some teeth from Tblisi in the Republic of Georgia. These remains are dated at between 900,000 and 1.6 million years ago.

All other non-African evidence of *Homo erectus* comes in the form of cultural artifacts dated at times that have been associated with that species from other locations. At the site of Soleihac in France are tools and animal remains dated at 800,000 years. Another French site, Terra Amata on the Riviera, has been proposed as a site where *H. erectus* built shelters and established a village around 400,000 years ago. This interpretation has recently been called into question. Someone lived there, but probably not in a village of huts. In Spain, at two adjacent sites called Torralba and Ambrona, dated at 400,000 years ago, are the remains of some large mammals, including elephants, along with some stone tools that suggest a hunting or, more probably, a scavenging site. Until, however, we locate definite fossils of *H. erectus* from Europe, we can only conclude that the species was there but was not widespread.

tundra: A treeless area with low-growing vegetation and permanently frozen ground.

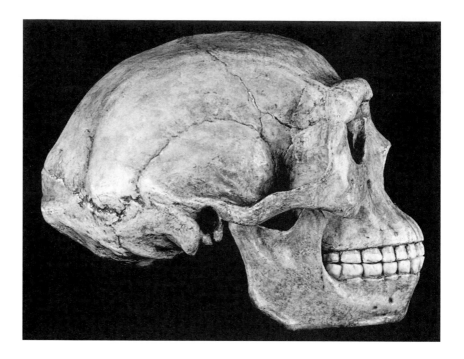

FIGURE 11.8
A cast of one of the "Peking Man" skulls, lost during World War II.

Recently, some new questions have been asked, and some new data offered that suggest changes to the traditional picture of *H. erectus* described above. Some of the early *H. erectus* fossils from the Turkana region of Africa, particularly ER 3733 and the "Turkana boy" (see Figures 11.2 and 11.4), have been described as having features that are more consistent with a possible human ancestor than do the other specimens of *H. erectus*. The long, low skull shape and bone thickness of most fossils assigned to the species seem like specialized traits that evolved later, not like traits that a species between *Australopithecus* and modern humans would have. The two Turkana skulls are thinner and higher in profile. It has thus been suggested by a few paleoanthropologists that they represent yet another species, *Homo ergaster* ("work man," a reference to the associated tools), that is the ancestor of both *Homo erectus* and, later, *Homo sapiens* (Tattersall 1993). Here, I will stay with the majority position and consider these fossils as *Homo erectus*.

The second possible change involves the dates of some of the Java *H. erectus* finds and, thus, the timing of the evolution and spread of the species. Using new, more accurate versions of the potassium/argon dating technique, researchers have redated the Sangiran *erectus* fossils to 1.6 mya and the Modjokerto remains to 1.8 mya—twice as old as previously thought, and at least as old as the oldest African *erectus* fossil. This could mean that *H. erectus* evolved somewhere other than Africa. But all previous hominid fossils come only from Africa, so it's unlikely that *erectus* evolved anywhere but there.

That leaves two plausible explanations. Perhaps *H. erectus* actually first appeared in Africa earlier than any of the fossils we have. Remember how rare fossilization is. The other possibility is simply that the expansion of *H. erectus* began very shortly after they first evolved. Science writer James Shreeve (1994:86) notes that Java is 10,000 to 15,000 miles from Africa, depending upon the route, and that Indonesia was connected to Asia at the time by the lower sea levels of the Pleistocene. If *erectus* walked just a mile a year, it would only have taken about 15,000 years to reach Java. That's still pretty fast, considering that they did not necessarily move one mile every year *in the right direction*. I think that, if the dates are correct, they probably mean that *H. erectus* is older than we now assume based on existing fossils.

Another important new date concerns the Java site of Ngandong. There is evidence that some of the *erectus* fossils there may be as young as 100,000 years. If so, there were populations of *erectus* still around well after modern *Homo sapiens* had evolved, in which case *Homo erectus* would have been a very long-lived species, indeed.

THE BEHAVIOR OF *HOMO ERECTUS*

What do we know about the lives of *H. erectus?* One of their most striking achievements is their elaboration on the stone tool-making technique associated with *Homo habilis.* While *habilis* took a few flakes off a core, just enough to make the "business end," *erectus* flaked the entire stone, controlling the shape of the whole core tool. This tool tradition is called **Acheulian,** after the site in France where it was first identified. The core tool produced by the Acheulian technique is the **hand axe.** It is symmetrical, edged and pointed, and **bifacial** (flaked on both sides) (Figure 11.9). It was the all-purpose tool of its time, used for any number of tasks from butchering to cutting wood. My colleague, archaeologist Ken Feder, calls them "Swiss Army rocks."

In addition to hand axes, *H. erectus* also made tools with straight, sharp edges called cleavers. Moreoever, making a hand axe or cleaver produces a great many flakes—as many as fifty usable ones by one estimate—so *H. erectus* also made flake tools, used either unmodified or further worked to produce a desired shape.

The hand axe appeared in Africa about 1.5 mya and lasted for over a million years. They spread throughout Africa and into Europe. They are, however, rarely found in Asia. Instead, Asian *erectus* populations, like those at Zhoukoudian, made what are called choppers, with flakes removed

Acheulian: A toolmaking tradition associated with *Homo erectus* in Africa and Europe.

hand axe: A bifacial, all-purpose stone tool, shaped somewhat like an axe head.

bifacial: A stone tool that has been worked on both sides.

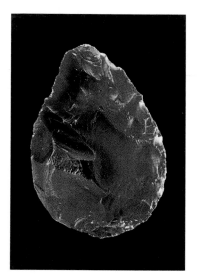

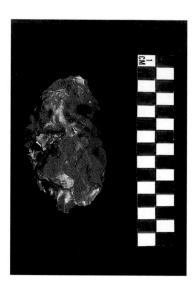

FIGURE 11.9
Bifacially flaked hand axes became one of history's most popular tools and were found in a variety of sizes showing varying degrees of quality.

from one side, and chopping tools with flakes removed from both sides (Figure 11.10).

Perhaps the most striking behavioral advance associated with *Homo erectus* is the purposeful use of fire. There is some evidence, though it is disputed, for the use of fire in Africa at 1.5 mya and France at 750,000 years ago. A rock shelter in Thailand has yielded evidence dated at 700,000 years ago. The earliest well-accepted date (although even it is not without its skeptics) is from the cave at Zhoukoudian sometime after 500,000 years ago (Binford and Chuan 1985; Binford and Stone 1986).

Fire, of course, provides heat, and so it is not surprising that some of the earliest evidence comes from cold northern areas. Fire also provides protection from animals and can be used for cooking, making meat more easily chewed and digestible. But in the long run, perhaps its most important use is as a source of light. Science writer John Pfeiffer (1969) suggests that fire could extend the hours of activity into the night and provide a social focus for group interaction. Sitting around the campfire at night was when people experimented, created, talked, and socialized. Fires have these functions in human cultures today. Moreover, the use of fire may well have given people a psychological advantage, a sense of mastery and control over a force of nature and a source of energy. As Pfeiffer says in the title of his article, "When *Homo erectus* Tamed Fire, He Tamed Himself."

Was *Homo erectus* a hunter of big game, as often portrayed, or did this species continue to scavenge for most of the meat in its diet? At the 400,000 year-old Spanish sites of Torralba and Ambrona, two hills on

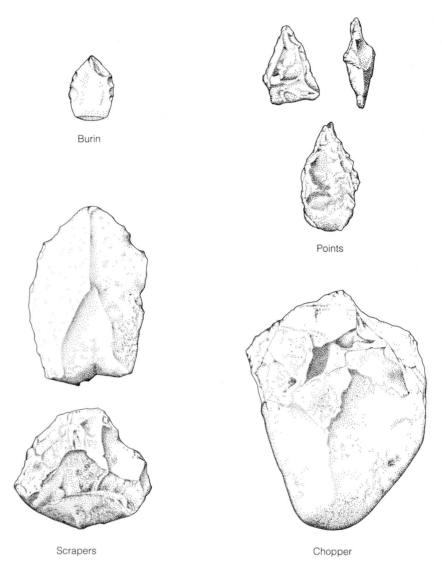

Burin

Points

Scrapers

Chopper

FIGURE 11.10
Flake tools associated with
Homo erectus from the cave
at Zhoukoudian.

either side of a mountain pass, are the remains of fifty elephants and over sixty other game animals (see Figure 9.9). The traditional interpretation is a rather elaborate reconstruction of a cooperative hunt, indeed, of several seasons of cooperative hunting (see, for example, Time-Life Books 1973). In this scenario, the animals were stampeded, possibly with the use of fire, into a bog where they were killed and butchered. The pieces of the carcasses were then taken to a campsite where they were further cut up, cooked, and eaten. There are some tools at the sites.

Is there evidence for this interpretation? A taphonomic analysis of 3000 bones from these sites found that 95 percent of them were so damaged that the search for specific evidence of human activity was impossible (Shipman and Rose 1983). Scratches on many of the bones, once thought to be stone tool cut marks, turn out, on examination under a scanning electron microscope (SEM), to be merely the results of soil abrasion and root growth. Of the fifty-five bones that could be analyzed, the SEM showed only sixteen cut marks on fourteen bones. The marks are not in a pattern that indicates systematic butchering. There is even little evidence of carnivore tooth marks. Furthermore, the tools found at the site are not associated with the elephants, but with the leg bones and mandibles of horses, deer, and wild cattle—the very parts of the animals that would be gathered by scavenging. At best, it appears that *H. erectus* was present at these sites and cut some meat off animal carcasses found there. There is no compelling evidence for cooperative big game hunting.

Two other alleged kill sites, at Olduvai Gorge and Olorgesailie in Africa, similarly give rise to elaborate interpretations of cooperative big game hunting, but they too are based on questionable evidence. The bones found at these sites are more indicative of scavenging than large-scale hunting. (For a good, detailed discussion, see Johanson and Shreeve 1989, Chapter 8.)

Finally, what about the intellectual and linguistic skills of *H. erectus?* As noted, the average cranial capacity of *erectus* was just a little short of the modern human minimum, and individual *erectus* remains fall within the modern human range. It's difficult to be certain what this fact means. After all, the modern range of 1000 to 2000 ml. means that some people have brains twice the size of others, but there is no evidence that within this range brain size has anything to do with intelligence. Was *H. erectus,* then, just a little bit less intelligent than we are?

Anthropologist Ralph Holloway (1980, 1981) has looked at the structure of *H. erectus* brains. He does this using the fact that the inside of the skull reflects, rather specifically, some of the features of the brain it once held. By making **endocasts** of the inside surfaces of fossil crania, Holloway can produce images of the very brains of our ancestors (Figure 11.11). One intriguing find is that the brains of *H. erectus* were asymmetrical—the right and left halves of the brain weren't the same shape. This is found to some extent in apes, but to a greater extent in modern humans, because the halves of our brains perform different functions. Language and the ability to use symbols, for example, are in our left hemispheres, while spatial reasoning (like the hand-eye coordination needed to make complex tools) is in the right hemisphere. This hints that *H. erectus* also had hemisphere specialization, maybe even including the ability to communicate through a symbolic language.

Further evidence of language use by *H. erectus* comes from the use of the anatomy of the cranial base to reconstruct the vocal apparatus. Even though the vocal apparatus is made up of soft parts, those parts are con-

FIGURE 11.11
Natural endocasts from South African australopithecines showing the degree of detail possible. Notice the blood vessels especially in the upper right cast. Such casts may also be made artificially and allow us to compare the brains of our ancestors with those of modern humans.

nected to bone, and so the shape of the bone is correlated with the shape of the larynx, pharynx, and other features (Figure 11.12).

Vocal tract reconstruction on the australopithecines indicates they are basically like apes, with the larynx and pharynx high up in the throat. While this allows them to drink and breathe at the same time (as human infants can do up to eighteen months), it does not allow for the precise manipulation of air that is required of modern human languages. The early hominids could make sounds, but they would have been like those of chimpanzees.

Homo erectus, on the other hand, had vocal tracts more like modern humans, postioned lower in the throat and allowing for a greater range and speed of sound production. Thus, *erectus* could have produced vocal communication that involved many sounds with precise differences among those sounds. Whether or not they did so is another question. But, given their ability to manufacture fairly complex tools, to control fire, and to survive in different and changing environmental circumstances, it stands to reason that *H. erectus* certainly had complex things to talk *about*. It is not out of the question that *erectus* had a communication system that was itself complex.

By any standards, *H. erectus*, although now extinct, was a smashing success. The species began nearly 2 million years ago in Africa and by

endocasts: Natural or human-made casts of the inside of a skull.

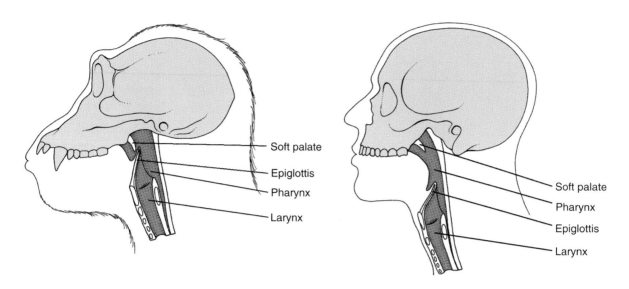

FIGURE 11.12

The vocal tracts of a chimp compared to a modern human's. The high placement of the chimp's makes it impossible for it to produce all of the sounds that are part of modern human languages.

perhaps 1.8 mya had spread as far as Java. By a half-million years ago, they had reached northern China and Europe. They lasted, in Africa and China, until a quarter-million years ago and may have persisted in Java until a mere 100,000 years ago. Their adaptations—now focused on learning, technology, and the cultural transmission of information—allowed them to exploit a number of different environments.

There is some debate over just how much *H. erectus* changed during its tenure on earth. There is a small increase in average cranial capacity over this time (about 180 ml.), as well as some refinement in hand axe-making technique and in flake tool variety. These changes, however, are small and slow, so the overall impression is one of stability—not a bad thing in evolutionary terms.

Somewhere between 400,000 and 200,000 years ago, there was another sudden surge in brain size, to an average matching our own. This may mark the beginning of our species. It also marks the beginning of perhaps the most complex part of our story.

SUMMARY

Somewhere around 2 million years ago, or perhaps earlier, a population of hominids, probably a population of *Homo habilis*, developed larger brains, along with bodies that were essentially modern in size and shape. They quickly became a new species, *Homo erectus*, and their adaptive abilities—

particularly their intellectual and technological achievements—enabled them to expand their population which, in turn, required them to radiate out in search of resources. By a half-million years ago, they had left evidence of their presence throughout Africa and in Asia and Europe. They lasted in Africa and China until 250,000 years ago and may have persisted in Java until as recently as 100,000 years ago.

Evidence of the intellectual potentials of *Homo erectus* comes from their average brain size of 980 ml., some indication of hemisphere specialization of their brains that may point to the use of symbolic language, and, most importantly, the products of those intellectual potentials. These products include their stone tools, their control and use of fire, and their obvious ability to adapt to a variety of different and changeable environments, including those related to the advance and retreat of the Pleistocene glaciers.

Because of its longevity and the fact that it seems to show stability (relative lack of change) during its tenure on earth, one may consider *Homo erectus* a successful species. It was clearly well-adapted to a large variety of environmental conditions and was adapted such that it maintained an equilibrium with its various environments, living off them but not altering them to such a degree that further biological change was necessitated. *Homo erectus* was almost certainly our ancestor. Exactly how we are related is part of the topic of the next chapter.

KEY TERMS

brow ridges	glaciers	hand axe
sagittal keel	tundra	bifacial
torus	Acheulian	endocasts
Pleistocene		

SUGGESTED READINGS

Many of the recommended works from the last chapter also cover the portion of the fossil record addressed here. See, especially, the books by Donald Johanson, Richard Leakey, and Ian Tattersall.

The story of the missing fossils of *Homo erectus* from China are the topic of C. Janus's *The Search for Peking Man*. Some of the new evidence about *Homo erectus* is nicely summarized in an article by James Shreeve, "Erectus Rising," from the September, 1994 issue of *Discover*.

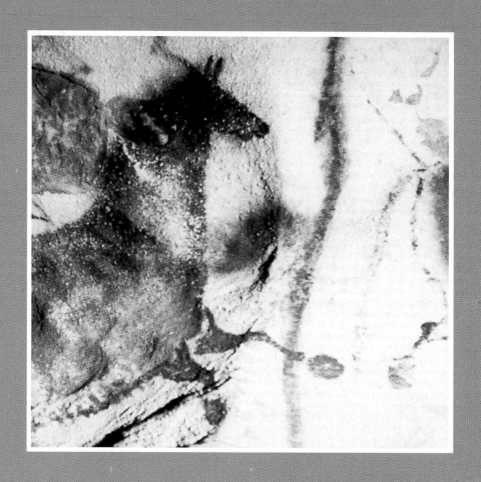

CHAPTER 1

THE EVOLUTION OF THE GENUS HOMO

The great tragedy of
Science—the slaying of
a beautiful hypothesis
by an ugly fact.
—Thomas Henry
Huxley

Williiam of Ockham (c. 1280–1349), an English philosopher, is credited with the principle popularly known as "Ockham's razor." The idea actually goes well back into human antiquity. Ockham said in effect that no more things should be presumed to exist than are absolutely necessary. A student of mine once translated this as "keep it simple."

Ockham's idea, also known as the law of **parsimony,** says that if several possible explanations exist to account for something in science or philosophy, *the simplest is the best*, at least as a starting point. It further means that explanations should be based on facts that are already known, rather than on facts that *may* exist. Of course, as new facts come to light, explanations will change, and we may find that the simplest explanation is not the best one.

Applied to the interpretation of the human fossil record, Ockham's razor means that we should begin by creating a tree of relationships among fossil species that has the fewest evolutionary lines allowed by the data. It also means that we should not create new taxonomic categories unless the data support them. Moreover, we should not suggest evolutionary relationships that include a species or other taxonomic unit that *may* someday be discovered even though no evidence exists for it at present.

Thus, I believe that the family tree (or bush) presented in Figure 10.16 is the most parsimonious given the existing data. Most anthropologists would have little or no objection to this model as a *possible* interpretation of that data.

Being simple, however, is not always that easy. There is no universal agreement on the dates of all the hominid fossils, nor on the interpretation of their phenotypic features or their taxonomic categories. There are at least a half-dozen different trees for the early hominids, each—to whoever proposed it—the most parsimonious. It is my intention that you understand the tree presented in the last chapter and that you should then be able to understand all the others, if you choose to get deeper into the subject. The "correct" answer, if we can ever find it, awaits more data from the fossil record.

If it is hard for us to agree on the fossils that represent the first two and a half million years of the human record, it gets worse when we address the latest two million. The reason is simple: This is the time during which our genus evolved. The data from these fossils matter to us because they will tell us just who we are and where we came from.

Is *Homo sapiens* a million or more years old? Half a million? A mere quarter of a million? Did we evolve from our immediate ancestors on a worldwide scale, or are we the descendants of a small and recent population from Africa? The arguments in favor of each of these ideas, and others, can get rather heated. The data are looked at closely, in every detail. Time and again, someone's "beautiful hypothesis" is slayed by some new "ugly fact." At stake is the very identity of our species. So, we will address all of the following questions:

> **When and where did the first *Homo sapiens* evolve? Why do we refer to them as "archaic"?**
>
> **Who were the Neandertals and what do we really know about their biology and culture?**
>
> **When and where did the first "anatomically modern" *Homo sapiens* evolve? How are they different biologically, geographically, and culturally from previous forms?**
>
> **How are all these forms related?**

THE FIRST *HOMO SAPIENS*

As we get closer to the present in the fossil record, we recover more and better preserved remains. This gives us more data, but it also makes it harder to generalize. We don't know everything about each fossil. We may not have an accurate age estimate for each. Different authorities may interpret the same fossil differently, and they have different ideas as to just how all these data fit together. And, as noted previously, by the time we are considering the evolution of *Homo sapiens*, we are considering the evolution of ourselves, and this matters to us.

Understanding the numerous pieces of data in the *Homo sapiens* fossil record and the ideas about what they all mean can be a complicated matter. In this and the following two sections, we will cover the fossils themselves: what has been found, where and when, and what we have concluded about the physical and behavioral adaptations of these ancestors. For the moment, we will use the traditional names for the fossil groups.

In the last section, we will consider some of the current competing ideas about how all these fossils are evolutionarily related and, thus, what they *should* be called.

Beginning perhaps as early as 400,000 years ago, fossil skulls start showing up that display another significant increase in brain size. All their cranial capacities are within the modern human range and their average is around 1300 ml., a more than 30 percent increase over the average for *Homo erectus*. The brains are also differently proportioned from those of *erectus*, with greater emphasis on the forebrain, reflected in part by steeper foreheads. This is important because the frontal lobes of the human brain are the areas thought to be most involved in control of voluntary movements, speech, attention, social behavior, planning, and reasoning.

parsimony: Use of the simplest explanation in formulating a scientific hypothesis.

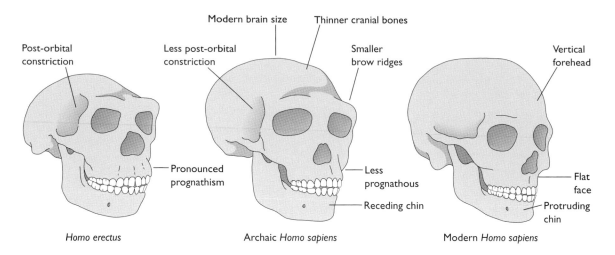

FIGURE 12.1
Cranial features of *Homo erectus*, archaic *Homo sapiens*, and modern *Homo sapiens*.

TABLE 12.1
Archaic *Homo Sapiens* Fossils

Country	Locality	Fossils	Age	Brain Size (in ml)
Germany	Steinheim	Cranium	200,000–240,000	1200
	Bilzinsleben	Cranial fragments	228,000	
	Ehringsdorf	Cranial fragment	225,000	
	Mauer	Mandible	<450,000	
England	Swanscombe	Occipital cranium	225,000	1300
Greece	Petralona	Cranium	160,000–240,000	1230
France	Arago	Cranium and fragmentary remains of seven individuals	250,000	1200
Hungary	Vértesszölös	Occipital fragment	200,000	1250
Zambia	Kabwe (Broken Hill)	Cranium, additional cranial, and post-cranial remains of several individuals	125,000	1280
Tanzania	Ndutu (Olduvai)	Cranium	>200,000	1100
Ethiopia	Bodo	Cranium	200,000–400,000	
South Africa	Elandsfontein	Cranium		
India	Nardama	Cranium		1300
China	Yingkou	Nearly complete skeleton	250,000	
	Dali	Cranium	250,000	1200

In addition, compared to *H. erectus,* the bones of the cranium are thinner, the overall size of the face is reduced, the profile is less prognathous, the brow ridges, though still present, are less pronounced, and the **postorbital constriction,** characteristic of *erectus,* is lessened (Figure 12.1). For all these reasons, but especially because of the brain size and shape, these fossils have been included in our species, *Homo sapiens.*

Still, these *Homo sapiens* are not like any living member of our species. Their foreheads are not as vertical as ours, they are more prognathous, they retain brow ridges, the faces are still proportionately larger, and they have the receding chins of previous hominids. Their postcranial skeletons, though essentially like ours, are often much more rugged and muscular, especially in certain regional populations. To recognize these differences, these early members of the species have been labeled "archaic" *Homo sapiens.* We, then, are "anatomically modern" *Homo sapiens.* Table 12.1

> **postorbital constriction:** A narrowing of the skull behind the eyes, as viewed from above.

Neandertals

Country	Locality	Fossils	Age	Brain Size (in ml)
Germany	Neandertal	Skullcap		1250
France	La Chappelle	Skeleton		1620
	Fontéchevade	Cranial fragments of several individuals	100,000	1500
	La Ferrassie	Eight skeletons	>38,000	1680
	La Chaise	Cranium	126,000	
	Biache St. Vast			
	Saint Césaire	Skeleton	<34,000	
Yugoslavia	Krapina	Cranial and post-cranial fragments of more than forty-five individuals	100,000	1300
Morocco	Jebel Irhoud	Two crania, mandible	100,000	1400
Ethiopia	Omo	Numerous cranial and postcranial fragments	130,0000	1435
Tanzania	Ngaloba		100,000	
South Africa	Florisbad	Cranium	40,000	
Israel	Tabun	Skeleton, mandible, and postcranial fragments	60,000	1270
	Amud	Skeleton	70,000	1740
	Kebara	Postcranial skeleton		
Iraq	Shanidar	Nine partial skeletons	70,000	1600
			Mean	1355.00

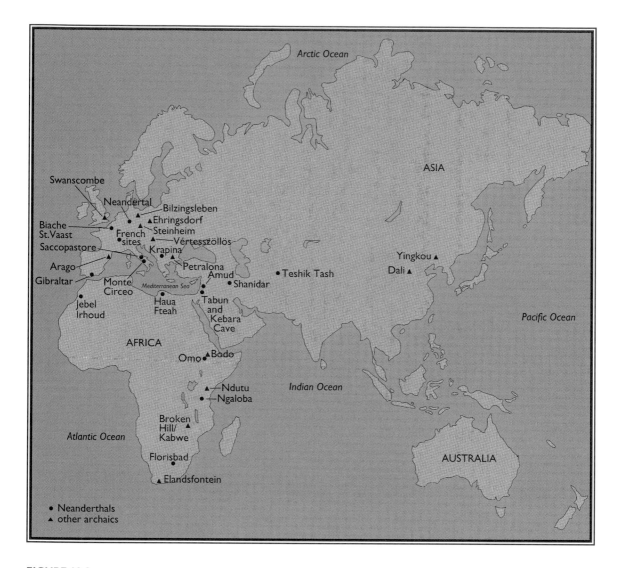

FIGURE 12.2

Map of archaic *Homo sapiens* sites.

gives the major fossil finds of archaic *H. sapiens*, and Figure 12.2 is a map showing the locations of the fossil sites. Figure 12.3 shows several of the more important early archaic fossils.

Despite a fairly large number of well-preserved fossils, we have few remains of the cultural achievements of early archaic *Homo sapiens*. We don't have a lot of evidence of what they were doing with those big brains. But the one thing we do know indicates that their brains gave them another leap in imagination and technical ability.

About 200,000 years ago, while continuing to make Acheulian hand axes and tools from the resultant flakes, archaics invented a new way to

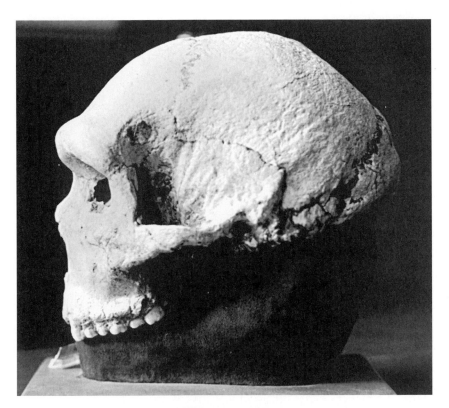

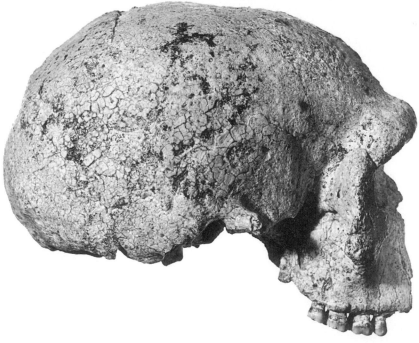

FIGURE 12.3
The skulls from Petralona, Greece, and Steinheim, Germany (below) are good examples of early archaic *Homo sapiens*. Note the more rounded shape and higher forehead as compared to *Homo erectus*. At the same time, note the retention of heavy brow ridges.

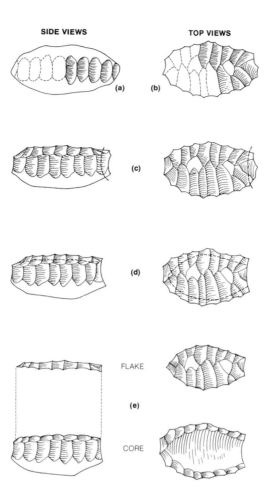

SIDE VIEWS   TOP VIEWS

(a)   (b)

(c)

(d)

FLAKE

(e)

CORE

FIGURE 12.4
(Above) The Levallois technique: (a) produce a margin along the edge of the core, (b) shape the surface of the core, (c, d) prepare the surface to be struck (the "striking platform"), (e) remove the flake, and return to step b for additional flake removal.
(Below) Photograph of a Levallois core and tool (replica).

FIGURE 12.5
The original Neandertal skullcap from Germany. The cranial vault held a very large brain, but the brow ridges indicate an obvious difference from modern humans.

manufacture stone tools. It appears first in Africa and later in Europe. This technique, called the prepared core technique or **Levallois** (after the location in France where it was first discovered), involves the careful preparation of the rough stone so that a number of flakes of a desired shape (up to four or five) may be taken off. These flakes were then used for cutting, scraping, and piercing. Figure 12.4 shows the steps involved in Levallois tool-making and a photograph of a replica of a prepared core tool.

No doubt the archaics had other cultural adaptations to help them deal with the changeable environments of the Pleistocene, as well as the ability to reason out solutions to the problems of survival that they encountered. We certainly know this was true for one famous group of later archaics from Europe, North Africa, and the Middle East.

THE NEANDERTALS

The **Neandertals** (see Figure 12.2 and Table 12.1) were named after one of the first human fossils ever found, a skullcap from the Neander River Valley in Germany recovered in 1856—even before Darwin wrote *Origin of Species* (Figure 12.5). (In German, *thal* means valley. It was always pronounced "tal" and recent spelling changes have dropped the silent "h." Both spellings, however, are still used.)

The Neandertals have had an interesting history in anthropology. At one time they were considered brutish, hunched-over, dim-witted members of a dead-end side branch of human evolution. At other times they

Levallois: Tool technology involving striking uniform flakes from a prepared core.

Neandertals: The populations of "archaic" *Homo sapiens* from Europe and the Middle East.

FIGURE 12.6
An old reconstruction from the Field Museum in Chicago (left) reinforces stereotypes of Neandertal as brutish, hairy, stooped-over distant cousins. In contrast, anthropologist Carleton Coon depicted a Neandertal in modern dress to attempt to show that the differences between us and them were only minor.

have been thought of as an ancient, just slightly different-looking form of modern *Homo sapiens*. We now know that both these theories are exaggerations (Figure 12.6).

The crania of the Neandertals are strikingly different from any modern human (Figure 12.7). They have, essentially, more pronounced versions of the cranial features of archaic *H. sapiens*. Their cranial capacities ranged from about 1300 ml. to 1740 ml., well within the modern range. But their foreheads were still sloped, the backs of their skulls were broad, and the sides were bulging. The brow ridges were still large, but were smaller at the sides than in *Homo erectus*, and they were filled with air spaces (called the frontal sinuses) unlike the solid ridges of *erectus*. The brow ridges of the Neandertals were also rounded over each eye, rather than forming a

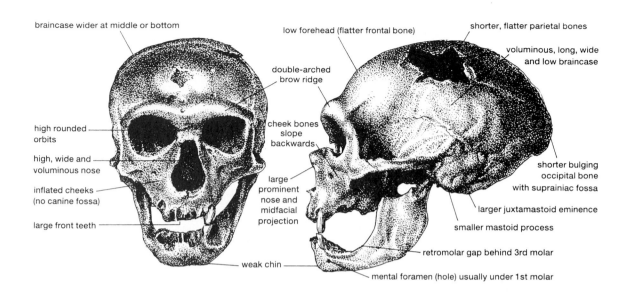

braincase wider at middle or bottom

low forehead (flatter frontal bone)

shorter, flatter parietal bones

voluminous, long, wide and low braincase

double-arched brow ridge

high rounded orbits

cheek bones slope backwards

high, wide and voluminous nose

shorter bulging occipital bone with suprainiac fossa

inflated cheeks (no canine fossa)

large prominent nose and midfacial projection

larger juxtamastoid eminence

large front teeth

smaller mastoid process

retromolar gap behind 3rd molar

weak chin

mental foramen (hole) usually under 1st molar

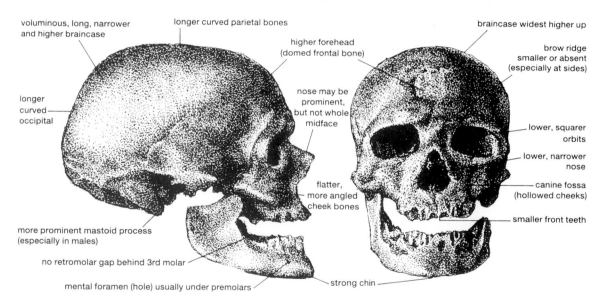

voluminous, long, narrower and higher braincase

longer curved parietal bones

braincase widest higher up

higher forehead (domed frontal bone)

brow ridge smaller or absent (especially at sides)

longer curved occipital

nose may be prominent, but not whole midface

lower, squarer orbits

lower, narrower nose

canine fossa (hollowed cheeks)

flatter, more angled cheek bones

smaller front teeth

more prominent mastoid process (especially in males)

no retromolar gap behind 3rd molar

mental foramen (hole) usually under premolars

strong chin

FIGURE 12.7
Cranial features of Neandertal (above) compared to modern *Homo sapiens*.

straight line, as in earlier archaics. The face was large and prognathous, with a broad nasal opening and widely set eyes. The chin was receding.

From the neck down, there are also striking differences. The bones of the Neandertals, even the finger bones, were more robust and had heavier muscle markings than their modern counterparts (Figure 12.8). The Neandertals were stocky, muscular, powerful people. This is seen even in the

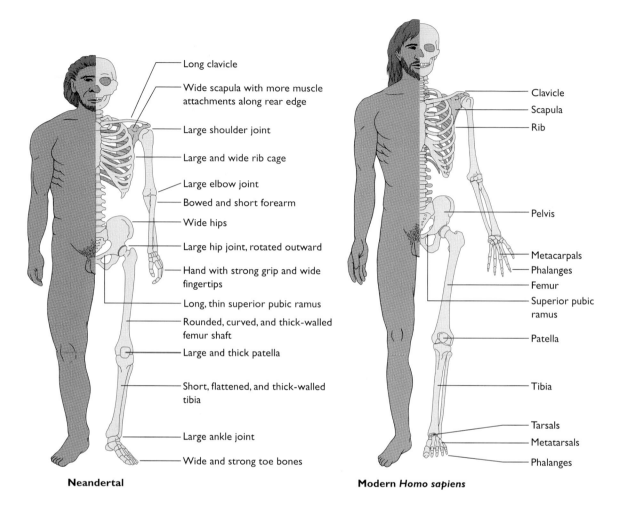

Long clavicle

Wide scapula with more muscle attachments along rear edge

Large shoulder joint

Large and wide rib cage

Large elbow joint

Bowed and short forearm

Wide hips

Large hip joint, rotated outward

Hand with strong grip and wide fingertips

Long, thin superior pubic ramus

Rounded, curved, and thick-walled femur shaft

Large and thick patella

Short, flattened, and thick-walled tibia

Large ankle joint

Wide and strong toe bones

Neandertal

Clavicle
Scapula
Rib

Pelvis

Metacarpals
Phalanges
Femur
Superior pubic ramus

Patella

Tibia

Tarsals
Metatarsals
Phalanges

Modern *Homo sapiens*

FIGURE 12.8
Skeletal features of Neandertal male compared to modern male.

bones of Neandertal children, so it is assumed to be a result of inheritance, not simply of a hard-working lifestyle.

Although very strong and stocky, the Neandertals were relatively short. Estimates put the average for males at 5 feet 6 inches and for females at 5 feet 3 inches. Some of this short stature is a result of relatively short lower legs. The lower arms were short as well. All these physical features hint at adaptations to a strenuous lifestyle and to cold climates. Shorter, heavier bodies with short limbs conserve heat better than narrow, long-limbed bodies. As evidence, the limbs of the Neandertals of the warmer Middle East are relatively longer than of those living in Ice-Age Europe, who faced some of the extreme climates of the glacial advances.

Neandertal fossils date from 130,000 to 34,000 years ago (see Table 12.1). During this time, it has been proposed they were responsible for a number of important cultural achievements. What do we know about their behavior?

Unifacially retouched Mousterian flakes from France.

Among the well-established accomplishments of the Neandertals is an elaboration on the Levallois stone tool-making technique. Called the **Mousterian** tradition, after the site of Le Moustier in France, it involved the careful retouching of flakes taken off cores. These flakes were sharpened and shaped by precise additional flaking, on one side or both, to make specialized tools (Figure 12.9). One authority has identified no less than sixty-three tool types (Bordes 1972).

Several specific uses of Mousterian tools have been inferred from microscopic wear pattern analysis on specimens from the Kebara Cave site in Israel. Archaeologist John Shea (1989) notes wear patterns that indicate animal butchering, woodworking, bone and antler carving, and working of animal hides. There are also wear patterns like those produced by the friction of a wooden shaft against a stone spear point. The Neandertals may have been the first to **haft** a stone point.

Though there is still debate on whether or not the Neandertals were big game hunters or mostly scavengers, there is no doubt that they were dependent on animals that abounded during the Pleistocene—animals

Mousterian: The culture associated with the European Neandertals.

haft: To attach a handle or shaft.

like reindeer, deer, ibex (a wild goat), aurochs (wild ox), horse, woolly rhinoceros, bison, bear, and elk. Bones of these creatures have been found in association with Neandertal remains.

From Neandertal times, we find some of the earliest possible evidence of abstract belief. This evidence comes in the form of burials of the dead. Though many of the "burials" have now been attributed to natural causes, at least thirty-six Neandertal sites show evidence of intentional interment of the dead, and in some graves were remains of offerings—stone tools, animal bones, and, possibly, flowers (Figure 12.10).

FIGURE 12.10
The Neandertal burial from La Ferrassie, France. The body was interred in the flexed position with knees drawn up to the chest, perhaps to mimic sleep.

There is some debate, however, over whether or not these Neandertal burials had ritual significance. Did they represent belief in an afterlife or reverence for the physical remains of the deceased, or were the people simply disposing of a corpse? The inclusion of animal bones in the graves may have been the result of the bones of both Neandertals and other animals being dragged by predators and scavengers into caves at the same time and subsequently buried by natural processes. The pollen found in a Neandertal grave at Shanidar, Iraq, may not have been from flowers placed in the grave, but may have been brought in by the burrowing action of rodents, carried in by water, or blown in by wind at the time of burial. The jury is still out on this issue. But, as far as we know, the Neandertals were the first to bury their dead, for whatever reason they did so.

Along the same lines, evidence has traditionally been cited for a Neandertal cave bear "cult" in Europe. The cave bear, now extinct, was a huge, impressive species, about 12 feet tall when standing upright. Caves in Switzerland and France are supposed to contain a number of cave bear skulls placed in special stone chests or in niches in the cave walls. But these interpretations were apparently wishful thinking on the part of early investigators. Re-analysis of the site descriptions indicate that the placement of the skulls was the result of natural processes—clusters of rocks or cave-ins. Moreover, none of the bear bones show any signs of cut marks. This intriguing story has fallen to scientific investigation.

It has also been suggested that Neandertals were among the first to care for their elderly, ill, and injured. The famous "Old Man" of La Chapelle-aux-Saints in France (Figure 12.11) has been interpreted as aged, lacking most of his teeth, and having a debilitating case of arthritis. That he survived for a time with these infirmities indicates that he was cared for by his group.

Recent reexamination, though, shows that much of his tooth loss was after death and that his arthritis may not have been quite as debilitating as previously thought. Nor was he really old. He died when he was less than forty, probably rather quickly, as did the vast majority of Neandertals. Care of the elderly was probably not something they had to contend with very often.

At the same time, there is a skeleton of a man from Shanidar, Iraq, that shows signs of injuries that may have resulted in blindness and paralysis of one arm. He lived with this condition for some time and, therefore, was obviously cared for by his comrades.

Finally, we have the question of the linguistic abilities of the Neandertals. Some investigators have reconstructed the vocal tract of Neandertals based on the structure of the underside of the cranium and have concluded that they were not capable of making all the vowel sounds of modern humans. On the other hand, a recently found hyoid bone—a horseshoe-shaped bone in the throat—from the Neandertal site of Kebara

FIGURE 12.11
The "Old Man" of La Chappelle, showing rather extreme expressions of Neandertal traits of size and robusticity.

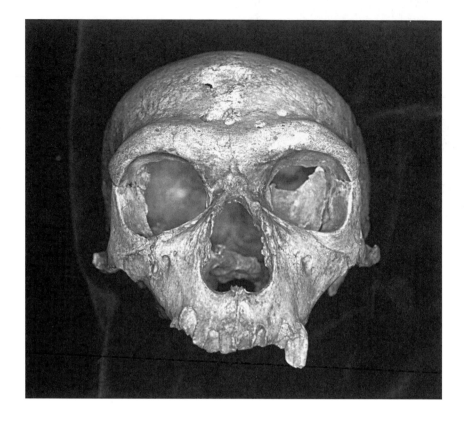

in Israel appears fully modern. This would mean that the vocal tract of the Neandertals *was* like ours and that they *could* make all the sounds of which we are capable. The point, of course, is—as we said for *Homo erectus*—that the Neandertals had sufficiently complex things to talk *about* and just how they did so is less important than the fact that they did talk.

Archaic *Homo sapiens* were successful in adapting to different environments and, in the case of the Neandertals, harsh and demanding climates. They were clearly intelligent. We will no doubt find more fossils of archaics in new areas in the future, but they weren't like any humans alive today. To begin the story of anatomically modern *Homo sapiens*, we once again return to Africa.

MODERN HUMANS

Starting perhaps as early as 120,000 years ago, fossils with modern features appeared, first in Africa and later in the Middle East, Europe, and Asia.

TABLE 12.2
A Sample of Early Modern *Homo Sapiens* Fossils

Country	Locality	Age
South Africa	Klasies River Mouth	120,000 (?)–84,000
	Border Cave	115,000 (?)–62,000
Ethiopia	Omo	130,000
Israel	Qafzeh	120,000–92,000
	Skhul	101,000–81,000
Germany	Stetten	36,000
France	Cro-Magnon	<30,000
	Abri Pataud	>27,000
China	Zhoukoudian	18,000–10,000
Australia		50,000

Later still, humans migrated to Australia, the islands of the Pacific, and to the New World. Table 12.2 lists the earliest finds of modern *H. sapiens* from Africa, the Middle East, Europe, and Asia. Figure 12.12 maps the locations of those finds.

We call these fossils "anatomically modern" because they lack some of the features that were characteristic of earlier hominids and because they possess features common to humans today. Gone is the prognathous profile. The modern human face is essentially flat. There are no heavy brow ridges. The skull is globular rather than elongated and the forehead is more nearly vertical. The face is smaller and narrower, and there is a protruding chin. The postcranial skeleton is less robust. Refer back to Figures 12.7 and 12.8, and look in the mirror. Figure 12.13 shows some of the more important early "anatomically modern" *H. sapiens* fossils.

With modern anatomy came further advances in technology and expressions of modern behavior patterns. Although much of the tool technology of early moderns resembles that of archaics, artifacts from one of the oldest anatomically modern sites do show an important advance. From Klasies River Mouth in South Africa, dated to perhaps 120,000 years ago, come long, bifacially worked spear points made from stone blades. These were flaked from cores by the "punch" technique (Figure 12.14). Here, a pointed punch, usually made of antler, is placed on the core and then struck with a stone hammer. This directs the force of the blow more precisely so that longer, narrower, thinner flakes of predictable shape may be taken off. The same technique shows up much later in Europe.

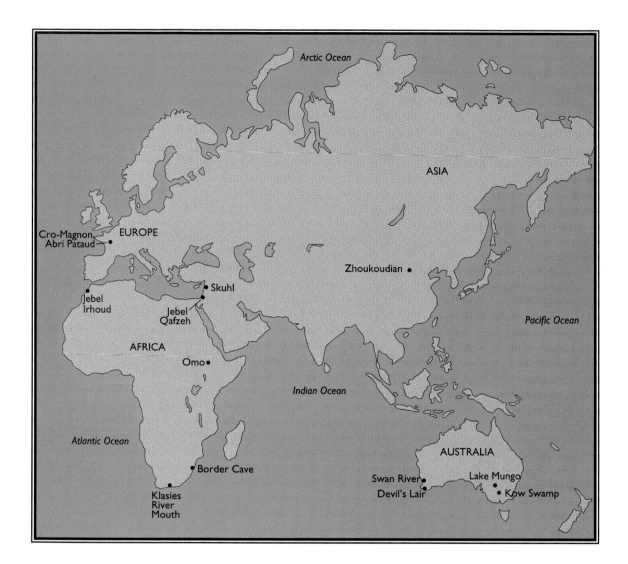

FIGURE 12.12

Map of early modern *Homo sapiens* sites.

The Klasies River site also provides evidence that the people there may have hunted adults of such large animals as cape buffalo and eland, a large antelope. Both these animals can weigh up to a ton. Certainly, they also scavenged and may have hunted only weak or old individuals of these dangerous species. But it appears that there is good evidence of at least limited big game hunting, and so that behavior, it seems, can be associated with the entrance of anatomically modern humans.

By the time the Neandertals have disappeared, about 30,000 years ago, modern *Homo sapiens* have spread all over the Old World, even as far as Australia, and we enter a cultural period called the Upper Paleolithic, known first through findings in Europe. This period is marked by

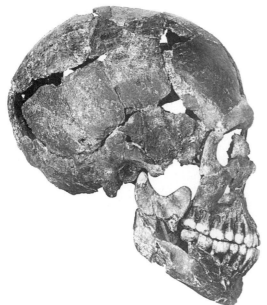

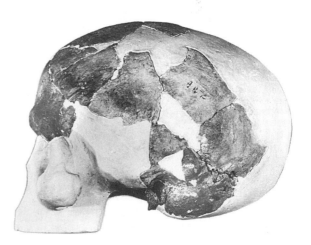

FIGURE 12.13
Examples of early modern *Homo sapiens* (clockwise from upper left): Skuhl, Israel; Jebel Irhoud, Morocco; Border Cave, South Africa; Jebel Qafzeh, Israel. The Border Cave skull is entirely modern and lends support to the Replacement Hypothesis. The Moroccan cranium is intermediate between archaics and moderns and so supports the Multiregional model (see Figure 12.19).

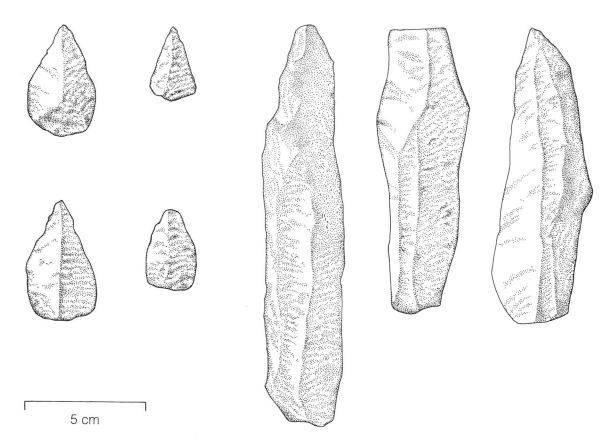

5 cm

FIGURE 12.14
Blade tools from Klasies
River Mouth in South Africa.

FIGURE 12.15
Bifacially flaked Solutrean
spear points, some of the fin-
est stonework ever seen.

FIGURE 12.16
Upper Paleolithic artifacts, including a shaft straightener with carved animals (top), a harpoon carved from antler (left), and an example of the famous Venus figurines (lower right) that may have served as fertility symbols.

several important cultural innovations. Blades struck off cores become so precisely and beautifully made as to be virtual works of art. In fact, some blades are so thin and delicate we think they may have been just that (Figure 12.15).

Tools in the Upper Paleolithic were also made from bone, antler, and ivory. Some are practical, such as harpoons, spear points, and shaft straighteners. Some have symbolic significance. Even some of the utilitarian items are decorated (Figure 12.16). Indeed, art is seen in the Upper Paleolithic in some of its most striking and beautiful forms. Over a hundred cave sites, mostly in France and Spain, have yielded paintings of animals that rival anything produced today (Figure 12.17). There are also carvings in stone, bone, antler, and ivory, among the most famous of which are the so-called Venus figurines, usually thought to be fertility symbols (Figure

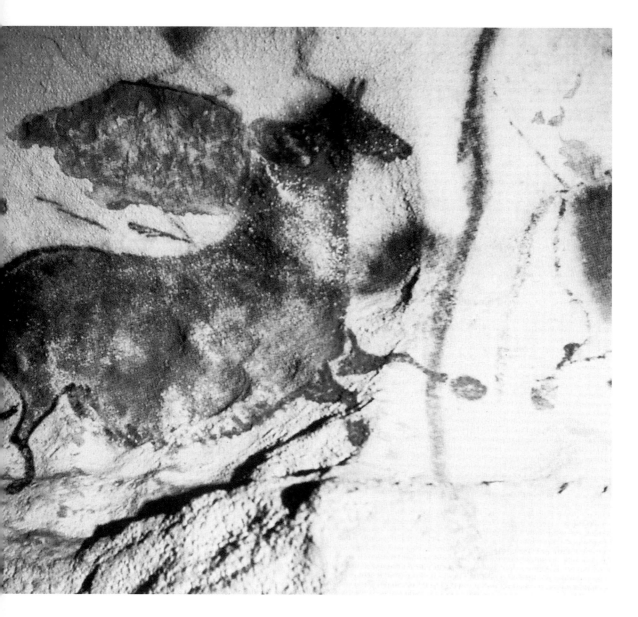

FIGURE 12.17

The galloping horse from the cave of Lascaux in France. Note how the left front leg is separated from the horse's body, adding the three dimensional appearance of the figure. Such art is anything but "primitive."

12.16). There is even an engraved antler from about 32,000 years ago that may have been a calendar based on phases of the moon.

During the Upper Paleolithic, big game hunting becomes a way of life, especially for people living in glacial climates with limited plant resources. People no longer rely on caves or rock shelters for places of habitation, but begin manufacturing shelters. From Mal'ta, for example, an

18,000-year-old site in south-central Russia, come the remains of a hut built on a wood frame supported by woolly mammoth bones and reindeer antlers and covered with animal hides.

Around 15,000 years ago, and possibly earlier, humans moved into North America, coming across a land bridge between Siberia and Alaska, which was exposed when the sea level dropped during glacial periods. They soon moved throughout the continent and on into South America. Modern *Homo sapiens* had populated every land mass on the planet except Antarctica.

How may we summarize what we know about the biological types of humans that have been included in genus *Homo*? Figure 12.18 gives the basic data. Obviously, though, an important question remains, and it is one of the most controversial, important, and, unfortunately, complex questions in anthropology today: How are all types of *Homo* related? How should they be classified taxonomically to reflect those relationships? In other words, just where does our species come from?

THE ORIGIN OF MODERN *HOMO SAPIENS*

Anthropologists have, both figuratively and literally, taken a magnifying glass—actually, a microscope—to all the data we have about our genus in order to determine how all the species of the genus *Homo* are related. This has resulted in a large number of articles that advocate one or another point of view, or that summarize and evaluate the various hypotheses. I will direct you to some of these references at the end of the chapter. The arguments can be detailed and confusing (even to other professional an-

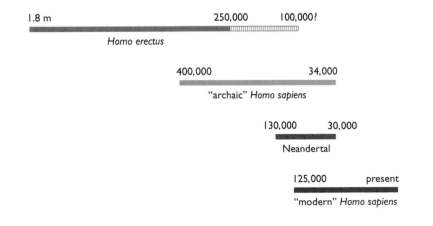

1.8 m   250,000   100,000?

Homo erectus

400,000   34,000

"archaic" *Homo sapiens*

130,000   30,000

Neandertal

125,000   present

"modern" *Homo sapiens*

FIGURE 12.18
Members of genus *Homo* and their dates.

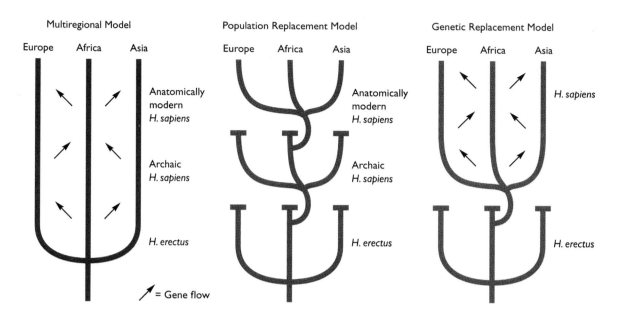

FIGURE 12.19
Models for the origin of
modern *Homo sapiens*.

thropologists), and the attempted summaries sometimes use different diagrams and different names for the hypotheses, and they vary in the detail
included in their explanations.

At the risk of adding yet another explanation, let me try to reduce
the competing hypotheses (or "models") down to their essential elements
in a way that relates them directly to the material we have discussed so
far.

There are two basic hypotheses: 1) the **Multiregional Hypothesis** and
2) the **Replacement Hypothesis.** The second of these, I think, comes in
two importantly different versions that depend on *what* is being replaced—
people or genes (Figure 12.19).

The Multiregional Hypothesis

Advocated most strongly by Milford Wolpoff of the University of Michigan (1989, and in Frayer et al. 1993), this model claims that modern
Homo sapiens evolved in various geographical regions from local archaic
populations or even from populations of *Homo erectus*. Of course, it is
impossible for several isolated lines to evolve in exactly the same direction,
or for isolated populations to remain a single species. So the Multiregional
model includes sufficient gene flow (the arrows in Fig. 12.19) to retain

species integrity and to share evolving traits among the various regional groups.

Thus, new and adaptive phenotypic features that may have begun in one part of the species's range would have spread, through interbreeding, across the entire range, pulling along the widespread populations toward the modern human biological condition.

If this hypothesis is correct, then certain data are expected. Recall from Chapter 1 that this is the part of the scientific method called deduction, where a hypothesis is tested. To support this hypothesis we should find:

1. transitional forms, that is, fossils that show the change from one stage to the next in all geographic regions;

2. that modern traits appear somewhat simultaneously all over the Old World range of the species;

3. that traits characteristic of a particular region today (we might, for the moment, call these "racial" traits) can be traced back to ancient forms in that region;

4. that the modern human species is highly genetically diverse, since it is an old species with distinct populations that have had a lot of time to accumulate genetic differences; and

5. that the genetic variation within each human group is about the same, since they have all been evolving together.

If this hypothesis is supported, then all the different species of genus *Homo* are actually members of the same species and should be called, according to the rules of taxonomic nomenclature, by the earlist name used. Thus, they would all be *Homo sapiens*.

The Population Replacement Hypothesis

This model is often associated with Christopher Stringer of the Natural History Museum in London (Stringer and Andrews 1988, Stringer and Gamble 1993). This replacement idea keeps *Homo erectus* as a separate species and states that modern humans evolved from archaics in only one location, Africa, and then spread, replacing the archaic populations when they came in contact, presumably because the moderns were better adapted.

Deductive predictions for this model would be:

1. that transitional forms would be found only in one place, the area of origin (in this case, Africa);

Multiregional Hypothesis: The idea that anatomically modern humans evolved independently in several different geographical areas.

Replacement Hypothesis: The idea that anatomically modern humans evolved in one area and spread out from there.

2. that modern traits should appear first in one location and then later elsewhere as the modern population spread;

3. that outside the area of origin, modern and archaic populations should overlap in time, since they are separate groups and the process of replacement would not be instantaneous;

4. that humans should have relatively little genetic diversity since the species is young; and

5. that modern populations should differ in amount of genetic variation, the most diversity being found in the region where moderns *first* evolved since this would be the oldest group and thus the one that had the most time to accumulate genetic variation.

If this hypothesis is correct, then anatomically modern *Homo sapiens* are a different species from archaic *Homo sapiens,* and the two groups would require different species names. Modern humans would remain *Homo sapiens. Homo neanderthalensis* has been suggested for the archaics since it was used early on. (Notice that the "h" is back in "neanderthalensis" here. That's because it was spelled that way when first used as a species name. The rules are stringently adhered to.)

The Genetic Replacement Hypothesis

Also called the Assimilation Model (Smith et al. 1989), this is a sort of compromise between the other two. It says that modern human *traits* first evolved, possibly in Africa, among an archaic group, and then spread, through gene flow, into other archaic populations. Because the modern traits were more adaptively advantageous, they were retained by natural selection, eventually replacing the archaic features.

This model would be supported by a combination of the deductive predictions of the other models. It accounts for the fossil, archaeological, and genetic evidence that modern *Homo sapiens* first evolved in one place, Africa. It would also be reasonable that the modern traits would then gradually spread out from Africa, arriving later in other locations.

At the same time, the Genetic Replacement model allows for some degree of similarity between modern populations and ancient populations in a particular region, an idea called "continuity." Not all features would necessarily be replaced by new ones through gene flow. Some old traits might not have been particularly adaptively important one way or the other and so may have simply remained. Other old traits may, in fact, *have* been locally adaptive and so would continue to be selected for.

Under this model, since there is gene flow between populations with archaic traits and populations with modern traits, these populations have to be considered members of a single species. Thus, we may refer to them both simply as *Homo sapiens*.

It should be noted that there are other versions of this model. Some, for example, consider archaics and moderns as a single species, but suggest that the Neandertals are separate (Aiello 1993). Others break archaics into two species, Neandertals and others, both different species from modern *H. sapiens* (Tattersall 1993). Because the evidence is inconclusive, we will consider the Neandertals a regional population of archaic *H. sapiens*, whatever we end up calling that group.

Now, what does the evidence show? The fossil evidence is complex and detailed and it can be interpreted in completely opposite ways by different investigators. Remember, we are really at the stage here of accumulating data and generating and testing hypotheses. There is, however, fairly widespread agreement that the fossils point to the evolution of modern features first in Africa and then later elsewhere (see the dates in Table 12.2). This supports both replacement hypotheses.

Wolpoff has made a strong case for regional continuity, especially in Asia and perhaps Australia, where some modern features are said to resemble features from the Sangiran *Homo erectus* fossils from Java. Some eastern European fossils are also said to show continuity. Continuity supports the Multiregional and the Genetic Replacement Hypotheses.

On the other hand, dates from the Middle East show that two important modern fossils, Skhul and Qafzeh from Israel, actually predated Neandertal archaics in the area and then shared the region with them for perhaps 60,000 years until the archaics disappeared. In western Europe, moderns also appear to replace archaics, though fairly quickly in that region. The Population Replacement model is supported by these data.

The archaeological record is also ambiguous. In Europe and the Middle East, there seems at first to be little difference in the tools of archaics and early moderns. The sophisticated tools and art works of the Upper Paleolithic come much later. There appears to be a slow overall trend of improvement that would support multiregional rather than population replacement evolution. The cultural data, however, do point to an origin in Africa via the discovery of the advanced "punch" technique from Klasies River Mouth at about 100,000 years ago. The Genetic Replacement model could account for all these data.

The strongest potential evidence for replacement comes from genetics. We can compare species, and populations within species, for their genetic differences (see Chapter 9). Genetic differences are the results of the accumulation of mutations over time. The more genetically variable a population is, the older it probably is. The more mutations that distinguish two groups, the longer those two groups have been evolutionarily separate.

Genetic data from living populations show that the human species is quite genetically homogeneous. There is less variation in our populous and widespread species than in the great ape species (Stringer and Andrews 1988). Our species, therefore, does not appear to be very old. Moreover, when regional populations are compared for their individual degrees of genetic variation, the most diverse populations are from sub-Saharan Africa, an indication that populations in this part of the world are the oldest modern humans.

A boost to genetic studies came from the use of **mitochondrial DNA (mtDNA)**. The mitochondria (see Figure 3.1) are the energy factories of the cells. They convert energy stored in nutrients into a form that the cells can use to power their functions. Mitochondria have their own DNA, distinct from the DNA in the cell's nucleus, even to the point of having differences in which amino acid that a particular codon codes for. In fact, the mitochondria are thought to have once been separate organisms that, early in the history of life, formed a **symbiotic** bond with larger cells. Each human cell contains thousands of mitochrondria.

The importance of mtDNA comes from the fact that the actions of the mitrochrondia are mostly run by the DNA in the nucleus of the cell. The mtDNA, while still having some function, can thus accumulate mutations that may not be selectively important. The reproductive success of the organism is not as dependent upon the exact genetic makeup of its mitochondria as it is the genes in its nuclei. Furthermore, the mtDNA mutates five to ten times faster than nuclear DNA, and the mutation rate appears to be fairly constant. So, mtDNA changes rapidly and the changes—the mutations—are less likely to disappear through selection than are mutations of nuclear DNA. And one more benefit: mtDNA is only inherited through females. Sperm cells have mitochondria, but they are not normally involved in fertilization. This simplifies the tracing of mtDNA inheritance. You inherited your mtDNA from your mother. It is not a combination, as is your nuclear DNA, of the genes of both parents.

Thus, if populations are compared for their mtDNA, we would seem to get a more accurate assessment of their genetic differences, and thus their evolutionary differences, than if we used nuclear DNA. Mitochondrial DNA studies support the idea that the human species is genetically homogeneous and, therefore, relatively young. No human groups differ by even as much as 1 percent of their mtDNA. Chimpanzees may be ten times as variable in their mtDNA as we are.

One of the first studies to apply mtDNA to the questions at hand was done by Rebecca Cann, Mark Stoneking, and the late Allan Wilson

(Cann et al. 1987). They analyzed the mtDNA from 147 women from around the world and constructed, through a computer program, a tree of relationships among the groups represented by these women (Figure 12.20). The tree shows that the group from sub-Saharan Africa was relatively distinct from the others and was the most internally diverse. This is what the Population Replacement Hypothesis would predict.

Moreover, these researchers were able to suggest a date for the appearance of modern human mtDNA. Archaeological and biological evidence indicate that New Guinea was settled by a small number of original migrants about 40,000 years ago. Comparing the mtDNA of the New Guinea sample with that from Africa showed the African sample to be five times more diverse. Thus, mtDNA mutations have been accumulating in Africa 5 × 40,000 years, or 200,000 years. This date is in line with the fossil evidence for the first appearance of modern human traits.

The research group concluded that we can all trace our mtDNA back to an African woman who lived about 200,000 years ago. This idea, as a result, came to be called the "Eve" hypothesis. Naturally, at least *one* male had to be involved, and it is most likely that we can all trace our *nuclear* genetic ancestry back to a small population of African men and women. The mtDNA lines, inherited only through females, all died out with the exception of one, just as last names passed through males can die out if families have only girls or no children at all.

Recently, parts of this interpretation have been questioned. Even if mtDNA is mostly adaptively neutral and has a fairly constant mutation rate—and there is evidence against both of these ideas—it turns out that there are far more computer-generated family trees than the one depicted in Figure 12.20, depending upon just how the analysis is done. It has been suggested, in fact, that there may be millions of different trees that can reasonably put all the genetic data into a set of relationships. These trees differ in the relationships among the groups represented, and they do not all agree on which group is ancestral to the others. Many, but not all, still "suggest" an African origin in the fairly recent past (Hedges et al. 1992:739).

Even more recently, a new study has been reported that compared thirty-eight men from different parts of the world for a section of their Y chromosomes. This is the chromosome that carries the code for male characteristics and so is only passed on through men. The study found very little genetic difference among the men in the sample and concluded that this similarity translated to an origin of modern populations at about 270,000 years ago.

Given all these sometimes contradictory data and the diverse interpretations derived from them, what *can* we conclude about the origin of

mitrochondrial DNA (mtDNA): The genetic material found in the cells' mitochondria, rather than in the cell nucleus.

symbiotic: A relationship between members of two different species.

FIGURE 12.20
Computer generated tree showing the lines of descent of the 147 women sampled in the study described. Note the cluster of women of African descent at lower right and the proposed ancestor based on the genetic distinctions between African and non-African women. Recent studies have generated very different trees showing different relationships.

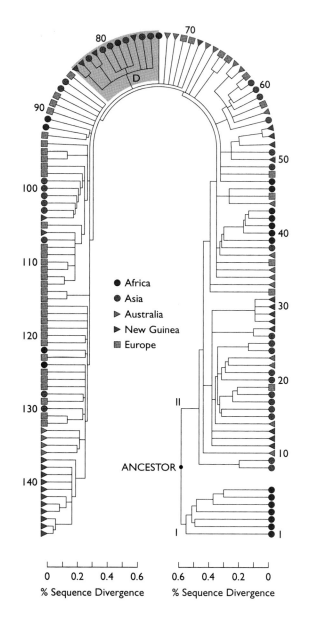

- ● Africa
- ● Asia
- ▶ Australia
- ▶ New Guinea
- ▣ Europe

ANCESTOR ●

% Sequence Divergence

% Sequence Divergence

the species to which we all belong? I think that, for the moment, the most parsimonious interpretation is the Genetic Replacement model. Some data support the Multiregional idea. Others support the Population Replacement idea. The Genetic Replacement model can find support in a combination of these data.

This model requires the appearance of modern traits in first one place and then their spread throughout the species to other regions. Both these requirements seem well supported by the evidence. The model also allows some regional continuity of traits and, at the same time, evidence of the replacement of archaic features by modern ones. This is possible if the traits and their genes, rather than whole populations, are being replaced. The homogeneity of our species as a whole, and the greater genetic variablility within sub-Saharan African groups, argues for a fairly recent evolution of *Homo sapiens* in general and an even more recent evolution of the specific traits associated with anatomically modern humans. These data argue against an antiquity going back to *Homo erectus* times, as the Multiregional model proposes.

Naturally, I may be wrong. Others disagree and base their assessment on a different reading of the very same data. New data will no doubt alter the whole discussion. For now, though, I propose that the simplest way to diagram the whole of human evolution is as shown in Figure 12.21. We have already discussed Australopithecus, Paranthropus, and *Homo habilis*. It seems clear that *Homo erectus* is a separate species and the most logical guess is that it evolved from a population of *H. habilis*. Though there are strong arguments that archaic *Homo sapiens* and anatomically modern *Homo sapiens* are different species, until there is better evidence, the most parsimonious view is to consider them a single species, *Homo sapiens*, that

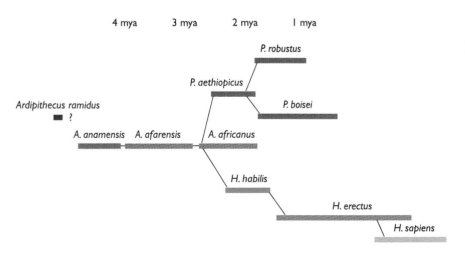

FIGURE 12.21
A proposed family tree of the hominids.

displays evolutionary change through time. The fascinating thing about science, however, is that the discovery of a single fossil or a well argued new interpretation could make me change my mind overnight.

SUMMARY

While *Homo erectus* was spreading successfully through the Old World, even dealing with the harsh and changeable climates of the Pleistocene, another evolutionary event took place. Once again, the earliest evidence for this event comes from Africa, perhaps as early as 400,000 years ago. This is the beginning of our species, *Homo sapiens*, marked by brains of modern human size but with cranial features still retaining some primitive or "archaic" characteristics. A regional group from Europe and the Middle East, the Neandertals, are also noted for their robust, muscular, and strong bodies.

The bigger brains and more precise and varied tools of early *Homo sapiens* apparently gave them an adaptive edge over *Homo erectus*, who they replaced. Like *erectus* before them, they spread through the continents of the Old World. Their success was aided, no doubt, by a more complex social organization. We see hints of this in the behavior of some of the Neandertals.

Finally, *Homo sapiens* of modern appearance showed up around 100,000 years ago. Once again, the earliest evidence comes from Africa. Whether anatomically modern *H. sapiens* are a different species from the archaics is still a matter of debate. What does seem clear, however, is that either modern human groups or modern human traits fairly rapidly spread and the archaic features disappeared. Modern *Homo sapiens* carried with them in their radiation such behaviors as big game hunting, complex tool technology, and the first good evidence of artistic symbols. By 15,000 years ago, our species could be found in nearly every habitable place on earth.

KEY TERMS

parsimony

postorbital
   constriction

Levallois

Neandertals

Mousterian

haft

Multiregional
   Hypothesis

Replacement
   Hypothesis

mitochondrial DNA
   (mtDNA)

symbiotic

SUGGESTED READINGS

A collection from scientific journals of original articles covering the human fossil record is *The Human Evolution Source Book* edited by Russell L. Ciochon and John G. Fleagle. Included are the major works from both sides of the Multiregional vs. Replacement debate. This issue is also addressed by several technical articles in the March, 1993 issue of *American Anthropologist*.

Christopher Stringer and Clive Gamble have written a readable and well-illustrated book focusing on the Neandertals but covering also the whole debate about archaic and modern humans. It's called *In Search of the Neanderthals: Solving the Puzzle of Human Origins*. Be aware, however, that they are major supporters of the Replacement model.

More detail on the evolution and spread of *Homo sapiens* can be found in Brian Fagan's *The Journey from Eden: The Peopling of Our World*.

For the most up-to-date detail on the archaeological record of early humans, see Kenneth Feder's *The Past in Perspective: An Introduction to Human Prehistory*.

THE STUDY
OF LIVING
POPULATIONS

From distant climes,
o'er widespread seas
we come . . .
—George Barrington

Ve have followed the evolutionary history of the hominids up to the modern human species—*Homo sapiens*—in its anatomically modern biological state. But the story of hominid evolution doesn't end just because we finally arrive at modern humans. Evolution continues to take place *within* each species of organism. A species undergoes change through time, even as it remains a single species. Remember the peppered moths from Chapter 4.

About 400,000 years ago (if the Genetic Replacement model I favored in the last chapter is correct), the basic nature of our species was established. Since then, all the processes of evolution have still been in operation, acting on the human "theme" and changing us over time and across geographic space. As we divided ourselves into groups based on ethnic identity, nationality, language, and religion, we provided those evolutionary processes with new and varying breeding populations or demes. Since evolution takes place in populations, the nature of those cultural groups also affected the further evolution of our whole species. So did the behaviors—the cultural systems—of the people in the populations. In other words, our biology and our culture are interrelated and affect one another.

As biological anthropologists, then, we are interested not only in how we evolved, but also in what we evolved into, and how we have continued to evolve in the recent past and are evolving even today. In this chapter, we will look at some of the ways bioanthropologists study living peoples in terms of genetic change, evolution within populations, the nature of our populations, the adaptive differences among populations, and, finally, our individual life histories. We will address these questions:

> **How do we recognize genetic changes in populations, and identify and study their causes?**
>
> **What basic data do we gather in order to describe human populations? What sorts of trends can we see in populations within our species?**
>
> **In what ways have humans adapted to the varying environments in which we live?**
>
> **What are the results of our species' evolution on the life histories—the "personal evolution"—of the human individual?**

GENES IN POPULATIONS

In Chapter 4, I introduced the concept of allele frequency. The technical definition of evolution is *change in allele frequency through time*. A process of evolution is any process that alters the frequencies with which alleles of genes appear in a population. Can we use allele frequency more specifically by applying actual allele frequency numbers in our study of human evolution?

The example of evolution we focused on in Chapter 4 was sickle-cell anemia. Let's expand that example. Suppose we can test a population for the sickle-cell genotypes at two points in time. Our first test gives the following numbers (based on an example in Relethford 1994):

AA (normal hemoglobin)	50 people
AS (sickle cell trait)	100 people
SS (sickle cell anemia)	50 people
Total =	200 people

(A and S are *alleles of a single gene*, the *Hb* gene for hemoglobin).

Now, when we return to test the population at some point in the future, we find the following numbers:

AA	35 people
AS	100 people
SS	10 people
Total =	145 people

Obviously, some change has taken place in the frequency (%) of the genotypes and in the total population size. Have the allele frequencies changed as well? In other words, has evolution taken place? To calculate the allele frequencies you add up the total number of each allele and divide by the number of alleles in the population, which would be twice the number of people since each person has two alleles at each locus. Thus, for the first test, the number of A alleles is:

$(50 \times 2) + 100 = 200,$
> since each AA person has two A alleles and each AS heterozygote has one.

The frequency of A alleles in the population is thus:

200 / 400 (since each of the 200 people has two alleles) = .50 (50%).

As you can see, the frequency of the S allele is also .50 (50%), using the same reasoning.

Now, calculate the allele frequencies in the second test, after the obvious change in genotype frequency and number of people has taken place. Using the same procedure:

freq. of A = $(35 \times 2) + 100 / 145 \times 2 = .59$ (59%)

freq. of S = $(10 \times 2) + 100 / 145 \times 2 = .41$ (41%)

(The results are rounded for simplicity.)

The frequency of the A allele has increased and that of the S allele has decreased. Evolution, by technical definition, is taking place.

The reason for this change is obvious because we understand sickle cell anemia. Those individuals with the SS genotype have a fatal disease, so only 20 percent (10 out of 50) of them survived between the two tests. Those with the AA genotype don't have sickle cell but may succumb to malaria. Here there was a 70 percent survival rate (35 out of 50) for the AA genotype. All of the heterozygotes survived since they had nonfatal symptoms of sickle cell and also possessed an immunity to malaria.

If, however, we did not already understand the situation, the calculation of these figures would show that *something* was happening and would indicate in which direction the change was taking place. It would be clear in this case that one of the two alleles is increasing in frequency because both homozygote genotypes are decreasing in number to different degrees. As a result of *this*, the heterozygote genotype is becoming more common. We would then have to try to figure out why.

Suppose, however, we can only examine the population once, as is often the case. How could we possibly see evidence for change over time? There is a formula, known as the **Hardy-Weinberg equilibrium,** that provides us with a tool. The formula is an example of a *null hypothesis*, a condition where nothing occurs. If you can state the conditions of *no* change, you can then compare them to a real situation and see whether or not change is taking place and, if it is, state the nature and direction of that change. The Hardy-Weinberg formula assumes that the genotype frequencies in a population will remain the same under certain conditions. These conditions are that there is random mating (that is, everyone stands an equal chance of mating with anyone else of the opposite sex), and that there is no gene flow, no drift, no mutation, and no natural selection for any allele over another. In other words, none of the processes of evolution is taking place.

For example, using our two alleles for hemoglobin, A and S, we designate the frequency of A as p, and the frequency of S as q. (These letters, although they may make it a bit confusing at first, are used because of a mathematical convention.) So, for our population example:

$p = .59$ and $q = .41$

Now, we calculate the probability (the chance) of creating each of the possible genotypes based solely on the percentages of the two alleles. The probability is the product (the result of mutiplication) of the frequencies of the alleles. How often a genotype is produced depends on how often the alleles of that genotype appear in the first place. Thus, the following applies:

GENOTYPE	PRODUCT OF FREQUENCIES
AA	$p \times p = p^2$
AS	$p \times q = pq$
SA	$q \times p = qp$
SS	$q \times q = q^2$

$$AS \text{ and } SA = 2pq$$

The heterozygote is counted twice because there are two ways of producing it, depending upon which allele comes from which parent. Because all genotypes are now accounted for,

$p^2 + 2pq + q^2 = 1$ (or 100%). This is the Hardy-Weinberg formula.

We can now return to our population and see what its genotype frequencies would be if they were based only on the frequencies of the alleles, that is, if there were no evolutionary processes taking place and the percentages of the genotypes were strictly a matter of chance. For the AA genotype, for example, we calculate p^2 as .59 $\times$ .59, which equals .3481. Now multiply this by the population size, 145, to show how many people would be *expected* to have this genotype if no evolution were taking place: 145 $\times$ .3481 = 50. Looking back, however, we *observed* that only 35 people possessed this genotype.

Do the rest of the calculations and summarize the results as in the table below.

GENOTYPE	EXPECTED FREQUENCY	EXPECTED NUMBER	OBSERVED NUMBER
AA	$p^2 = .59^2 = .3481$	.3481 $\times$ 145 = 50	35
AS	$2pq = .59 \times .41 \times 2$ $= .4838$	.4838 $\times$ 145 = 70	100
SS	$q^2 = .41^2 = .1618$	.1618 $\times$ 145 = 24	10

(The numbers in the expected and observed columns should add up to the same figure but don't exactly because of rounding.)

The observed numbers of people possessing each genotype are not the same as those expected if chance alone were determining them. In evolutionary terms, then, our sample population is not in Hardy-Weinberg equilibrium. Something else is going on, namely, some evolutionary processes are in action.

In real life, we would still have to run certain statistical tests on our results because even if the expected and observed numbers do not match, they could still be the results of chance. For the record, I ran one such test, called Chi-Square, and found that the above results are not a matter of chance. They are, in mathematical terms, statistically significant.

Hardy-Weinberg equilibrium: The formula that shows genotype frequencies in a population under hypothetical conditions of no evolutionary change.

At any rate, we can note the direction of the differences. Again, comparing expected with observed, we see that there are large drops in the numbers of people with the AA and SS genotypes, and a large increase in those with the AS genotype. This hints that the heterozygote was being selected for and that the two homozygotes were being selected against. We know, of course, that this is the case with sickle cell anemia in malarial areas.

Calculating allele frequencies and using them to see evolution in action, as in the examples above, is a powerful tool when the genetic mechanism for a trait is known, as it is for sickle cell anemia. It allows us to understand change over time in a particular genetic system. But what about traits for which the genetic mechanism is unknown? Is there any way these can contribute to our understanding of evolution in living populations?

EVOLUTION IN POPULATIONS

When I conducted my study of evolutionary processes among the Hutterites, I used **dermatoglyphics,** the study of the parallel ridges on the skin of the fingers, palms, toes, and soles. I focused on those of the fingers—in other words, fingerprints. I was not collecting data about the small features that make each individual's fingerprints absolutely unique from everyone

FIGURE 13.1
Fingerprint features used as anthropological data.

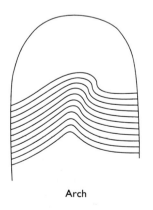

Arch

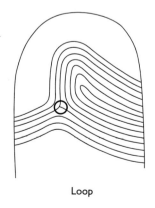

Loop

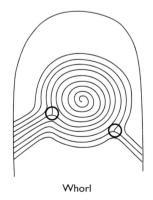

Whorl

◯ = Triradii

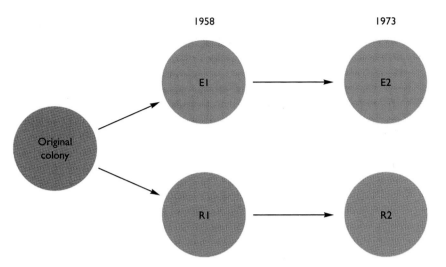

FIGURE 13.2
Hutterite colonies in the study described. E and R are code letters I used to identify each colony, the first letters of their names.

else's. Rather, I was looking for the frequencies of various types of fingerprint patterns and for data about the size of the patterns, called ridge count. This is measured by counting the number of ridges between a reference point, the triradius, and the center of the pattern (Figure 13.1).

This research is an example of another way of examining evolution in living populations. If we know the genetic mechanism for a trait, as in the sickle cell example, we can see if the gene or genes for that trait change through time, that is, if they evolve. However, we don't know the genetic mechanism that gives rise to fingerprints, or, for that matter, the genetic mechanism for most phenotypic traits. But by comparing measures of phenotypic traits between populations and between groups within a population, we may estimate the degrees of genetic difference among these groups and thus gauge the extent to which the various processes of evolution are taking place. We use phenotypic traits—even if the exact genetic mechanisms are unknown—as **genetic markers.**

We know that one's fingerprints are under some genetic control since certain features, especially ridge count, are similar among members of a family line. Moreover, certain unusual dermatoglyphic traits have been correlated with abnormalities of known or suspected genetic origin. We also know, however, that other fingerprint traits are affected by prenatal environmental factors or simply by chance. Not knowing what genes are involved, I obviously couldn't calculate allele frequencies and run Hardy-Weinberg tests, so how did I use these markers?

In 1973, I collected fingerprint data from everyone in each of two Hutterite colonies that were the results of the splitting of an original colony in 1958 (Figure 13.2). As you recall from Chapter 1, I was interested

dermatoglyphics: The study of the parallel ridges and furrows on the finger tips, palms, toes, and soles.

genetic markers: Traits of genetic origin used to compare populations and estimate genetic differences.

FIGURE 13.3
Diagram of tests run and expected results.

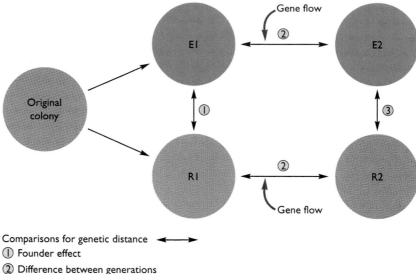

Comparisons for genetic distance
① Founder effect
② Difference between generations
③ Difference after one generation

in examining the effects of gene flow and genetic drift. I examined 133 sets of fingerprints for pattern type, pattern size, and a few other variables (about 1330 individual prints—although many of the men in this farming society had fewer than ten fingers). I then statistically compared the fingerprint data of various subgroups to get a numerical *approximation* of the genetic distances among them. I used different methods of analysis to see if some dermatoglyphic data were better than others for estimating genetic distance.

First, I was specifically interested in seeing how much genetic change was brought about by splitting (fissioning) the population. This would measure the form of genetic drift known as the founder effect (see Chapter 4). Second, I wondered how much change takes place between generations, and how much of that change is the result of the fact that about half of the mothers of the second generation had moved into the two colonies after marriage (gene flow). Natural selection was ruled out as a cause of change since there is no evidence that it makes any difference in reproductive success what ridge patterns you have and how big they are. Nor do people choose mates based on their fingerprints.

I felt I could apply what I found to a broader perspective on human evolution. The Hutterites nicely mirror the nature of many human populations during much of our history—small groups of interrelated families that may well have split and merged in various ways as they moved about in search of resources.

I proposed two major hypotheses (Figure 13.3). First, I guessed that there would be a founder effect after the original population split in 1958 to create two new populations. That is, I hypothesized that the new populations would be genetically different from one another as a result of being founded by nonrepresentative samples of the original (see Chapter 4). I did not think the effect would be particularly extensive, however, since splitting a sample into two equal halves lessens the chance of a major difference between them. In addition, all the families involved were descended from seven brothers, so there would not be a whole lot of genetic variation to begin with.

In the second hypothesis, I expected a significant effect from gene flow, making the next generations after the split (E2 and R2 in Figure 13.3) different from their parental generations (E1 and R1). I therefore expected the second generations of the two colonies to be even more different from one another than were the two founded colonies. As noted in Chapter 4, nearly three-quarters of the mothers of the second generation "flowed" into the colonies of their husbands at marriage, and families with one of these women accounted for about half the children of the second generation. A lot of new genes were brought into each colony and all of the women carrying those genes became parents. The parents should be distinctly genetically different from the nonparents—a form of selection, although not based on adaptedness.

What did I find? For the first hypothesis, the data showed evidence of a founder effect, but there was more difference between the two founded populations than I expected. You obviously can't base a whole conclusion on one small study, but my results did suggest that fission and the founder effect could be important processes not only within the Hutterites but in the small, interrelated human populations that they represent.

My second hypothesis was not supported by the evidence. The two second generation populations were *more* similar to one another than were the founder populations. This was surprising at first but then the reason became clear.

The colonies from which the flow group women came were all the same subgroup of Hutterites. The Hutterites are divided into three subgroups. Since about World War I, these groups have been **endogamous**— members only marry within their group. Thus, the women were more closely related than if they had come from the Hutterite population in general.

Moreover, since the two colonies I studied were geographically close, the colonies from which the women came were also geographically close. Hutterites often find their mates in colonies they regularly visit. This increased the chances that the flow group women were themselves closely related. The genes flowing into the two colonies were similar so the dif-

endogamous: Restricting marriage to within a certain social group.

ferences between the colonies was lessened over time, even over a single generation. Differences among populations, then, can increase and decrease, back and forth, depending upon how the memberships of those populations are organized and exactly who marries whom. Culture, in other words, influences biology.

Finally, I observed which statistical tests most closely matched the predicted results (once I had figured out that gene flow *decreased* the genetic distance). I was able to suggest that ridge count (the size of the patterns) was the best dermatoglyphic feature to use as a genetic marker.

This dermatoglyphic study of the Hutterites is just one example of a population genetic study. It does, however, show the ways in which we can go about making genetic comparisons among various populations, and how we can then analyze the evolutionary processes behind the differences we find.

This example also points out the importance of collecting and organizing data about the populations we study. How do we do this and what can we learn from such data about the nature of the human species as a whole and of the groups into which we have divided ourselves?

DESCRIBING POPULATIONS

The statistical study of the size and makeup of human populations, and of changes in those measures, is called **demography.** Normally studied in detail by the fields of human or cultural geography, demographic data are nonetheless of importance to biological anthropologists. Populations are, after all, the units of evolutionary change, and so the nature of the groups we study cannot be separated from the evolutionary processes that affect those groups. The Hutterite example clearly shows this.

The most obvious thing we need to know about a population is its size—how many people there are. Since we're interested in change over time, we also want to know to what extent and in what direction the size of a population has changed during a given period.

For example, we know that the population of Europe dropped from about 70 million in 1347 to 45 million by 1352—a 35 percent decrease over a mere five years. It then took 118 years (until 1470) for Europe to once again achieve a population of 70 million.

On the other hand, the number of Hutterites in North America increased from about 300 in 1875 to about 30,000 at present. This is a 100 fold increase in 120 years.

We need to determine what causes such changes and, for that matter, any population changes anywhere. Clearly, there are three variables in-

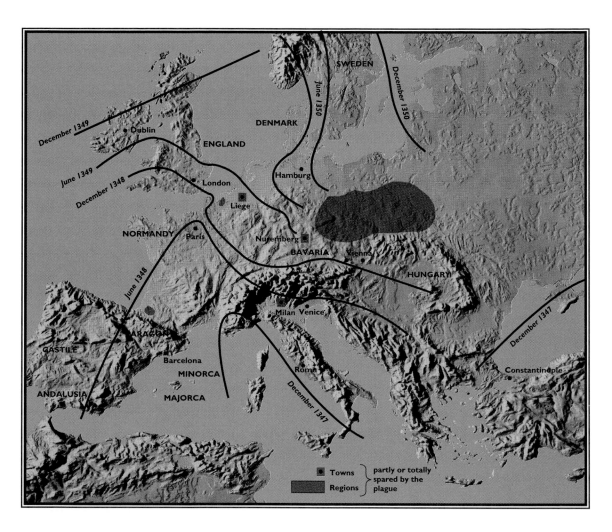

Towns
Regions
partly or totally
spared by the
plague

FIGURE 13.4
The progression of the Black Death across Europe in the fourteenth century, an event that, in five years, killed over one-third of Europe's people.

volved: births, deaths, and migration into or out of the population. When the birth rate exceeds the death rate, the population size increases. It decreases when the death rate is greater. Only in rare cases is migration a major factor, though it certainly may play a significant role.

In the case of fourteenth-century Europe, we know that the drop in population was the result of plague, mostly bubonic plague, a fatal bacterial disease carried by fleas that are, in turn, transported by rats. A major outbreak began in Italy in 1347 and spread rapidly across Europe over the next five years, killing 25 million people. The period came to be known as the Black Death (Figure 13.4). No birth rate could have made up for this. The fact that it took longer to replace the 25 million than to kill them off results from two facts. There were further, though smaller, out-

demography: The study of the size and makeup of populations.

breaks of plague over the next century that kept the death rates high. Second, a phenomenal growth rate of around 100 persons per thousand would have been required each year to put the population back in only five years. By comparison, the U.S. growth rate for 1970 was only about nine persons per thousand. (Growth rate is birth rate minus death rate.)

Bubonic plague is older than the fourteenth century and is still around today. It spread so quickly in Europe during those years because of the dense populations of many of Europe's cities and because of the extensive trade networks that linked those cities. Rats that carried the fleas moved easily from place to place, and the bacteria easily moved from person to person. Culture affected a biological event, and the connection went the other way as well. Many aspects of European culture were affected by the Black Death—everything from economy to art.

The increase in the Hutterite population in North America can be attributed to the high birth rate among this group. They have, on average, 10.4 children per family, one of the highest recorded for any population. This results in a birth rate of about 46 births per thousand. The death rate is about 4 per thousand, yielding a growth rate of 42 per thousand. This high rate is the result of Hutterite religious beliefs—their firm adherence to the biblical injunction to "be fruitful and multiply"—and, most likely,

FIGURE 13.5

Age-sex graph of Hutterite colonies used in my study. This is typical of such graphs for the Hutterites in general.

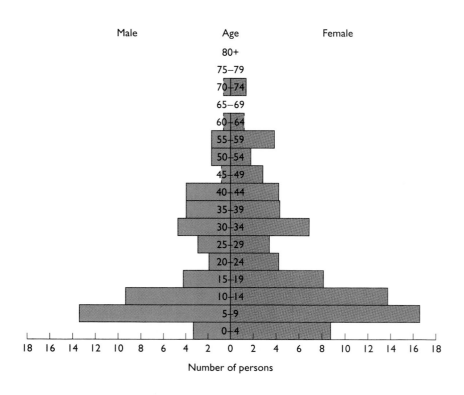

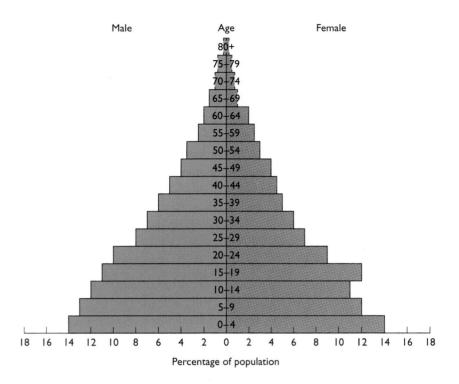

Male   Age   Female

FIGURE 13.6
Age-sex graph for developing
nations, with an emphasis on
large numbers of children.

Percentage of population

because of the healthy lifestyle they lead that includes hard work in non-urban areas and excludes drugs and all but occasional alcohol.

We are also interested in the composition of populations. How many people are there of each sex, in each age group, and in various other ethnic, occupational, economic, and religious groups. We can display these data with a pyramid diagram. Figure 13.5 shows the age-sex structure of the Hutterite colonies I studied. The data here are typical for all Hutterites.

As you might expect for a group with such a high reproductive rate, the graph is wider on the bottom, showing that there are more children than adults. The fact that there are many more children between ages five and nine than between zero and four may indicate that the growth rate is slowing, at least in these colonies.

That females outnumber males (79 to 54) may indicate any number of factors that would have to be examined more closely. Perhaps male death rates are higher. They are in the general population. It could also be that, despite what I was told and what I calculated, I *did not* get to see everyone in the colonies. Maybe some of the men did not want to participate and I never knew they existed.

Now, compare the graph for the Hutterites with one representing developing nations—nations like Mexico, where industrialization is fairly recent (Figure 13.6). This age-sex graph also shows larger numbers of chil-

FIGURE 13.7

Age-sex graph for developed nations, which have fewer children and longer life expectancy.

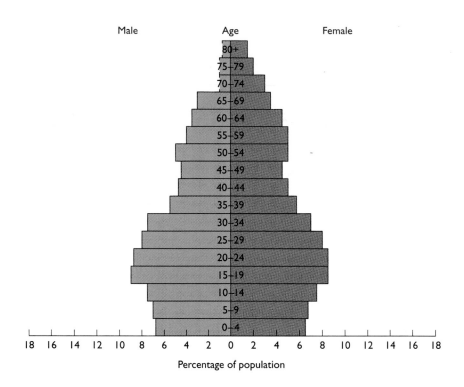

dren but, unlike the Hutterite graph, the numbers of adults rapidly decrease with age. This reflects higher death rates, especially as one gets older.

For adults, the Hutterites more closely resemble a graph for developed nations, like the United States, that have been industrialized for some time (Figure 13.7). Here the numbers of adults do not decrease as quickly with age, indicating that people in developed countries live longer in general. Regarding children, however, the developed nations differ from the Hutterites in having lower birth rates.

What are the cultural connections here? As we noted, the Hutterites are responding to their religious beliefs by having many children. Their communal, self-sufficient lifestyle can accomodate large families, and their practice of splitting colonies prevents local overpopulation.

Developing nations have high mortality rates. This provides one incentive to produce as many children as possible simply to try to offset the deaths. In addition, birth control technology is not always available and there may be cultural rules against it. But, although the bottom of the pyramid diagram is wide for such populations, it narrows down quickly. Because of poor medical care and poor nutrition and sanitation, people have a decreasing chance of living into the next age group.

In developed countries, there is increasing motivation to limit population and there is access to the means of birth control. Moreover, the quality of medical care, diet, and lifestyle in general allow people to live longer. Thus, the nearly vertical shape of the diagram.

Finally, what can we say from demographic statistics about the human species in general? One thing is for certain—our total population is going to increase. Since the beginning of farming and animal domestication some 12,000 years ago, the rate of increase of the human population has accelerated, jumping sharply with the Industrial Revolution of the eighteenth century (Figure 13.8). At current growth rates, the world population, now about 5.6 billion, is expected to reach 6.25 billion by the year 2000 and 8.5 billion by the middle of the next century.

In addition to a growing population, the structure of the population of the next century will change. As birth rates and death rates continue to drop in developed nations, and, perhaps, as other nations become increasingly developed, the age-sex pyramids will become top-heavy. There will be more older people than younger people. This will radically change the social and economic nature of such cultures.

Both of these changes carry implications that are beyond the scope of this book. Clearly, though, they will require responses and actions that will put a very different face on the world of the next generation, and that will profoundly affect *Homo sapiens* of the twenty-first century.

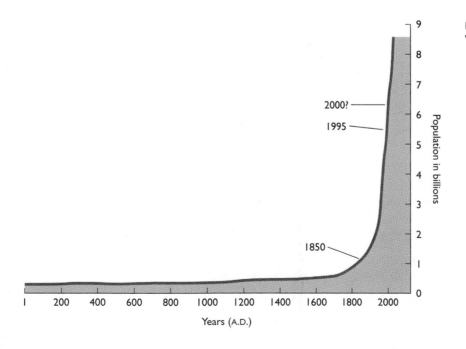

FIGURE 13.8
World population curve.

FIGURE 13.9
Cultural adaptation. The famous igloo of the Inuit has
many ingeneous features that
make it remarkably adapted
to life in a harsh climate.

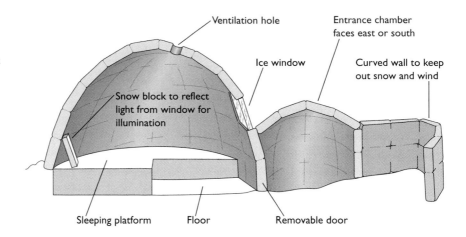

FIGURE 13.9
Cultural adaptation. The famous igloo of the Inuit has
many ingeneous features that
make it remarkably adapted
to life in a harsh climate.

HUMAN ADAPTATIONS

Living human populations inhabit every continent on the planet except
Antartica (and there are small, temporary groups of people who live there,
mostly doing scientific research). We have to deal with just about every
imaginable set of environmental circumstances the earth possesses, and
we have been doing this for just about as long as modern *Homo sapiens*
has existed. Indeed, our predecessor, *Homo erectus*, also successfully moved
into a wide range of climatic conditions.

One would expect, therefore, that different populations of our species
would be differently adapted to those various environments. Obviously,
most of our adaptations are cultural. We build shelters, manufacture clothing, make tools, and invent various technological devices that are specifically geared to the environmental conditions with which we have to
contend (Figure 13.9).

Human populations also differ in their physical appearance and in
features of their physiology. Our species displays **polymorphisms**—variations in phenotypic traits that are the results of genetic variation (that is,
multiple alleles). Are some of these polymorphisms adaptive responses to
different environments?

Species Adaptations

As members of the same species, all humans must certainly share many
adaptations to variable conditions. One important environmental variable
is temperature. All humans sweat as a means of dissipating heat from the

body. As noted in Chapter 10, our relative hairlessness may be an adaptation to promote the quick evaporation of sweat. On the other hand, when it becomes too cold, we shiver, our metabolic rate increases, and our blood vessels alternately widen and narrow to increase or decrease the flow of blood, and therefore warmth, to various body parts.

Similarly, we are all exposed to ultraviolet radiation from the sun. An excess of UV can damage skin cells, alter the cells' DNA causing skin cancer, and adversely affect the body's immune system. To protect tissues from UV damage, specialized skin cells called **melanocytes** produce the pigment **melanin** and deliver it to the upper layer of skin where it absorbs UV radiation. Melanocytes respond to increased UV levels by increasing their melanin production and darkening the skin. This, of course, is tanning. Even dark-skinned individuals can exhibit a tanning response.

Humans, however, live in such a variety of conditions—including those related to temperature and ultraviolet radiation—that these species-wide responses may not be sufficient to adapt all populations to their environments.

Variation in Adaptations

Humans have settled in places from the hottest deserts and rain forests to the coldest reaches above the Arctic Circle. No matter how much we may sweat, shiver, increase our metabolic rate, and change the shape of our blood vessels, it may not be enough to deal with some environmental extremes. For example, there is no difference in the number of sweat glands among human populations. Regardless of regional temperature, we all pretty much have the same number. There are, however, other adaptations to temperature that do vary with location.

Populations that inhabit hot climates tend to be very linear in build, and those in cold areas tend to be stockier (Figure 13.10). This is because the linear individual has a greater surface area and so loses heat more rapidly, whereas the stockier person has a smaller surface area, and so retains heat better. There is also a tendency for people in cold climates simply to be bigger in general than those in hot climates since, obviously, the larger person would have more of their body mass away from the surface and so retain heat more efficiently.

Ultraviolet radiation varies with latitude. Sunlight strikes the earth more directly at the equator, and at more of an angle the farther one gets from the equator. Hitting at an angle, the solar radiation also travels through more atmosphere and thus more UV is absorbed by ozone in northern latitudes. Not only do humans have the ability to tan in response to increased UV levels, but, as is obvious to us all, populations are genetically programmed for differences in skin color, and these differences also

polymorphisms: Variations in phenotypic traits that are the results of genetic variation.

melanocytes: Specialized skin cells that produce the pigment melanin.

melanin: The pigment that is largely responsible for human skin color.

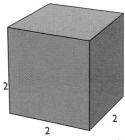

Volume = 2 × 2 × 2 = 8 in.^{3}
Surface area = (2 × 2)(6 sides)
= 24 in.^{2}
(Numbers in inches)

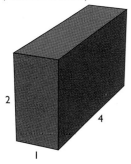

Volume = 1 × 2 × 4 = 8 in.^{3}
Surface area = (1 × 2) (2) +
(1 × 4) (2) +
(2 × 4) (2)
= 28 in.^{2}

FIGURE 13.10
The body build of the Inuit (left) is adapted to heat retention, while that of the Masai cattle herder from Kenya is built to promote heat loss. (Above) The relationship between surface area and shape for two solids of equal volume. This explains the adaptations of the two men pictured.

vary by latitude. In general, peoples closer to the equator have darker skin. Skin color gradually gets lighter in populations away from the equator (Figure 13.11).

It is generally agreed that the relationship between dark skin and high levels of UV radiation is an example of an adaptive response. Because of the damaging effects of UV, peoples in or near the equator have undergone selection for permanently higher levels of melanin production. Darker skinned people do not have more melanocytes than lighter skinned ones, just more melanin. An implication of this, of course, is that dark skin was the original human skin color, since—at least according to the latest evidence—our species first evolved in equatorial Africa.

The question then becomes, why did populations who moved away from the equator evolve lower melanin production and therefore lighter

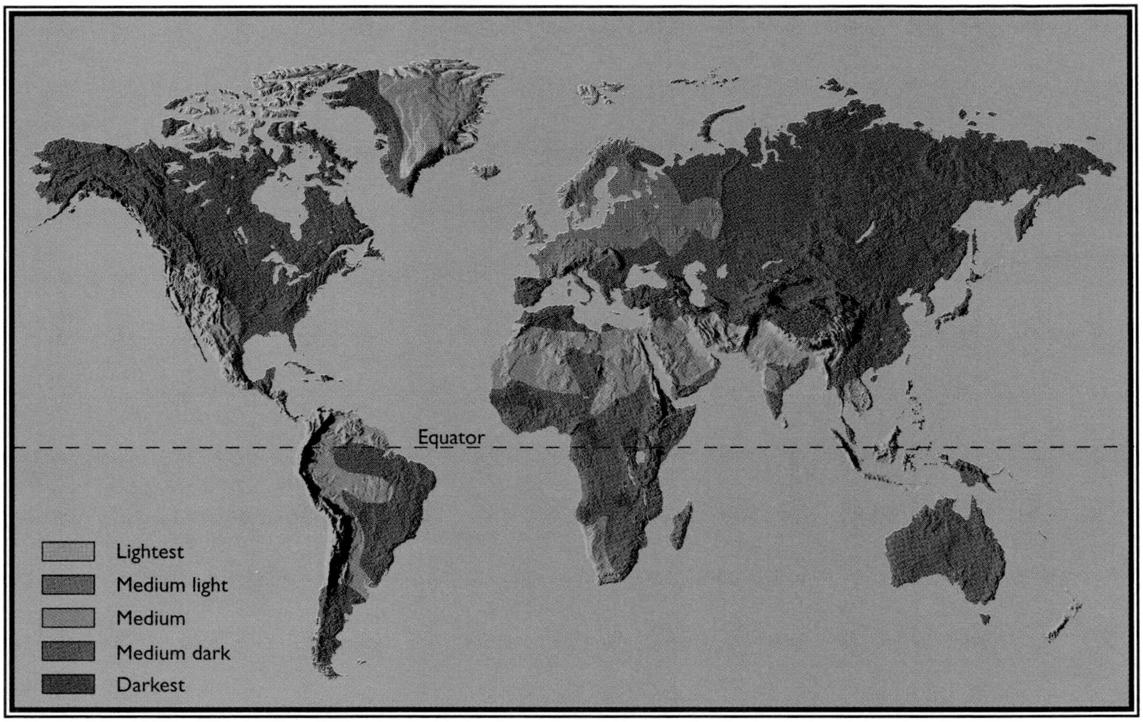

FIGURE 13.11
Skin color distribution.
Darker skin is concentrated
in equatorial regions.

skin? It is easiest to say that since dark skin was no longer needed it became light. Evolution, however, does not really work this way. More likely, there was an adaptive reason why lighter skin was actively selected *for*.

A common answer has to do with vitamin D production. Vitamin D can be synthesized by the body, in the lower layers of skin, when a precursor of the vitamin is activated by UV radiation. This vitamin is important in regulating the absorption of calcium and its inclusion in the manufacture of bone. Deficiency in vitamin D can lead to a condition of skeletal deformity known as rickets in children. There is an adult version of the abnormality as well. Bones with rickets are also more prone to breakage and deformity of the pelvis can make childbirth difficult.

It has been thought that, as populations moved away from the equator, those with darker skin could not manufacture sufficient vitamin D for normal bone growth and maintenance. Those with lighter skin, therefore, were at an adaptive and, thus, a reproductive advantage. Over time, lighter skin became the normal, inherited condition in these groups. Skin color was thus seen as a balancing act—dark enough to protect from the damaging effects of UV and light enough to allow the beneficial effects.

The vitamin D part of this explanation has, however, recently been questioned. Rickets is associated with recent urban populations (in narrow city streets, children get little direct sunlight), and is seldom found in rural areas. There is little evidence for it in the fossil record. Moreover, although dark skin does slow down the production of vitamin D, it can still allow for sufficient synthesis to maintain healthy levels. Vitamin D synthesis may not have been a selective factor for our ancestors.

Now, of course, we can also obtain vitamin D through vitamin supplements and by adding it to milk. It is also found in fish liver oils and egg yolks. A correlation between dark skinned urban populations and rickets—once proposed as evidence for the adaptive connection—may be based more on socioeconomic matters resulting in poor diet than on skin color differences directly.

Another possibility for an active selective factor for light skin concerns injury to the skin from cold. Data from the military suggest that darker skin is more prone to damage from frostbite than is lighter skin (Post et al. 1975). Selection for light skin may not be related to ultraviolet radiation but to temperature, while selection for darker skin remains related to UV.

As these examples of body build and skin color demonstrate, our species, despite its ability to adapt through culture to a wide array of environments, has still undergone natural selection for and against certain features in response to those environments. The discussion of sickle cell anemia from Chapter 4 is another example. Although we might like to think we have buffered ourselves against this process of evolution, it has occurred in modern *Homo sapiens* and it continues to affect populations of our species.

Are All Polymorphisms Adaptively Important?

We can see, in the distribution of body build and skin color, some obvious correlations with environmental factors that lead us rather directly to our conclusions about the adaptive significance of these polymorphic traits. Other human polymorphisms, on the other hand, seem distributed among our populations in such a way that there is no obvious relationship to environmental circumstances.

The distribution of blood types in the ABO system (see Chapter 3) is a perfect example (Figure 13.12) of a polymorphism unrelated to the environment. There seems to be no "rhyme or reason" to how the various frequencies of the phenotypes are disbursed around the world. Type A, for example, is totally absent among some native South American groups, but is found in frequencies over 50 percent in parts of Europe, native Australia, and among a few native North American groups, where, however, it is

FIGURE 13.12
Approximate frequency distributions of type A and type B blood, demonstrating the lack of a pattern in the distribution of this polymorphism.

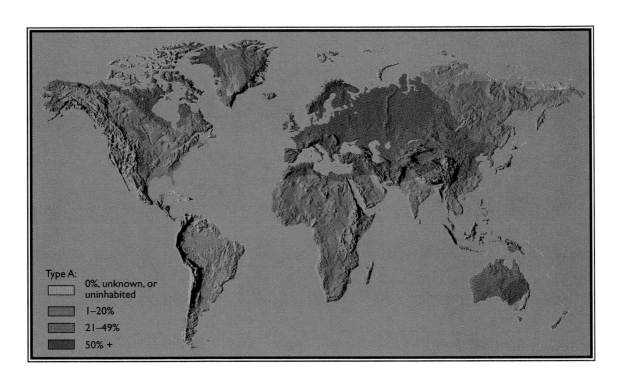

Type A:
- 0%, unknown, or uninhabited
- 1–20%
- 21–49%
- 50% +

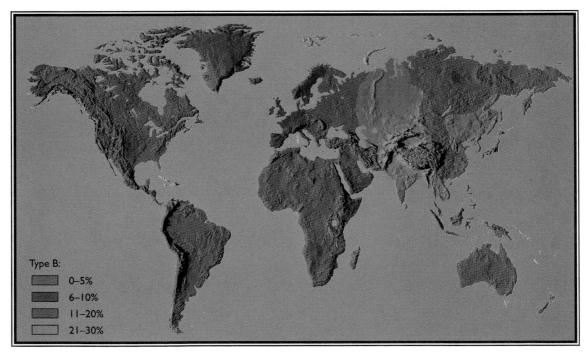

Type B:
- 0–5%
- 6–10%
- 11–20%
- 21–30%

TABLE 13.1
ABO Blood Group Phenotypes and Antibodies

Genotypes	Phenotypes	Antigens	Antibodies
AA AO	A	A	anti-B
BB BO	A	A	anti-A
AB OO	AB O	A, B none	none anti-A, anti-B

generally found among less than a quarter of the population. Type O, the most common world wide, still ranges from 40 percent in parts of Asia to 100 percent among some native South Americans.

Are the variations of this genetic trait adaptively neutral; that is, do they make no difference in terms of differential reproductive success? We believe this to be the case for some other blood group systems. (There are about thirty different blood group systems besides the ABO system; that is, different chemical phenotypes in the blood that are the results of different genes with multiple alleles.)

The actual phenotypic trait involved in the ABO system is the presence or absence of certain proteins, called antigens, on the surface of the red blood cells. In addition, your blood plasma contains, from shortly after birth, other proteins that react against the alternate version of your antigen. For example, if you have antigen A, then antigen B is the alternate version. These other proteins are called **antibodies.** Table 13.1 shows how these are expressed in the ABO system.

The reactions between antigens and antibodies is the reason that blood used for transfusions must match the blood type of the recipient. As a type A person, if I received a transfusion of type B blood, my anti-B antibodies would recognize the B antigen of the transfused blood as foreign to my system. My antibodies would bind with the antigens on the transfused red blood cells and destroy the cells by causing them to burst (hemolyze). If extensive enough, this reaction could lead to shock or kidney failure. In emergencies, however, a person of any blood type may receive type O, since O has no antigens and therefore would stimulate no reaction.

Since antibodies of various sorts are important components of our bodies' immunological system, disease is one obvious factor to examine for an adaptive significance of the ABO polymorphism. Some microorganisms possess antigens that are similar to the A and B antigens, so perhaps certain blood types are predisposed to fight off certain infectious diseases. At the same time, if an infecting microorganism possesses antigens that are similar to your own, then your system may not be stimulated to produce the proper antibodies against the organism, making you more susceptible to that disease.

Some correlations between blood type and susceptibility to diseases have been suggested. Type A has been associated with bronchial pneumonia, smallpox, and typhoid, and type O has shown correlations with bubonic plague. Among the data that support some connections among these factors is the low frequency of type O in India, where there is a long history of frequent plague epidemics.

It should also be noted that there is some evidence that mosquitos are more attracted to type O persons. If so, then diseases carried by mosquitos, such as malaria, would also be influenced, although indirectly, by blood type.

There are correlations as well between blood types and noninfectious gastrointestinal diseases. Type O persons appear to have a greater chance of duodenal and stomach ulcers and type A persons of stomach cancer. Most people have blood group antigens in their body fluids, including their gastric juices, as well as in their blood, and so there may well be some reactions between these antigens and chemicals in the digested food one eats. The reactions may have a positive or negative effect on the digestive process itself, or they may lead to some irritation of the digestive tract. Thus, certain blood types may have been selected for, and others against, depending upon what foods were typically consumed in certain areas by certain populations.

Along the same lines, there may also be reactions between blood antigens in the digestive tract and some intestinal bacteria. Individuals of certain blood types may be more or less affected by bacterial ailments like infant diarrhea. Such ailments are major factors in infant mortality in many parts of the world. Thus, they are important selective factors, and any polymorphism that influenced the severity of these problems could be selected for or against.

What do blood type correlations tell us? Certainly these data indicate that a selective role for the ABO system is possible, especially with diseases that affect people during or before their reproductive period. We must demonstrate, however, that selection is, in fact, taking place. The fact that we have gained some control over some of the diseases in question limits our ability to study them in the present and so we have to rely, as with the plague connection, on historical records.

Moreover, we must establish a cause-and-effect relationship between antigen and disease, and we must show if, and under what conditions, this would make enough of a difference to affect reproductive success. The ABO system is also found in chimps and gorillas, so the origin of the

antibodies: Proteins in the immune system that react to foreign antigens.

polymorphism itself may be hidden in our evolutionary past. Some of the more important connections are with diseases of dense urban populations. Thus selection for certain blood types, and their distribution, may be a fairly recent phenomenon.

As this single example shows, the topic is a complex one. We asked at the beginning of this section: Are all polymorphisms adaptively important? The answer to that question is: We don't know for sure. Human polymorphisms need to be examined for their selective contributions to populations within the species. We may find, however, that some of our variable traits make no difference at all, or at least make no difference now.

THE BIOANTHROPOLOGY OF INDIVIDUALS

Individuals don't evolve, at least not in the sense that we are using the term here. And yet, we are interested in growth rates, developmental rates, and the timing of important events in the lives of individual members of our species. Why is this important to bioanthropology?

FIGURE 13.13

Distance curve for height and age.

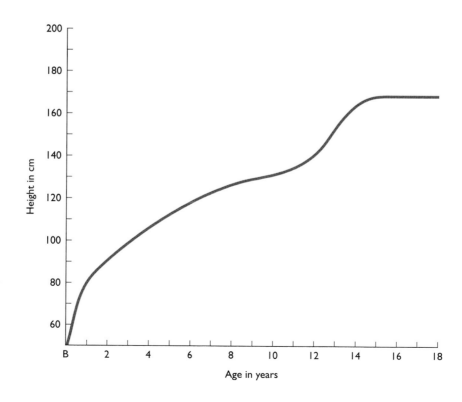

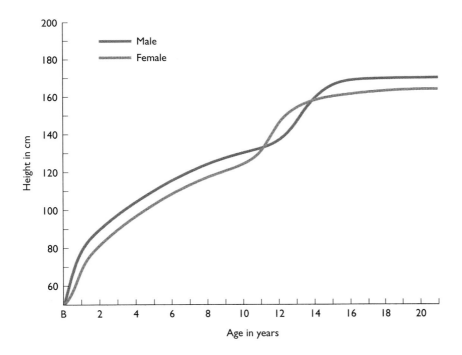

FIGURE 13.14
Distance curves for height and age in males compared to females.

First of all, we are interested in these topics simply because they are part of our species' makeup. Studying just the adults of a species does not tell us everything about that species. We need to know such things as how developed an individual is at birth, how fast it reaches certain levels of growth, when it becomes sexually and physically mature, how long its reproductive span is, and how long it lives. We also look at rates at which certain components of the body grow and compare them to one another, and we compare all these data for different populations within a species and for different groups within populations—like males and females.

For example, we may plot a curve that shows the height of the members of a human population at certain ages (Figure 13.13). This type of curve is called a **distance curve.** We see from such a curve that change in height as people mature is not steady but alters its rate at different stages. The sudden increase in height in early adolescence is obviously related to puberty and is called, in fact, the "adolescent growth spurt."

We all remember that the adolescent growth spurt did not occur at the same time in members of the two sexes. This and other differences in growth rate can be seen by comparing distance curves for males and females (Figure 13.14). These differences will be discussed in the next chapter.

These changes can be seen in another way by plotting the rate of change for different ages. This is called a **velocity curve,** and measures how fast changes are taking place, in this case, how many centimeters per

distance curve: A graph that compares some variable at different points in time.

velocity curve: A graph that compares rate of change in some variable at different points in time.

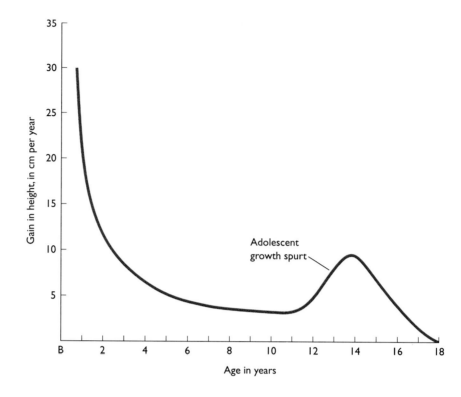

FIGURE 13.15
Velocity curve for data in
Figure 13.13.

year the plotted individual is growing (Figure 13.15). Note the increase (acceleration) of growth rate at early adolescence.

Not every part of the body, of course, grows at the same rate. Figure 13.16 compares height with brain size, using percent of final adult size as a scale. Note that, unlike height, the fastest brain growth is in the first few years of life.

These and many other data analyses show us the patterns of growth of our species in general and of different populations and groups within the species. Observing these patterns leads to other reasons for being interested in this topic. First, we want to know what factors influence the differences we see between populations of our species, and the changes within populations at different points in time.

Two obvious influences on populations are nutrition and medical care. In societies where people are properly nourished, for example, girls grow faster, reach sexual maturity earlier, and achieve a larger adult body size. Over the last century, better nutrition and medical care have even made adult height greater and the age of sexual maturity earlier in the United States. There are still differences in age of **menarche** between poor women and those of more affluent means within this country.

At the same time, however, age at **menopause** is no different in populations of different nutritional and medical levels, nor has better food

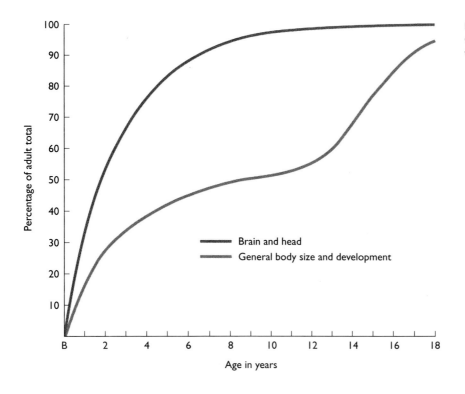

FIGURE 13.16
Curves for height compared to brain growth.

and health expanded the overall human lifespan, which remains about a hundred years at most (Hill 1993). Culture can affect some aspects of our stages of life but not others.

Finally, we are interested in life course data because it may help explain how we evolved. A new study called **life history** collects such data and compares it within and between groups of organisms to try to draw some general rules about the life histories of living things and therefore explain the differences between them.

To give but one example (Hill 1993), we see major differences in the life histories of modern humans and our closest kin, the chimpanzees. Chimps reach sexual maturity about four years earlier than humans, but humans have an adult lifespan (from maturity to death) that is four times as long as a chimpanzee (forty-two years compared to fourteen), and in human females, half of that time is spent in a postreproductive stage. Chimps, on the other hand, reproduce pretty much all their adult lives. Yet, despite the longer time we have to reproduce, humans still reproduce more often than chimps.

Life history studies are trying to explain these differences and are also trying to establish when the human life history pattern first evolved. It appears, by looking at the dental development pattern of the "Taung child" (*Australopithecus africanus*), that this genus did not share our life

menarche: A woman's first menstrual period.

menopause: The end of a woman's reproductive cycle.

life history: The study that examines the timing of life cycle events such as fertility, growth, and death.

history and may have been more similar to chimpanzees (Smith 1993). These studies are still in their infancy, but should provide further insight in the future into this important and relatively unstudied aspect of our evolutionary history.

SUMMARY

While a major focus of bioanthropology is on the evolutionary history of the hominids, the nature of the product of that evolution—modern *Homo sapiens*—is also important. We study living populations of our species from several different yet interrelated approaches.

If we know the genetic mechanism for a particular phenotypic trait, we can calculate the frequencies of the alleles of the gene involved and then see what changes in allele frequency take place in populations over time. Since evolution is technically defined as change in allele frequency, this allows us to see if evolution is in operation for that phenotype and to try to determine what processes of evolution are involved. The use of the Hardy-Weinberg equilibrium lets us do this even if we cannot examine a population at several different time periods.

Even if we don't know the genetic mechanism of a trait, we may still use that trait as a genetic marker, provided it is under some genetic control. By statistically comparing populations, or groups within a population, for a marker trait, we may estimate their genetic distances. In this way, we can hypothesize what sorts of evolutionary changes are taking place.

The use of demographic variables for size and composition of populations lets us describe the groups we study and observe changes in those variables that may denote certain biological or cultural trends. Indeed, when we analyze such data, we see that the biology of demographic changes is intimately linked to cultural variables of and around the studied populations.

Since humans live in such a wide range of environmental circumstances, it stands to reason that human groups would have different adaptations to those environments. Most adaptations of our species are cultural, but we still exhibit a number of polymorphic traits. There is evidence that our variation in these traits is the result of natural selection at some point in our evolution to climatic and other environmental variables.

Finally, we understand that we need to study not only adult members of our species but also the growth and development of immature members as they are in the process of becoming adults. When certain changes take place and how fast they do so are part of our species' characteristics. Understanding how these changes and rates of change differ from those of other species is beginning to shed more light on the nature and course of our evolution.

KEY TERMS

Hardy-Weinberg equilibrium	demography	distance curve
dermatoglyphics	polymorphisms	velocity curve
genetic markers	melanocytes	menarche
endogamous	melanin	menopause
	antibodies	life history

SUGGESTED READINGS

We just really skimmed the surface of the study of population genetics. For a more detailed treatment, with specific reference to humans, see *Human Variation and Human Microevolution* by Jane Underwood. For some classic examples of human population studies, try *The Structure of Human Populations* edited by G. A. Harrison and A. J. Boyce.

If you would like to know more about dermatoglyphics, the standard work is *Finger Prints, Palms, and Soles* by Harold Cummins and Charles Midlo.

There are many texts available that cover human demography. Richard Tullar's *The Human Species* gives a nice introduction, as does John Relethford's book of the same name.

For more detail on human polymorphisms and their adaptive significance, see Stephen Molnar's *Human Variation: Races, Types, and Ethnic Groups,* and for a well-known work that covers all of these topics and more, try *Human Biology* by Harrison, Weiner, Tanner, and Barnicot.

CHAPTER

14

HUMAN
BIOLOGICAL
DIVERSITY

... scrutiny of the
actual facts shows that
there are only *three
primary colors peculiar
to the human body;* . . .
ruddy, black and brown.
—John Clark Ridpath
(American, 1894)

In the previous chapter we discussed some human polymorphic traits. The distribution of some, like skin color, points fairly clearly to an explanation involving natural selection to varying environmental conditions. Others, like blood type, are distributed in such a way as to make them seem adaptively neutral, or, at least, the adaptive significance is complex and not immediately obvious.

If our interest in phenotypic variation among modern humans was limited to describing and explaining the distribution of polymorphisms, we would still have a challenging task. But our biological variation has further meaning to us. Our variable traits—of adaptive significance or not—are distributed with some geographic regularity, enough so that one can very often tell from what part of the world a person comes.

People look European, or Asian, or African, or American Indian. We can often be more specific: People from Japan don't look like people from China. Swedes don't look like Italians. Masai from East Africa don't look like the San (Bushmen) from the Kalahari. Inuit don't look like Maya (Figure 14.1).

We seem to have evidence, in other words, that our species is divided into some number of fairly distinct subgroups. The term usually applied to such groups is *race*. It seems, on the surface, a logical assumption. Indeed, for much of the history of anthropology, a focus has been on discovering just how many human races there are and on identifying them.

However—and I'll give away the "punch line" right here—races, on a biological level, don't exist within the human species. Races *are* real, but are cultural categories. Cultures respond to and interpret objective reality—in this case human biological and cultural diversity—and create subjective categories that have meaning within given cultural systems. A good example of this process, and a somewhat more clear-cut one, is the way in which different cultures interpret the two categories of sex, male and female.

These ideas require more detailed examination, and such an examination is, perhaps, one of the more important contributions of biological anthropology. Let's look at the following questions:

How are the two human sexes interpreted differently by different cultures? How can we use this as a model for examining "racial" variation?

Is race a valid biological concept?

Are there human biological races?

What, then, are human races?

How can bioanthropology contribute to understanding some of the problems that the idea of race has presented?

FIGURE 14.1
Can you tell where each of these people comes from by their physical features?

SEX AND GENDER

Most human beings are unambiguously either biologically male or female. As noted in Chapter 9, we exhibit sexual dimorphism—varying phenotypic traits that distinguish the two sexes. These range from traits directly involved with our different reproductive roles all the way to those physical features that allow anthropologists to determine the race of a skeleton.

Human males, on average, are larger and more heavily muscled than females. They have relatively larger hearts and lungs, a faster recovery time from muscle fatigue, higher blood pressure, and greater oxygen-carrying capacity. Males are more susceptible than females to disease and death at all stages of life. During the first year of life, one-third more males die, mostly from infectious disease. Males are also more likely to have speech disorders, vision and hearing problems, ulcers, and skin disorders.

Females have a greater proportion of body fat than do males. They mature faster at almost all stages of life, most notably exhibiting earlier puberty and adolescent growth spurt. They are less likely than males to be thrown off their normal growth curve [see Figure 13.14] by disease or other factors, and, if they are, will recover more quickly than males. Although females appear to have a greater tendency than males to become obese, males suffer more from the effects of too much weight—strokes, for example. Females seem to be more sensitive to touch and pain and perhaps to higher sound frequencies, and they are said to be better at locating the sources of sounds. (For more detail, see Barfield 1976.)

Although these dimorphic features are not completely understood or even well established, the trends they show do suggest an adaptive explanation. Many of the characteristics of the human male are aimed at sustained, stressful physical action at the expense, however, of overall health. Females are healthier, become sexually mature earlier, and they seem more sensitive to stimulation of the senses. These traits might be geared toward their reproductive and child-rearing roles. Perhaps some basic themes of primate dimorphism (we find the size and strength differences in apes as well) were retained and some others selected for in our early ancestors as their small, cooperative bands (described in Chapter 10) confronted the challenges of life on the savannas.

At any rate, although there is some individual and regional variation in the degree and nature of our sexually dimorphic traits, in general we rarely have any difficulty telling the **sex** of another human being. Male and female are two biological categories that are objectively real and are common to all human groups.

As these two real categories are incorporated into various cultural systems, however, differences arise. The identity, place, and role of males

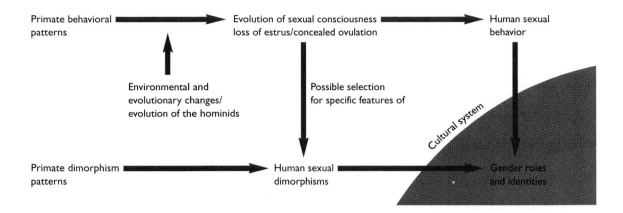

Primate behavioral patterns → Evolution of sexual consciousness loss of estrus/concealed ovulation → Human sexual behavior

Environmental and evolutionary changes/ evolution of the hominids

Possible selection for specific features of

Cultural system

Primate dimorphism patterns → Human sexual dimorphisms → Gender roles and identities

FIGURE 14.2
The sexual identities and roles common to all members of the human species are translated by individual cultural systems into gender identities and roles.

and females under different cultural systems vary depending upon the nature of those systems—their economies, politics, family organizations, and abstract beliefs. Thus, *males* and *females* of the human species become the *men* and *women* of a particular society practicing a particular culture. We refer to the cultural interpretation of biological sex categories as **gender** (Figure 14.2).

From cultural anthropology we acquire data about the incredible range of variation in gender identity and role among the world's cultures. The variable factors include the roles of each gender in economic activities, differences in political and other decision-making power and influence, and expected norms of behavior.

For example, in the United States only a century ago, men were seen as the gender that properly had political, economic, and social power and that, therefore, should be educated. Women were far less likely to receive a college education, seldom held any sort of management position (if they did any work outside the home at all), and until 1920, were not even allowed to vote. Women were sometimes thought of as "the weaker sex." Obviously, things are different now, at least to a degree. As our culture has changed over the last hundred years, our gender roles and identities have changed to fit our evolving cultural system.

We refer to culturally defined categories as **folk taxonomies,** or cultural classifications. A society of people orders its world in ways that reflect objective reality as its people see and understand that reality, and that also meet its particular cultural needs and fit the totality of its cultural system.

To take an example from a different area, our society has a scientific viewpoint about the causes of disease. We understand that diseases are the results of natural processes, and one way we classify them is by the nature of their cause. Diseases are genetic, bacterial, viral, parasitic, environmen-

sex: The biological categories and characteristics of males and females.

gender: The cultural categories and characteristics of men and women.

folk taxonomies: Cultural categories for important items and ideas.

FIGURE 14.3
Hijras, emasculated men who dress and behave like women, make up a third gender category in India. These hijras are blessing a child, one important ritual function they perform.

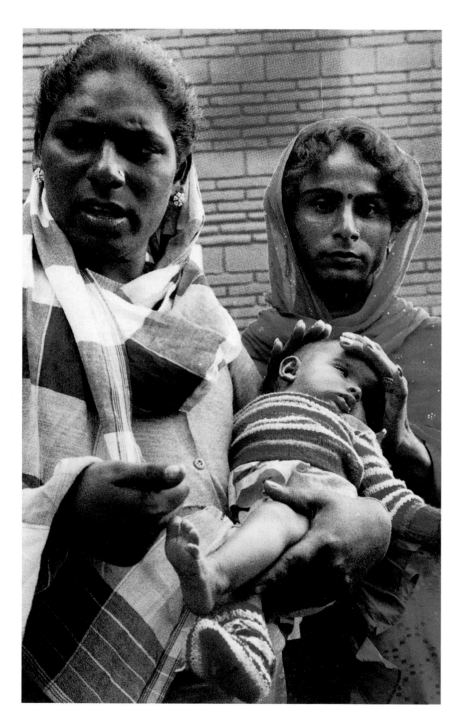

tal (drugs, radiation, pollutants), nutritional, congenital (where the development of the embryo is disrupted), emotional, and so on.

The Fore (Fo-RAY), a farming people of Papua New Guinea (Lindenbaum 1979), also classify disease by cause, but the causes are very different. The Fore believe that all disease is the result of the malicious intent of either sorcerers or spirits. Life-threatening diseases are thought to be caused by sorcery—malevolent action of one person against another. This reflects the political and economic tensions, rivalries, and jealousies that have become prevalent parts of Fore lives. Less severe diseases are caused by nature spirits inhabiting important places or by the ghosts of the recently deceased. These diseases are punishments for violating important norms with regard to nature or the dead. Very minor illnesses are attributed to a person's having violated some social rule among the living. The Fore folk taxonomy for disease, though it differs a great deal from our own, makes perfect sense within the context of the Fore cultural system.

Similarly, folk taxonomies for gender differ to a great degree among the cultures of the world even though we are all dealing basically with two sexes and two gender categories. We need to note, however, that biological sex is not always unambiguous. There are people born with underdeveloped sexual characteristics or with characteristics (including genitalia) of both sexes. In addition, there are those who are ambivalent toward their own sexual identity. As a result, some cultures recognize more than two genders.

A striking example is the *hijras* of India (Nanda 1990). The word means "not men," and, indeed, *hijras* are men who have been surgically emasculated. They make up a third gender, and they have very specific identities and roles within the culture of Hindu India. Although often mocked and ridiculed because of their exaggerated feminine expressions and gestures, they are also in demand as performers at important rituals such as marriages and births (Figure 14.3).

A less extreme example comes from a number of American Indian cultures where some men dressed as women and assumed the occupations and behaviors of women. Such men have been referred to by the term *berdache*. In some cases, they engaged in sexual relations with other men, and certain rituals could be performed only by them. In the cultures in which they were found, *berdaches* were not considered abnormal but were thought of as another gender. (Since *berdaches*, a French derivation of a Persian word, has derogatory implications, anthropologists have recently suggested the use of either specific terms from native languages or the use of a generic term, "two-spirit" to cover any instance of multiple gender categories.)

It appears, then, that some societies acknowledge that certain of their members are, or think of themselves as, ambiguous with regard to the two standard sex categories. These societies have evolved third or even fourth

FIGURE 14.4

The caribou, *Rangifer tarandus*. This woodland caribou of Alaska and Canada is sometimes classified as subspecies *Rangifer tarandus caribou*. Well adapted to a wide range of environments, among the caribou's traits are hollow outer guard hairs that give it extra bouyancy for swimming and extra insulation for warmth. This feature makes caribou hides a favorite material among the Inuit for making parkas.

gender classifications to accommodate them, and these classifications have developed defined places, identities, and roles within those societies' cultures. Sex is biological. Gender is a folk taxonomy. So, as we will see, is race in humans.

RACE AS A BIOLOGICAL CONCEPT

The processes of evolution assure that each species of living thing possesses genetic variation and displays some degree of phenotypic variation. Some species are more variable than others, depending upon the nature of the species' geographic distribution and the variety of specific environments to which its members are adapted.

As noted in Chapter 5, some species are said to be specialized. They inhabit a relatively small geographic area or are adapted to a highly specific set of ecological circumstances—a narrow niche. Such species, of course, tend to be relatively genetically and phenotypically homogeneous. Natural selection has selected for essentially the same characteristics in all members of specialized species. A classic example is the koala that lives only in Australia and eats primarily the leaves of the eucalyptus tree. We would not expect koalas to show a whole lot of variation, and they don't.

A species that inhabits a wide geographic range and is adapted to many specific niches is said to be generalized. Selection will promote different versions of the species' basic traits in response to the environments found in different parts of its range. Such species are more variable.

To remain a single species, of course, all males and females of the group must be potentially capable of interbreeding. There must be sufficient gene flow to prevent one or more groups from becoming completely isolated. Gene flow, however, is not always even. Members of a species may be clustered into breeding populations or demes (see Chapter 4). More genes are exchanged within demes than between different demes, often because some geographic barrier prevents extensive gene flow or because the environments to which the species are adapted come in clusters themselves with gaps between them that limit steady genetic exchange (see Figure 4.6).

Demes may be thought of as an important stage in many cases of speciation. If a deme becomes so isolated that virtually no genes are exchanged, if its environment is different enough to cause selection for a distinct set of traits, and if enough time elapses, the deme may eventually become a separate species, unable to interbreed with what were formerly other demes of the same species.

If, however, isolation is not complete or the conditions above have not been going on for a long enough time, the demes may represent phenotypically distinguishable regional populations within the same species. Such a species is said to be **polytypic** ("many types"), and such demes may be referred to as **subspecies** or **races.**

For example, reindeer of Europe and Asia and caribou of North America are classified as a single species, *Rangifer tarandus* (Figure 14.4). Now isolated from one another in separate hemispheres, the reindeer and caribou were no doubt once able to interbreed when Alaska and Siberia were joined during the Pleistocene, connecting the Old and New Worlds. Reindeer and caribou, then, have been separated for only a few thousand years, generally not enough time for speciation to have occurred. Enough time has elaspsed, however, for the two populations to become physically distinguishable. They may be considered subspecies or races of a single species.

The North American population of this species has been further classified into at least four subspecies, the result of their distribution in different environments of Alaska, Canada, and Greenland. These subspecies, some woodland and some tundra dwellers, are distinguishable by such

polytypic: A species with physically distinguishable regional populations.

subspecies: A physically distinguishable population within a species.

races: In biology, the same as subspecies. In culture, cultural categories to classify and account for human diversity.

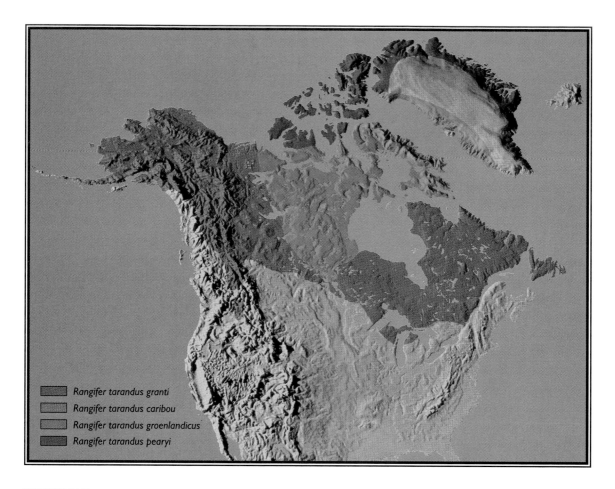

Rangifer tarandus granti
Rangifer tarandus caribou
Rangifer tarandus groenlandicus
Rangifer tarandus pearyi

FIGURE 14.5

North American populations of caribou are considered by some to represent subspecies or races.

features as size, antler shape, and coat color (Figure 14.5). There are, then, five named subspecies or races of *Rangifer tarandus*, at least one in the Old World and four in the New World.

The utility of the race/subspecies concept, however, has been questioned. The identification and naming of subspecific groups is rather arbitrary. Zoologists Paul Ehrlich and Richard Holm (in Montagu 1964) noted two problems with the idea. First, we need to decide *what* phenotypic traits we should choose in defining racial groups within a species. Are all traits equally useful, or are some more useful than others? If so, which ones?

Second, we need to decide *how* much difference in phenotypic characters should be recognized as amounting to subspecific difference. A certain number of traits? A particular degree of difference in the measurements of certain traits?

One might well be justified in calling the caribou and reindeer subspecies, but their complete isolation in separate hemispheres for the last

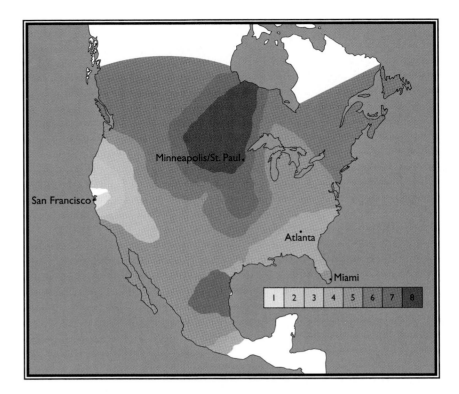

FIGURE 14.6
Distribution of size variation in male house sparrows, determined by sixteen skeletal measurements. The larger the number, the larger the sparrow. The classes, however, are arbitrary. If a line is drawn from Atlanta to St. Paul or from St. Paul to San Francisco, the size variation in the sparrows is distributed as a cline, a continuum of change from one area to another. Notice also that the birds tend to be larger in the north, another example of this adaptation to cold (see Chapter 13).

10,000 years might mean they are on the way to becoming separate species. This state is better acknowledged with the use of the term **semispecies**— populations at an intermediate state between being a single interbreeding group and being different species. They still *can* interbreed (it has been done artificially), but they *don't*.

The four North American races pose a different problem. Because all the groups of caribou do exchange genes as members of a single species, it really becomes a matter of judgment as to whether their different environments, geographic ranges, and phenotypic features constitute distinct enough differences to warrant subspecific or racial designations.

Recent books in evolutionary biology seem either to treat race as one of the steps toward the evolution of new species (for example, Mettler et al. 1988) or do not mention either "subspecies" or "race" at all (for example, Ridley 1993). Indeed, the latter makes the point that all species show some variation among their populations and that, more often than not, the distribution of this variation is in the form of a **cline**—a continuum of change from one area to another, as opposed to sudden and absolutely distinct changes (Figure 14.6). Many biologists, then, do not recognize the subspecies or race concept as a valid description for what actually occurs in a natural species. With these views in mind, we can now address the question of human biological races.

semispecies: Populations of a species that are completely isolated from one another but have not yet become truly different species.

cline: A geographic continuum in the variation of a particular trait.

ARE THERE HUMAN RACES?

Based upon the discussion above, the easiest answer would be to say that, because there are many who find no validity in the biological concept of race to begin with, there simply *cannot* be any human races. But the human species does display a number of visible polymorphic traits, many of which show some regularity in terms of their geographic distribution (see again Figure 14.1). Could we, then, be like the caribou of North America—distributed in distinct enough breeding populations that the concept *could* be applied, arbitrary though it may be? After all, we have applied it, even in anthropology.

We may formalize the conditions required for subspecific classification by those who apply the concept. These conditions are (1) some degree of population isolation with limited gene flow, (2) environments different enough to promote adaptive selection in different directions, (3) genetic variation among the populations, and (4) enough time. How well does our species meet these criteria?

The latest evidence (Chapter 12) indicates that *Homo sapiens* has been around for about 400,000 years. This is, theoretically, enough time even for speciation to have occurred if all the other conditions were met. However, since modern humans first arose and while we have been spreading and moving about, no human population has been isolated long enough, or to a complete enough degree, to allow even moderately separate and independent genetic events to take place. During all this time, humans have in fact become increasingly mobile, and it seems fair to say that we exchange genes at most every opportunity.

To be sure, cultural rules of endogamy exist, and they do tend to genetically isolate certain populations at certain times. The rules, however, change, and the political, ethnic, and religious populations defined by the rules change through time. The rules, in addition, are not always fully upheld. Endogamy is a temporary condition.

Gene flow, then, is the norm for our species, and, as widespread as we are, we still manage to exchange enough genes—through intermediary populations—even between the most far-flung of our peoples. As Stephen Jay Gould puts it, "I do not belong to a separate species from my brethren in Brazil just because I have never been there" (1992:43).

What about different environments? As noted in the previous chapter, some (if not many) of our polymorphisms may be attributed to natural selection in response to differing environmental circumstances. But culture is our major adaptive mechanism. Even where natural selection has had an effect on certain traits of our species—such as skin color or maybe blood type—these adaptive differences are minor compared to our major adaptation of culture, with its values, social systems, and technologies.

The cultural adaptation was well developed and part of our hominid line long before modern humans arose. Think of the place of culture in the success of *Homo erectus*. Our big brains—the basis for the cultural potential—are shared by all modern humans and are so basic to our modern identity that they are unlikely to show much major variation. Furthermore, the products of the cultural ability—social systems, beliefs, technologies—act as a buffer against much of the effect of biological natural selection. Had I been a Neandertal only 40,000 years ago, I might well have been selected out long ago, even if my group took care of me. But, today, my eyeglasses, blood pressure medication, and an emergency appendectomy—among other things—have kept me going well beyond average Neandertal life expectancy. Culture, in a sense, *is* our environment. Thus, it may well be said that we all share that environment and that there is, therefore, little environmental variation in our species.

Finally, as recent genetic studies have shown, we are not a very genetically diverse species to begin with. About 75 percent of all human genes are monomorphic (having only one allele); that is, all humans are identical for three-quarters of the human **genome** (Lewontin 1982:120). This is a higher percentage than in chimpanzees. The genetic variation that does exist—the remaining 25 percent of our genes multiple alleles—is actually fairly evenly distributed. Richard Lewontin (1982:123) calculates that if some great cataclysm left only Africans alive, that remnant of the human species would still retain 93 percent of the total genetic variation of the former population of the species, although certain traits, like skin color, would have different *average* expressions.

The human species, then, fails in theory to meet the criteria for division into subspecies. And we may strengthen the argument by looking at the variable traits themselves. Examined closely, we see that no real boundaries exist between trait expressions. Although I divided skin color into five categories for the sake of the map on Figure 13.11, those divisions were arbitrary. Skin color does not change abruptly as the map may imply. It changes gradually in populations closer to or farther from the equator. In other words, skin color is distributed as a cline. It does not come in neat packages with clear geographic limits. Neither, for example, does blood type, as a look at Figure 13.12 clearly shows.

Moreover, when we compare the distributions of human polymorphisms, we see that the distributions are "discordant." The distribution of one trait rarely matches the distribution of any other. Thus, a subspecific or racial division based on the distribution of one trait will invariably differ from that based on another (Fig. 14.7, and compare again Figures 13.11 and 13.12). At the biological level, then, *human variation exists, but human races don't.*

Does this mean, however, that our species is one gigantic "stew" of people with no discernable groups and thus no way to trace and understand

genome: The total genetic endowment of a species.

FIGURE 14.7
Diagram of discordant variation. Each layer represents the geographic variation in one polymorphism. Each "core" represents a sample of individuals from a particular area. Notice that each core is different and that any other four cores would also be different. The expression of one trait does not predict a particular expression of another. There are no natural racial divisions based on specific combinations of traits.

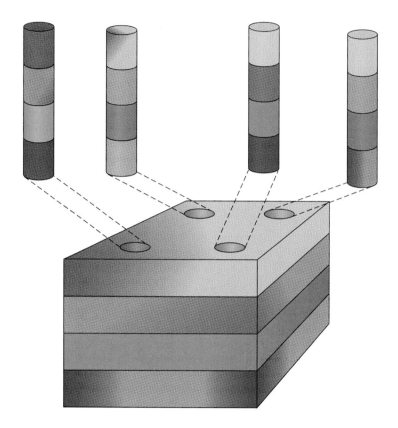

the history of our populations? Whereas phenotypic traits only serve to confuse the matter, our increasing knowledge of genetics does allow us to compare living populations to one another, to understand what genetic variation does exist, and to begin to build a family tree determining where populations originated, how they are related, and how they spread.

Such an analysis is essentially an extension of that done with mitochondrial DNA as described in Chapter 12. Figure 12.20 showed a tree of relationships among populations from which the mtDNA samples were drawn. Those data were limited, however. A more extensive study was done by L. L. Cavalli-Sforza and colleagues (summarized in Cavalli-Sforza 1991) that used more than 100 different inherited traits of 3000 individuals taken from 1800 populations. The study compared proteins, the direct products of the genes. A second study used actual DNA code sequences. There was marked agreement among the analyses.

Once again, genetic analysis strongly suggests that *Homo sapiens* arose in Africa and then spread out through a series of major migrations (Fig. 14.8). Moreover, distribution of genes coincided to a great degree with the distribution of languages. Languages and genetic populations can be correlated because, as human populations split and separate, "each fragment evolves linguistic and genetic patterns that bear marks of shared branching points. . . . [Furthermore], linguistic differences [and the cultural differences they reflect] may generate or reinforce genetic barriers between populations. Hence, some correlation is inevitable" (Cavalli-Sforza 1991:109). Figure 14.9 is a simplified diagram of this correlation.

We can conclude that our species does not sort itself into clear-cut and profoundly different racial or subspecific groups. We are too mobile, too genetically homogeneous, and too culturally adapted. But the richness of our genetic, ethnic, and cultural variety is not lost within some worldwide melting pot. There *are* human populations, identified by correlated biological and, mostly, cultural factors. And this brings us to the next question.

FIGURE 14.8
Movement and timing of modern *Homo sapiens* from its first appearance in Africa. These data are based on DNA comparisons of modern populations as described in the text.

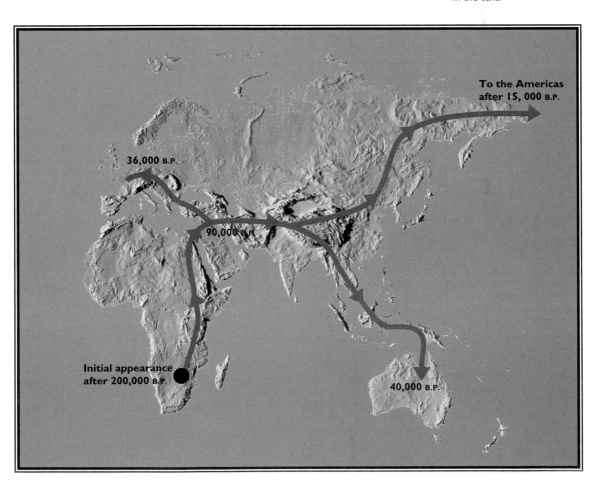

FIGURE 14.9
Chart of the correlation between genetic and linguistic groups in modern humans. The living populations listed are a representative sample. Note that where populations live close to one another under similar environmental conditions, as is the case for Ethiopians and Southwest Asians, they may speak languages of the same group even though they are genetically different.

Genetic Groups	Living Populations	Linguistic Groups
African	San	Khoisan
	Masai	Nilo-Saharan
	Mbuti	Niger-Congo
	Ethiopian	Afro-Asiatic
Caucasoid	Southwestern Asian	
	Mediterranean	Indo-European
	Northern European	
	Indian	
American	North American	Amerind
	Central American	
	South American	
Arctic	Eskimo	Eskimo-Aleut
	Siberian	
Northeast Asian	Japanese	Altaic
	Korean	
	Tibetan	Sino-Tibetan
Mainland Island Southeast Asian	Southern Chinese	
	Indonesian	
	Philippine	Austronesian
	Polynesian	
Pacific Islands	Melanesian	Indo-Pacific
	New Guinean	Australian
	Australian	

WHAT, THEN, *ARE* HUMAN RACES?

Like gender categories, human races are folk taxonomies. Several years ago I gave one of my classes a weekend assignment to ask ten people, preferably from different backgrounds and of different ages and both sexes, two questions: How many races are there? What are they?

Nearly all the responses were versions of a familiar set of categories: "white," "black," and "yellow," or "Caucasian," "Negro," and "Oriental," or some other terms that varied with the individual. The similarity of most responses is an indication that some basic taxonomy is shared among members of our culture.

However, there was some interesting variation in the responses as well. One respondent said there were three races, "black," "white," and "Polish." Jews were considered a race by some, as were Hispanics. A few people, who I guessed had done some reading on the subject, added American Indians and native Australians to the usual three. This showed that, despite the similarities, there was no universally agreed upon classification, as there would be for some scientific fact like the number of planets in the solar system or the names of dog breeds. Specific responses were as variable as the individual backgrounds of the respondents.

Cultures classify other people relative to themselves. Isolated societies with some knowledge that others exist will have a very simple racial classification: us and them. As knowledge accumulates among more mobile or cosmopolitan groups and as the relations among people become more varied, the classifications become more complex. Knowledge about other groups includes such things as their cultural practices, their relations with your group, and their physical appearance. Thus, a racial taxonomy also carries implications about a society's attitude toward others. In short, race—which differs from society to society—is a folk taxonomy, used by a particular society, at a particular time, for particular, culturally based reasons.

The categories of race that we in the United States recognize are no exception. The categories' origins can be traced to European knowledge and attitudes first acquired during the Age of Exploration. European explorers, using mostly water transporation, were limited in the range and distribution of human variation they could observe. They sampled points along the continuum of human variation. Because points along a continuum can differ greatly from one another, depending upon how far apart they are, it appeared that human variation fell into a number of relatively discrete categories (Figure 14.10).

In addition, the peoples contacted were not seen as simply different human beings; instead, they were compared to and ranked against European peoples, usually unfavorably. They were, after all, of different appearance, with different cultures, often with less complex technologies, and—this was important to the Europeans—with non-Christian religions. Furthermore, the motivation for the explorers' voyages was less to acquire knowledge than to find new territories, sources of labor, spices, and gold. A dominant attitude was built in to the European's relationships with these new peoples. Witness the way in which Europeans would claim new

FIGURE 14.10
Columbus's first contact with natives of the New World. To the Europeans, the Indians were so strikingly different in physical and cultural features that it was natural to consider them as a distinct category of human. (From a seventeenth-century Spanish version of a 1594 engraving by de Bry. The Granger Collection.)

lands "in the name of the crown," entirely ignoring the fact that there were already people to whom the lands belonged. Obviously, it was thought, the indigenous people were too primitive to really have laws of ownership.

The racial folk taxonomy that resulted from these cultural events was formalized, and thus made more real, by Linnaeus. In the final edition of his taxonomy in 1758, he included *Homo sapiens* and divided the species into varieties or races. Not surprisingly, he recognizes four races of humans (five if you count a category called "wild man," apparently a catch-all to account for populations, mostly mythical, that did not fit the other four). His main races are American, European, Asiatic, and African, and his descriptions of these races are a blend of biological generalizations and, as Stephen Molnar says (1992:10), "personality profiles" based on European perspectives. Here is Linnaeus's description of Africans, for example:

> Black, phlegmatic [sluggish], relaxed. Hair black, frizzled; skin silky; nose flat; lips tumid [swollen]; crafty, indolent, negligent. Anoints himself with grease. Governed by caprice [impulse]. (Kennedy 1976:25).

Europeans, of course, were "brawny," "gentle," "inventive," "covered with cloth vestments," and "governed by laws" (Kennedy 1976:25).

Because the history of the United States has been so influenced by European cultures, it stands to reason that the European folk taxonomy with regard to race—the categories and the attitudes they implied—was carried over and affected our country's culture. Our racial categories are real. They may not reflect universal biological reality on the species level, but they do have meaning within our cultural system, for better or for worse.

RACE, BIOANTHROPOLOGY, AND SOCIAL ISSUES

The issue of race in the human species is not just a matter of whether or not to apply the biological concept of subspecies. Would that it were. Rather, the idea of race can be, and is, used to make prejudgments about people and to determine a person's place in society, often without regard to that person's individual characteristics. This is **racism.** The moral dimension of this problem, though it should be important to everyone, is not something we can or should deal with in a brief book about science. We may, however, show how bioanthropology, through the use of science, can examine some claimed connections between racial categories and biological traits. In so doing, we can help make ourselves more informed about just what race is and what it is not.

Let's briefly look at one topic. If your goal is to limit the social place and power of a particular group, one of the strongest arguments you can propose is that the population in question possesses some unalterable biological difference that inherently limits their abilities and therefore justifies their lower social position. Slavery in the United States was often justified by the claim that the black slaves were biologically less intelligent than the whites and therefore could never hope to attain the dominant race's social, political, and intellectual level. Claims like this have been quite common, even during the last century (Gould 1981).

Such broad statements about race and intelligence, or even race and evolutionary level, are so clearly motivated by social and economic situations as to be at least questionable, if not obviously false. Perhaps more

racism: Judging an individual based solely on his or her racial affiliation.

dangerous, however, are the more subtle correlations whose propositions are based on scientific investigation. Ideas that sound scientific are often treated more seriously, especially because, even today, many people feel that science is something so complex and obscure that only a handful can really understand it. Many people take the position that if something sounds scientific and they don't get it, it must be valid.

Such is the case for the claimed connection between the American black and white races and IQ (intelligence quotient). The most famous (or infamous) example is educational psychologist Arthur Jensen's 1969 article in the *Harvard Educational Review* titled "How much can we boost IQ and scholastic achievement?" The article is 123 pages long and quite scientific in its wording, logic, and methodology, and it includes a lengthy mathematical formula or two. (As a result, many people, both supporters and critics of Jensen's work, have never bothered to actually read it.)

A focus of Jensen's article was on the documented fact that American black children score, on average, fifteen points lower on IQ tests than American white children. Jensen wondered why programs aimed at the obvious solution of culturally enriching children's lives had basically failed. Some studies showed that the fifteen-point IQ difference remained. Hence, the title of his article (emphasis mine for the right intonation): "How much *can* we boost IQ and scholastic achievement?"

Jensen embarks on a scientific investigation. His first conclusion is that IQ tests measure something called *g*, or general intelligence—a biological, inherited entity. This entity, *g*, has a **heritability** of .80 (80 percent). This means that 80 percent of the variation in intelligence within a population is explained by genetic differences. Only 20 percent is the result of members of that group having been brought up in different cultural environments. (It bears restating that heritability measures the amount of *variation within a group* that is due to genetic differences. It does not measure the amount of genetic control of a trait in an individual. It does not say that 80% of my intelligence is genetically determined.)

The obvious conclusion, then, is that the difference in intelligence between the two racial groups in question must be largely the result of some genetic difference, and, thus, all the cultural enrichment programs in the world can only have a limited effect. The answer to the question in Jensen's title is, "Not much." He states, "No one has yet produced any evidence based on a properly controlled study to show that representative samples of Negro and white children can be equalized in intellectual ability through statistical control of environment and education" (1969:82–83).

Jensen went further, however. He compared scores from different parts of IQ tests and concluded that the different IQs of blacks and whites is the result of their having different kinds of intellectual abilities. Whites are better at problem solving and abstract reasoning, while the abilities of blacks are focused on memorization, rote learning, and trial-and-error experience. His ultimate conclusion was that education should be as individualized as possible, taking into account not only individual differences in ability and skill but these racially based differences as well.

As you can imagine, Jensen's article caused a great deal of controversy. He was labeled a racist, and, certainly, those with racist leanings embraced his work enthusiastically. I don't know what Jensen's social attitudes were, but I can look at his article from a scientific point of view, drawing especially on what we have learned from anthropology.

First, the idea that IQ tests measure some innate mental ability is fraught with problems. It has been said that IQ tests measure the ability to take IQ tests. This is not, as it sounds, just a sarcastic remark. IQ tests, in fact, measure particular knowledge and abilities that are largely learned through one's culture. They are valuable. They may, in fact, point out some learning disability that may turn out to be biologically based. Because they measure the kinds of skills required by education in our culture as well as by many occupations, they do have predictive value as to one's success within those aspects of our cultural system.

We do not even know, however, what intelligence is. How can we—through a test given in a cultural language, in a cultural setting, with cultural problems—apply a single number to such a complex and multifaceted concept? When we do this, we call it **reification.** With IQ scores we have reified intelligence—translated a complex idea into a single entity, in this case, a number, which we then use to classify people into groups such as different learning tracks in schools.

Let's put this another way. As anthropologist Jonathan Marks suggests, there is a difference between *ability* and *performance* (Marks 1995: 240 ff.). One's score on an IQ test is a score of one's performance. Certainly some internal factor—one's innate intellectual abilities, whatever those are—plays a part in one's performance on an IQ test. But that performance is also affected by all sorts of external factors. In test taking, for example, one's cultural background, quality of education, personality, home life, even one's mood on the day of the test can all effect one's performance on a test. We cannot, therefore, infer innate abilities from the score on a test, any more than we can, say, infer a person's athletic abilities from their performance in one game. We cannot do so, in part, because there *are* so many external influences; and we have no way of accounting for them, controlling them, or even knowing what they are. More importantly, though, to make such an inference from IQ is to reify intelligence—to take the measurement of performance on a test and assume that it is also a measurement of an innate ability. As Marks puts it, "We can't measure ability; we can only measure performance" (1995: 241).

But what about the claimed heritability of IQ? This is a complicated issue (see Gould 1981 for the best discussion), but there is one major

heritability: The amount of variation of a particular trait within a population that is caused by genetic differences.

reification: Translating a complex set of phenomena into a single entity such as a number.

problem we can point out here. Heritability studies—estimating the genetic and environmental components of the phenotypic variation in a population—are done regularly, but these studies are done on organisms like fruit flies, where the genetic mechanisms for phenotypic traits are well known (and can even be manipulated) and where the environmental variables can be controlled in detail. Numbers may be placed on these genetic and environmental variables which may then be plugged into the heritability formula. This is the formula that Jensen reproduces in his article.

To apply the heritability formula to humans, however, is virtually impossible. What numbers can we place on the external environmental variables that affect us? How, in other words, can we reify culture? What number is applied to having a culturally enriched childhood, to being a member of a minority group, or to having a poor early education?

Heritability has been *estimated* for humans based on twin studies. Because identical twins have no genetic variation between them, any phenotypic difference, including intelligence, must be the result of environmental differences. IQ scores of identical twins are generally very similar, even in twins raised separately, and this seems to indicate that environment has little effect on intelligence. We must remember, however, that IQ does not measure intelligence, but rather performance on an exam. Therefore, IQ is measuring, to a great extent, the results of environmental influences in the first place and not the results of genetic endowment. Even in twins raised apart, it may well be that their environments are similar enough to result in similar IQ scores. On those rare occasions when identical twins are separated shortly after birth, it would be likely that they are raised in homes of similar socioeconomic level and so they receive educations of similar quality. It cannot be denied that identical twins are probably similar in whatever those innate abilities are that we call intelligence, but studies based on the IQ scores of such twins are reflecting a whole lot more than those innate abilities.

To further claim that two races have different kinds of intellectual abilities is to ignore the very nature of the modern human species. This claim says that there is a major degree of difference in the very abilities—to solve problems or to formulate abstractions and generalizations—that are a hallmark of our species' evolution. Certainly, we express individual variation in some of these abilities, and some of this variation may well be based on some sort of biological difference. I have no doubt that Beethoven and Einstein had some fundamental innate processes going on in their brains that I don't. But to think that natural selection would promote, in two different groups, profoundly different expressions of the major adaptive mechanism of a species makes little sense in light of what we know about the workings of adaptive evolution.

Finally, if you are looking to make biological comparisons between two groups, the groups need to be biologically defined. American whites and American blacks are decidedly not biological races. We have already established that race is not a biological concept for the human species (or, perhaps, for any other species) in the first place. What variation does exist is distributed in such a way as to make distinct, discrete groups of *Homo sapiens* nonexistent. We perceive differences in these two groups—average skin color, major geographic area of origin, frequency of diseases like hypertension, and even frequency of some genes such as that for sickle cell anemia—but the groups themselves are cultural. There's simply not much genetic difference, certainly not on the level of genes for different intellectual abilities. Indeed, it has been estimated that about 15 percent of all genes in African Americans have come from European Americans because of the extent of gene flow between the two populations over the last several hundred years (Lewontin 1982).

An analogy may make this discussion about race and intelligence a little clearer. Just as there is a documented difference in the average IQ scores of European Americans and African Americans, it is also a fact that most professional basketball players are black, and, today, the biggest stars of the game are African Americans like Michael Jordan, Shaquille O'Neal, and Charles Barkley, to name just a few. The sport has become virtually associated with that racial group. It could be reasonably inferred from this fact that blacks are innately better basketball players than whites. But how reasonable is that inference, really? (For a more detailed discussion of this analogy, see Marks 1995: 240 ff.)

For one thing, we cannot infer a generalization about a whole group of people from a small sample. Professional basketball players are those who, due in large measure to some innate abilities, excel at the skills required for the game. In no way does it follow that all blacks have those skills, no more than it follows that all white European men have the ability to write the Ninth Symphony. It does not even follow that blacks are *more likely* to possess those skills than whites.

Why, then, the prevalence of blacks in the sport? Sports involve innate skills, but they are also performances and, as such, are influenced by complex external factors. The difference in socioeconomic status of those identified as white and black has made a difference in the opportunity that people have to play certain sports. In fact, just a few generations ago, most professional basketball players were white, because, except for boxing, blacks had little or no opportunity to participate in professional sports.

Even now that sports are open to all groups, the effects of those socioeconomic differences have an influence. To practice the skills of basketball, one needs only a hoop of some sort, an area to play, and a ball. These prerequisites can be found in every neighborhood. Swimming pools, golf gear, tennis courts, even baseball equipment are not as inexpensive nor as readily available. Moreover, with career choices more limited for black youths than for whites, an easily practiced sport becomes an increasingly popular focus. There may well be many white youths who have the innate abilities of a Jordan, O'Neal, or Barkley, but more athletically inclined black youths are interested in a career in basketball and so pursue it. Thus, more men who become professional basketball players are black.

Similarly, the difference in performance on IQ tests can be seen as heavily influenced by the socioeconomic limitations imposed on African Americans for the past several centuries, limitations that have resulted in separate and often poor quality education, limited access to various forms of cultural enrichment, and even the psychological effects of being identified as members of a minority group. These are all intangible factors that are impossible to fully control or even identify. Scores on IQ tests certainly involve some aspect of a person's innate intellectual abilities, but, again, because of all these external factors, we cannot infer those abilities from the results of test performances. And we certainly cannot make a biological generalization about a culturally defined group of people based on those performance results.

Our folk taxonomies are powerful and influential. We respond to them often without realizing that they are *our* culture's way of ordering *our* world and are not necessarily scientific universals. The influence of the American folk taxonomy for race can easily be seen in Jensen's work. By understanding what race is, and what it's not, and by applying what we know about the workings of genetics and evolution, we may see the fallacies of this particular piece of research. This perspective is an important one for helping us deal with the other issues of race that confront us almost daily.

SUMMARY

Human societies need to find order in, and to make sense of, the environments in which they live. Objective reality is, thus, translated into categories that have meaning within particular cultural systems. We call these categories folk taxonomies.

So important are the relationships between the sexes and the relative places in society of males and females that different cultural systems have evolved very different folk taxonomies for sex. These are gender roles and identities and, in some societies, may even include more than two genders if those societies have the need to formally classify persons of ambiguous sex or sexuality.

That humans in general display variable traits is obvious, on some level, to all societies, and so all cultural systems also include folk taxonomies for race. On a biological level, however, races or subspecies do not exist for our species. Indeed, the concept is falling from use in biology in general. But even if we attempt to apply the race concept to humans, we find that the biological nature of our species does not lend itself to division into clear-cut, discrete units.

So powerful is the folk taxonomy for race that our categories take on a reality beyond that which is warranted, and we find that we use them as cues to tell us how to think about other groups of people and how to treat them. We can all too easily confuse culture and biology, and this effect can even be seen in scientific investigations, such as those that look for some biological racial difference in the cultural measure of intelligence called IQ.

KEY TERMS

sex	subspecies	genome
gender	races	racism
folk taxonomies	semispecies	reification
polytypic	cline	

SUGGESTED READINGS

A good book on sex and gender from an anthropological perspective is *Female of the Species* by M. Kay Martin and Barbara Voorhies. Despite the title, it is really about both sexes and all the gender categories found in various cultural systems. The fascinating case of India's hijras is documented in *Neither Man Nor Woman: The Hijras of India* by Serena Nanda.

On race, I highly recommend Stephen Molnar's *Human Variation: Races, Types, and Ethnic Groups* for a text covering the entire issue as a part of anthropology. It includes sections on our polymorphic traits. Another treatment of the same subject, but from a biologist, is Richard Lewontin's *Human Diversity*. The newest book on the subject, and the one that includes an extended discussion of race and athletic ability, is Jonathan Marks's *Human Biodiversity: Genes, Race, and History*.

For a collection of articles on the nonexistence of human biological races, see *The Concept of Race* edited by Ashley Montagu, and for a nice treatment of the history of race studies, try Kenneth A. R. Kennedy's *Human Variation in Space and Time*.

The best book on racism, emphasizing an examination of scientific attempts to find correlations between race (and sex) and intelligence is Stephen Jay Gould's *The Mismeasure of Man*.

CHAPTER

15

BIOLOGICAL ANTHROPOLOGY: APPLICATIONS AND LESSONS

We too are part of
history's seamless web.
—Reinhold Niebuhr

As I am writing this, many flags in the country are still being flown at half-staff for the victims of the Oklahoma City bombing of April 19, 1995. The death toll stands at over 160. Many of the bodies were difficult to identify because they were literally blown apart by the blast, leaving only fragments.

One of the people involved in the grim task of identifying the dead was forensic anthropologist Clyde Snow, himself an Oklahoman. Though certainly not to everyone's taste, such work is one of the ways that biological anthropology can make a tangible contribution to our lives. It is, of course, unfortunate that such skills are needed. But they are, and the work of identifying human remains and, sometimes, of identifying the cause of their deaths, is an important one, bringing some comfort to the survivors and justice to the slain.

Although we feel that the work of all biological anthropologists is useful in its contribution to knowledge, there are some practical ways in which our field can be applied and some lessons we can learn from our unique perspective on our species. In this last chapter, we will address the simple question:

What are some of the applications and lessons of biological anthropology?

FORENSIC ANTHROPOLOGY: READING THE BONES

Forensic means relating to courts of law or public discussion, or, referring to the application of science to legal matters. The skills we use to retrieve information from ancient skeletons (see Chapter 9) has also proved useful in retrieving information from more modern ones—the victims of violent crimes and accidents. Forensic anthropology is increasingly called upon to examine skeletal remains and the conditions under which they were found so as to determine identity, time and cause of death, and any other information that may prove helpful to law enforcement agencies. In turn, some of the methods that have been developed by forensic anthropologists have been applied to older remains that are of strictly scientific, rather than legal, interest.

Perhaps the best-known case of the latter is the well-publicized "Ice Man." He was found by hikers in September, 1991, at over 10,000 feet in the Alps, just on the Italian side of the border with Austria. He had been naturally mummified by the dehydrating action of the cold and the wind and was in a remarkable state of preservation. This became all the more

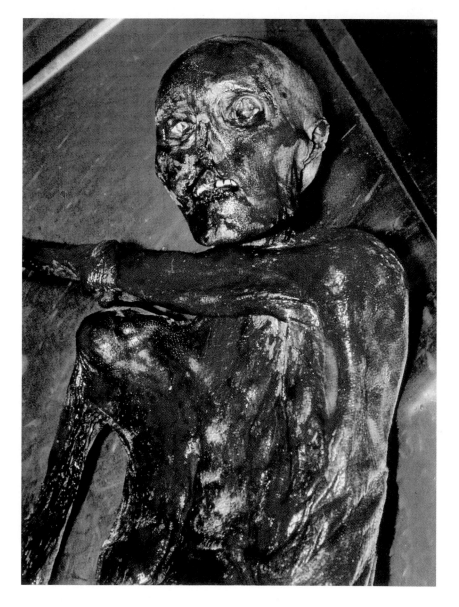

FIGURE 15.1
The Ice Man's body, pre-
served for over 5000 years
in the Italian Alps, was naturally mummified by cold and
wind. Pressure from the ice
disfigured his nose and lip
and pushed his left arm into
this odd position. We are
still learning about his life
and death from his preserved
body, which includes his
brain and internal organs.

remarkable when carbon-14 dating of the body itself, and of grass with which he had stuffed his boots, provided a date of 3300 B.C. The body was over 5000 years old.

The Ice Man was found with a fascinating array of artifacts, including much of his clothing and some tools. Details on these may be found in the references I'll give at the end. Here, we'll concentrate on the body itself (Figure 15.1).

Investigators x-rayed the body and, using techniques we discussed in Chapter 9, determined that it was that of a male about 5 feet 2 inches tall who died in his late twenties or thirties. Oddly, he had only eleven pairs of ribs, instead of the usual twelve, and eight of these had been broken at one time or another but were healed, or were healing, at the time of his death. He had arthritis of the neck, lower back, and right hip, and the joints of his knees and ankles were worn. There is some evidence of hardening of the arteries, and his lungs were blackened, probably by smoke from open fires.

There are odd sets of parallel lines on the Ice Man's lower back, left thigh, and right ankle that resemble tattoos. One hypothesis is that these are related to the arthritic and joint pain he probably suffered in those areas. Some cultures are known to use hot brands as treatments for such ailments.

There is a good deal of wearing down of the Ice Man's teeth, some of which can be clearly seen on his upper incisors. This probably indicates that he used his teeth as tools, perhaps for leather working, and that he ate a tough diet including dried meat and the products of flour from grains that had been mixed with sand to aid in grinding. Both practices are known from the archaeological record.

His diet, however, may not have been particularly good. Patterns on a fingernail recovered later (the others had fallen off) are consistent with signs of periods of reduced nail growth from disease or malnutrition.

How did the Ice Man die? We may never know for sure, but we may make a good guess. There was no evidence that insects had laid any eggs on his body, and some sloe berries were found along with him. These facts point to his death in late summer or early fall, when insect reproductive activity has ceased and when the berries are available. It is a time when the weather in that area can turn suddenly and unexpectedly bad. Given his ill health and possible poor diet, he may simply have been caught in foul weather and froze to death.

Finally, in part to put to rest the inevitable questions about a possible fraud, mitochrondrial DNA analysis was performed. It indicated that the Ice Man was a European and that he was related to living populations from the northern Alps. Techniques of reconstruction have even given us an idea of what he looked like (Figure 15.2).

All this information, and more, can be gleaned about a mummified corpse over fifty centuries old. When the Ice Man died, writing was just being invented in Mesopotamia, the great pyramids of Egypt had yet to be built, and the lives of Socrates, Julius Caesar, and Jesus were over 3000 years in the future.

As famous as the Ice Man is, we do not, of course, know his name. Forensic studies, however, have provided us with new information about some famous people whose names we are very familiar with. For example, forensic anthropologist William Maples (Maples and Browning 1994) has helped identify the skeletal remains of the assassinated Russian Tsar Nicholas II and his family. The bones did not, by the way, include those of Anastasia, the Tsar's daughter, said to have survived and escaped to the West.

Maples has examined the remains of U. S. President Zachary Taylor to prove that he was not murdered by arsenic poisoning. He has also helped identify the true remains of Spanish conquistador Francisco Pizarro and proved that a mummy reported to be Pizarro's was actually someone else's.

Clyde Snow identified a skeleton found in Brazil as that of Nazi war criminal Josef Mengele. The standard information about the skeleton fit what was known about Mengele, but Snow clinched it by superimposing images of the skull over photographs of the man known as the "Angel of Death." They matched, and the identification was verified shortly after when Mengele's dental records were discovered. Snow has also been involved in a review of the assassination of John F. Kennedy and has, as mentioned earlier, searched in Bolivia for the remains of the famous outlaws Butch Cassidy and the Sundance Kid, so far without success.

More important, however, than these cases of the rich and famous are those involving the remains of common, everyday people who, for one reason or another, need to be identified and, perhaps, who require justice. Clyde Snow has, for example, examined and tried to identify the remains of some of the more than 10,000 people who "disappeared" during the military rule in Argentina from 1976 to 1983. His evidence has been used to help prosecute some of those responsible. He has done similar work in the Philippines and in the Middle East, and he has helped identify the victims of airline crashes, such as the one that took place in Chicago in 1979 killing 273 people.

Smaller tragedies, however, are not outside the activities of the forensic anthropologist. For a typical example, we can look at one of Clyde Snow's cases, a case that, ironically, began around Oklahoma City (Snow and Luke 1970). In the summer of 1967, two young girls, aged five and six years, disappeared in the Oklahoma City area within a few weeks of one another. In November of that year, two hunters found some bones, including a human cranium, in a rural area outside the city. The bones were scattered on the surface. Further investigation, however, revealed a crude grave that contained more bones and children's clothing. An extensive excavation was conducted. Among the several hundred bones eventually recovered—most of which belonged to various nonhumans— were those of a young child. Snow investigated further to see if the bones could reveal a specific identity and perhaps a cause of death. There was a

good chance that these were the bones of one of the missing girls. Perhaps the remains of both the missing girls were present.

Snow determined that the bones had been buried fairly recently. They still had the greasy texture of fresh bone, and there were no signs of weathering that would indicate they had been there over winter. Although the bones had been damaged by scavengers, there were no rodent gnaw marks on them. Rodents gnaw well weathered bones as sources of minerals and protein. The bones were recent, but how recent?

They were completely skeletonized, but this could certainly have happened during the previous summer. It was shown that, in Oklahoma's climate, a child's body would be reduced to bone within two to six weeks. There were spider webs and other signs of insect activity in the skull, so it was determined that the bones had been completely exposed before cold weather set in and those creatures became inactive. Burial had occurred in early September at the latest.

Soon, the possibility that more than one human was represented was ruled out. The cause of death was a problem, though. Much of the skeleton was missing, and the bones that remained were found scattered about. Some of the bones were damaged, and some teeth were missing. None of this, however, could be clearly attributed to trauma before death or purposeful dismemberment afterward. More likely, it was the result of decom-

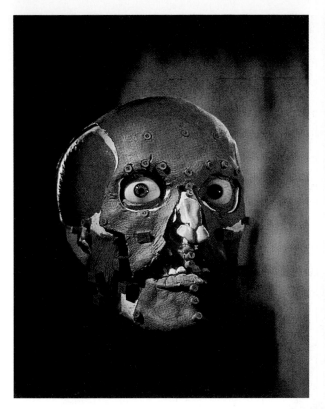

FIGURE 15.2
Artist John Gurche reconstructed the face of the Ice Man. He began with measurements, computer images, X rays, and CAT scans and produced a model of the Ice Man's skull. Next, he added clay to resemble the mummified face and then, like a plastic surgeon, rebuilt the face, reconstructing the nose and adding fatty tissue and muscles (represented by the red pegs) using anatomical data and his own interpretation from anthropological training.

position and the work of carnivorous scavengers that dug up the grave, scattered the bones, and carried off those with fleshy parts.

Determining the sex of the skeleton was difficult. No pelvis was found, nor was there enough of the remainder of the skeleton to make a good assessment for a preadolescent. The clothing found was that of a little girl, however.

Both the missing girls were white, and the presence of a Carabelli's cusp on one of the remaining teeth pointed to that population. Carabelli's cusp is a small dental feature found in about 50 percent of U. S. whites, 34 percent of blacks, and only 5 percent to 20 percent of American Indians. The incisors were not shovel-shaped, a form found in over 80 percent of American Indians. It was important to rule out American Indians since Oklahoma has a high Native American population. Some remaining hair verified the assessment, as its color and shape were those common to white populations.

Age was determined through cranial sutures, epiphyseal union, and dental eruption and development (see Chapter 9). In addition to the four separate bones of the cranial vault, each bone itself grows in separate pieces. The occipital, at birth, is in four pieces, which fuse together at four or five years of age. The occipital found was completely fused with no trace of sutures.

The epiphyses at the proximal (closest to the body) femur and radius, and the distal (farthest from the body) humerus were all open. These close at seventeen, fourteen, and fourteen years respectively. Taken with the evidence from the occipital, an age range of four to about fifteen was determined. This was narrowed to five to twelve years by looking at further sites of bone union in the vertebral column.

Both first permanent molars were fully erupted. The central incisors were missing, but the size and form of the sockets indicated that they too had erupted. Taking into account the range of variation at which eruption occurs among individuals, these data provided an age range of about five and a half to eight years. In addition, teeth, of course, develop below the gum line before they erupt, and X rays of the child's teeth further narrowed the age range to about six to eight years. The evidence, then, favored the skeleton being that of the older girl. Finally, stature was estimated using formulas that compare the length of various long bones to total height. The skeleton was estimated to have belonged to someone about 50 inches tall. The older missing girl was about that height, while the younger was 8 inches shorter.

Snow concluded that the remains probably belonged to one of the two missing girls. There had been no other unsolved cases of missing girls of that age from the area in several years. The bones most likely were those of the six year old. Sadly, the remains of the other girl have not been found, and no suspect has been identified. But Snow's forensic work helped strengthen the identification, which would have been little more than a good guess without the precise information he was able to extract by reading the bones.

LESSONS FROM THE PAST

Besides applying the skills of the biological anthropologist to legal matters, we may also apply the perspective of our discipline to areas of modern life. Our evolutionary perspective tells us that we are not a species that suddenly appeared a few million years ago nor are we, as modern humans, what evolution was somehow directed toward all along.

Rather, humans evolved from previous primate species. We are variations on the primate theme. We retain many of the major primate characteristics, and our unique features are still based on them. Moreover, in no way can we say that the modern manifestation of our species is the culmination or the best-adapted form of our evolutionary line. We have manipulated our environment, our very biology, and our behavior through culture, so our present environment may not be the one to which our species was biologically adapted. We may well learn a few valuable lessons by taking a closer look at what we were like in the past, before culture played so great a part in our lives.

For instance, anthropologists Marcia Thompson and David Harsha (1984) have looked at the daily routines of people in modern industrial societies such as ours and compared them with people in nonindustrial cultures and with tropical nonhumans. They conclude that, in the common structure of our work days, we are violating a pattern that evolved in our tropical ancestors and cousins that programs us for a two-peaked rhythm of daily activity, one peak in the late morning and another in the late afternoon, with a lull in between. That period of tiredness we often feel after lunch may have nothing to do with eating.

Tropical animals and people in many human societies take an afternoon break that originally may have been a response to the heat of the midafternoon sun but may now in humans be a real biological decrease in activity level. After all, they note, other bodily functions—more than 100 physiological and performance variables—fluctuate in predictable cycles during the twenty-four hours of our day. Thus, the afternoon nap is a natural phenomenon. (I knew it!)

Thompson and Harsha suggest that the best way we could respond to this, given that most of us can't nap, at least during weekdays, would be to move lunch back a few hours to correspond to the afternoon lull. As it is, we often take lunch during one of our peak activity periods. By taking into account a possible biological pattern, we might make ourselves more productive in our modern cultural environment.

Another anthropologist, James McKenna (Small 1992), has looked at sleep behavior of other primates and of people in other cultures and has noted that it is common for young babies to sleep with their parents. In the West, we have long been advised that babies should sleep by themselves, probably as a response to our emphasis on independence and the idea that the parents' lives, perhaps especially in bed, are separate from that of their children.

McKenna suggests that, in fact, infant nonhuman primates and human babies seem better off psychologically and physically if they sleep with their parents. In humans, this may even extend to help in learning to breathe properly. For humans, speech is so important that we have two kinds of breathing—automatic and controlled—and we need to learn to switch between kinds. In addition, remember that the vocal tract of infants is different from adult humans and is like those of chimpanzees in being higher in the throat at first. As the vocal tract begins to drop early in life, the baby goes through a great physical change.

These two facts—the development of the two kinds of breathing and the physical change in the vocal tract—may explain Sudden Infant Death Syndrome (SIDS), where babies inexplicably die in their sleep. It is thought that, perhaps because of miscues in regulating breathing, these babies stop breathing and fail to wake up so they can start again. Sleeping with a parent may help prevent this because such situations cause the baby to wake up periodically in response to the parent's movement and so the infant learns better how to jump between kinds of breathing. McKenna notes that SIDS is twice as common in the United States as in Japan, where infants normally sleep with parents.

We may also learn lessons about disease. The evolutionary perspective that sheds light on the nature of sickle cell anemia may also be applied to other diseases, especially those associated with particular populations. Biologist Jared Diamond (1991) offers an intriguing evolutionary explanation for the high frequency of Tay-Sachs disease among Eastern European (Ashkenazic) Jews and their descendents. Tay-Sachs is a lethal disease caused by a recessive gene. In homozygotes, it results in the body's inability to produce an enzyme that breaks down a particular fatty substance. This substance accumulates in nerve cells and literally destroys the victim's nervous system. Most sufferers die by age four. The disease is incurable and cannot be prevented.

Tay-Sachs has a frequency of about one in 400,000 worldwide but is found in one of every 3600 Ashkenazim. Other Jewish populations have Tay-Sachs no more often than the general population. The usual explanation for this incredibly high frequency is the founder effect. The founders of the Ashkenazic populations happened to have a high frequency of the gene, which then persisted through genetic drift, aided by the fact that it was usually hidden from natural selection as a recessive. Some of the other ten diseases that are overrepresented among Ashkenazim have been explained in this way (Glausiusz 1995) as has the high frequency of Tay-Sachs in a Pennsylvania Dutch population (see Chapter 4).

But Diamond contends that the founders of the Ashkenazim were large populations, and that their communities in Eastern Europe were widespread. The founder effect has significant results only in small populations. In the numerous and widespread communities, drift would have increased the frequency of the gene in some but decreased it in others. In addition, since these communities were first founded almost a thousand years ago, one would expect natural selection to have had sufficient time to decrease the frequency of this lethal gene to that found in the general population.

Moreover, it seems as if there are several different mutations along the same segment of DNA that can cause Tay-Sachs, and that two of them are overrepresented among the Ashkenazim. It is unlikely that the same random evolutionary events could have happened twice. In addition, two of the other diseases that are more common in Eastern European Jews than in the general population also result from the excess accumulation of fatty substances.

Diamond suggests that, as with sickle cell, the heterozygous condition for Tay-Sachs must confer some selective advantage. He notes that Ashkenazic Jews were confined to towns for much of the last 2000 years. They were forbidden to own land and so lived as businessmen in confined, urban areas. (This is the origin of the term *ghetto*.) A common ailment in such towns was TB (tuberculosis). In the early twentieth century, for example, TB caused up to 20 percent of all deaths in Eastern Europe. One study, however, indicates that relatively few Jews died from TB (one in 306 people for whom data were available, a far cry from 20 percent). Thus, a reasonable hypothesis is that heterozygotes for Tay-Sachs, who do not exhibit symptoms of the disease, nevertheless have slightly elevated levels of the fatty substance, and this—for reasons that are still unknown—may provide some immunity to TB.

Though the cause-and-effect relationship has not been established, this hypothesis provides a basis for further investigation and is an example of how our knowledge of evolutionary processes can provide a possible answer to a question involving modern human populations.

Finally, S. Boyd Eaton and Melvin Konner propose that the major chronic illnesses that we in the industrialized West suffer from are caused by a "mismatch between our genetic constitution" and factors in our

FIGURE 15.3

The !Kung San (the ! represents a click sound) from the Kalahari Desert in Namibia and Botswana are, of course, fully modern humans. Yet their way of life, until recently that of hunters of wild game and gatherers of wild plants, can give us a window into the lives of our ancestors before the invention of farming and animal domestication. Here, members of a !Kung family are on the move, carrying with them their children, tools, weapons, and other possessions. The lives of the !Kung have been forever changed by political and military events in southern Africa.

modern lifestyles including diet, exercise, and exposure to such things as alcohol and tobacco. Our genes, they suggest, "must now function in a foreign and, in many ways, hostile Atomic Age [environment]" (Eaton and Konner 1985:1).

They note that some studies indicate that our ancestors who lived before the advent of farming, about 12,000 years ago, were taller and more heavily muscled than we are. Their teeth also showed a much smaller percentage of dental caries (tooth decay). By looking at the lives of recent hunter-gatherer groups, we may, suggest the authors, have a "window" into the world of our Stone-Age ancestors (Figure 15.3). (They are careful, of course, to caution that recent hunter-gather groups are fully modern humans with technologies, such as the bow and arrow, that were not available until about 15,000 years ago.) One thing we note right away is that such people have a lower incidence of coronary heart disease, emphysema, hypertension, and cancer of the breast, prostate, colon, and lung.

When the diets of fifty hunter-gatherer groups were analyzed, it was seen that, on average, they ate more red meat than we do now. This sounds bad at first, until we understand that wild game has much less saturated fat than do domestic animals, and most of that is "structural" fat (rather than "storage" fat), which is largely polyunsaturated—not the harmful kind, in other words. Thus, our ancestors ate about three times the protein we do, but only about half the fat.

Most of the plant foods eaten, because they were wild and unprocessed, had a higher nutritional value, fewer calories, more complex carbohydrates (rather than simple ones that turn to fat), more fiber, and less salt (a contributor to hypertension). They drank mostly water and seldom were exposed to alcohol and tobacco.

Additionally, rather than concentrating on one sort of exercise, our ancestors were more like "decathlon athletes," responding to the harsh physical demands of their lives with a varied "exercise program" that changed daily and seasonally.

The lessons from all this are obvious and are, indeed, suggestions we hear all the time. We know we're supposed to eat low fat foods, cut down on salt, get plenty of fiber, and exercise regularly. Evolution, though, provides an explanation and rationale for following those suggestions.

SUMMARY

Biological anthropology studies the human species, past and present, from the perspective of evolutionary processes, change, and adaptation. To understand how these affected our ancestors, we have developed skills that allow us to squeeze an amazing amount of information out of the meager skeletal remains that those ancestors left us. These skills are now being increasingly recognized and used by law enforcement agencies in the identification and analysis of skeletal remains of missing persons and accident and murder victims. Forensic anthropology is a fast-growing specialty within our field.

Our evolutionary perspective can also be useful in more abstract ways. By understanding the nature of our adaptations as a species, we may evaluate some of our behaviors and practices in light of the recent cultural environment we have made for ourselves. We find that some of our cultural adaptations may be out of step with our biological ones. Using the evolutionary viewpoint to look at daily biological rhythms, sleep patterns, the nature of our breathing, diseases that affect us, our diet, and our exercise habits—among other aspects of our lives—may enable us to change how we do things so as to be more in line with how our species is actually adapted and, in so doing, improve our lives.

In the end, however, it must be noted that, to be useful and important, information need not have a practical, concrete application. There is nothing wrong with the idea of knowledge for its own sake, and, certainly, learning about our species—where we came from, what processes brought about our evolution, who we are and where we fit in the natural world—should be important to us as individuals and as members of our own society and the society of all the world's peoples.

SUGGESTED READINGS

The Ice Man story is summarized in a new book by Konrad Spindler, *The Man in the Ice*. Paul Bahn's review of that book, which adds some additional information, is in the May/June 1995 issue of *Archaeology* magazine. The June 1993 issue of *National Geographic* includes an article, "The Ice Man," by David Roberts that covers the Ice Man as well as some of the related archaeology of his time and place.

On forensic anthropology, see *Dead Men Do Tell Tales* by William R. Maples and Michael Browning and *Bones: A Forensic Detective's Casebook* by Douglas Ubelaker and Henry Scammell.

The Clyde Snow case, covered in this chapter, is recounted in detail in "The Oklahoma City Child Disappearances" by Snow and James Luke, in Podolefsky and Brown, *Applying Anthropology*, and a profile of Snow is in the December 1988 issue of *Discover* in a piece by Patrick Huyghe called "No Bone Unturned."

Glossary of Human and Nonhuman Primates

Adapidae (ah-da′-pih-day)   Group of early primates from the then connected land mass of North America and Europe, dating to more than 50 mya and thought to be ancestral to prosimians, such as lemurs and lorises.

Aegyptopithecus (ee-gyp′-toe-pith′-ah-cuss)   Fossil species of an extinct monkey with several apelike traits. Discovered in Egypt and dating to more than 25 mya, it may represent a form of primate ancestral to Old World monkeys and apes.

Anthropoidea (an-throw-poi′-dee-ah)   One of the two suborders of the order Primates (the other is Prosimii). Means "humanlike" and includes monkeys, apes, and humans.

Ardipithecus ramidus (ar-di-pith′-ah-cuss rah′-mi-dus)   The newest hominid, from Ethiopia and dated at about 4.4 mya. It is based on skeletal fragments and teeth. Not yet fully accepted, it is thought by its discoverers to represent the earliest species in the hominid line. Thus, the species name meaning "root" in the local language.

Australopithecus afarensis (os-trail-oh-pith′-ah-cuss ah-far-en′-sis)   Fossil species from East Africa, the oldest well-established species in the hominid line. Dated from 4 mya to 3 mya, *afarensis* had a small, chimp-sized brain but walked fully upright.

Australopithecus africanus (os-trail-oh-pith′-ah-cuss ah-frih-cane′-us)   A fossil hominid species from South Africa dated from about 3 mya to 2.3 mya. It is similar to A. *afarensis* and may well be a direct evolutionary descendant of the earlier species. It retains the chimp-sized brain and is fully bipedal.

Australopithecus anamensis (os-trail-oh-pith′-ah-cuss a-na-men′-sis)   The newest species of this genus and the newest hominid species. Found in Kenya and dating from 4.2 to 3.9 mya, it is the earliest well-documented fully bipedal hominid.

Catarrhini (cat-ah-rhine′-eye)   One of two infraorders of suborder Anthropoidea (the other is infraorder Platyrrhini, the New World monkeys). Catarrhini is the infraorder of the Old World monkeys, apes, and hominids. Along with the geographical distinction, catarrhines can be distinguished from platyrrhines by their narrow nose shape, fewer number of premolar teeth, and lack of a prehensile tail.

Cercopithecoidea (sir-co-pith-ah-coy′-dee-ah)   The superfamily of all monkeys of Europe, Africa, and Asia.

Gigantopithecus (ji-gan-toe-pith′-ah-cuss)   Genus name for fossil apes, from 12 to perhaps 1 mya in China, India, and Vietnam. They may have reached a height of 12 feet when standing erect, and may have weighed 1200 pounds, thus the largest primate known.

Hominidae (ho-mih′-nih-day)   The family of modern and extinct human species, defined as the primates that are habitually bipedal. Members of this group are called hominids.

Hominoidea (ho-min-oy′-dee-ah)   The superfamily that includes the large, tailless primates: apes and hominids, living and extinct.

Homo erectus (ho'-mow ee-wreck'-tuss) Fossil hominid species dating from at least 1.8 mya to perhaps as late as 100,000 years ago. First appearing in Africa, *H. erectus* was the first hominid species to expand beyond that continent. Fossils are found throughout Africa and Asia, and there is archaeological evidence from Europe. Members of this species had a brain size average about two-thirds that of modern humans, made advances in stone tool technology, and late in their existence were able to control fire.

Homo ergaster (ho'-mow er-gas'-ter) A proposed new species that includes the earliest *H. erectus* fossils from East Africa. They are said to be sufficiently different that they represent a separate species that was ancestral to both *H. erectus* and, later, *Homo sapiens*. This idea is not widely accepted at the moment.

Homo habilis (ho'-mow ha'-bill-us) Fossil hominid species dating from about 2.2 to 1.5 mya and found in East Africa. Fully bipedal, and with an average brain size of 680 ml, *H. habilis* was the first confirmed hominid stone tool maker. Because this was the first hominid with a brain larger than that of a chimpanzee, and because of the association with stone tools, this is thought to be the earliest member of our genus, *Homo*.

Homo neanderthalensis (ho'-mow knee-an-dir-tall-en'-sis) Name once applied to the Neandertals, indicating that they were a different species from *Homo sapiens*. In the past, this was based on an exaggeration of some of the differences between them and modern humans. At present, there is a debate as to whether or not they do represent a separate species or are simply the European and Middle Eastern populations of "archaic" *Homo sapiens*. If it is determined that they are part of a distinct species, the name might be reinstituted.

Homo sapiens (ho'-mow say'-pee-ens) Taxonomic name for modern humans. There is some debate as to whether or not this name covers certain fossil forms. See ***Homo sapiens,*** archaic and ***Homo sapiens,*** anatomically modern).

Homo sapiens, **anatomically modern** (ho'-mow say'-pee-ens) Humans with fully modern traits, who appeared about 200,000 years ago in Africa and spread from there. The modern average human brain size is about 1400 ml, with a broad range

of 1000 to 2200 ml for normal adults. It is now debated whether this group represents a separate species from archaic *Homo sapiens* or simply possesses modern traits. See *Homo sapiens,* archaic.

Homo sapiens, **archaic** (ho'-mow say'-pee-ens) Fossil hominids dating from 400,000 years ago to about 35,000 years ago. Their average brain size of 1200 ml is about the same as modern humans, but they possess a number of primitive cranial features. The name usually includes the Neandertals, who also had extremely robust postcranial skeletons. It is now being debated as to whether they represent early members of *Homo sapiens* or are a separate species. See ***Homo sapiens,*** anatomically modern and ***Homo neanderthalensis.***

Hylobatidae (high-low-bat'-ah-day) Family that includes the gibbons and siamangs, the arboreal, so-called lesser apes of Southeast Asia. They are highly efficient brachiators.

Omomyidae (oh-mow-me'-ah-day) A group of early primates that lived in the then connected land mass of North America and Europe. Dating to more than 50 mya, they are thought to be ancestral to tarsiers and may have been ancestral to Anthropoidea as well.

Ouranopithecus (oo-ran'-oh-pith'-ah-cuss) An ape form from Greece dated at 9 or 10 mya. Based on some hominid-like features, it is thought by some to be a member of the ape line that led to the hominids.

Papio (pah'-pee-oh) A genus within superfamily Cercopithecoidea (the Old World monkeys) comprised of the several species of baboons, large monkeys living in social groups on the African savannas.

Paranthropus aethiopicus (par-an'-throw-pus ee-thee-o'-pih-cus) Species from East Africa dating from 2.8 to 2.2 mya. They are the first members of the so-called robust hominids, having large, rugged features associated with chewing, although their other features, including brain size, are very similar to members of genus *Australopithecus*. Many authorities still include them in that genus. It is thought they were adapted to tough, gritty, hard vegetable foods. The most famous, and first, specimen of this species was the "Black Skull."

Paranthropus boisei (par-an′-throw-pus boys′-ee-eye)　The East African robust hominid from 2.2 to 1 mya. It had large features associated with chewing, although less pronounced than in *P. aethiopicus.* The first specimen was "Zinjanthropus." Sometimes included in genus *Australopithecus.*

Paranthropus robustus (par-an′-throw-pus row-bus′-tus)　The Southern African robust hominid, dated from 2.2 to 1.5 mya. It is marked by robust chewing features, although they are less robust than in either *P. aethiopicus* or *P. boisei.* The postcranial skeleton and the brain size remain similar to those of *Australopithecus.* It is sometimes included in that genus.

Platyrrhini (plat-ee-rhine′-eye)　One of two infraorders of the suborder Anthropoidea (the other is suborder Catarrhine, the Old World monkeys, apes, and hominids). Platyrrhines include the New World monkeys. Members of this group can be told apart from the catarrhines by their broad nose shape, greater number of premolar teeth, and by the fact that several species have prehensile tails.

Pongidae (pon′-jih-day)　Family of the so-called great apes, the orangutans of Southeast Asia, and the gorillas, chimpanzees, and bonobos of Africa.

Primates (pry-mate′-ees)　Order within class Mammalia. Large-brained, arboreal mammals with stereoscopic color vision and grasping hands (and sometimes feet). Includes prosimians, monkeys, apes, and hominids.

Prosimii (pro-sim′-ee-eye)　One of two suborders of the order Primates (the other suborder is Anthropoidea). Prosimians are the more primitive of the two suborders in that they retain features of some of the oldest primate fossils. Many lack color vision, are nocturnal, and have limited opposability of the thumb.

Sivapithecus (she′-vah-pith′-ah-cuss)　The general group name of fossil ape forms from Africa, India, Pakistan, Turkey, Greece, Hungary, and China, dated from 15 to 12 mya. Specifically, the genus thought to be ancestral to the orangutan.

Glossary of Terms

absolute dating technique Dating technique that gives a specific age, year, or range of years for an object or site. See **relative dating technique.**

Acheulian A toolmaking tradition associated with *Homo erectus* in Africa and Europe. Includes hand axes, cleavers, and flake tools.

adapted When an organism is in a state of adjustment to a particular environment through its anatomy, physiology, and behavior.

adaptive radiation The evolution and spreading out of related species into new niches.

allele frequency The percentage of times a particular **allele** appears in a population. Same as **gene frequency,** but is the preferred term.

alleles Variants of a genetic **locus.** Most loci possess more than one possible allele, the different alleles conveying different instructions for the development of a certain **phenotype** (for example, different blood types).

altruistic Behavior that benefits others without regard to one's own needs or safety. An example of the kind of behavior that sociobiology attempts to explain in evolutionary terms. Altruistic behavior may have evolved because it promotes the **inclusive fitness** of one's genes.

amino acid The chief component of **proteins.** Each "word" in the genetic code stands for a specific amino acid.

analogies Traits shared by two or more species that are similar in function but unrelated evolutionarily, for example, the wings of a bird and the wings of an insect. See **homology.**

anthropology The **holistic** study of the human species. Anthropology includes the study of human biology, human physical **evolution,** human cultural evolution, and human adaptation.

antibodies The **proteins** in the immune system that react to foreign **antigens.**

antigens The **proteins** used by the body's immune system that distinguish between "self" and "non-self." The antigens of the ABO blood group systems are examples.

applied anthropology The use of **anthropology** to address current practical problems and concerns.

arboreal Refers to organisms that are **adapted** to life in the trees.

archaeology Subfield of **anthropology** that studies the human cultural past.

asexually Reproducing without sex, by fissioning or budding.

belief systems Ideas that are taken on faith and cannot be scientifically tested. Examples are religions, philosophies, and ethical and moral beliefs. See **scientific method.**

bifacial A stone tool that has been worked on both sides.

biological anthropology Subfield of **anthropology** that studies humans as a biological species.

bipedal Walking on two legs.

brachiation Locomotion using arm-over-arm swinging.

breeding populations Populations within a **species** that are genetically isolated to some degree from other populations. See **deme.**

brow ridges Heavy, bony ridges over the eyes.

carbon dating A **radiometric** dating technique using the decay rate of a radioactive form of carbon found in organic remains.

catastrophists Those who believe the history of the earth is explained by a series of global catastrophes, either natural or divine in origin. See **uniformitarianism.**

chromosomal mutations Refers to **mutations** of a whole **chromosome** or a large portion of a chromosome.

chromosomes Strands of **DNA** in the nucleus of a cell.

cladistics A classification system based on order of evolutionary branching, rather than on present similarities and differences. See **taxonomy.**

cline A geographic continuum in the variation of a particular trait.

codominant When both **alleles** of a pair are expressed in the **phenotype.**

codons The sections of **DNA** that code for specific **amino acids.**

comparative anatomy Comparing the anatomical features of various species, an idea usually attributed to Georges Cuvier. Used to reconstruct a **fossil species** from fragmentary remains.

competitive exclusion When one **species** out-competes others for the resources of a particular area.

core tools Tools made by taking flakes off a stone nucleus. See **flake tools.**

crossing over When sections of **chromosomes** switch between members of a chromosome pair. A source of genetic variation by breaking up linked **loci.** See **linkage.**

cultural anthropology Subfield of **anthropology** that focuses on human cultural behavior and cultural systems.

culture Ideas and behaviors that are learned and transmitted. Also, the system made up of the sum total of these ideas and behaviors that is unique to a particular society of people. Nongenetic means of adaptation.

Darwinian gradualism The view, held by Darwin, that **evolution** is slow and steady with cumulative change. See **punctuated equilibrium.**

deduction Suggesting specific data that would be found if a **hypothesis** is true. This is a step in the **scientific method** involving the testing of hypotheses. See **induction.**

deme Populations within a **species** that are genetically isolated to some degree from other populations. Same as **breeding population,** but sometimes implies physical distinctions.

demography The study of the size and makeup of populations.

deoxyribonucleic acid (DNA) The molecule that carries the genetic code.

dependency Here, the period after birth during which offspring are dependent upon adults.

dermatoglyphics The study of the parallel ridges and furrows on the finger tips, palms, toes, and soles, commonly referred to as finger prints, palm prints, etc.

distance curve A graph that compares the measure of some variable at different points in time, for example height and age. See **velocity curve.**

diurnal Active during the day.

DNA See **deoxyribonucleic acid.**

dominance hierarchy A social pattern seen in animal species where there are recognized individual differences in power, influence, and access to resources and mating. Found in many **primate** species.

dominant In a **heterozygous** pair of **alleles,** the one that is expressed in the **phenotype.**

endocasts Natural or humanmade casts of the inside of a skull. The cast reflects the surface of the brain and allows us to study the brains even of extinct species.

endogamous Restricting marriage to within a certain social group.

environmental Any nongenetic influence on the phenotype. Also refers to the conditions under which an organism exists, to include climate, altitude, other species, food sources, and so on.

enzymes The **proteins** that control chemical processes.

estrus The period of fertility. The signals indicating this condition to males of the species. A popular synonym is "in heat."

ethology The study of the natural behavior of animals under natural conditions.

evolution Systematic change through time, usually with reference to biological species but may also refer to changes within cultural systems.

fission A process of **evolution** that involves the splitting up of a population to form new populations.

fitness The relative adaptiveness of an individual organism, measured ultimately by reproductive success. See **adapted.**

flake tools Tools made from the flakes removed from a stone core. See **core tools.**

folk taxonomies Cultural categories for important items and ideas. **Gender** and **race** are examples of folk taxonomies.

foramen magnum The hole in the base of the skull through which the spinal cord emerges and around the outside of which the top vertebra articulates.

forensic anthropologist One who applies anthropology to legal matters. Usually used with reference to the identification of skeletal remains and the assessment of time and cause of death.

fossils Remains of life forms of the past.

founder effect A process of **evolution.** Genetic differences between populations produced by the fact that genetically different individuals established (founded) those populations.

gamete sampling A process of **evolution.** The genetic change caused when genes are passed to new generations in frequencies unrepresentative of those of the parental generation. An example of **sampling error.**

gametes The cells of reproduction, commonly sperm and egg.

gender The culturally defined categories and characteristics of men and women. The translation of **sex** into a **folk taxonomy.** See **sex.**

gene flow A process of **evolution** that involves the exchange of genes among populations through interbreeding.

gene frequency The percentage of times a particular **allele** appears in a population. See **allele frequency.**

gene pool All the **alleles** in a population.

generalized Refers to **species** that are adapted to a wide range of **environmental niches.** Such species tend to be genetically and physically variable. See **specialized.**

genes Those portions of the **DNA** molecule that code for specific traits. Roughly a synonym for **locus.**

genetic markers Traits of genetic origin used to compare populations and estimate genetic differences.

genome The total genetic endowment of a **species.**

genotypes The **alleles** possessed by an organism.

glaciers Massive sheets of ice that expand and move. Found on the polar ice caps and in mountains.

grooming The cleaning of the fur of another animal; promotes social cohesion. Common among **primates.**

haft To attach a handle or shaft, such as to a spear point.

half-life The time needed for one-half of a given amount of a radioactive substance to decay.

hand axe A **bifacial,** all-purpose stone tool, shaped somewhat like an axe head. First invented by *Homo erectus* and usually associated with that species.

Hardy-Weinberg equilibrium The formula that shows **genotype** frequencies in a population under hypothetical conditions of no evolutionary change.

heritability The amount of variation of a particular trait, within a population, that is caused by genetic, as opposed to **environmental,** differences.

heterozygous Having two different **alleles** in a gene pair. See **homozygous.**

holistic Assuming an interrelationship among the parts of a subject. **Anthropology** is a holistic discipline.

hominids Modern human beings and our ancestors, defined as the primates who stand erect; technically, the members of family Hominidae.

homologies Traits shared by two or more **species** through inheritance from a common ancestor. An example would be the arms of a human and the wings of a bat. We assume many behaviors that are similar in humans and chimpanzees are also homologies.

homozygous Having two of the same allele in a genetic pair. See **heterozygous.**

human ecology Specialty that studies the relationships between humans and their environments.

hunter-gatherers Societies that rely upon naturally occurring sources of food. They have no domestic plants or animals except, perhaps, dogs.

hypotheses Educated guesses to explain natural phenomena. In the **scientific method,** hypotheses must be testable. See **theory.**

inclusive fitness The idea that **fitness** is measured by the success of one's genes, whether those genes are possessed by the individual or by that individual's relatives. Fitness, in other words, "includes" *your* adaptive success as well as that of your relations.

independent assortment When genetic **loci** on different **chromosomes** segregate to **gametes** independently of one another. A source of genetic variation. See **segregation.**

induction Developing a general explanation from specific observations. The step in the **scientific method** that generates **hypotheses.** See **deduction.**

inheritance of acquired characteristics The incorrect idea, associated with Lamarck, that an organism can acquire adaptive traits during its lifetime and that these traits can be passed on to its offspring.

inorganic A molecule not of **organic** origin.

intelligence The relative ability of the brain to acquire, store, access, and process information.

Levallois Tool technology involving striking uniform flakes from a prepared core. See **core tools** and **flake tools.**

life history The study that examines the timing of life cycle events such as fertility, growth, and death.

linkage When genetic **loci** occur on the same **chromosome** and are therefore inherited together. See **crossing over.**

locus (pl. loci) The location on a **chromosome** of the genetic code for a specific trait. This term has become preferable to the use of **gene.**

macromutations Any **mutations** with extensive and important physical results. The mutations for sickle cell anemia and Down syndrome are examples.

meiosis The process of cell division in which **gametes** are produced, each gamete having one-half the normal complement of **chromosomes** and, therefore, with only one **allele** of each original pair.

melanin The pigment that is largely responsible for human skin color.

melanocytes Specialized skin cells that produce the pigment **melanin.**

menarche A woman's first menstrual period.

Mendelian genetics The basic laws of inheritance, discovered by Gregor Mendel in the nineteenth century.

menopause The end of a woman's reproductive cycle.

messenger ribonucleic acid (mRNA) The molecule that carries the genetic code out of the nucleus for translation into **proteins.** See **transfer RNA.**

mitosis The process of cell division that results in two exact copies of the original cell.

mitrochondrial DNA (mtDNA) The genetic material found in the cells' mitochondria, rather than in the cell nucleus. The mtDNA does not play a role in inheritance and thus may give a more accurate measure of the genetic differences among populations.

monogenic A trait coded for by a single **locus.** The ABO blood group system is a monogenic trait.

Mousterian The culture associated with the European **Neandertals.**

Multiregional Hypothesis The idea that anatomically modern humans evolved independently in several different geographical areas. See **Replacement Hypothesis.**

mutation Any mistake in an organism's genetic material.

natural selection Evolutionary change based on the differential reproductive success, or **fitness,** of individuals within a **species.**

Neandertals The populations of "archaic" *Homo sapiens* from Europe and the Middle East.

niche The environment of an organism and its adaptive response to that environment. Has been referred to as an organism's "ecological address."

nocturnal Active at night.

notochord A still cartilagenous rod that supports the body and protects the dorsal nerve. The evolutionary precursor of the vertebral column.

nucleotide The basic units or buildings blocks of the **DNA** and **RNA** genetic code. Made up of a sugar, a phosphate, and one of the four bases of the code, designated G, C, A, and T (or U).

omnivore An organism with a mixed diet of animal and vegetable foods.

opposability   The ability to touch (oppose) the thumb to the tips of the other fingers.

organic   The carbon-rich molecules that make up living organisms. Also, referring to living organisms. See **inorganic.**

osteology   The study of skeletal anatomy and function.

paleoanthropology   Specialty that studies the human fossil record.

Pangea   The supercontinent that included parts of all present-day land masses. It formed around 280 million years ago and began breaking up around 200 mya.

parsimony   Use of the simplest explanation in formulating a scientific **hypothesis.**

particulate   The idea that biological traits are controlled by individual factors rather than by a single all-encompassing hereditary agent.

petrified   A **fossil** that has turned to stone. As the **organic** material decays, it is slowly replaced by minerals leaving a cast in stone of the organism or some of its parts.

phenotype   The chemical or physical results of the genetic code.

photosynthesis   The process whereby plants manufacture their own nutrients from carbon dioxide and water, using chlorophyll as a catalyst and sunlight as an energy source.

physical anthropology   The traditional name for **biological anthropology.**

plate tectonics   The movement of the plates of the earth's crust caused by their interaction with the molten rock of the earth's interior. The cause of continental drift.

Pleistocene   The geological time period, from 1.6 million to 10,000 years ago, characterized by a series of glacial advances and retreats. See **glaciers.**

point mutations   Any **mutations** of single **codons.** The mutation that causes sickle cell anemia is an example.

polygenic   A trait coded for by more than on **locus.** Skin color is a polygenic trait.

polymorphisms   Variations in phenotypic traits that are the results of genetic variation. Human skin color is a polymorphic trait; human clothing styles are not polymorphic because they are not genetic.

polytypic   A species with physically distinguishable regional populations.

postorbital constriction   A narrowing of the skull behind the eyes, as viewed from above.

potassium/argon (K/Ar) dating   A **radiometric** dating technique using the decay rate of radioactive potassium, found in volcanic rock, into stable argon gas.

prehensile   The ability to grasp.

primates   Large-brained, tree-dwelling mammals with three-dimensional color vision and grasping hands. Humans are primates.

primatology   Specialty that studies nonhuman **primates.**

prognathism   The jutting forward of the lower face and jaw area.

progressive   In **evolution,** the now discounted idea that all change is toward increasing complexity.

prosimian   A member of the group of **primates** with the most primitive features, that is, that most closely resemble the earliest primates.

protein   One of the family of molecules that makes cells and carries out cellular functions. Proteins are made of **amino acids.**

protein synthesis   The process by which the genetic code puts together **proteins** in the cell.

provenience   The precise location of something; here, of **fossils** or archaeological artifacts.

pseudoscience   Scientifically testable ideas that are not tested, but are taken on faith, even if shown to be false. **Scientific creationism** is a pseudoscience.

punctuated equilibrium   The view that species tend to remain stable and that evolutionary changes occur fairly suddenly. See **Darwinian gradualism.**

quadrupedal   Walking on all fours.

races   In biology, the same as **subspecies.** In culture, cultural categories to classify and account for human diversity. See **folk taxonomy.**

racism   Judging on individual based solely on his or her racial affiliation.

radiometric   Refers to the decay rate of a radioactive substance. See **carbon dating** and **potassium/argon dating.**

recessive   The **allele** of a **heterozygous** pair that is not expressed. For a recessive allele to be expressed it must be **homozygous.**

recombination The reconstitution of **allele** pairs at fertilization from the **gametes,** which each carry only one-half of each parent's genetic endowment. See **segregation.**

reification Translating a complex set of phenomena into a single entity such as a number. IQ test scores are an example.

relative dating technique Dating technique that indicates the age of one item in comparison to another. **Stratigraphy** provides relative dates by indicating that one layer is older or younger than another.

Replacement Hypothesis The idea that anatomically modern humans evolved in one area and spread out from there. See **Multiregional Hypothesis.**

reproductive isolating mechanisms Any difference that prevents the production of fertile offspring between members of two populations. Necessary for the production of separate **species.**

reproductive strategies Behaviors that evolve to maximize an individual's reproductive success.

RNA See **messenger ribonucleic acid** *and* **transfer ribonucleic acid.**

sagittal keel A sloping of the sides of the skull toward the top, as viewed from the front.

sampling error When a sample chosen for study does not accurately represent the population from which the sample was taken.

savanna The open grasslands of the tropics. The savannas of Africa are, according to latest evidence, where **hominids** first evolved.

scavenge To eat the flesh of an animal that is already dead.

science The method of inquiry that requires the generation, testing, and acceptance or rejection of **hypotheses.**

scientific creationism The belief in a literal biblical intepretation regarding the creation of the universe, with the connected belief that this view is supported by scientific evidence. An example of a **pseudoscience.**

scientific method The process of conducting scientific inquiry. See **science.**

segregation In genetics, the breaking up of allele pairs in the production of **gametes.** See **recombination.**

semispecies Populations of a **species** that are completely isolated from one another but have not yet become truly different species.

sex The biological categories and characteristics of males and females. See **gender.**

sexual dimorphism Physical differences between the sexes of a **species.** See **sex.**

sexually Reproducing by combining genetic material from two individuals. See **asexually.**

sites Any places that contain evidence of human presence.

sociobiology The scientific study that examines evolutionary explanations for behaviors of **species,** including humans. It particularly focuses on social behaviors, showing how they can be affected by **natural selection.**

specialized Species adapted to a narrow range of **environmental niches.** See **generalized.**

speciation The **evolution** of new **species** from existing species.

species A group of organisms that can produce fertile offspring among themselves but not with members of other groups. A closed genetic population, usually physically distinguisable from other populations.

stereoscopic vision Three-dimensional vision; depth perception.

strata (sing. **stratum**) Layers; here, the layers of rock and soil under the surface of the earth.

stratigraphy The study of the earth's **strata.**

subspecies Physically distinguishable populations within a **species.** See **races.**

symbiotic A relationship between members of two different **species**; often, but not necessarily, a mutually beneficial relationship.

symbolic Here, a communication system that uses arbitrary but agreed-upon sounds and signs for meaning.

systematists See **taxonomists.**

taphonomy The study of how the remains of organisms become part of the paleontological record. How **fossils** form and what processes affect them through time.

taxon Any category within a taxonomic classification. See **taxonomy.**

taxonomists Those who classify and name living organisms.

taxonomy A classification based on similarities and

differences. In biology, the science of categorizing organisms and of naming them so as to reflect their relationships.

theory A **hypothesis** that has been well supported by evidence and testing. In **science,** theory is a positive term.

torus A bony ridge at the back of the skull, where the neck muscles attach.

transfer ribonucleic acid (tRNA) The form of **RNA** that lines up amino acids along **mRNA** to make proteins. See **messenger RNA.**

trephination The cutting of a hole in the skull, presumably to treat some illness. Refers to the practice within societies with prescientific knowledge.

tundra A treeless area with low-growing vegetation and permanently frozen ground. Located in the Artic, tundra conditions were found during the **Pleistocene** in the vacinity of **glaciers** far to the south.

uniformitarianism The idea that present-day geological and biological processes can also explain the past history of the earth and its life. The processes are "uniform." See **catastrophism.**

velocity curve A graph that compares rate of change of some variable at different points in time; for example, rate of growth at different ages. See **distance curve.**

vertebrates Organisms with backbones.

zygote The fertilized egg before cell division begins.

Bibliography

Aiello, L. C. 1993. The fossil evidence for modern human origins in Africa: A revised view. *American Anthropologist* 95 (1): 73–96.

Appleman, P. 1970. *Darwin: A Norton Critical Edition*. New York: Norton.

Attenborough, D. 1979. *Life on Earth*. Boston: Little, Brown.

Bahn, P. G. 1995. Last days of the iceman. *Archaeology* May/June, 1995: 66–70.

Barfield, A. 1976. Biological Influences on Sex Differences in Behavior. In *Sex Differences*, ed. M. S. Teitelbaum. Garden City, N.Y.: Anchor Press/Doubleday.

Bass, W. 1971. *Human Osteology: A Laboratory and Field Manual of the Human Skeleton*. Columbia: Missouri Archaeological Society.

Binford, L. 1985. Ancestral life ways: the faunal record. *Anthroquest* 32 (1): 15–20.

Binford, L. and K. Chuan. 1985. Taphonomy at a distance: Zhoukoudian, "The Cave Home of Beijing Man." *Current Anthropology* 26:413–43.

Binford, L. and N. M. Stone. 1986. Zhoukoudian: A Closer Look. *Current Anthropology* 27:435–76.

Binford, L. R. 1987. *Bones: Ancient Men and Modern Myths*. Orlando, Fla.: Academic Press.

Boesch, C., and H. Boesch-Achermann. 1991. Dim forest, bright chimps. *Natural History* (September, 1991): 50–57.

Bordes, F. 1972. *A Tale of Two Caves*. New York: Harper & Row.

Bowlby, J. 1990. *Charles Darwin: A New Life*. New York: Norton.

Bramblett, C. A. 1994. *Patterns of Primate Behavior*, 2nd ed. Prospect Heights, Ill.: Waveland Press.

Cann, R. L., M. Stoneking, and A. C. Wilson. 1987. Mitochondrial DNA and human evolution. *Nature* 325:31–36.

Cavalli-Sforza, L. L. 1991. Genes, peoples, and languages. *Scientific American* 265:104–10.

Ciochon, R., J. Olsen, and J. James. 1990. *Other Origins: The Search for the Giant Ape in Human Prehistory*. New York: Bantam Books.

Ciochon, R. L., and J. G. Fleagle, eds. 1993. *The Human Evolution Source Book*. Englewood Cliffs, N.J.: Prentice Hall.

Coppens, Y. 1994. East side story: the origin of humankind. *Scientific American* 270:88–95.

Cowen, R. 1995. *History of Life*, 2nd ed. Boston: Blackwell Scientific Publications.

Cummins, H., and C. Midlo. 1961. *Finger Prints, Palms, and Soles: An Introduction to Dermatoglyphics*. New York: Dover.

Darwin, C. R. 1898. *On the Origin of Species by Means of Natural Selection*, 6th ed., 1872. New York: Appleton.

De Bonis, L., and G. D. Koufos. 1994. Our ancestor's ancestor: Ouranopithecus is a Greek link in human ancestry. *Evolutionary Anthropology* 3 (3): 75–83.

de Waal, F. B. M. 1995. Bonobo sex and society. *Scientific American* 272:82–88.

Diamond, J. 1991. Curse and blessing of the ghetto. *Discover* (March): 60–65.

Dobzhansky, T. 1970. *Genetics of the Evolutionary Process*. New York: Columbia University Press.

Eaton, S. B., and M. Konner. 1985. Diet: Paleolithic genes and twentieth century health. *Anthroquest*, The L. S. B. Leakey Foundation, 1985.

Edey, M., and D. Johanson. 1989. *Blueprints: Solving the Mystery of Evolution*. Boston: Little, Brown.

Fagan, B. 1994. *In the Beginning: An Introduction to Archaeology*, 8th ed. New York: HarperCollins.

Fagan, B. M. 1990. *The Journey from Eden: The Peopling of Our World*. London: Thames and Hudson.

Feder, K. L. 1990. *Frauds, Myths and Mysteries: Science and Pseudoscience in Archaeology*. Mountain View, Calif.: Mayfield Publishing.

Feder, K. L., and M. A. Park. 1993. *Human Antiquity: An Introduction to Physical Anthropology and Archaeology*, 2 ed. Mountain View, Calif.: Mayfield Publishing.

Fedigan, L. M., and L. Fedigan. 1988. *Gender and the study of primates: Curricular Module for the Project on Gender and Curriculum*. Washington, D.C.: American Anthropological Association.

Ferris, Timothy. 1988. *Coming of Age in the Milky Way*. New York: William Morrow and Company.

Fleagle, J. G. 1988. *Primate Adaptation & Evolution*. San Diego: Academic Press.

Fossey, D. 1983. *Gorillas in the Mist*. Boston: Houghton Mifflin.

Frayer, D. W., M. H. Wolpoff, A. G. Thorne, F. H. Smith, and G. G. Pope. 1993. Theories of modern human origins: The paleontological test. *American Anthropologist* 95 (1): 14–50.

Galdikas, Biruté. 1995. *Reflections of Eden: My Years with the Orangutans of Borneo*. Boston: Little, Brown and Co.

Gish, Duane T. 1979. *Evolution: The Fossils Say No!* San Diego: Creation-Life Publishers.

Glausiusz, J. 1995. Unfortunate drift. *Discover* (June): 34–35.

Goodall, J. 1971. *In the Shadow of Man*. Boston: Houghton Mifflin.

Goodall, J. 1986. *The Chimpanzees of Gombe: Patterns of Behavior*. Cambridge, Mass.: Belknap Press.

Goodall, J. 1990. *Through a Window: My Thirty Years with the Chimpanzees of Gombe*. Boston: Houghton Mifflin.

Gore, R. 1989. Extinctions. *National Geographic* 175 (6): 662–699.

Gore, R. 1993. Explosion of life. The Cambrian period. *National Geographic* 184 (4): 120–136.

Gould, S. J. 1977. *Ever Since Darwin*. New York: Norton.

Gould, S. J. 1980. *The Panda's Thumb*. New York: Norton.

Gould, S. J. 1981. *The Mismeasure of Man*. New York: Norton.

Gould, S. J. 1983. *Hen's Teeth and Horse's Toes*. New York: Norton.

Gould, S. J. 1985. *The Flamingo's Smile*. New York: Norton.

Gould, S. J. 1989. *Wonderful Life: The Burgess Shale and the Nature of History*. New York: Norton.

Gould, S. J. 1991. *Bully for Brontosaurus*. New York: Norton.

Gould, S. J. 1992. What Is a Species? *Discover* (December): 40–45.

Gould, S. J. 1993. *Eight Little Piggies*. New York: Norton.

Gould, S. J. 1993. *The Book of Life*. New York: Norton.

Gould, S. J. 1994. The evolution of life on the earth. *Scientific American* 271 (4): 84–91.

Gould, S. J. 1995. Of tongue worms, velvet worms, and water bears. *Natural History* 104 (1): 6–15.

Greene, J. C. 1959. *The Death of Adam*. New York: Mentor Books.

Harris, C. L. 1981. *Evolution: Genesis and Revelations*. Albany: State University of New York Press.

Harrison, G. A., and A. J. Boyce, eds. 1972. *The Structure of Human Populations*. Oxford: Clarendon.

Harrison, G. A., J. S. Weiner, J. M. Tanner, and N. A. Barnicot. 1977. *Human Biology: An Introduction to Human Evolution, Variation, Growth, and Ecology*, 2d ed. Oxford: Oxford University Press.

Hedges, S. B., S. Kumar, K. Tamura, and M. Stoneking. 1992. Technical comments. *Science* 255:737–39.

Hill, K. 1993. Life history theory and evolutionary anthropology. *Evolutionary Anthropology* 2 (3): 78–88.

Holloway, R. 1980. Indonesian "Solo" (Ngandong) endocranial reconstructions: Preliminary observations and comparisons with Neandertal and Homo erectus groups. *American Journal of Physical Anthropology* 53:285–95.

Holloway, R. 1981. The Indonesian Homo erectus brain endocasts revisited. *American Journal of Physical Anthropology* 55:503–21.

Hostetler, J. A. 1974. *Hutterite Society*. Baltimore: Johns Hopkins University Press.

Janus, C. 1975. *The Search for Peking Man*. New York: Macmillan.

Jensen, A. R. 1969. How much can we boost IQ and scholastic achievement? *Harvard Educational Review* 39 (1, Winter): 1–123.

Johanson, D. C., and M. A. Edey. 1981. *Lucy: The Beginnings of Humankind*. New York: Simon and Schuster.

Johanson, D., and J. Shreeve. 1989. *Lucy's Child: The Discovery of a Human Ancestor*. New York: William Morrow and Company.

Jolly, A. 1985. *The Evolution of Primate Behavior*. New York: Macmillan.

Jolly, A. 1988. Madagascar's lemurs: On the edge of survival. *National Geographic* 174 (2): 132–161.

Kano, T. 1990. The bonobos' peaceable kingdom. *Natural History* (November 1990): 62–71.

Kennedy, K. A. R. 1976. *Human Variation in Space and Time*. Dubuque, Iowa: Wm. C. Brown.

Kingston, J. D., B. D. Marino, and A. Hill. 1994. Isotopic evidence for neocene hominid paleoenvironments in the Kenya rift valley. *Science* 264:955–959.

Lack, D. 1947. *Darwin's Finches: An Essay on the General Biological Theory of Evolution*. Cambridge: Cambridge University Press.

Leakey, R., and R. Lewin. 1992. *Origins Reconsidered: In Search of What Makes Us Human*. New York: Doubleday.

Lemonick, M. D. 1994. One Less Missing Link. *Time* (October 3): 68–69.

Lewontin, R. 1982. *Human Diversity*. New York: Scientific American Books.

Lindenbaum, S. 1979. *Kuru Sorcery: Disease and Danger in the New Guinea Highlands*. Mountain View, Calif.: Mayfield.

Lyell, C. 1873. *The Geological Evidences of the Antiquity of Man*. London: Murray.

Maples, W. R., and M. Browning. 1994. *Dead Men Do Tell Tales*. New York: Doubleday.

Marks, J. 1995. *Human Diversity: Genes, Race, and History*. New York: Aldine de Gruyter.

Martin, M. K., and B. Voorhies. 1975. *Female of the Species*. New York: Columbia University Press.

Mettler, L. E., T. G. Gregg, and H. E. Schaffer. 1988. *Population Genetics and Evolution*. Englewood Cliffs, N.J.: Prentice Hall.

Molnar, S. 1992. *Human Variation: Races, Types, and Ethnic Groups*, 3d ed. Englewood Cliffs, N.J.: Prentice Hall.

Montagu, A., ed. 1964. *The Concept of Race*. New York: Collier Books.

Morris, H. M. 1974. *The Troubled Waters of Evolution*. San Diego, Calif.: Creation-Life Publishers.

Mowat, F. 1987. *Woman in the Mists*. New York: Warner Books.

Nanda, S. 1990. *Neither Man Nor Woman: The Hijras of India*. Belmont, Calif.: Wadsworth.

Napier, J. R., and P. H. Napier. 1985. *The Natural History of the Primates*. Cambridge, Mass.: M.I.T. Press.

Nichols, M., J. Goodall, G. B. Schaller, and M. G. Smith. 1993. *The Great Apes: Between Two Worlds*. Washington, D.C.: National Geographic Society.

Orgel, L. E. 1994. The origin of life on the earth. *Scientific American* 271 (4): 76–83.

Park, M. A. 1979. Dermatoglypics as a Tool for Population Studies: An Example. Unpublished doctoral dissertation, Dept. of Anthropology: Indiana University, Bloomington.

Park, M. A. 1982–83. Palmistry: Science or handjive? *The Skeptical Inquirer* VII (2): 21–32.

Passingham, R. 1982. *The Human Primate*. New York: W. H. Freeman.

Pfeiffer, J. 1969. *The Emergence of Man*. New York: Harper & Row.

Podolefsky, A., and P. J. Brown, ed. 1994. *Applying Anthropology: An Introductory Reader*. Mountain View, Calif.: Mayfield Publishing.

Post, P. W., F. Daniels, Jr., and R. T. Binford. 1975. Cold injury and the evolution of "white" skin. *Human Biology* 47:65–80.

Relethford, J. H. 1994. *The Human Species: An Introduction to Biological Anthropology*, 2nd ed. Mountain View, Calif.: Mayfield.

Ridley, M. 1993. *Evolution*. Boston: Blackwell Scientific Publications.

Rischer, C. E., and T. A. Easton. 1992. *Focus on Human Biology*. New York: HarperCollins.

Roberts, D. 1993. The Ice Man. *National Geographic* 183 (6): 36–67.

Sagan, C. 1977. *The Dragons of Eden: Speculations on the Evolution of Human Intelligence*. New York: Random House.

Schadewald, R. 1981–82. Scientific creationism, geocentricity and the flat earth. *The Skeptical Inquirer* VI (2): 41–48.

Schadewald, R. 1986. Creationist pseudoscience. In *Science Confronts the Paranormal*, ed. Kendrick Frazier. Buffalo, New York: Prometheus Books.

Schultz, E., and R. Lavenda. 1994. *Anthropology: A Perspective on the Human Condition*. Mountain View, Calif.: Mayfield Publishing.

Sharer, R. J., and W. Ashmore. 1993. *Archaeology: Discovering Our Past*, 2nd ed. Mountain View, Calif.: Mayfield Publishing.

Shea, J. 1989. A functional study of the lithic industries associated with hominid fossils in Kebara and Qafzeh Caves, Israel. In *The Human Revolution: Behavioural and Biological Perspectives in the Origins of Modern Humans*, eds. P. Mellars and C. Stringer: 611–25. Princeton, N.J.: Princeton University Press.

Shipman, P. 1981. *Life History of a Fossil: An Introduction to Taphonomy and Paleoecology*. Cambridge, Mass.: Harvard University Press.

Shipman, P. 1984. Scavenger hunt. *Natural History* 93(4):20–27.

Shipman, P. 1986. Scavenging or hunting in early hominids: Theoretical frameworks and tests. *American Anthropologist* 88:27–43.

Shipman, P., and J. Rose. 1983. Evidence of butchery and hominid activities at Torralba and Ambrona: An evaluation using microscopic techniques. *Journal of Archaeological Science* 10:465–74.

Shreeve, J. 1994. Erectus rising. *Discover* (September): 80–89.

Small, M. F. 1992. A reasonable sleep. *Discover* (April): 83–88.

Smith, B. H. 1993. Life history and the evolution of human maturation. *Evolutionary Anthropology* 1 (4): 134–142.

Smith, F. H., A. B. Falsetti, and S. M. Donnelly. 1989. Modern human origins. *Yearbook of Physical Anthropology* 32:35–68.

Smith, J. M. 1984. Science and myth. *Natural History* 93 (11): 10–24.

Smuts, B. 1985. *Sex and Friendship in Baboons*. Hawthorne, N.Y.: Aldine de Gruyter.

Snow, C. C., and J. L. Luke. 1970. The Oklahoma City child disappearances: forensic anthropology in the identification of skeletal remains. In *Applying Anthropology*, ed. A. and P. J. Brown Podolefsky. Mountain View, Calif.: Mayfield.

Spindler, K. 1995. *The Man in the Ice*. New York: Harmony Books.

Stanford, C. B. 1995. To catch a colobus. *Natural History* 104 (1):48–55.

Stringer, C., and C. Gamble. 1993. *In Search of the Neanderthals: Solving the Puzzle of Human Origins*. London: Thames and Hudson.

Stringer, C. B., and P. Andrews. 1988. Genetic and fossil evidence for the origin of modern humans. *Science* 239:1263–68.

Strum, S. 1987. *Almost Human*. New York: Random House.

Tattersall, I. 1993. *The Human Odyssey: Four Million Years of Human Evolution*. New York: Prentice Hall.

Tattersall, I. *The Fossil Trail: How We Know What We Know About Human Evolution*. New York: Oxford University Press.

Teitelbaum, M. S., ed. 1976. *Sex Differences*. Garden City, N.Y.: Anchor Press/Doubleday.

Thompson, M. J., and D. W. Harsha. 1984. Our rhythms still follow the African sun. *Psychology Today* (January): 50–54.

Time-Life Books, eds. 1973. *The First Men*. New York: Time-Life Books.

Tullar, R. M. 1977. *The Human Species: Its Nature, Evolution, and Ecology*. New York: McGraw-Hill.

Ubelaker, D., and H. Scammell. 1992. *Bones: A Forensic Detective's Casebook*. New York: HarperCollins.

Underwood, J. H. 1979. *Human Variation and Human Microevolution*. Englewood Cliffs, N.J.: Prentice Hall.

Vrba, E. S. 1993. The pulse that produced us. *Natural History* 102 (5): 47–51.

Weaver, K. F. 1985. The search for our ancestors. *National Geographic* 168:560–623.

Weaver, Robert F. 1984. Changing life's genetic blueprint. *National Geographic* (December): 818–47.

White, T. D., G. Suwa, and B. Asfaw. 1994. Australopithecus ramidus, a new species of early hominid from Aramis, Ethiopia. *Nature* 371 (22 September): 306–312.

White, T. D., and P. A. Folkens. 1991. *Human Osteology*. San Diego: Academic Press.

Wildlife News. 1995. A New Species of Chimpanzee? (2, Winter.) African Wildlife Foundation.

Wilford, J. N. 1994. Fog thickens on climate and origin of humans. *New York Times* May 17: C1, C8.

Wilson, Edward O. 1992. *The Diversity of Life* (College Edition with Study Materials). New York: Norton.

Wolpoff, M. 1989. Multiregional evolution: The fossil alternative to Eden. In *The Human Revolution: Behavioural and Biological Perspectives in the Origins of Modern Humans*, ed. P. Mellars and C. Stringer. Princeton, N.J.: Princeton University Press: 62–108.

Woodruff, D. S., and P. A. Morin. 1995. Geneticists out on a limb. *Natural History* 104 (1): 54.

Photo and Illustration Credits

Chapter 1 CO-1, © David L. Brill, 1976; Fig. 1.1, From John Hostetler. Hutterite Society. 1974. Reprinted by permission of the Johns Hopkins University Press; Fig. 1.3, © William F. Keegan; Fig. 1.4, © William F. Keegan; Fig. 1.5, Photograph by Michael Kodas/ The Hartford Courant, 7/25/93.

Chapter 2 CO-2, Courtesy Kenneth Feder; Fig. 2.1, © Julia Margaret Cameron/National Portrait Gallery, London; Fig. 2.2, © David Muench 1995; Fig. 2.3, Courtesy Kenneth Feder; Fig. 2.4, Courtesy of The U.S. Geological Survey; Fig. 2.6, © Robert F. Sisson/ National Geographic Society.

Chapter 3 CO-3, © David Robert Austen; Fig. 3.4, © David Robert Austen.

Chapter 4 CO-4, © Michael Tweedie/ Photo Researchers, Inc.; Fig. 4.1, © Fritz Prenzel/Animals Animals/Earth Scenes; Fig. 4.2, Photograph courtesy of the March of Dimes Birth Defects Foundation; Fig. 4.3, © Michael Tweedie/Photo Researchers, Inc.; Fig. 4.3, © Michael Tweedie/Photo Researchers, Inc.; Fig. 4.9 (left), © Bill Longcore, Science Source/Photo Researchers, Inc.; Fig. 4.9 (right), © Ken Eward, Science Source/Photo Researchers, Inc.

Chapter 5 CO-5, © Zig Leszczynski/ Animals Animals/Earth Scenes; Fig. 5.2 (top left), © Stephen Dalton/Animals Animals/Earth Scenes; Fig. 5.2 (top right), © Zig Leszczynski/Animals Animals/Earth Scenes; Fig. 5.2 (bottom), © Robert Lubeck/Animals Animals/Earth Scenes; Fig. 5.3, Reprinted by permission of the publishers from The Diversity of Life by Edward O. Wilson, Cambridge, Mass.: The Belknap Press of Harvard University Press, Copyright © 1992 by Edward O. Wilson; Fig. 5.5, Negative # 319836. Courtesy Department of Library Services.

American Museum of Natural History; Fig. 5.8, Courtesy Janet M. Beatty.

Chapter 6 CO-6, "The Age of Reptiles," a mural by Rudolph F. Zallinger. Copyright © 1966, 1975, 1985, 1989, Peabody Museum of Natural History, Yale University, New Haven, Connecticut, USA; Fig. 6.2, © Fred Bavendam/Peter Arnold, Inc.; Fig. 6.5, Marvin Mattelson, © National Geographic Society; Fig. 6.7, "The Age of Reptiles," a mural by Rudolph F. Zallinger. Copyright © 1966, 1975, 1985, 1989, Peabody Museum of Natural History, Yale University, New Haven, Connecticut, USA; Fig. 6.8, © Arthur Gloor/Animals Animals/Earth Scenes.

Chapter 7 CO-7, © Ron Garrison/The Zoological Society of San Diego; Fig. 7.1, Reprinted by permission of Blackwell Science, Inc.; Fig. 7.3, © Frans Lanting/Minden Pictures; Fig. 7.5, Courtesy Marine World Africa USA/ Darryl Bush; Fig. 7.7 (top left), © Gerard Lacz/Animals Animals/Earth Scenes; Fig. 7.7 (top right), © Gerard Lacz/Animals Animals/Earth Scenes; Fig. 7.7 (bottom left), © Gerard Lacz/ Animals Animals/Earth Scenes; Fig. 7.7 (bottom right), © David Young-Wolff/PhotoEdit; Fig. 7.8, Michael A. Park; Fig. 7.9, © Joe MacDonald/Animals Animals/Earth Scenes; Fig. 7.9, © Stewart Halperin/Animals Animals/ Earth Scenes; Fig. 7.12, © Frank R. Sladek/Animals Animals/Earth Scenes; Fig. 7.13, © Zoological Society of San Diego; Fig. 7.14, © Andrew L. Young; Fig. 7.15, © Fred Whitehead/Animals Animals/Earth Scenes; Fig. 7.16, Courtesy Kenneth Feder; Fig. 7.17 (top left), © Ron Garrison/The Zoological Society of San Diego; Fig. 7.17 (top right), Michael A. Park; Fig. 7.17 (bottom left), © Steve Turner/Animals Ani-

mals/Earth Scenes; Fig. 7.17 (bottom right), © Ron Garrison/The Zoological Society of San Diego; Fig. 7.18, Jane Goodall, Courtesy National Geographic Society; Fig. 7.19, Michael A. Park.

Chapter 8 CO-8, © Irven DeVore/Anthro-Photo; Fig. 8.2, © T.W. Ransom/ /Biological Photo Service; Fig. 8.3, © Irven DeVore/Anthro-Photo; Fig. 8.4, © Zig Leszczynski/Animals Animals/ Earth Scenes; Fig. 8.5, © Kennan Ward/DRK Photo; Fig. 8.6, © Frans Lanting/Minden Pictures.

Chapter 9 CO-9, © James Amos/National Geographic Society; Fig. 9.1, From "The Antiquity of Human Walking" by John Napier. Copyright © April 1967 by Scientific American, Inc. All rights reserved.; Fig. 9.4 (left), From "The Antiquity of Human Walking" by John Napier. Copyright © April 1967 by Scientific American, Inc. All rights reserved.; Fig. 9.4 (right), From "The Antiquity of Human Walking" by John Napier. Copyright © April 1967 by Scientific American, Inc. All rights reserved.; Fig. 9.5, Identification of Pathological Conditions in Human Skeletal Remains, Orter and Putschar, 1985: 195 and 98, Smithsonian Institution Press; Fig. 9.6, © E. E. Kingsley 1984/Science Source/Photo Researchers, Inc.; Fig. 9.7, © James Amos/National Geographic Society © 1993; Fig. 9.8, From Price and Feinman, Images of the Past. Mayfield Publishing Company: Mountain View, CA.; Fig. 9.10, Courtesy of the Greenland National Museum and Archives; Fig. 9.11, From C.K. Brain. 1981. Who Were the Hunters or the Hunted? Chicago: The University of Chicago Press. Reprinted with permission of the publisher.; Fig. 9.12, Reprinted with per-

mission from J.J. Yunis et al., "The Striking Resemblance of High-Resolution G-Banded Chromosomes of Man and Chimpanzees, Science, 208 (1980), 1145-1149. Copyright 1980, American Association for the Advancement of Science.
Chapter 10 CO-10, © John Reader/ Photo Researchers, Inc.; Fig. 10.2, From "The Early Relatives of Man" by Elwyn L. Simons. Copyright © July 1964 by *Scientific American, Inc.* All rights reserved.; Fig. 10.3, From R.D. Martin, *Primate Origins and Evolution: A Phylogentric Reconstruction.* Princeton University Press: Princeton, NJ, 1990, p. 61.; Fig. 10.4, © David L. Brill, 1985; Fig. 10.6, Courtesy Dr. Ian Tattersall, American Museum of Natural History, from *The Human Odyssey*; Fig. 10.7, © David L. Brill, 1985; Fig. 10.9, © 1994 Tim D. White/David L. Brill; Fig. 10.10, © Science Photo Library/ Photo Researchers, Inc.; Fig. 10.11 (left), © Institute of Human Origins; Fig. 10.11(right), © Donald C. Johanson/Institute of Human Origins; Fig. 10.13, © John Reader/Photo Researchers, Inc.; Fig. 10.13, Negative # 4744(5). Photo by D. Finnin/C. Chesek. Courtesy Department of Library Services, American Museum of Natural History; Fig. 10.14, Redrawn with permission from: Bernard Campbell, *Human Ecology,* 2ed. (Hawthorne, NY: Aldine de Gruyter) © 1983, 1995 by Bernard Campbell; Fig. 10.17, © The National Museums of Kenya; Fig. 10.18, Micrographs courtesy of Dr. Frederick E. Grine, SUNY, Stony Brook. Photographed by Chester Tarka; Fig. 10.19, Courtesy Transvaal Museum, D.C. Panagos; Fig. 10.20 (all), © The National Museums of Kenya; Fig. 10.21, © Eric Delson; Fig. 10.22, © The National Museums of Kenya; Fig. 10.23, Courtesy Dr. Pat Shipman.
Chapter 11 CO-11, © David L. Brill, 1985; Fig. 11.2, © The National Museums of Kenya; Fig. 11.4, © David L. Brill, 1985; Fig. 11.5, © Jan Roletto; Fig. 11.6, Data compiled from Bowen 1978; Bradley, 1985; and Flint 1971;

Fig. 11.7, Negative # 319781. Courtesy Department of Library Services, American Museum of Natural History; Fig. 11.8, Negative # 315446. Photo by Charles H. Coles. Courtesy Department of Library Services, American Museum of Natural History; Fig. 11.9 (left), © Boltin Picture Library; Fig. 11.9 (center and right), Courtesy Kenneth Feder; Fig. 11.10, From "Peking Man" by Wu Rukand and Lin Shenglong. Copyright © June 1983 by *Scientific American, Inc.* All rights reserved; Fig. 11.11, © John Reader/ Science Photo Library/Photo Researchers, Inc.; Fig. 11.12, Reprinted from Roger Lewin, *In the Age of Mankind: A Smithsonian Book of Human Evolution* (Washington, DC: Smithsonian Institution Press), page 181, by permission of the publisher, Copyright 1989.
Chapter 12 CO-12, © Mario Ruspoli/ Caisse Nationale des Monuments Historiques et de Site Paris/S.P.A.D.E.M.; Fig. 12.3 (left), Courtesy Dr. Christopher B. Stringer; Fig. 12.3 (right), Courtesy State Museum for Nature, Stuttgart, Germany; Fig. 12.4, After Bordaz 1970; Fig. 12.4, Courtesy Dr. Ian Tattersall from *The Human Odyssey*; Fig. 12.5, © Landschaftsverband Rheinland; Fig. 12.6, © The Field Museum, Neg # A66700, Chicago; Fig. 12.6, From *In Search of the Neanderthals* by Christopher Stringer and Clive Gamble. Published with permission of the publisher, Thames and Hudson Ltd.; Fig. 12.7, From *In Search of the Neanderthals* by Christopher Stringer and Clive Gamble. Published with permission of the publisher, Thames and Hudson Ltd.; Fig. 12.8, From *In Search of the Neanderthals* by Christopher Stringer and Clive Gamble. Published with permission of the publisher, Thames and Hudson Ltd.; Fig. 12.9, Courtesy Kenneth Feder; Fig. 12.10, Courtesy Phototheque du Musée de l'Homme, Paris. M. Lucas, photographer; Fig. 12.11, Courtesy Milford Wolpoff, University of Michigan at Ann Arbor; Fig. 12.13 (top left), Peabody Museum, Harvard University. Photograph by Hillel Burger. Photo

No. N26470; Fig. 12.13 (top right); Courtesy Phototheque du Musée de l'Homme, Paris; Fig. 12.13 (bottom left), Courtesy of Laboratory of Vertebrate and Human Paleontology, Paris. B. Vandermeersch; Fig. 12.13 (bottom right), Photo by A.R. Hughes. Courtesy Professor P.V. Tobias, University of the Witwatersrand, Johannesburg, South Africa; Fig. 12.15, Courtesy Kenneth Feder; Fig. 12.16, Negative # 39686. Photo by Kirschner. Courtesy Department of Library Services. American Museum of Natural History; Fig. 12.17, © Mario Ruspoli/Caisse Nationale des Monuments Historiques et de Sites, Paris/S.P.A.D.E.M.; Fig. 12.20, Courtesy Mark Stoneking, Pennsylvania State University.
Chapter 13 CO-13, © Bruce Dale/National Geographic Society; Fig. 13.4, From Matthews and Platt, *The Western Humanities,* Mayfield Publishing Company: Mountain View, CA, 1995; Fig. 13.10 (left), Negative # 231604. Photo by D.B. MacMillan. Courtesy Department of Library Services. American Museum of Natural History; Fig. 13.10 (right), © Bruce Dale/National Geographic Society.
Chapter 14 CO-14, © David Young-Wolff/PhotoEdit; Fig. 14.1 (top left), © David Young-Wolff/PhotoEdit; Fig. 14.1 (top right), © David Young-Wolff/PhotoEdit; Fig. 14.1 (bottom left), © Michelle Bridwell/PhotoEdit; Fig. 14.1 (bottom right), © Rhoda Sidney/PhotoEdit; Fig. 14.3, Courtesy Dr. Serena Nanda, John Jay College; Fig. 14.4, © Johnny Johnson/DRK Photo; Fig. 14.5, Maps redrawn from originals by permission of the Canadian Museum of Nature, Ottawa; Fig. 14.6, Reprinted by permission of Blackwell Science, Inc.; Fig. 14.9, Data from Cavalli-Sforza 1991; Fig. 14.10, © The Granger Collection.
Chapter 15 CO-15, © Liaison Agency Inc./National Geographic Society; Fig. 15.1, © Liaison Agency Inc./National Geographic Society; Fig. 15.2 (all), © Kenneth Garrett/National Geographic Society; Fig. 15.3, © Irven DeVore/ Anthro-Photo.

Index

Italicized page numbers indicate illustrations. Page numbers in bold indicate glossary terms.

ABO blood group system, 45, 278-282, *279*, *280*
absolute dating techniques, **159**-161, *160*
Acheulian, **217**
acquired characteristics, inheritance of, 28-29, **29**
Adam and Eve, 20
Adapidae, *174*, 175
adaptation
  arboreal, 78, 115, 121-123
  bipedalism as, 187-192
  defined, 28, 32
  environmental correlations, without, 278-282, *279*, *280*
  and environmental separation, 32, 73
  and fitness, 31
  human, 128, 274-282, *274*, *279*, 300-301, 323
  mammalian, 107
  pace of, 80-83, *81*, *82*
  primate, 115
  radiation, adaptive, 77-79, *78*, *79*
  relative to specific environment, 58, 66
  and speciation, 73
  and taxonomic categories, 106-107
  and variation, 31, 56-58, *57*
adapted, 28, **29**

adaptive radiation, **77**-79, *78*, *79*
adolescent growth spurt, 283, *283*, *284*, 292
Aegyptopithecus, 175, *176*
Africa
  chimpanzee behavioral variation in, 143
  climatic zones of, and evolution, 188, *188*, 191, *192*, 197
  and dating age of earth, 91
  genetic diversity of populations of, 252, 253
  genetic variation of humans and, 301
  hominid origin in, 121, 178, 181, 192, 206, 209, 216-217
  hominoids of, 123, 176, 178
  Homo erectus in, *207*, *208*, 209, 210, 216-217
  Homo sapiens (archaic) in, 228-229
  human origin in, 214, 240, 249, 250, 251, 252, 253
  hunter-gatherers of, recent, *326*
  leopard kills in, ancient, *162*, 163
  Levallois tool-making method in, 233
  malaria and, 65, 67
  monkeys of, 121
  polygynous society of, 16
  prosimians in, 79, 118
  sickle cell anemia and, 63, *63*, 66, 67
  sites in, 156, *156*, 157, 175, 181, 182, 183, 193, 198, 199, 200, *208*, 210

African Americans
  and claims about intelligence, 307-312
  gene flow and, 311
  and sickle cell anemia, 63, *63*, 66-67
  and sports, 311-312
  teeth of, 322
age
  determination of, 152, *152*, 210, 322
  of species, and genetic diversity, 251-252
  See also dating techniques
aging
  care for the, 239
  mutations and, 55
Alaska, 296, 297
Algeria, *207*, *208*
allele frequency, 54-**55**, 56
  calculating change over time, 260-264
alleles, 43-44, **45**
altruistic behavior, 134-**135**
Ambrona site, Spain, *158*, 201, 215, 218-220
American Indians
  blood types among, 278-279, *278*
  gender categories of, multiple, 295
  teeth of, 322
American Sign Language (AMESLAN), 126
amino acids, **41**
Amphioxis, *106*
analogies, **133**
Anaximander, 20

Animalia kingdom, defined, 105
Anthropoidea suborder, 118,
    119-120
anthropoids, 119-126
anthropology
    applied. *See* applied anthropol-
        ogy
    archaeology, **11**
    biological. *See* biological
        anthropology
    choosing populations to study, 6
    cultural, **11**
    defined, **9**, *10*
    fear of first contact in, 2-3
    focus on race of, 290
    paleoanthropology, **11**,
        157-161, *158*
antibodies, 280, **281**
antigens, **45**, 280
ants, 133-134, 136
apes
    bipedalism of, occasional, 111,
        144, 145, 187
    characteristics of, 123-126,
        123-125
    and cladistics, 167, *167*
    evolution of, 176-178, *177*
    sexual dimorphism of, 152
    See also individual species
applied anthropology, **11**
    examples of, 6-9, *7*, 323-327
    forensic, 12, **13**, 166, 316,
        316-323
arboreal, 78, **79**
archaeology, defined, **11**
Archeopteryx, 79, 80
Ardipithecus ramidus, 181-183,
    182, 190, 191
Argentina, 12, 319
Aristotle, 21
Arizona, 85
art, of Upper Paleolithic,
    244-246, 245-246
asexually, **93**
Ashkenazic jews, and Tay-Sachs
    disease, 324-325
Asia
    blood types in, *279*, 280
    glaciers covering, 213, *213*

Homo erectus in, *207, 208*, 217
Homo sapiens (archaic) in, *228*
and human origin models, 251
primate evolution in, 173, 175,
    177
primates of, 109, 121, 123
prosimians in, 79, 118, 119,
    119, 120
sickle cell anemia in, 63
Assimilation Model. *See* Genetic
    Replacement Hypothesis
asteroid, collision with earth of,
    26, 58, 97-98
Australia
    blood types of natives, 278, *279*
    and dating age of earth and
        life, 91-93, *92*
    homogeneous characteristics in,
        297
    human fossil sites in, *241*
    and human origin models, 251
    mammalian traits in, 106
Australopithecus, 179-180, 196,
    197, 221
*Australopithecus afarensis, 180,
    181*, 183-187, *184, 187*,
    192-193
    Lucy skeleton, 183, *183*
Australopithecus africanus, 178,
    180, *181*, 193, 285-286
    Taung Baby, 178, 285
Australopithecus anamensis, 183
axolotl, 74, *75*

baboons
    behaviors of, related to human,
        135, 139-140
    estrus in, *127*, 139
    savanna adaptation of, 190-191
    social structure of, 113, *115*,
        136-140, *137, 138*
    See also primates
Barkley, Charles, 311
bases, 39, 40, 41
basketball, 311-312
bats, 109, 132-133, *133*
behavior
    of baboons, 136-140, *137, 138*
    biological vs. learned, 134-136

of bonobos, 143-146, *144*
of chimpanzees, 135, 140-143,
    143, 145-146
flexible, 134
genetically coded, 133-134, 135
homologous and analogous,
    135-136
skeletal structure revealing, 154
belief systems
    defined, **15**
    of Neandertals, 238-239, *238*
    scientific creationism and,
        83-86
    social importance of, with sci-
        ence, 15-16, *17*, 85-86
    study of earth separated from,
        27
Bellantoni, Nick, 6-8
berdaches, 295
Bible, knowledge of natural world
    and, 20-21, 23, 27, 33,
    84-85
bifacial, **217**
Big Bang, 90, *91*
Binford, Lewis, 200
biological anthropology
    defined, 10-12, *10*, **11**
    diversity of studies, 11-12
    primatology and, 104
    and science, 12
biological change. *See* evolution
biology
    vs. learned behaviors, 134-136
    and race, 296-299, *298*,
        300-303, *302*, 307
    and intelligence, 308-312
bipedalism, **111**
    adaptation of, by hominids,
        187-192
    of apes, occasional, 111, *144*,
        145, 187
    of humans, 111, 126
    Laetoli footprints showing, 187,
        187
    skeletons and fossils revealing,
        154, 185
birds
    and adaptive radiation, 77-78,
        78, 79

birds (*continued*)
cline of, *299*
dinosaurs, descended from,
77-78, *79,* 80, 99, *100*
Black Death, 268-270, *269*
Black Skull (*Paranthropus aethiopicus*), 194-195, *194*
blending, as inheritance concept,
38, 44
blood type
ABO system, 45, 278-282, *278,*
280
alleles determining, 45
body heat
and body build, 236, 275, *276*
conservation, 236, 275
dissipation of, 189, 274-275
Bolivia, *12,* 319
bonobos, *124, 144*
bipedalism of, 125, *144,* 145,
187
and chimpanzees, branch of
line from, 145, 166
evolutionary change of, 191
and humans, branch of line
from, 107, *108*
sexual behaviors of, 145, 190
social structure of, 143-146,
190, 191
taxonomy of, *105,* 107, *117,*
123, 167, *167*
Border Cave site, South Africa,
243
brachiation, *123,* **123**
brain
ape, 125
chimpanzee, 140
complexity of, 112
Homo erectus, 220
Homo sapiens (archaic), 227,
230
human, 112, *113,* 301, 310
primate, 112
shape of, 220, 227
brain size (cranial capacity)
Australopithecus, 199
Australopithecus afarensis, 185
Australopithecus africanus, 193
chimpanzee, 125
Homo erectus, 208, 209-210,

210, 214, *215,* 220-221,
221, 222
Homo habilis, 199-200
Homo sapiens (archaic), 227,
228-229
human, 112
Paranthropus, 193, 199
Paranthropus aethiopicus, 194
Paranthropus boisei, 196
Paranthropus robustus, 195
as relative, 112
Brazil, 76
breathing, 221, 324
breeding populations, 59, **59**-60
brow ridges, **209**
Bryce Canyon, Utah, *25*
bubonic plague, 268-270, *269,*
281
Buffon, Georges, 23-24, *34*
burial of the dead, 238-239, *238*

calendar, engraved antler, 246
Cambrian Explosion, 93
Canada
caribou of, 296, 297
Hutterite colonies of. *See* Hutterites
sickle cell anemia in, 66-67
Cann, Rebecca, 252-253
Carabelli's cusp, 322
carbon dating, **159**-160
caribou, *296,* 297-299, *298*
Carnivora, 107
carnivores, **155**
comparing behaviors among,
135-136
hominids scavenging kills of,
189, 191, 200, 201
teeth type of, 155
Cassidy, Butch and the Sundance
Kid, *12,* 319
Catarrhini, 120-121
catastrophism, 23, 25-26, 27, 29
catastrophists, **23**
cats, 118, *151,* 155
Cavalli-Sforza, L. L., 302-303
cave bear cults, 239
caves
art in, 245-246, *246*

and cave bear cults, 239
hominids as prey, found in,
162, 163
Homo erectus use of, 214
cells
meiosis of, 46-47, *47*
mitosis of, 46, *46*
mutations of individual in, 55
as proteins, 39
structure of, *39*
Central America, 79
Cercopithecoidea, 121, *122*
chain of being, 21, 23, 28
change
catastrophism, 23, 25-26, 27,
29
as new idea, 20-22, *22*
uniformitarianism, 23-**25,**
26-27, 28, 29
See also evolution
Chicago, Illinois, airline crash in,
319
Chile, 175
chimpanzees, *124*
bipedalism of, 125, 187
characteristics of, 125-126
chromosomes, number of, 46
dependency period of, 127
diet of, 125-126, *142,* 143, 189
and humans
behaviors related to, 135,
140, 141, 145-146
evolutionary relationship to,
107, *108,* 145, 165, 166,
281-282
genetic similarity to, 53, 165,
165, 166
hunting by, 126, *142,* 143, 189
lifespan of, 285
mtDNA, variability of, 252
sexual maturity of, 285
social structure of, 113, *116,*
140-146, *141, 142*
taxonomy of, *105,* 107, *117,*
123, 167, *167*
tool uses of, 125-126, *125,* 143
vocal apparatus of, *222*
See also bonobos; primates
China
ape fossils in, 177

Homo sites in, *207, 208, 212, 214-215, 228, 241*
choppers, 217-218
Chordata, 106, *106*
chromosomal mutations, 55, *55*
chromosomes, **39**, 46-48, 55
   evolutionary relationships revealed by, 164-166, *165*
cladistics, **109**, 166-167, *167*
classification. See taxonomy
class, taxonomic, 106
cleavers, 217
climatic zones and evolution
   in Africa, 188, *188*, 191, *192*, 197
   and body type, 275
   during Pleistocene, 213-214
cline, 299, **299**
coal burning, and peppered moth, 57
codominant, 44-**45**
codons, **39**-41, *40*
Columbus, *306*
comet, collision with earth of, 26, 58, 97-98
communication
   of apes, 126
   of baboons, *138*
   of bonobos, 145
   of chimpanzees, *116*, 141
   language. See language
   of primates, 115, *116*
comparative anatomy, defined, 23
competitive exclusion, **197**
Connecticut
   grave excavation in, 6-8, *7, 8*
   Pleistocene conditions of, 214
continental drift, 95-97, *96*
continuity of traits, 250-251
Coon, Carlton, *234*
core tools, **199**
courtship behaviors, and speciation, 72
cranial capacity. See brain size
cranial shape
   Ardipithecus ramidus, 182
   Australopithecus afarensis, 180, *184, 185*
   Australopithecus africanus, 178, *179, 180*, 193

Homo erectus, 209, 209, 210, 228
Homo habilis, 180, 199, 200
Homo sapiens (archaic), *228, 229, 231, 233, 234-235, 235*
   human, *152, 210, 228, 235*
   early, *241, 243*
   Neandertal, *233, 234-235, 235*
Paranthropus aethiopicus, 194-195, 194
Paranthropus boisei, 180, 196, *197*
Paranthropus robustus, 180, 195, *196*
   sexual dimorphism and, *152*
Sivapithecus, 177
cranial suture closure, *153*
creationism, scientific, 83-86, *85,* **85**
crimes, identifying suspects in, 166
crossing over, **47**
cultural adaptations, 274, *274,* 300-301
cultural anthropology, **11**
culture
   and biology, as interrelated, 260
   defined, **9**
   as evidence of intelligence, 128
   folk taxonomies, 293-295
   and gender. See gender
   as human adaptation, 128, 274, *274,* 300-301, 323
   as learned, 9-10
   and sickle cell anemia, 67
   as variable, 10
cusps, tooth, 176, *176,* 322
Cuvier, Georges, 23, 26, 27, 29, *34*
cytoplasm, *39, 40,* 41

Dart, Raymond, 157, 159, 178
Darwin, Charles, *20*
   and delay in publishing his ideas, 32, 58-59
   evolution, developing theory of, 29-33, *31*

   on speciation, 80, 83
   as synthesizer of ideas, 20, 27, 34
   See also evolution
Darwin, Erasmus, 28
Darwinian gradualism, 80-81, *81, 82*
dating techniques, *158,* 159-161, *160*
   absolute, 159
   radiometric, 159-161
   relative, 159
   uniformitarianism and, 26-27, *26*
   See also age
daughter cells, 46, *46*
dead, burial of, 238-239, *238*
deduction, defined, **13**
demes, 59, **59**-60, 297
demography, 268, **269**
dental apes, 176
dental eruption, *153,* 322
deoxyribonucleic acid. See DNA
dependency, 112, **113**
depth perception, 110, *111*
developed nations, age-sex structure of, 272-273, *272*
developing nations, age-sex structure of, 271-272, *271*
Diamond, Jared, 324
diet
   of chimpanzees, 125-126, *142,* 143, 189
   effect of, on populations, 284-285
   of hominids, 188-189, 191, 193, 195, 200, 201
   of hunter-gatherers, 327
   of primates, 109
   on savannas, 188-189
   and teeth, evidenced by, 155, 176, 177, 193, 195, *195,* 318
   See also food finding; meat eating
dinosaurs, 98-99
   birds descending from, 77-78, *79,* 80, 99, *100*
   extinction of, 97-98
   fossils of, 156, *157*

dinosaurs (*continued*)
 time lines of origins, *94, 95,* 97
discordant variation, 301, *302*
disease
 blood type, and correlations to, 281-282
 bubonic plague, 268-270, *269*
 folk taxonomies of, 293-295
 genes located for, 166
 genetic. *See* genetic disease
 modern lifestyles and, 325-327
 rickets, 277-278
 sexual dimophism and, 292
 skeletal evidence of, 155, *155,* 239
distance curve, *282, 283,* **283**
diurnal, 78, **79**
DNA (deoxyribonucleic acid)
 defined, **39**
 evolutionary relationships revealed through, 165-166, *165*
 fossils, extracting from, 164
 genetic analysis by, *302, 303*
 mitochondrial, 252-253, *254,* 318
 and origin of life, 93
 protein synthesis and, 41
 structure of, 39, *40*
dogs, 38, 46, 53, *53,* 109, 110, 135, 155
dolphins, 109
dominance hierarchy, **113**
dominant, **44-45**
donkeys, 53
Down Syndrome, 55, *55*
Dubois, Eugene, 214

earth
 age of, 21, 23, 24, 25, 84, 91
 cataclysmic change on, 25-26, 58
 continent formation on, 95-97, *96*
 time lines of life on, 92-99, *92, 94, 95*
Eaton, S. Boyd, 325-327
ecology. *See* human ecology

Egypt
 mummification in, 161
 sites in, 175
endocasts, 220, *221,* **221**
endogamous, **267**
energy, control of, 206
England
 peppered moth adaptation, 56-58, *57*
 sites in, *228*
environment
 adaptation to. *See* adaptation
 adaptive radiation and, 77-79, *78, 79,* 212-213
 vs. genetics, 45-46
 in human evolution, 188-191, *188,* 197-198
 mutations resulting from, 55
 niches of, and speciation, 53, 72
 and skin color, 45-46
environmental, **45**
enzymes, **39**
epiphyseal union, *153*
ER 3733, *209,* 216
error. *See* mutations
essentialism, 21
estrus, 127, *127,* 139, 145
ethics. *See* belief systems
Ethiopia, sites in, 157, 181, 182, 183, 194, 200, *228, 241*
ethology, 136, **137**
Europe
 Bible, literal interpretation of, 20-21, 23-24
 and Black Death, 268-270, *269*
 blood types in, 278, *279*
 glaciers covering, 213, *213*
 Homo erectus in, *207, 208,* 215, 217
 Homo sapiens (archaic) in, 228-229
 and human origin models, 251
 Levallois tool-making method in, 233
 monkeys of, 121
 peppered moth adaptation, 56-58, *57*
 primate evolution in, 173, 175, 178

prosimians in, 79
racial folk taxonomy of, 305-307, *306*
racism of, about human origins, 214
reindeer of, 297, 298-299
sickle cell anemia in, 63, 66
Tay-Sachs disease in, 324-325
tuberculosis in, 325
European Americans
 gene flow and, 311
 and intelligence testing, 308-311
 and sickle cell anemia, 66
 teeth of, 322
Eve hypothesis, 253
evolution
 adaptation. *See* adaptation
 allele frequency and, 54-55
 complexity and, 28, 32
 controversy about, 27, 29, 32, 58-59, 84-86
 defined, **21**, 55
 detecting in populations, 260-268, *264-266*
 diagrams of, *31, 58*
 history of ideas of, 20-33, *28, 34*
 of hominids. *See under* hominids
 modes of, 80-83, *81, 82*
 mutation and, 55-56
 primate, 172-178, *173, 174, 176, 177*
 processes of, 68. *See* gene flow; genetic drift; mutation; natural selection
 relationships of
  genetics indicating, 164-167, *165, 167*
  taxonomy indicating, 107-109, *108*
 and scientific method, 13, 14
 species as basic unit of, 52-55
 theory of, 52
 time lines of, 90-99, *91-96*
excavation, 157-159, *158*
exercise, 327
extinctions
 adaptive radiation and, 77, *78*

as commonplace, 32, 58
of dinosaurs, 97-98, 98-99
fossils as evidence of, 21
of hominids, 196-198
mass, 23, 25-26, 97-98
as nonexistent, 29
and uniformitarianism, 24, 26

faces, and recognition of individual, 113, *114*
facts and science, 12, 13
family, taxonomic, 107
farming, and malaria increase, 67
Fayum site, Egypt, 175
Feder, Ken, 217
Fedigan, Linda, 12
female and male differences. *See* male and female differences
fingerprints, tracking evolution with, 5, 11, 264-268, *264-266*
fire, use of, 206, 218, 219
fission, **61**
fitness, **31**
flake tools, **199**, 217, *219*, 222, 237, *237*
folk taxonomies, **293-295**
gender as, 292-293, *293*, 295
human races as, 290, 304-307, 312
food finding
and bipedalism, 188-189
Homo erectus and, 209, 212
food sharing, 126, 143, 145, 190, 192
foramen magnum, 178, **179**
forensic anthropologist, **13**
forensic anthropology, 12, **13**, 166, 316, 316-323
Fore people, 295
forests, bipedalism and, 182-183, 190-191
Fossey, Dian, 140
fossils
cause of death, information on, 163
dating of. *See* dating techniques
defined, 21

formation of, 161-163, 175
location and recovery of, 156-159, *156*, *157*
and mass extinctions, 97
recent, as interpreted differently, 226, 227
founder effect, **61-62**, 266-267, 325
foxes, 136
France, sites in, 215, 217, *228-229*, 238, 239, *240*, *241*, 245
friendship, 113, 138, 139
frostbite tendency, and skin color, 278

Galápagos islands, finches of, 77, 78
galaxies, 90, 91
Galdikas, Biruté, 140
Galileo, 15, 16
gametes, 46-48, *47*, **47**, *48*, 62
isolation of, and speciation, 73
mutations in, 55
gamete sampling, 62, **63**
Garden of Eden, 20
gender
as culturally determined, 292-**293**, *293*, 295
third and fourth categories of, 294, 295-296
gene flow, 58, 59, **59**-60, *60*, 297
and Hutterite example, 60, 266-268
and models of human origin, 248-249, *248*, 250-251
as norm for humans, 300
gene frequency, **55**. *See* allele frequency
gene pool
defined, **57**
mutation and, 56, *58*
generalized, **77**
genes
chemical process of, 38-42, *39*, *40*
defined, **39**, 41
disease, identified in, 166
and Mendel's simplification, 43

and reproduction, 46-48, *46*, *47*
and trait expression, 43-45
See also alleles
Genesis, Book of, 20-21, 23, 84-85, 104
genetic code, defined, 39
genetic diseases
dominant alleles and, 44
genes located for, 166
sickle cell anemia. *See* sickle cell anemia
Tay-Sachs, 62, 324-325
genetic drift, 58, 61-62, *61*
and Hutterite example, 61, 62, 266-267
genetic markers, **265**
Genetic Replacement Hypothesis, *248*, 250-256
genetics
chemical process of, 38-42, *39*, *40*
evolutionary relationships, reconstructing with, 164-167, *165*, *167*
Genetic Replacement model of human origin, *248*, 250-255, *254*
heritability, and intelligence, 308-310
Mendelian, 33, 38, 43, **43**-48, *47*, *48*
populations, analyzing with. *See under* populations
traits. *See* traits
genome, **301**
genotypes, 44, **45**
geographic ranges, and speciation, 53, 73, 297
geological periods, 94, *173*, *212*, *213*, **213**-214, 217
geological processes
fossil strata exposed through, 157
plate tectonics, **95**-97, *96*
Rift Valley formation, and evolution, 191, *192*
Georgia, Republic of, 215
Germany, sites in, *228-229*, *231*, 233, *241*
gibbons, 117, 123, *123*

Gigantopithecus, 109, *110,*
    177-178
giraffes, 29
glaciers, *212, 213,* **213**-214
Gombe Stream National Park,
    Tanzania, 140, 143
Goodall, Jane, 140, 143, 146
gorilla, *124*
    bipedalism of, 125
    characteristics of, 125, 126,
        140
    genetic similarity to humans,
        140
    skeletal structure, *151, 154,*
        185, *185*
    taxonomy of, *105, 107, 108,*
        117, 123, 167, *167*
Gould, Stephen Jay, 82-83, 164,
    300
gradualism, Darwinian, 80-81, *81,*
    82
Grand Canyon, Arizona, *85*
gravity, theory of, 13-14, *14*
Greece, sites in, 177, *228, 231*
Greeks
    concepts of, influencing evolu-
        tion, 21, 23, 28
    evolution proposed by, 20
Greenland, 91, 161, *162,* 297
grid systems of excavation, *158,*
    159
grooming, **115,** *116,* 118-119,
    119, 141, 145
growth rate, population, 270
growth rates, individual, 282-286,
    282-285
Gurche, John, *320-321*

haft, **237**
hairlessness, 189
half-life, **160**
hand axe, **217**-218, *218*
Hardy-Weinberg equilibrium,
    262-264, **263**
Harsha, David, 323
Harvard Educational Review, 308
Hawaii, grave movement to, 6-9,
    7, 8

health, skeletal remains revealing,
    155, *155,* 318
hearing, 109, 110
heat. *See* body heat
heaven, belief systems, and sci-
    ence, 15-16
hemoglobin, 42, 63-64
heritability, 308-310, **309**
heterozygous, 44, **45**
Hexian site, China, *208,* 215
hierarchies
    among baboons, 136-139, *138*
    among bonobos, 145
    among chimpanzees, 140-141
    dominance, **113**
higher power, 15, 16
hijras, of India, *294,* 295
Hippocratic Oath, 15
holistic approach, defined, **9**
Hominidae, 126, 166-167,
    179-180
hominids
    bipedalism of, 154
    characteristics of, 126-128
    defined, **73,** 126
    diet of, 188-189, 191, 193, 195,
        200, 201
    and ecological isolation, 72
    evolution of, 178-187, *179-185,*
        192-201, *192-199, 201,*
        255
    bipedalism in, *186,* 187-192,
        188
    fossils of, locating, 156, 157,
        159
    origin of, 121, 178, 181, 192,
        206, 209, 216-217
    pace of evolution of, 81
    sexual dimorphism of, 152
    social structure of, 139-140,
        146, 190, 192
Hominoidea, 121-123
hominoids
    tooth cusp pattern, 176, *176*
    traits of, 121-126, *123*
Homo, 179-180, 196, 197, 198,
    247, *247*
Homo erectus, 207, 208, 209
    body size, 210, *211*

cranial shape and capacity,
    208, 209-210, *210,*
    220-221, *221,* 222
distribution of, 206-207, *207,*
    208, 210-213, 214,
    221-222
ER 3733, *209,* 216
fire, use of, 218, 219
fossil evidence of, 214-217,
    215, 216
and human origin models, 248,
    248, 249, 255
Java Man, *208,* 214, *215*
language capability of, 220-221
new data and, 216-217
Peking Man, 214-215, *216*
scavenging meat, 218-220
social structure of, 210-212,
    218-220
success of, 207, 221-222
tool use of, 209, 210, 217-218,
    218, 219, 222
Turkana boy, 216
Homo ergaster, 216
Homo habilis, 180, 181, 198-201,
    198, 199, 201, 217
    skull 1470, *199*
homologies, 132, *133,* **133**
Homo sapiens (anatomically mod-
    ern). *See* humans
Homo sapiens (archaic)
    cranial capacity and shape,
        227-229, *228-229*
    distribution of, *228-229,* 230
    Homo ergaster as ancestor, 216
    and human origin hypotheses,
        248-251, *248,* 255-256
    Neandertals. *See* Neandertals
    tool use by, 230-233, *232*
homosexuality, 145
homozygous, 44, **45**
Hooke, Robert, 21, 23, 26, 27, 34
horses, 53
"How much can we boost IQ and
    scholastic achievement"
    (Jensen), 308, *309*
Hubbard Glacier, Alaska, *212*
human ecology, defined, **11**
Human Genome Initiative, 166

humans (modern *Homo sapiens*)
 adaptation of, 128, 274-282,
  274, 279, 300-301, 323
 ancestor of, 253
 and apes
  evolutionary relationship to,
   107, *108,* 145, 165, 166,
   281-282
  genetic similarity to, 53, 140,
   165, *165,* 166
 behaviors of, compared with
  other species, 134-136,
  139-140, 141, 145-146
 as bipedal. *See* bipedalism
 brain of, *113*
 brain size, 112
 breathing of, 221, 324
 chromosomes, number of, 46
 dependency of, 127
 early, 240-247, *241-246*
  fossils of, 240-241, *241*
  Homo erectus and, 217
  tool technologies of, 241,
   244, 245, 245
 fossil evidence of, 251
 gene flow and. *See* gene flow
 growth rates of, 282-286,
  282-285
 infants, sleeping with parents,
  324
 intelligence of, 128
 lifespan of, 284-285
 migration of, 247, 302, *303*
 movements of, 126
 naps, need for, 323-324
 origins
  in Africa, 214, 240, 249,
   250, 251, 252, 253
  European discomfort with,
   214
  models for, 248-256, *248,*
   254, 255
 reproduction of, 127-128
 sexual behaviors of, 127-128,
  190
 skeletal structure, 150, *151,* 152
 taxonomy of, 105, *105,* 107,
  117, 167, *167*
 teeth of. *See under* teeth

 vocal apparatus of, 221, *222,*
  324
 world population of, 273, *273*
Hungary, sites in, *228*
hunter-gatherers, **13**
 studies of modern, 12, 325-327,
  326
hunting
 behaviors of, humans compared
  with various, 135-136
 by chimpanzees, 126, *142,* 143,
  189
 by early hominids, 189
 by early humans, 242, 246
 by *Homo erectus,* 218-220
 by Neandertals, 237-238
Hutterites, 2-6, *4, 5*
 demographics of, 268, 270-272,
  270
 fingerprint study of, 264-268,
  265, 266
 gene flow and, 60, 266-268
 genetic drift and, 61, 62,
  266-267
Hutton, James, 24, 26, 27, *34*
Huxley, Thomas Henry, 32
hybrids, and species separation,
  53, 73
Hylobatidae, 123
hypotheses, **13**-15

Ice Ages. *See* Pleistocene
Ice Man, 316-318, *317, 320-321*
inclusive fitness, 134-**135,** 139,
  143
independent assortment, **47**
India
 gender categories of, multiple,
  294, 295
 sickle cell anemia in, 63
 sites in, 109, 177, *177, 228*
individuals, recognition of, 113,
  114
induction, **13**
infraorder, 117
inheritance
 of acquired characteristics,
  28-29, **29**

 as blending, 38, 44
 as particulate, 38
 process of, 46-48
 See also heritability
inorganic, **93**
insect wings, 132-133, *133*
intelligence, 112, **113,** 309
 and race, 307-312
intelligence quotient. *See* IQ
Inuits
 body build of, 276
 cultural adaptation of, *274*
 mummification of, 161, *162*
IQ test performance, and race,
  308-312
Iraq, sites in, *229, 239*
Israel, sites in, *229,* 237, 239-240,
  241, 243, 251
Italy, sites in, 316

Japan, and Peking Man, 215
Java
 migration to, 217
 sites in, *207, 208,* 212, 214,
  216-217
Java Man (*Homo erectus*), *208,*
  214, *215*
Jebel Irhoud site, Morocco, *243*
Jebel Qafzeh site, Israel, *243*
Jensen, Arthur, 308-309, 312
Jews, and Tay-Sachs disease,
  324-325
Johanson, Donald, 11-12, 183
John Paul II (pope), 15
Jordan, Michael, 311
Judeo-Christian belief system, and
  scientific method, 20-21,
  23, 27, 33, 84-85, 107
Jurassic Park, 164

Kebara Cave site, Israel, 237,
  239-240
Kennedy, John F., 319
Kenya, sites in, 183, 194, *199,*
  200, *208,* 209, 210, *211,*
  216
kingdoms, taxonomic, 105

Klasies River Mouth site, South
     Africa, 241, 242, *244*, 251
koalas, 297
Konner, Melvin, 12, 325-327
!Kung, *326*

La Chapelle-aux-Saints site,
     France, 239, *240*
Laetoli footprints, 187, *187*
Lamarck, Jean Baptiste de, 28-29,
     31-32, *34*
language
   of apes, 126
   culture, determined by, 9-10,
        11, 134
   gene distribution and, 302-303,
        304
   Homo erectus, capability of,
        220-221
   of humans, 128, 221
   of Neandertals, capability of,
        239-240
   See also communication
Lantian site, China, 208, 215
Lascaux cave site, France, *246*
Laurasia, 173
laws. *See* belief systems
Leakey, Louis, 156, 196, 198, 199
Leakey, Mary, 156, 186, 198, 199
Leakey, Richard, 200
lemurs, 109, 119, 175
leopards, 136, *162*, 163, 189
Levallois technique, *232*, **233**,
     237
Lewontin, Richard, 301
life, origin in time, 91-95, *92-95*
life history, **285**-286
lifespans, 285
linkage, **47**
Linnaeus, Carolus. *See* Linné,
     Karl von
Linné, Karl von, 105, 107,
     306-307
lions, 53, 135, 136
locomotion
   bipedal. *See* bipedalism
   brachiation, 123, *123*
   human limbs and, 126
   primate, 111

locus (pl. loci), **41**. *See* genes
lorises, *119*, 175
Lucy (*Australopithecus afarensis*),
     183, *183*
Lyell, Charles, 24, 25, 26-27, *34*

McKenna, James, 324
macromutations, 74, **75**
Madagascar, prosimians in, 79,
     109, 111, 118, 119,
     175-176
malaria, *65*, 66-67, 281
Malaysia, 123
male and female differences
   behavioral. *See* gender; repro-
        ductive strategies
   physical. *See* sexual dimorphism
Mal'ta site, Russia, 246-247
Mammalia, 106
mammals
   adaptive radiation of, 78-79,
        99
   defined, 106-107
   extinction, surviving mass,
        98-99
   reproductive strategies of, 135
   skeletal structures of, compared,
        151
Maples, William, 319
Marks, Jonathan, 309
marmosets, 111
meat eating
   behaviors of species surround-
        ing, 135-136
   by chimpanzees, 125, 126, *142*,
        143, 189
   by hominids, 189, 191, 193,
        200-201, 218-220
   See also hunting
medicine
   effect on populations, 284, 301
   ethics of, 15
   and interrelatedness of life, 83
   prehistoric, 155, *155*
meiosis, 46-47, *47*, **47**, 48
melanin, **275**
melanocytes, **275**
menarche, 284, **285**
Mendel, Gregor, 33, *34*, 38

Mendelian genetics, 33, 38, *43*,
     43-48, *47*, 48
Mengele, Josef, 319
menopause, 284, **285**
messenger ribonucleic acid
     (mRNA), *40*, **41**
Mexico
   axolotl of, 74, *75*
   collision with comet or aster-
        oid, 97-98
Middle East
   and human origin models, 251
   monkeys of, 121
   sickle cell anemia in, 63
   sites in, 175, *228-229*
migration
   of *Homo erectus*, 212-213, 214
   of humans, 247, 302, *303*
Milky Way Galaxy, 91
Mississippi Delta, age of, 26-27,
     26
mitochondria, 39, 252
mitochondrial DNA (mtDNA),
     252-**253**, 254, 318
mitosis, 46, *46*, **47**
Modjokerto site, Java, 208, 216
Molnar, Stephen, 307
monkeys
   adaptive radiation of, 78-79
   hunted by chimpanzees, *142*,
        143
   New World, 79, 121, *122*, 175
   Old World, 121, *122*, 175-177,
        176
   taxonomy of, *117*
monogenic, 42, **43**
Montana, 173
morals. *See* belief systems
Morocco, sites in, *207*, 208, *229*,
     243
mosquitos
   and blood type, 281
   and malaria, 66, 67
mother-infant units
   baboon, 137, 139
   bond of, 134, 140
   chimpanzee, 140, 141-142
   human, and breathing, 324
   special status of, 113, *115*, 140
mouse lemur, 109

Mousterian tradition, *237*, **237**
mRNA. *See* messenger ribonu-
        cleic acid
mtDNA. *See* mitochondrial DNA
mules, 53
Multiregional Hypothesis, *243*,
        248, 248-**249**, 251, 255
mummification, 161, *162*, 316,
        317
mutations
    defined, **45**, 52
    evolutionary differences as-
        sessed with, 251-253
    as evolutionary process, 55-56,
        58
    macromutations, 74, **75**
    sickle cell anemia, 63-67, *64*,
        66

natural selection
    defined, **31**
    evolution, as major process of,
        31-32, 56-59, *58*
    and mutations, 56
    and speciation, 32, 80-83, *81*,
        82
    and variation. *See* variation
    See also genetics *and related en-
        tries*
Neander River Valley site, Ger-
        many, 233
Neandertals
    appearance of, *154*, 233-236,
        234-236, *240*
    cultural achievements of,
        236-240, *237*, *238*
    defined, **233**
    Old Man of La Chapelle-aux-
        Saints, 239, *240*
New England
    cemeteries of, 7
    fossilization in, 161
    Pleistocene conditions of, 214
New Guinea, mtDNA sampling
        and, 253
Newton, Isaac, 20
New World monkeys, 79, 121,
        122, 175
Ngandong site, Java, *208*, 217

niche, **53**
Nicholas II (tsar of Russia), 319
Noah and the flood, 20, 21
nocturnal, 78, **79**
North America
    blood types among natives of,
        278-279, *278*
    carbibou of, *296*, 297-299,
        298
    glaciers covering, *212*, 213-214,
        213
    Hutterite colonies of. *See* Hut-
        terites
    migration into, 214, 247
    primate fossils in, 173, 175
    prosimians extinct in, 79
    sickle cell anemia in, 66-67
notochord, 106, *106*, **107**
nucleotide, **39**
nucleus, of cell, 39, *40*, 41
nutrition, effect of, on popula-
        tions, 284-285

Ockham's razor, and human fossil
        record, 226
Ockham, William of, 226
Oklahoma City
    bombing, 316
    disappearances in, 319-323
Old Man of La Chapelle-aux-
        -Saints (Neandertal), 239,
        240
Oldowan tools, 198-199, *198*
Olduvai Gorge, Tanzania, 156,
        156, 198, 200, 208, 210
Old World
    hominoids, 121-126
    monkeys, 121, *122*, 175-177,
        176
    and New World, compared,
        121
    primate evolution in, 175-178,
        176, *177*
    prosimians of, 79, 175
omnivore, **155**
Omomyidae, *174*, 175
Omo site, Ethiopa, 157
O'Neal, Shaquille, 311
On the Origin of Species by Means

of Natural Selection (Dar-
        win), 32-33, 59, 72
opposability, **111**, 118, 121, 126
Opukahaia, Henry, grave excava-
        tion of, 6-9, *6-8*, 161
orangutans, *124*
    ancestor of, 177, *177*, 178
    characteristics of, 125, 126
    prehensile grip of, *112*
    relation to humans, 140
    skull of, *177*
    taxonomy of, *117*, 123
order, defined, 107
organic, **93**
origins, human. *See under* humans
osteology, 150, **151**
Ouranopithecus, 177

Pakistan, ape fossils of, 177, *177*
paleoanthropology, **11**, 157-161,
        158
Paleolithic, Upper, 242-247, *245*,
        251
palmistry, 83-84
panda bears, 164
Pangea, **97**
Paranthropus, 179-181, 193-194,
        195, 196, 197
Paranthropus aethiopicus, Black
        Skull, 194-195, *194*
Paranthropus boisei, 180, *181*, 196,
        197
    Zinjanthropus, 196, *196*, 198,
        199
Paranthropus robustus, 180, *181*,
        195, *196*
parsimony, 226, **227**
particulate, 38, **39**
pea plants, experiments with,
        43-44, *43*, 45, 46, 47
Peking Man (*Homo erectus*),
        214-215, *216*
pelvis, sexual dimorphism in, 152,
        152
Pennsylvania Dutch, and
        Tay-Sachs disease, 62
peppered moth, 56-58, *57*
Permian era, 94, 97
Petralona site, Greece, *231*

petrified, **157**
Pfeiffer, John, 218
phenotypes, **44-45**
    See also traits
Philosophie Zoologique (Lamarck),
    28-29
philosophy
    Greek, 21, 23, 28
    and society. *See* belief systems
photosynthesis, **93**
phylum, defined, 106
physical anthropology, **11**. *See* bi-
    ological anthropology
physics, 172
pigeons, 31
Pithecanthropus erectus. *See* Java
    Man
Pizarro, Francisco, 319
plate tectonics, **95-97**, 96
Plato, 21
Platyrrhini, 120-121
Pleistocene, *212, 213,* **213-214,**
    217
point mutations, **55**
pollen, and evidence of burials,
    239
pollinators, and speciation, 72
pollution and adaptation, 56-58,
    57
polygenic, 42, *42,* **43**
polymorphisms, **275**
    adaptive importance of,
        278-282, *279, 280*
    discordant distribution of, 301,
        302
polytypic, **297**
Pongidae, 123, 166-167
pongids, 123-126, *124, 125*
Pope, Alexander, 104
Population Replacement Hypoth-
    esis, 248, 249-250, *251,*
    253
populations
    age of, and genetic variability,
        251-252
    age-sex structure of, 271-273,
        271-273
    defined, 52
    demes, 59, 297

gene flow between. *See* gene
    flow
genetic analysis of, 302
    with allele frequencies, 260-264
    by mtDNA, 252-253, *254*
    with dermatoglyphics, 264-268,
        264-266
    genetic drift in. *See* genetic
        drift
    growth rates of individuals
        within, 282-286, *282-285*
    size of, 268-271, *269, 273, 273*
postorbital constriction, **229**
potassium/argon (K/Ar) dating,
    160-161
prehensile, **111,** *112,* 132
    New World monkeys, tails of,
        121, *122*
    prosimian abilities, 118-119
primates
    adaptive radiation of, 78-79
    behaviors common among, 135
    characteristics of, 109-115,
        110-116
    coloration of, 113, *114*
    defined, **11**
    distribution of living, *118*
    evolution of, 172-178, *173,*
        174, 176, 177
    intelligence of, 112
    movement of, 111, *112*
    as prey, *162, 163,* 189
    reproduction of, 111-112
    senses of, 109-110, 111, *111*
    social structure of, 113-115,
        114-116, 139-140
    taxonomy of, 117-126, *117,*
        119, 120, 122-125
    vision of, 109-110, *111*
    See also individual species; pro-
        simians
primatology, defined, **11**
Principles of Geology (Lyell), 27
prognathism, **185**
progressive, 28, **29,** 32
proof, and scientific method, 13
prosimians
    characteristics of, 118-119
    defined, **79**

displacement of, 78-79,
    175-176
reproduction of, 111-112, 119
senses of, 110, 118
taxonomy of, *117*
Prosimii suborder, 118, 175
proteins, *39, 40,* 41
    evolutionary relationships re-
        vealed through, 164-165
protein synthesis, **41**
provenience, **159**
Provo Canyon, Utah, *22*
psuedoscience, 83-86, *85*
PTC (phenylthiocarbamide), and
    taster trait, 44
pubic symphysis, and age, *153*
punch technique, 241, *244,* 251
punctuated equilibrium, 81-**83,**
    82
Punnett Square, 48, *48*
pygmy chimp. *See* bonobos

Qafzeh site, Israel, *251*
quadrupedal, **111**

races, **297**
    biological meaning of, 297-299,
        298
    human
    biological evidence and,
        300-303, *302,* 310-311
    cultural reality of, 307
    as folk taxonomy, 290,
        304-307, 312
    intelligence and, claims about,
        307-312
    See also skin color
racism, **307**
    of Europeans, about human or-
        igins, 214
    and Jensen's work, 309
radiometric dating techniques,
    159-161, *160*
recessive, **44-45**
recombination, **47**
reification, **309**
relative dating techniques, **159**

relativity, theory of, 13
religion
  Bible, literal interpretation of, 20-21, 23, 84-85
  colonies based in. *See* Hutterites
  and European racial categories, 305
  and grave excavation, 6, 8, 9
  and society. *See* belief systems
Replacement Hypothesis, *243*, **249**
  Genetic Replacement, *248*, 250-256
  Population Replacement, *248*, 249-250, 251, 253, 255
reproduction
  asexual, 46, *46*, 93
  mammalian behaviors surrounding, 135
  primate behaviors surrounding, 111-112, 139, 141
  sexual
    consciousness of, 127-128, 145, 190, 192
    estrus and, 126-127, *127*
    genetics of, 46-48, *47*, *48*
    isolating mechanisms of, 72-75, *74*, *75*
    origin of, 93
    and species definition, 53
  See also reproductive success
reproductive isolating mechanisms, 72-75, **73**, *74*, *75*
reproductive strategies, **135**, 139, 140-143
reproductive success
  mutations and, 56
  natural selection fostering, 31, 59, 81
  sexual consciousness and, 190
  strategies for, 135, 139, 140-141
rhesus monkey, *122*
rickets, 277-278
Rift Valley, Africa, 191, *192*
RNA, *40*, *41*, 93
Russia, sites in, 246-247

sagittal crest, 185, *185*, 193, 194, *194*, 195
sagittal keel, **209**
salamanders, 74, *75*
sampling error, **61**
Sangiran site, Java, *208*, 216
Sarich, Vincent, 164, 165
Saskatchewan, Hutterite colonies of. *See* Hutterites
savannas, 136, *137*, **137**, 139
  bipedalism evolving in, 188-190
scanning electron microscope (SEM), 200, *201*, 220
scavenge, **189**
science
  belief systems distinguished from, 15-16, 83-86
  Christianity's influence on, 20-21, 23, 33, 107
  defined, 12, **13**
  ideas sounding like, 308
  ignoring data in, 43, 45
  and uniformitarianism, 24-26
  See also individual sciences
scientific creationism, 83-86, 85, **85**
scientific method, defined, **13**-15
sea levels, lowering of, 214, 217, 247
seasonal mating, and speciation, 72
segregation, of gene pairs, 46-**47**
semispecies, **299**
SEM. *See* scanning electron microscope
senses, of primates, 109-110, *111*
sex, biological, 292, **293**
  ambiguous, 295
sex cells. *See* gametes
sexual diphormism, **153**
  in *Australopithecus afarensis*, 183-184
  of humans, 292, 295
  human skeleton exhibiting, 152, *152*
sexuality
  bonobo, 145, 190
  hominid, 190, 192
  human, 127-128, 190

sexually, **93**
sexual maturity, 127, 284, 285, 292
sexual reproduction. *See* reproduction: sexual
Shanidar site, Iraq, 239
shelter
  and cultural adaptation, 274, *274*
  early humans and, 246-247
  Homo erectus and, 212, 215
Shipman, Pat, 200
shovel-shaped teeth, 322
Shreeve, James, 217
siamangs, *117*, 123
sickle cell anemia, 55, 63-67, *63*, *64*, *66*
  and allele frequencies, 261-264
Simons, Elwyn, 12
single-celled organisms
  and origin of life, 91-93, *92*, *94*
  reproduction of, 46, *46*, 93
sites, 156, **157**
Sivapithecus, 177, *177*, 178
skeletal structure
  Australopithecus afarensis, 183, 185
  Homo erectus, 209-210, *210*, *211*
  Homo sapiens (archaic), 229, 235-236, *236*
  humans, 150, *151*, 152, *152*, *153*-155, 236
  early, 241
  mammalian, compared, *151*
  Neandertal, 235-236, *236*
  prosimians, *174*
skeletons
  identification of, 8-9, 12, 316, 319-323
  information obtained from, 150-155, 318
  reconstructing soft tissue based on, 154, *320-321*
skin color
  as adaptive trait, 275-278, *277*
  as cline, 301

skin color (*continued*)
  environmental influences on,
    45-46
  as polygenic trait, 42, *42*, 45-46
  See also races
Skuhl site, Israel, *243*, 251
skull 1470 (*Homo habilis*), *199*
skull, sexual dimorphism in, 152,
  152
skull shape. *See* cranial shape
slavery, 307
smell, sense of, 109, 110, 118
Smith, John Maynard, 16
Smuts, Barbara, 12
Snow, Clyde, 12, 316, 319-323
social structure
  of baboons, 136-140
  of bonobos, 143-146, 190, 191
  of chimpanzees, 113, *116*,
    140-146, *141*, *142*
  of gibbons and siamangs, 123
  of hominids, 139-140, 146,
    190, 192
  of humans, 128
  of primates, 113-115, *114-116*,
    123, 139-140
  sexuality and, 145, 190
  See also culture
social structure of, 128
sociobiology, 134, **135**
socioeconomic status
  and IQ tests, 309, 310, 312
  and race, 307, 311-312
Soleihac site, France, 215
South Africa
  migration into, 247
  sites in, *228-229*, 241, *241*, *243*
South America
  blood types among natives of,
    278, *279*, 280
  new species and, 76, 77
  primates of, 111
Spain, sites in, *158*, 201, 215,
  218-220, 245
sparrows, 299
specialized, **77**
speciation
  adaptive radiation and, **77**-79,
    78, *79*

defined, **73**
natural selection as process, 32,
  80-83, *81*, *82*
numbers of, and discovery, 76
pace of, 80-83, *81*, *82*
reproductive isolating mechanisms and, 72-75, *74*, *75*,
  297
species
  chromosomes, variation in
    number of, 46
  classification of. *See* taxonomy
  defined, **9**, 53
  demes of, 59-60, *59*
  evolution, as basic unit of, 52,
    53-55, *54*
  extinction of. *See* extinctions
  generalized, 297
  new. *See* speciation
  number of living, 75, 76
  polytypic, 297
  similarity of all, 76-77
  specialized, 53, 296-297
sports, 311-312
Steinheim site, Germany, *231*
Steno, Nicholas, 22, 23, 26, 27,
  34
stereoscopic vision, 110, *111*,
  118
Stoneking, Mark, 252-253
stone tools. *See* tool technologies
strata, 22, **23**
stratigraphy
  defined, 22, *22*, **23**, 25
  practical use of, 156-157, *158*,
    159
Stringer, Christopher, 249
stromatolites, 92-93, *92*
Strum, Shirley, 12
suborder, 117
subspecies, **297**-299, *298*, 300
Sudden Infant Death Syndrome
  (SIDS), 324
superfamily, 117
supreme being, 15, 16
Switzerland, 239
symbiotic, 252, **253**
symbolic, **129**
systematists, 53

tanning response, 275
Tanzania, sites in, 140, 143, 156,
  156, 200, *207*, *208*,
  228-229
taphonomy, **163**
tarsier, 119, *120*, *174*, 175
taster trait, 44, 48, 54-55, 62
Taung Baby (*Australopithecus africanus*), 178, 285
taxon, **117**
taxonomists, **53**
taxonomy
  cladistics, **109**, 166-167, *167*
  defined, **105**
  evolutionary relationships in-
    ferred from, 107-109,
    108
  Linnaean, 105-109, *105*, *106*,
    108
  See also under individual species
Taylor, Zachary, 319
Tay-Sachs disease, 62, 324-325
Tblisi, Republic of Georgia, 215
teeth
  cusps of, 176, *176*, 322
  diet evidenced by, 155, 176,
    177, 193, 195, *195*, 318
  hominid, 182, *182*, 183, 185,
    193, 194, 195, *195*, 200
  hominoid, 176, *176*
  human
    dental eruption of, *152*, 322
    omnivore type, 155
    shapes of, 322
  of hunter-gatherers, 326
  of New World/Old World pri-
    mates, 121
termite "fishing stick," 125, *125*,
  143, 198
Terra Amata site, France, 215
testing and testability, 13-16,
  83-84
theory, defined, **13**
Thompson, Marcia, 323
thought, capacity for, 133-134
tigers, 53
Time, 167-168
time, origins of life and universe
  in, 90-99, *91-96*

tool technologies
  Acheulian, **217**
  of chimpanzees, 125-126, *125*, 143
  of *Homo erectus*, 209, 210, 217-218, *218*, *219*
  of *Homo habilis*, 198-199, 200-201, 217
  of *Homo sapiens* (archaic), 230-233, *232*, 237, *237*
  and human origin models, 251
  humans, of early, 241, *244*, 245, *245*
  Levallois technique, *232*, **233**, 237
  Mousterian tradition, *237*, **237**
  of Neandertals, 237, *237*
  non-human hominids, 199
  punch technique, 241, *244*, 251
Torralba site, Spain, 215, 218-220
torus, **209**
traits
  alleles determining. *See* alleles
  coding for, 41-42
  differences in, and speciation, 73
  different genetics for similar, 164
  environment and. *See* environmental influences
  and Genetic Replacement model of origins, 250-251
  homologous and analogous, 132-133, *133*
  polymorphisms. *See* polymorphisms
  and race, 298, 299, 301
  sickle cell, 65-66
  taster, 44, 48, 54-55, 62
  and taxonomic categories, 106-107
transfer ribonucleic acid (tRNA), 40, **41**
transmutation of species, 27. *See* evolution
trephination, *155*, **155**
Trinil site, Java, *208*, 214
Trisomy 21, 55, *55*

tRNA. *See* transfer ribonucleic acid
tuberculosis, 325
tundra, 214, **215**
Turkana boy, 216
Turkana site, Kenya, 183, 194, *199*, *208*, 209, 210, *211*, 216
Turkey, ape fossils of, 177, *177*
twin studies, and heritability, 310
two-spirits, 295
typhoid, 6, 9

ultraviolet (UV) radiation, and melanin production, 275-277, 278
uniformitarianism, 23-**25**, 26-27, 28, 29
United States
  European racial folk taxonomy and, 307
  sickle cell anemia in, 66-67
universe
  age of, conflicting data on, 172
  history of, 90-91, *91*, 99-100
Upper Paleolithic, 242-247, *245*, 251
Ussher, James (archbishop), 21, *34*
Utah, *22*, *25*
UV. *See* ultraviolet (UV) radiation

values
  attached to dominant/recessive genes, 44
  of belief systems, and science, 15-16, 17, 86-86
variation
  and adaptation, 31, 56-58, *57*
  as already present, 31, 58
  as arising when needed, 29, 31
  cline, distribution as, 299, *299*
  discordant, 301, *302*
  and mutation, 52, 55-56
  polymorphisms. *See* polymorphisms

as random, 32
as raw material for natural selection, 30, 31
sexual reproduction and, 46-48, *47*, *48*
velocity curve, **283**-284, *284*
Venus figurines, 245, *245*
versus chimp, 123
vertebrates, **93**, 106
Vietnam, ape fossils in, 177
vision, of primates, 109-110, *111*, 118
vitamin D production, and skin color, 277-278
vocal apparatus, 220-221, *222*, 239-240, 324
Vries, Hugo de, 52

Wallace, Alfred Russel, 32, *34*
warfare, chimpanzee, 143
water, on savanna, 212
whales, brain size of, 112
wheat plants, chromosomes, number of, 46
will, Lamarckian, 28-29, 32
Wilson, Allan, 164, 165, 252-253
Wilson, Edward O., 73, 76
Wolpoff, Milford, 248, 251
wolves, 53, *105*, 107, *108*, 135
woolly spider monkey, *122*
Wyoming, sites in, 173

Y-5 cusp pattern, 176, *176*
Yucatán, Mexico, collision with comet or asteroid, 97-98
Yugoslavia, sites in, *229*

Zaire, 143
Zambia, sites in, *228*
Zhoukoudian cave site, China, *208*, 214-215, 216, *219*
Zinjanthropus (*Paranthropus boisei*), 196, *196*, 198, 199
zygote, 46-**47**, *48*